WAR

WAR

Studies from

PSYCHOLOGY
SOCIOLOGY
ANTHROPOLOGY

Edited by

LEON BRAMSON
and
GEORGE W. GOETHALS

BASIC BOOKS, *Inc., Publishers*

NEW YORK / LONDON

Preface

This book is an attempt to bring together classical and contemporary writings by psychologists, sociologists, and anthropologists on the causes of war. The editors are convinced that no single approach to such a complex problem can lay claim to completeness. With this volume, however, they hope to encourage a fresh look at the possibilities of the social sciences' regarding the topic by making available an introduction to such studies. It goes without saying that such an effort also constitutes an attempt to define the limits of these approaches.

The careful reader will notice that these writings tell us some interesting things about social science as well as war. For example, the problems of theory and method—of inquiry, broadly conceived—which are characteristic of the different fields of study are represented here in microcosm. The advantages and limitations of the different approaches of the disciplines are reflected in the attempt to apply them in studying the causes of war. Also, these writings characteristically show social scientists trying to grapple with what is commonly recognized as the greatest dilemma of the modern age. For most of them a detached objectivity is a condition of their craft, yet here they emerge as sufficiently involved and committed to focus on a historic issue. This effort illustrates an inconsistency in social science itself. Although they generally view themselves as naturalists in the positivist tradition, these thinkers are also morally sensitive men whose interest in war has stemmed from a desire to improve the lot of humanity. Their self-image as impartial and detached observers is maintained in spite of the fact that the quality of their involvement with the subject matter is different from the involvement of, say, the chemist in his laboratory with the compounds in his test tubes. But this charming inconsistency is not damaging to their work; rather, their moral concern has served to channel their scientific energies. They have mustered the utmost detachment of which they are capable in the service of their moral commitment. Perhaps the paradox points to the fact that humaneness may be an essential characteristic of the best students of human behavior.

The editors believe that the effort to understand war as *behavior* is indispensable to the comprehension of the nature of the phenomenon and its widespread appeals. For it is a paradox of history that, particularly in the past two centuries, many thinkers have had a good word to say for war. Nor have the philosophers of bellicosity been limited to continental Europe. Prominent Americans who regarded war as a moral tonic for citizens of a healthy nation included Theodore Roosevelt and Oliver Wendell Holmes. Some of the contributors to this volume have found it curious that many among the most civilized peoples of the modern world should have greeted the onset of war with cries of joy. This aspect of war is one which social scientists might well be expected to study. Since they are examining war as behavior, many have asked whether there are real satisfactions to be found in war, both ancient and modern, which might afford a clue as to why so many people have embraced the military experience because it represents life's potentialities raised to the highest power. To ask such questions, however, is to fly in the face of conventional opinion. Today it is not considered polite or reasonable to admit a taste for war, as it was so frequently in the nineteenth and early twentieth centuries. But it is the virtue of these social scientists that they are asking the kind of question concerning the causes of war which conventional opinion might not readily generate. If war is to be controlled in our time, the answers to the questions asked by these students of human behavior are likely to provide an indispensable part of the basis of an enduring peace.

Having said this much, it would be wise to anticipate an objection from a student of international affairs. "The causes of war," he might declare, "are to be found in the conflicts of competing national units in an international system." The implication of such a hypothetical statement is that political analysis alone is relevant in accounting for modern war. Such a statement, although partly true, is dangerously false if it attempts to reduce the range of behavior to the realm of politics and arrogate to the "master science" the study of the causes of war. For it is human beings, individually and in concert, who declare and fight wars, and the architects of future peace must not ignore this aspect of the causes of war. This is not to deny the importance of political analysis or to assert that the findings of social scientists must be set into a larger historical and social context to be of maximum usefulness. But whoever takes the view that only political analysis is relevant in considering modern war must then take account of the implied irrelevance of the fact that man is an animal, albeit a highly developed one; that war has had many obvious appeals to large sectors of modern populations; and that war has had and continues to have a number of social and economic functions which stand in the way of achieving that peace among nations for which we all hope. To ignore these facts is to risk a one-dimensional view of the world's most pressing problem.

There is another, related objection to the approaches represented here. "The next war," a student of military technology might say, "will begin by someone's pushing a button. It will all be over in twenty-four hours. This has nothing to do with the pattern of causes of previous warfare." This hypothetical objection suggests a paraphrase of the charge frequently leveled at generals—that they fight wars with the weapons and concepts of the previous one—that social scientists are asking questions about the causes of the previous war rather than the next one. There is no doubt that the horror of modern war is caused by the application of essentially industrial techniques to warfare. But even in an era of push-button rocketry—perhaps even more so—the dimensions discussed by the contributors to this volume are highly relevant. They may be more relevant because they attempt to deal with human irrationality. Current thermonuclear technology and delivery systems make irrationality a key element in the possibilities associated with the causes of war. However, the objection has some weight if interpreted as a critique of the attempt to understand the appeals of war in the nuclear era. Such an attempt has more relevance to the contemporary cold war than to the almost unthinkable prospect of a hot thermonuclear one. Such a war is not unthinkable to a large number of the leaders, as well as the rank and file, of many contemporary nations. Large numbers of people with a tendency toward what Erik H. Erikson has called totalistic responses among both leaders and followers in important sectors of many modern societies could intensify an already dangerous and inherently unstable international situation. Paradoxically, this might be especially true in democratic countries where such individuals and groups might make their weight felt through the channels for the expression of public opinion. Thus it is not only in totalitarian states that totalistic responses might lead a nation closer to war.

This collection is intended to serve as an introduction to the continuing efforts of social scientists to understand the causes of war. The students for whom it is primarily intended are members of a generation which has been spared a firsthand knowledge of war. Although we are grateful that this has been the case, it also leads to a special problem. In addition to combating conventional thinking on this question, there is a certain remoteness from the subject which creates special difficulties for Americans in particular. Protected by two oceans for over a century, the American people has never known what it means to be attacked and overrun by a foreign army. With the possible exceptions of the War of 1812 and the Civil War for restricted areas of the country, Americans have not known the meaning of occupation. They have been spared the horrors of twentieth-century war inflicted on civilian populations; they have never been bombed from the air, their cities have never been converted into shelters or laid waste, and the people have never been harnessed into total mobilization. American battle casualties have been light in comparison with those of other powers in the global struggles that have wracked our century. This is not to minimize the anguish of Americans at home and on the front lines during the past wars, but to emphasize that, for example, compared with the Russians, the Germans, the Japanese, the English, and the French, the collective toll has not been high. Nor have American political and social institutions been shattered by the impact of foreign war and occupation, as has been the case with so many other nations.

All this is to ring the changes on a familiar theme—American innocence. It is not only the current generation of students which is relatively remote from the actual experience of war, but the entire nation, which has been spared in comparison with others. The only way to transcend this innocence short of the actual experience, for which no sane person today would hope, is to try to get as close as possible to the subject matter at hand. This means that war in all its dimensions, as reported in personal documents, histories, and even fictional accounts, in art and literature as well as in chronicle, will help to bridge the gap. And since war has plagued mankind since before the beginning of recorded history, the interested student has much to learn from the insights and observations of those who have tried to understand it. These materials can be invaluable in making him sensitive to the central issues and problems awaiting those who would study war as behavior. Such study may be incumbent on those who would prepare for peace.

Acknowledgments

The editors wish to acknowledge the assistance of the following people: James Breay, research assistant during the summer of 1962, rendered invaluable service as a bibliographer and helped choose the selections; Elizabeth A. Feigon assisted with bibliography and made valuable editorial suggestions; Kathryn Puester provided administrative and secretarial assistance; Mary Lou Woodruff rendered secretarial help in the early stages of the project; Susan Self typed and assembled the final copy and supervised its completion; Howard Gardner helped with bibliography and with proofreading.

Editorial suggestions were contributed by Paul Bohannan, Mary Bramson, Dante Germino, John Ratté, David Riesman, and Edward Tiryakian. Bibliographical suggestions were made by Kenneth Bock, Stanley Hoffman, Tamotsu Shibutani, and Jan Thurlings.

The editors are grateful to the administrative committee of the Harvard Foundation for Advanced Study for a grant covering the expenses of a research assistant and secretarial help.

This book is a joint effort on the part of the editors, and final responsibility for it rests entirely with them.

March 1964   LEON BRAMSON
Cambridge, Mass.   GEORGE W. GOETHALS

Contents

PART I

Studies from Psychology

INTRODUCTION

In the popular view, psychology is a body of knowledge the central concern of which is the welfare of man. It should follow from this that psychologists have a great deal to say about a phenomenon such as war, which has negative effects on this welfare. Such, however, is not the case. What the psychologist says about war in comparison with what he says about many other less important phenomena is brief. Happily, this brevity has not been related to triviality; the relatively small collection of ideas from psychology concerning war is vitally important. Despite this, however, it is important to recognize why this contribution has been small, for it relates to some important aspects of psychology as a discipline. First, it should be recognized that psychology as an independent discipline is a product of the twentieth century. Psychological conceptions previous to that time had been part of philosophy and physiology. One of the concerns of youth is always the definition of identity, and psychology as a formal academic discipline has spent a major portion of its energies in defining its own subject matter. Properly speaking, psychology consists of the study of motivation, perception, and learning. Obviously this is quite different from the popular conception. Recently, when psychology came into its own as a discipline not only with a past but with a formal history, the definitions of the kinds of problems it could properly investigate and the kinds of people who could be considered psychologists became broader. At one time, for example, psychoanalysis and its practitioners were considered beyond the purview of the discipline. Presently psychoanalytic theory is seen not only as a practice but also as a fruitful source from which hypotheses for research may be derived. Thus the brevity of psychology's contribution to war is the result of the evolution of a discipline which began by rigorously limiting its scope and then proceeded to make that scope more inclusive.

In recent years the social psychologist in particular has had a great deal to say about the military establishment and its organization, the soldier and his morale or lack of it, and the intricacies of small group behavior as seen in the infantry squad or the bomber crew. Obviously these investigations relate to the problem of war; however, it is not within the scope of this particular collection to review the thinking of the social scientist as he investigates the problems of morale and organization, so much a part of the world of man at war. This collection takes a different point of departure. Its task is to reveal what the psychologist thinks about war and, further, the strategies he has adopted in thinking about it. Corollaries are, of course, the philosophical implications of these strategies. To borrow a phrase from Abraham Maslow, war is a "peak experience," and the way psychologists view it is important and may tell us much about why man behaves in this extreme fashion. Although the ideas about war are myriad, the strategies of inquiry are finite.

One approach to war is to suggest that it is part of man's fate. War represents an aspect of man's biological endowment. It suggests that man is as committed to seeking death as he is to seeking life. Closely related to this pessimistic point of view is another which shares the same negative orientation. This is the notion that war, the most extreme conflict possible between groups, represents a stage in an uncompleted evolutionary sequence. The optimistic note sounded by those who espouse this idea is that war in an evolutionary sense is a transitory phenomenon. However, in the here and now of our evolutionary journey, we are still faced with the grim reality of war. This point of view and the preceding one place heavy emphasis on war as part of whatever it is that man brings into this world with him either by genetic or cultural heritage.

Another approach suggests that war represents social learning gone awry. War is not some *mystique* inherent in the germ plasm, but is a distortion of the aggressive tendency learned early in life. War represents, to paraphrase Clausewitz, "the continuation of behavior in another context." It is the translation of personal aggression to the cultural sphere. Obviously this is an environmental rather than a genetic point of view. War is tragic because it can be avoided.

Others believe that, although war is not genetic nor the cultural actualization of a learned human trait, man strives continually to maintain in his world a condition of optimal stimulation. Such a point of view suggests that man craves excitement and at this stage in his history has found, to his misfortune, war a seductive solution to that need. The psychologist who presents this position is not naïve about the political and economic factors which contribute to a state of war; however, he places a priority on man's continual attempts to generate excitement for himself even at the risk of danger or death.

In one way or another all of these papers written by psychologists fall into the categories mentioned. Sooner or later there is a commitment to a general genetic or environmental position; sooner or later there is a conclusion as to whether man is capable of exerting control. The strategies may vary from polemic to basic research; however, the continually recurring themes deal with from whence war arises and man's capacity to control or be overcome by it.

One thing that may surprise the reader as he reads these papers is an idea enunciated by William James but found in others' writings. This is that war may be a good thing for the human race. War may actualize some of man's best traits, even though this actualization may occur in the midst of his most destructive experience. This search for the moral equivalent is implicit in many thinkers from William James to the present.

Some of these papers reveal an unsolved problem—the proper role of the social scientist in a democracy. It involves the complex problem of making clear those statements which are put forward in the role of the citizen as opposed to those in the role of the social scientist. This consideration colors Freud's letter to Einstein and Harry Stack Sullivan's paper on the necessity of formulating a psychiatry of peoples. In any event, the themes psychologists choose to treat and choose to avoid, the form in which they speak, and the matters on which they are silent are revealed in these papers.

Instinct Theories and
Comparative Psychology

One approach to war is to see it as part of man's animal heritage. Man the rational being retains vestigial animal traits of an irrational and destructive nature. William James and William McDougall contend that over many centuries man has gone through a social evolution which has substituted strategies of group action for direct personal aggression and retaliation. In extreme situations this group action can involve the behavior of war. James and McDougall have many points of view in common, and much of what they say is colored by paradox. On one hand, war is seen as meaningless, creating nothing but destruction and pillage; on the other hand, war is viewed as the stage on which some of the most laudatory human virtues are portrayed. McDougall states:

> The operation of the primal law will, therefore, have tended to secure that the successful rival of the patriarch should have strong instincts of sex and of pugnacity and a but moderately strong fear instinct, combined with the more developed mental organization that permits of deliberation and of control of the stronger impulses through the organized cooperation of the weaker impulses. That is to say, it was a condition which secured for the family community a succession of patriarchs each of whom was superior to his rivals not merely in power of combat, but also and chiefly in power of farsighted control of his impulses. Each such patriarch, becoming the father of the succeeding generation, will then have transmitted to it in some degree his exceptional power of self-control. In this way the primal

law, enforced by the fiercest passions of primitive man, may have prepared human nature for the observance of laws less brutally and ruthlessly enforced, may, in short, have played a great part in developing in
humanity that power of self-control and law-abidingness which was the
essential condition of the progress of social organization.

James might well have voiced the same sentiment, although in a different style.

James and McDougall are well aware of the destructive effects of war. They
are sympathetic to the problems of personal tragedy and extreme social disorganization. There is a paradox, however, in their point of view. This is that,
although they see war as a destructive force which must be eradicated, they
also see that in the past war has been the arena in which man could display
some of his most noble virtues and, further, in which social orders could be
changed. Thus, as they deal with the problem retrospectively, James and
McDougall see war as having accomplished some degree of social progress.
The important point is that they believe future wars would be utterly destructive and would not be related to any social evolution.

Both James and McDougall are essentially optimistic. They see the destructive past as a precursor of the constructive future. They see man as the possessor of traits which will eventually make war obsolete. For McDougall this
comes about as the instinct of pugnacity is replaced by the instinct of emulation:

> To this stage the most highly civilized communities are tending, in accord-
> ance with the law that the collective mind follows in the steps of evolution
> of the individual mind at a great interval of time. There are unmistakable
> signs that the pugnacity of nations is being supplanted by emulation; that
> warfare is being replaced by industrial and intellectual rivalry; that wars
> between civilized nations, which are replacing the mortal conflicts be-
> tween individuals and between societies dominated by the spirit of pug-
> nacity, are tending to become mere incidents of their commercial and
> industrial rivalry, being undertaken to secure markets or sources of
> supply of raw material which shall bring industrial or commercial ad-
> vantage to their possessor.
>
> The tendency of emulation to replace pugnacity is, then, a tendency to
> bring to an end what has been an important, probably the most important,
> factor of progressive evolution of human nature, namely, the selection of
> the fit and the extermination of the less fit (among both individuals and
> societies) resulting from their conflicts with one another.

For James this sequence comes when radical social reorganization provides
peaceful ways of expressing manly virtues; to employ James's own epigram,
when we discover and make real "the moral equivalent of war" through social
action.

Both James and McDougall explicitly and inferentially speak of man the animal as well as man the human being. D. O. Hebb raises this question in a startlingly different context. He turns his attention to a concern of high priority to American psychologists: to what extent can we learn anything valid about human behavior from the study of the so-called lower animals. In an essay written with W. R. Thompson, this strategy of studying behavior is evaluated.

There is a common opinion that understanding human behavior will result from the study of human behavior only, on the ground that proving something true of an animal does not prove it for man. The latter part of this statement is both correct and irrelevant. It implies that an empirical science proceeds by proof and disproof, which is a most misleading idea. . . .

The statement that animal experiment proves nothing for man does not go far enough; finding that something is true *of man* up till now, and for the limited sample of men that one has actually been able to test, cannot logically establish that it will be true of other men in the future, as Hume noted long ago. Finding that a psychotic behaves in a certain way does not prove anything about normal persons, but no one would argue from this that clinical studies have not helped in our understanding of the normal. In principle, study of animals has exactly the same status. . . . We concede that animal psychology has had its own myopic errors, but these have usually arisen when study is concentrated on some one laboratory animal, rat or cat, regarded simply as a convenient substitute for man and not as the object of comparative study.[1]

These comments demolish two extreme strategies in the study of human behavior. They reject the slavish and unimaginative extrapolation from animal data and the equally rigid adherence to what has been called the concept of "species-specific" behavior. They are saying that animal studies are important *primarily* because they lead us to view human behavior in a comparative context. Thus we become aware not only of similarities but, even more important, of differences.

Hebb and Thompson would be valuable if this were all that was brought forth in their essay; however, they go beyond this to offer a new dimension of thinking from this comparative knowledge. This places them in sharp contrast with James and McDougall. James and McDougall see man's problem, in essence, as being that of the animal in man delaying his progress toward a peaceful Arcadia. Hebb and Thompson see something else—it is the human qualities in the *animal* which cause the difficulty and create the peril. They expose to our consideration the precarious nature of man's emotional behavior

[1] D. O. Hebb and W. R. Thompson, "The Social Significance of Animal Studies," in Gardner Lindzey, ed., *Handbook of Social Psychology* (Cambridge, Mass.: Addison-Wesley Publishing Co., 1954), pp. 532–534.

and the social significance of this complex primate attribute. They see in man's emotional repertory and his particular needs the key to his happiness as well as to his naked survival. Like James and McDougall they see man as the product of his evolution, but the problems of his evolution lie not in its lack of progress but rather in man's limited ability to grasp the implications of this evolution.

◄◄◄ ►►►

WILLIAM JAMES

The Moral Equivalent of War *

The war against war is going to be no holiday excursion or camping party.
The military feelings are too deeply grounded to abdicate their place among
our ideals until better substitutes are offered than the glory and shame that
come to nations as well as to individuals from the ups and downs of politics
and the vicissitudes of trade. There is something highly paradoxical in the
modern man's relation to war. Ask all our millions, north and south, whether
they would vote now (were such a thing possible) to have our war for the
Union expunged from history and the record of a peaceful transition to the
present time substituted for that of its marches and battles, and probably
hardly a handful of eccentrics would say yes. Those ancestors, those efforts,
those memories and legends, are the most ideal part of what we now own together, a sacred spiritual possession worth more than all the blood poured out.
Yet ask those same people whether they would be willing in cold blood to start
another civil war now to gain another similar possession, and not one man or
woman would vote for the proposition. In modern eyes, precious though wars
may be, they must not be waged solely for the sake of the ideal harvest. Only

* Written for and first published by the Association for International Conciliation (Leaf-
let No. 27) and also published in *McClure's Magazine*, August, 1910, and *The Popular
Science Monthly*, October, 1910. Reprinted from William James, *Memories and Studies*,
pp. 267–296, by permission of Paul R. Reynolds and Son (Copyright 1911, Longmans,
Green & Co., New York).

when forced upon one, only when an enemy's injustice leaves us no alternative, is a war now thought permissible.

It was not thus in ancient times. The earlier men were hunting men, and to hunt a neighboring tribe, kill the males, loot the village, and possess the females was the most profitable, as well as the most exciting, way of living. Thus were the more martial tribes selected, and in chiefs and peoples a pure pugnacity and love of glory came to mingle with the more fundamental appetite for plunder.

Modern war is so expensive that we feel trade to be a better avenue to plunder, but modern man inherits all the innate pugnacity and all the love of glory of his ancestors. Showing war's irrationality and horror is of no effect upon him. The horrors make the fascination. War is the *strong* life; it is life *in extremis;* war taxes are the only ones men never hesitate to pay, as the budgets of all nations show us.

History is a bath of blood. The *Iliad* is one long recital of how Diomedes and Ajax, Sarpedon and Hector, *killed.* No detail of the wounds they made is spared us, and the Greek mind fed upon the story. Greek history is a panorama of jingoism and imperialism—war for war's sake, all the citizens being warriors. It is horrible reading, because of the irrationality of it all—save for the purpose of making history—and the history is that of the utter ruin of a civilization in intellectual respects perhaps the highest the earth has ever seen.

Those wars were purely piratical. Pride, gold, women, slaves, excitement were their only motives. In the Peloponnesian War for example, the Athenians ask the inhabitants of Melos (the island where the "Venus of Milo" was found), hitherto neutral, to own their lordship. The envoys meet, and hold a debate which Thucydides gives in full and which, for sweet reasonableness of form, would have satisfied Matthew Arnold. "The powerful exact what they can," said the Athenians, "and the weak grant what they must." When the Meleans say that, sooner than be slaves, they will appeal to the gods, the Athenians reply:

> Of the gods we believe and of men we know that, by a law of their nature, wherever they can rule they will. This law was not made by us, and we are not the first to have acted upon it; we did but inherit it, and we know that you and all mankind, if you were as strong as we are, would do as we do. So much for the gods; we have told you why we expect to stand as high in their good opinion as you.

Well, the Meleans still refused, and their town was taken. "The Athenians," Thucydides quietly says, "thereupon put to death all who were of military age and made slaves of the women and children. They then colonized the island, sending thither five hundred settlers of their own."

Alexander's career was piracy pure and simple, nothing but an orgy of power and plunder made romantic by the character of the hero. There was no rational principle in it, and the moment he died his generals and governors attacked one another. The cruelty of those times is incredible. When Rome finally conquered Greece, Paulus Aemilius was told by the Roman Senate to reward his soldiers for their toil by "giving" them the old kingdom of Epirus. They sacked seventy cities and carried off one hundred and fifty thousand inhabitants as slaves. How many they killed I know not, but in Aetolia they killed all the senators, five hundred and fifty in number. Brutus was "the noblest Roman of them all," but, to reanimate his soldiers on the eve of Philippi, he similarly promises to give them the cities of Sparta and Thessalonica to ravage if they win the fight.

Such was the gory nurse that trained societies to cohesiveness. We inherit the warlike type, and, for most of the capacities of heroism that the human race is full of, we have to thank this cruel history. Dead men tell no tales, and, if there were any tribes of other type than this, they have left no survivors. Our ancestors have bred pugnacity into our bone and marrow, and thousands of years of peace won't breed it out of us. The popular imagination fairly fattens on the thought of wars. Let public opinion once reach a certain fighting pitch, and no ruler can withstand it. In the Boer War both governments began with bluff but couldn't stay there; the military tension was too much for them. In 1898 our people had read the word "war" in letters three inches high for three months in every newspaper. The pliant politician McKinley was swept away by their eagerness, and our squalid war with Spain became a necessity.

At the present day, civilized opinion is a curious mental mixture. The military instincts and ideals are as strong as ever, but are confronted by reflective criticisms which sorely curb their ancient freedom. Innumerable writers are showing up the bestial side of military service. Pure loot and mastery seem no longer morally avowable motives, and pretexts must be found for attributing them solely to the enemy. England and we, our army and navy authorities repeat without ceasing, arm solely for "peace"; Germany and Japan it is who are bent on loot and glory. "Peace" in military mouths today is a synonym for "war expected." The word has become a pure provocative, and no government wishing peace sincerely should allow it ever to be printed in a newspaper. Every up-to-date dictionary should say that "peace" and "war" mean the same thing, now *in posse,* now *in actu.* It may even reasonably be said that the intensely sharp competitive *preparation* for war by the nations *is the real war,* permanent, unceasing, and that the battles are only a sort of public verification of the mastery gained during the "peace" interval.

It is plain that on this subject civilized man has developed a sort of double personality. If we take European nations, no legitimate interest of any one of them would seem to justify the tremendous destructions which a war to compass it would necessarily entail. It would seem as though common sense and reason ought to find a way to reach agreement in every conflict of honest interests. I myself think it our bounden duty to believe in such international rationality as possible. But, as things stand, I see how desperately hard it is to bring the peace party and the war party together, and I believe that the difficulty is due to certain deficiencies in the program of pacificism which set the militarist imagination strongly, and, to a certain extent, justifiably, against it. In the whole discussion both sides are on imaginative and sentimental ground. It is but one Utopia against another, and everything one says must be abstract and hypothetical. Subject to this criticism and caution, I will try to characterize in abstract strokes the opposite imaginative forces and point out what to my own very fallible mind seems the best utopian hypothesis, the most promising line of conciliation.

In my remarks, pacificist though I am, I will refuse to speak of the bestial side of the war regime (already done justice to by many writers) and consider only the higher aspects of militaristic sentiment. Patriotism no one thinks discreditable, nor does anyone deny that war is the romance of history. But inordinate ambitions are the soul of every patriotism, and the possibility of violent death the soul of all romance. The militarily patriotic and romantic-minded everywhere, and especially the professional military class, refuse to admit for a moment that war may be a transitory phenomenon in social evolution. The notion of a sheep's paradise like that revolts, they say, our higher imagination. Where then would be the steeps of life? If war had ever stopped, we should have to reinvent it, on this view, to redeem life from flat degeneration.

Reflective apologists for war at the present day all take it religiously. It is a sort of sacrament. Its profits are to the vanquished as well as to the victor, and, quite apart from any question of profit, it is an absolute good, we are told, for it is human nature at its highest dynamic. Its "horrors" are a cheap price to pay for rescue from the only alternative supposed, of a world of clerks and teachers, of coeducation and zoophily, of consumer's leagues and associated charities, of industrialism unlimited, and femininism unabashed. No scorn, no hardness, no valor any more! Fie upon such a cattleyard of a planet!

So far as the central essence of this feeling goes, no healthy-minded person, it seems to me, can help to some degree partaking of it. Militarism is the great preserver of our ideals of hardihood, and human life with no use for hardihood would be contemptible. Without risks or prizes for the darer, history would be insipid indeed, and there is a type of military character which everyone feels that the race should never cease to breed, for everyone is sensitive to its superiority. The duty is incumbent on mankind of keeping military characters in stock—of keeping them, if not for use, then as ends in themselves and as pure pieces of perfection—so that Roosevelt's weaklings and mollycoddles may not end by making everything else disappear from the face of nature.

This natural sort of feeling forms, I think, the innermost soul of army writings. Without any exception known to me, militarist authors take a highly mystical view of their subject and regard war as a biological or sociological necessity, uncontrolled by ordinary psychological checks and motives. When the time of development is ripe, the war must come, reason or no reason, for the justifications pleaded are invariably fictitious. War is, in short, a permanent human *obligation*. Gen. Homer Lea, in his recent book, *The Valor of Ignorance*, plants himself squarely on this ground. Readiness for war is for him the essence of nationality, and ability in it the supreme measure of the health of nations.

Nations, General Lea says, are never stationary—they must necessarily expand or shrink, according to their vitality or decrepitude. Japan now is culminating; and, by the fatal law in question, it is impossible that her statesmen should not long since have entered, with extraordinary foresight, upon a vast policy of conquest—the game in which the first moves were her wars with China and Russia and her treaty with England and of which the final objective is the capture of the Philippines, the Hawaiian Islands, Alaska, and the whole of our coast west of the Sierra passes. This will give Japan what her ineluctable vocation as a state absolutely forces her to claim, the possession of the entire Pacific Ocean; and, to oppose these deep designs, we Americans have, according to our author, nothing but our conceit, our ignorance, our commercialism, our corruption, and our feminism. General Lea makes a minute technical comparison of the military strength which we at present could oppose to the strength of Japan and concludes that the islands, Alaska, Oregon, and Southern California would fall almost without resistance, that San Francisco must surrender in a fortnight to a Japanese investment, that in three or four months the war would be over, and our republic, unable to regain what it had heedlessly neglected to protect sufficiently, would then disintegrate, until, perhaps, some Caesar should arise to weld us again into a nation.

A dismal forecast indeed! Yet not unplausible if the mentality of Japan's statesmen be of the Caesarian type of which history shows so many examples and which is all that General Lea seems able to imagine. But there is no reason to think that women can no longer be the mothers of Napoleonic or Alexandrian characters; and, if these come in Japan and find their opportunity, just such surprises as *The Valor of Ignorance* paints may lurk in ambush for us. Ignorant as we still are of the innermost recesses of Japanese mentality, we may be foolhardy to disregard such possibilities.

Other militarists are more complex and more moral in their considerations. The *Philosophie des Krieges* by S. R. Steinmetz is a good example. War, according to this author, is an ordeal instituted by God, who weighs the nations in its balance. It is the essential form of the state and the only function in which peoples can employ all their powers at once and convergently. No victory is possible save as the resultant of a totality of virtues, no defeat for which some vice or weakness is not responsible. Fidelity, cohesiveness, tenacity, heroism, conscience, education, inventiveness, economy, wealth, physical health, and vigor—there isn't a moral or intellectual point of superiority that doesn't tell when God holds his assizes and hurls the peoples upon one another. *Die Weltgeschichte ist das Weltgericht,* and Dr. Steinmetz does not believe that in the long run chance and luck play any part in apportioning the issues.

The virtues that prevail, it must be noted, are virtues anyhow, superiorities that count in peaceful as well as in military competition; but the strain on them, being infinitely intenser in the latter case, makes war infinitely more searching as a trial. No ordeal is comparable to its winnowings. Its dread hammer is the welder of men into cohesive states, and nowhere but in such states can human nature adequately develop its capacity. The only alternative is degeneration.

Dr. Steinmetz is a conscientious thinker, and his book, short as it is, takes much into account. Its upshot can, it seems to me, be summed up in Simon Patten's word, that mankind was nursed in pain and fear and that the transition to a pleasure economy may be fatal to a being wielding no powers of defense against its disintegrative influences. If we speak of the *fear of emancipation from the fear regime,* we put the whole situation into a single phrase, fear regarding ourselves now taking the place of the ancient fear of the enemy.

Turn the fear over as I will in my mind, it all seems to lead back to two unwillingnesses of the imagination, one aesthetic and the other moral; unwillingness, first, to envisage a future in which army life, with its many elements of charm, shall be forever impossible and in which the destinies of peoples shall nevermore be decided quickly, thrillingly, and tragically by force, but only gradually and insipidly by evolution; and, second, unwillingness to see the supreme theater of human strenuousness closed and the splendid military aptitudes of men doomed to keep always in a state of latency and never show themselves in action. These insistent unwillingnesses, no less than other aesthetic and ethical insistencies, have, it seems to me, to be listened to and respected. One cannot meet them effectively by mere counterinsistency on war's expensiveness and horror. The horror makes the thrill, and, when the question is of getting the extremest and supremest out of human nature, talk of expense sounds ignominious. The weakness of so much merely negative criticism is evident—pacificism makes no converts from the military party. The military partly denies neither the bestiality nor the horror nor the expense; it only says that these things tell but half the story. It only says that war is *worth* them; that, taking human nature as a whole, its wars are its best protection against its weaker and more cowardly self and that mankind cannot *afford* to adopt a peace economy.

Pacificists ought to enter more deeply into the aesthetical and ethical point of view of their opponents. Do that first in any controversy, says J. J. Chapman, *then move the point,* and your opponent will follow. So long as antimilitarists propose no substitute for war's disciplinary function, no *moral equivalent* of war, analogous, as one might say, to the mechanical equivalent of heat, so long they fail to realize the full inwardness of the situation. And as a rule they do fail. The duties, penalties, and sanctions pictured in the Utopias they paint are all too weak and tame to touch the military-minded. Tolstoi's pacificism is the only exception to this rule, for it is profoundly pessimistic as regards all this world's values and makes the fear of the Lord furnish the moral spur provided elsewhere by the fear of the enemy. But our socialistic peace advocates all believe absolutely in this world's values, and, instead of the fear of the Lord and the fear of the enemy, the only fear they reckon with is the fear of poverty if one be lazy. This weakness pervades all the socialistic literature with which I am acquainted. Even in Lowes Dickinson's exquisite dialogue,[1] high wages and short hours are the only forces invoked for over-coming man's distaste for repulsive kinds of labor. Meanwhile men at large still live as they always have lived, under a pain-and-fear economy—for those of us who live in an ease economy are but an island in the stormy ocean—and the whole atmosphere of present-day Utopian literature tastes mawkish and dishwatery to people who still keep a sense for life's more bitter flavors. It suggests, in truth, ubiquitous inferiority.

Inferiority is always with us, and merciless scorn of it is the keynote of the military temper. "Dogs, would you live forever?" shouted Frederick the Great. "Yes," say our Utopians, "let us live forever and raise our level gradually." The best thing about our "inferiors" today is that they are as tough as nails and physically and morally almost as insensitive. Utopianism would see them soft and squeamish, while militarism would keep their callousness, but transfigure it into a meritorious characteristic, needed by "the service" and redeemed by that from the suspicion of inferiority. All the qualities of a man acquire dignity when he knows that the service of the collectivity that owns him needs them. If proud of the collectivity, his own pride rises in proportion. No collectivity is like an army for nourishing such pride, but it has to be confessed that the only sentiment which the image of pacific cosmopolitan industrialism is capable of arousing in countless worthy breasts is shame at the idea of belonging to *such* a collectivity. It is obvious that the United States of America as they exist today impress a mind like General Lea's as so much human blubber. Where is the sharpness and precipitousness, the contempt for life, whether one's own, or another's? Where is the savage yes and no, the unconditional duty? Where is the conscription? Where is the blood tax? Where is anything that one feels honored by belonging to?

Having said thus much in preparation, I will now confess my own Utopia. I devoutly believe in the reign of peace and in the gradual advent of some sort of a socialistic equilibrium. The fatalistic view of the war function is to me nonsense, for I know that war-making is due to definite motives and subject to prudential checks and reasonable criticisms, just like any other form of enterprise. And when whole nations are the armies and the science of destruc-

[1] *Justice and Liberty* (New York: Doubleday, Page & Co., 1909).

tion vies in intellectual refinement with the sciences of production, I see that war becomes absurd and impossible from its own monstrosity. Extravagant ambitions will have to be replaced by reasonable claims, and nations must make common cause against them. I see no reason that all this should not apply to yellow as well as to white countries, and I look forward to a future when acts of war shall be formally outlawed between civilized peoples.

All these beliefs of mine put me squarely into the antimilitarist party. But I do not believe that peace either ought to be or will be permanent on this globe, unless the states pacifically organized preserve some of the old elements of army discipline. A permanently successful peace economy cannot be a simple pleasure economy. In the more-or-less socialistic future toward which mankind seems drifting, we must still subject ourselves collectively to those severities which answer to our real position upon this only partly hospitable globe. We must make new energies and hardihoods continue the manliness to which the military mind so faithfully clings. Martial virtues must be the enduring cement; intrepidity, contempt of softness, surrender of private interest, obedience to command must still remain the rock upon which states are built—unless, indeed, we wish for dangerous reactions against commonwealths fit only for contempt and liable to invite attack whenever a center of crystallization for military-minded enterprise gets formed anywhere in their neighborhood.

The war party is assuredly right in affirming and reaffirming that the martial virtues, although originally gained by the race through war, are absolute and permanent human goods. Patriotic pride and ambition in their military form are, after all, only specifications of a more general competitive passion. They are its first form, but that is no reason for supposing them to be its last form. Men now are proud of belonging to a conquering nation, and without a murmur they lay down their persons and their wealth, if by so doing they may fend off subjection. But who can be sure that *other aspects of one's country* may not, with time and education and suggestion enough, come to be regarded with similarly effective feelings of pride and shame? Why should men not someday feel that it is worth a blood tax to belong to a collectivity superior in *any* ideal respect? Why should they not blush with indignant shame if the community that owns them is vile in any way whatsoever? Individuals, daily more numerous, now feel this civic passion. It is only a question of blowing on the spark until the whole population gets incandescent and, on the ruins of the old morals of military honor, a stable system of morals of civic honor builds itself up. What the whole community comes to believe in grasps the individual as in a vise. The war function has grasped us so far, but constructive interests may someday seem no less imperative and impose on the individual a hardly lighter burden.

Let me illustrate my idea more concretely. There is nothing to make one indignant in the mere fact that life is hard, that men should toil and suffer pain. The planetary conditions once and for all are such, and we can stand it. But that so many men, by mere accidents of birth and opportunity, should have a life of *nothing else* but toil and pain and hardness and inferiority imposed upon them, should have *no* vacation, while others natively no more deserving never get any taste of this campaigning life at all—*this* is capable of arousing indignation in reflective minds. It may end by seeming shameful to all of us that some of us have nothing but campaigning and others nothing but unmanly ease. If now—and this is my idea—there were, instead of military conscription, a conscription of the whole youthful population to form for a certain number of years a part of the army enlisted against nature, the injustice would tend to be evened out, and numerous other goods to the commonwealth would follow. The military ideals of hardihood and discipline would be wrought into the growing fiber of the people; no one would remain blind, as the luxurious classes now are blind, to man's relations to the globe he lives on and to the permanently sour and hard foundations of his higher life. To coal and iron mines, to freight trains, to fishing fleets in December, to dish-washing, clothes-washing, and window-washing, to road-building and tunnel-making, to foundries and stokeholes, and to the frames of skyscrapers, would our gilded youths be drafted off, according to their choice, to get the childishness knocked out of them and to come back into society with healthier sympathies and soberer ideas. They would have paid their blood tax, done their own part in the immemorial human warfare against nature; they would tread the earth more proudly, the women would value them more highly, they would be better fathers and teachers of the following generation.

Such a conscription, with the state of public opinion that would have required it and the many moral fruits it would bear, would preserve in the midst of a pacific civilization the manly virtues which the military party is so afraid of seeing disappear in peace. We should get toughness without callousness, authority with as little criminal cruelty as possible, and painful work done cheerily because the duty is temporary and threatens not, as now, to degrade the whole remainder of one's life. I spoke of the moral equivalent of war. So far, war has been the only force that can discipline a whole community, and, until an equivalent discipline is organized, I believe that war must have its way. But I have no serious doubt that the ordinary prides and shames of social man, once developed to a certain intensity, are capable of organizing such a moral equivalent as I have sketched or some other just as effective for preserving manliness of type. It is but a question of time, of skillful propagandism, and of opinion-making men seizing historic opportunities.

The martial type of character can be bred without war. Strenuous honor and disinterestedness abound elsewhere. Priests and medical men are in a fashion educated to it, and we should all feel some degree of it imperative if we were conscious of our work as an obligatory service to the state. We should be *owned,* as soldiers are by the army, and our pride would rise accordingly. We could be poor, then, without humiliation, as army officers now are. The only thing needed henceforward is to inflame the civic temper as past history has inflamed the military temper. H. G. Wells, as usual, sees the center of the situation.

In many ways [he says], military organization is the most peaceful of activities. When the contemporary man steps from the street, of clamorous insincere advertisement, push, adulteration, underselling and intermittent employment into the barrack-yard, he steps on to a higher social plane, into an atmosphere of service and cooperation and of infinitely more honorable emulations. Here at least men are not flung out of employment to degenerate because there is no immediate work for them to do. They are fed and drilled and trained for better services. Here at least a man is supposed to win promotion by self-forgetfulness and not by self-seeking. And beside the feeble and irregular endowment of research by commercialism, its little shortsighted snatches at profit by innovation and scientific economy, see how remarkable is the steady and rapid development of method and appliances in naval and military affairs! Nothing is more striking than to compare the progress of civil conveniences which has been left almost entirely to the trader, to the progress in military apparatus during the last few decades. The house-appliances of today for example, are little better than they were fifty years ago. A house of today is still almost as ill-ventilated, badly heated by wasteful fires, clumsily arranged and furnished as the house of 1858. Houses a couple of hundred years old are still satisfactory places of residence, so little have our standards risen. But the rifle or battleship of fifty years ago was beyond all comparison inferior to those we possess; in power, in speed, in convenience alike. No one has a use now for such superannuated things.[2]

Wells adds that he thinks that the conceptions of order and discipline, the tradition of service and devotion, of physical fitness, unstinted exertion, and universal responsibility, which universal military duty is now teaching European nations, will remain a permanent acquisition when the last ammunition has been used in the fireworks that celebrate the final peace.[3] I believe as he does. It would be simply preposterous if the only force that could work ideals of honor and standards of efficiency into English or American natures should be the fear of being killed by the Germans or the Japanese. Great indeed is fear, but it is not, as our military enthusiasts believe and try to make us believe, the only stimulus known for awakening the higher ranges of men's spiritual energy. The amount of alteration in public opinion which my Utopia postulates

[2] *First and Last Things* (New York: G. P. Putnam's Sons, 1908), p. 215.
[3] *Ibid.,* p. 226.

is vastly less than the difference between the mentality of those black warriors who pursued Stanley's party on the Congo with their cannibal war cry of "Meat! Meat!" and that of the general staff of any civilized nation. History has seen the latter interval bridged over; the former one can be bridged over much more easily.

◄◄◄ ►►►

WILLIAM McDOUGALL

*The Instinct of Pugnacity**

The instinct of pugnacity has played a part second to none in the evolution of social organization, and in the present age it operates more powerfully than any other in producing demonstrations of collective emotion and action on a great scale. The races of men certainly differ greatly in respect to the innate strength of this instinct, but there is no reason to think that it has grown weaker among ourselves under centuries of civilization; rather, it is probable, as we shall see presently, that it is stronger in the European peoples than it was in primitive man. But its modes of expression have changed with the growth of civilization; as the development of law and custom discourages and renders unnecessary the bodily combat of individuals, this gives place to the collective combat of communities and to the more refined forms of combat within communities. It is observable that, when a pugnacious people is forcibly brought under a system of civilized legality, its members are apt to display an extreme and, to our minds, absurd degree of litigiousness.

The replacement of individual by collective pugnacity is most clearly illustrated by barbarous peoples living in small, strongly organized communities. Within such communities individual combat and even expressions of personal anger may be almost completely suppressed, while the pugnacious instinct finds its vent in perpetual warfare between communities whose relations remain subject to no law. As a rule, no material benefit is gained, and often none

* Reprinted from William McDougall, *An Introduction to Social Psychology*, chap. 11, by permission of the publisher (Copyright 1915, Methuen & Co., Ltd., London).

is sought in these tribal wars, which often result in the weakening and even the extermination of whole villages or tribes. Central Borneo is one of the few regions in which this state of things still persists. The people are very intelligent and sociable and kindly to one another within each village community, but, except in those regions in which European influence has asserted itself, the neighboring villages and tribes live in a state of chronic warfare; all are kept in constant fear of attack, whole villages are often exterminated, and the population is in this way kept down very far below the limit at which any pressure on the means of subsistence could arise. This perpetual warfare, like the squabbles of a roomful of quarrelsome children, seems to be almost wholly and directly due to the uncomplicated operation of the instinct of pugnacity. No material benefits are sought; a few heads, and sometimes a slave or two, are the only trophies gained; and, if one asks of an intelligent chief why he keeps up this senseless practice of going on the warpath, the best reason he can give is that, unless he does so, his neighbors will not respect him and his people and will fall upon them and exterminate them. How shall we begin to understand the prevalence of such a state of affairs if we regard man as a rational creature guided only by intelligent self-interest and if we neglect to take account of his instincts? And it is not among barbarous or savage peoples only that the instinct of pugnacity works in this way. The history of Christendom is largely the history of devastating wars from which few individuals or societies have reaped any immediate benefit and in the causation of which the instinct of pugnacity of the rulers, or of the masses of the peoples, has played a leading part. In our own age the same instinct makes of Europe an armed camp occupied by twelve million soldiers, the support of which is a heavy burden on all the peoples; and we see how, more instantly than ever before, a whole nation may be moved by the combative instinct—a slight to the British flag or an insulting remark in some foreign newspaper sends a wave of angry emotion sweeping across the country, accompanied by all the characteristics of crude collective mentation, and two nations are ready to rush into a war that cannot fail to be disastrous to both of them. The most serious task of modern statesmanship is, perhaps, to discount and to control these outbursts of collective pugnacity. At the present time custom is only just beginning to exert some control over this international pugnacity, and we are still very far from the time when international law, following in the wake of custom, will render the pugnacity of nations as needless as that of the individuals of highly civilized states and physical combats between them as relatively infrequent.

It might seem at first sight that this instinct, which leads men and societies so often to enter blindly upon deadly contests that in many cases are destructive to both parties, could only be a survival from man's brutal ancestry and that an early and a principal feature of social evolution would have been the eradication of this instinct from the human mind. But a little reflection will show us that its operation, far from being wholly injurious, has been one of the essential factors in the evolution of the higher forms of social organization and, in fact, of those specifically social qualities of man the high development of which is an essential condition of the higher social life.

It was said above that the earliest form of human society was in all probability the family, and, indeed, it is probable that in this respect primitive man did but continue the social life of his prehuman ancestors. But what form the primitive family had and in what way more complex forms of society were developed from it are obscure and much disputed questions. Hence any attempt to show how the human instincts played their parts in the process must be purely speculative. Nevertheless it is a legitimate and fascinating subject for speculation, and we may attempt to form some notion of the socializing influence of the instinct of pugnacity among primitive men by adopting provisionally one of the most ingenious of the speculative accounts of the process. Such is the account offered by Messrs. Atkinson and Andrew Lang, which may be briefly sketched as follows.[1] The primitive society was a polygamous family consisting of a patriarch, his wives, and children. The young males, as they became full-grown, were driven out of the community by the patriarch, who was jealous of all possible rivals to his marital privileges. They formed semi-independent bands hanging, perhaps, on the skirts of the family circle, from which they were jealously excluded. From time to time the young males would be brought by their sex impulse into deadly strife with the patriarch, and, when one of them succeeded in overcoming him, this one would take his place and rule in his stead. A social system of this sort obtains among some of the animals, and it seems to be just such a system as the fierce sexual jealousy of man and his polygamous capacities and tendencies would produce in the absence of any modifying law or moral tradition. This prohibition enforced by the jealousy of the patriarch is the *primal law*, the first example of a general prohibition laid upon the natural impulse of a class of human beings and upheld by superior force for the regulation of social relations.

We have seen . . . that jealousy is an emotion dependent upon the existence of a sentiment. Whether we have to recognize among the constituent dispositions of the sentiment an instinct of acquisition or possession is a difficult question to which we found it impossible to give a decided answer. But however that may be, it is clear that the principal constituent of the emotion of male jealousy, especially of the crude kind excited within the crude sentiment of attachment or ownership which the primitive patriarch entertained for his family, is anger; in the human, as well as many other species, the anger excited in connection with the sexual instinct is of the most furious and destructive intensity. If, then, we accept this hypothesis of the primal law, we must believe that the observance of this law was enforced by the instinct of pugnacity.

[1] "The Primal Law."

Now an instinct that led to furious and mortal combat between the males of any group might well determine the evolution of great strength and ferocity and of various weapons and defensive modifications of structure, as sexual characters, in the way that Darwin supposed it to have done in many animal species.[2] But it is not at first sight obvious how it should operate as a great socializing force. If we would understand how it may have done so, we must bear in mind the fact, so strongly insisted on by Walter Bagehot in his brilliant essay, "Physics and Politics," [3] that the first and most momentous step of primitive men toward civilization must have been the evolution of rigid customs the enforced observance of which disciplined men to the habit of control of the immediate impulses. Bagehot rightly maintained that the achievement of this first step of the moral ladder must have been a most difficult one; he wrote, "Law, rigid, definite, concise law was the primary want of early mankind; that which they needed above anything else, that which was requisite before they could gain anything else," that is, before they could gain the advantages of social cooperation.[4] Again, he wrote, "In early times the quantity of government is much more important than its quality. What is wanted is a comprehensive rule binding men together, making them do the same things, telling them what to expect of each other, fashioning them alike, and keeping them so. What the rule is does not matter so much. A good rule is better than a bad one, but a bad one is better than none." [5] When Bagehot goes on to tell us how law established law-abidingness, or the capacity of self-control, in human nature, his account ceases to be satisfactory, for he wrote when biologists still believed with Lamarck and Darwin and Spencer in the inheritance of acquired characters. That such inheritance is possible we may no longer assume, though very many writers on social topics still make the assumption, as Bagehot did, and still use it as the easy key to all problems of social evolution. For Bagehot simply assumed that the habit of self-control and of obedience to law and custom, forcibly induced in the members of succeeding generations, became an innate quality by transmission and accumulation from generation to generation. While, then, we may accept Bagehot's dictum that it is difficult to exaggerate the difference between civilized and primitive men (that is, really primitive men, not the savages of the present time) in respect to their innate law-abidingness and while we may accept also his view that the strict enforcement of law played a great part in producing this evolution, we cannot accept his view of the mode of operation of law in producing this all important change.

But the hypothesis of the primal law enables us to conceive the first step of the process in a manner consistent with modern biological principles. For

2 *The Descent of Man* (New York: D. Appleton & Co., 1872).

3 "International Scientific Series" (New York: D. Appleton & Co., 1901).

4 *Ibid.*, p. 21.

5 *Ibid.*, p. 25.

offense against the primal law meant death to the offender unless he proved himself more than a match for the patriarch. Hence the ruthless pugnacity of the patriarch must have constantly weeded out the more reckless of his male progeny, those least capable of restraining their sexual impulse under the threat of his anger. Fear, the great inhibitor, must have played a great part in inducing observance of the primal law, and it might be suggested that the principal effect of the enforcement of this law must have been to increase by selection the power of this restraining instinct. But those males who failed to engage in combat would never succeed in transmitting their too timorous natures to a later generation, for by combat alone could the headship of a family be obtained. Hence this ruthless selection among the young males must have led to the development of prudence rather than to the mere strengthening of the instinct of fear.

Now prudent control of an impulse implies a much higher type of mental organization, a much greater degree of mental integration, than is implied by the mere inhibition of an impulse through fear. No doubt the instinct of fear plays a part in such prudent control, but it implies also a considerable degree of development of self-consciousness and of the self-regarding sentiment and a capacity for deliberation and the weighing of motives in the light of self-consciousness. If an individual has such capacities, a moderate strength of the fear impulse will suffice to restrain the sex impulse more effectively than a very strong fear impulse operating in a less developed mind. The operation of the primal law will, therefore, have tended to secure that the successful rival of the patriarch should have strong instincts of sex and of pugnacity and a but moderately strong fear instinct, combined with the more developed mental organization that permits of deliberation and of control of the stronger impulses through the organized cooperation of the weaker impulses. That is to say, it was a condition which secured for the family community a succession of patriarchs each of whom was superior to his rivals not merely in power of combat, but also and chiefly in power of farsighted control of his impulses. Each such patriarch, becoming the father of the succeeding generation, will then have transmitted to it in some degree his exceptional power of self-control. In this way the primal law, enforced by the fiercest passions of primitive man, may have prepared human nature for the observance of laws less brutally and ruthlessly enforced, may, in short, have played a great part in developing in humanity that power of self-control and law-abidingness which was the essential condition of the progress of social organization.

If we consider human societies at a later stage of their development, we shall see that the pugnacious instinct has played a similar part there also. And in this case we are not compelled to rely only on speculative hypotheses, but can find inductive support for our inference in a comparative study of existing savage peoples.

When in any region social organization had progressed so far that the mortal combat of individuals was replaced by the mortal combat of tribes, villages, or groups of any kind, success in combat and survival and propagation must have been favored by, and have depended upon, not only the vigor and ferocity of individual fighters, but also, and to an even greater degree, the capacity of individuals for united action, good comradeship, personal trustworthiness, and the capacity of individuals to subordinate their impulsive tendencies and egoistic promptings to the ends of the group and to the commands of the accepted leader. Hence, wherever such mortal conflict of groups prevailed for many generations, it must have developed in the surviving groups just those social and moral qualities of individuals which are the essential conditions of all effective cooperation and of the higher forms of social organizations. For success in war implies definite organization, the recognition of a leader, and faithful observance of his commands, and the obedience given to the war chief implies a far higher level of morality than is implied by the mere observance of the primal law or of any other personal prohibition under the threat of punishment. A leader whose followers were bound to him by fear of punishment only would have no chance of success against a band of which the members were bound together and to their chief by a true conscientiousness arising from a more developed self-consciousness, from the identification of the self with the society, and from a sensitive regard on the part of each member for the opinion of his fellows.

Such conflict of groups could not fail to operate effectively in developing the moral nature of man; those communities in which this higher morality was developed would triumph over and exterminate those which had not attained it in equal degree. And the more the pugnacious instinct impelled primitive societies to warfare, the more rapidly and effectively must the fundamental social attributes of men have been developed in the societies which survived the ordeal.

It is not easy to analyze these moral qualities and to say exactly what elements of the mental constitution were involved in this evolution. In part the advance must have consisted in a further improvement of the kind we have supposed to be effected by the operation of the primal law, namely, a richer self-consciousness and increased capacity for control of the stronger primary impulses by the cooperation of impulses springing from dispositions organized about the idea of the self. It may also have involved a relative increase of strength of the more specifically social tendencies, namely, the gregarious instinct, the instincts of self-assertion and subjection, and the primitive sympathetic tendency; the increase of strength of these tendencies in the members of any social group would render them capable of being more strongly swayed by regard for the opinions and feelings of their fellows and so would strengthen the influence of the public opinion of the group upon each member of it.

These results of group-selection produced by the mortal conflicts of small societies and ultimately due to the strength of the pugnacious instinct are very clearly illustrated by the tribes of Borneo. As one travels up any one of the large rivers, one meets with tribes that are successively more warlike. In the coast regions are peaceful communities which never fight save in self-defense, and then with but poor success, whereas in the central regions, where the rivers take their rise, are a number of extremely warlike tribes whose raids have been a constant source of terror to the communities settled in the lower reaches of the rivers. And between these tribes at the center and those in the coast regions are others that serve as a buffer between them, being decidedly more bellicose than the latter but less so than the former. It might be supposed that the peaceful coast people would be found to be superior in moral qualities to their more warlike neighbors, but the contrary is the case. In almost all respects the advantage lies with the warlike tribes. Their houses are better built, larger, and cleaner; their domestic morality is superior; they are physically stronger, are braver, and physically and mentally more active and in general are more trustworthy. But, above all, their social organization is firmer and more efficient because their respect for and obedience to their chiefs and their loyalty to their community are much greater; each man identifies himself with the whole community and accepts and loyally performs the social duties laid upon him. And the moderately warlike tribes occupying the intermediate regions stand midway between them and the people of the coast as regards these moral qualities.[6]

Yet all these tribes are of closely allied racial stocks, and the superior moral qualities of the central tribes would seem to be the direct result of the very severe group-selection to which their innate pugnacity has subjected them for many generations. And the greater strength of their pugnacious instinct, which displays itself unmistakably in their more martial bearing and more fiery temper, is probably due ultimately to the more bracing climate of the central regions, which, by favoring a greater bodily activity, has led to more frequent conflicts and a stricter weeding out of the more inoffensive and less energetic individuals and groups.

Such tribal conflict, which in this remote region has continued up to the present time, has probably played in past ages a great part in preparing the civilized peoples of Europe for the complex social life that they have developed. Mr. Kidd has insisted forcibly upon this view, pointing out that the tribes of the central and northern regions of Europe, which have played so great a part in the later history of civilization, were subjected for long ages to a process of military group-selection which was probably of extreme severity and which rendered them, at the time they first appear in history, the most

---

[6] These statements are based not merely on my own observations during a sojourn of six months among these tribes, but also on the authority of my friend Dr. Charles Hose, who for more than twenty years has exercised a very remarkable influence over many of the tribes of Sarawak and has done very much to establish the beneficent rule of the rajah, H.H. Sir Charles Brooke, over the wilder tribes of the outlying districts.

pugnacious and terrible warriors that the world has ever seen.[7] This process must have developed not only the individual fighting qualities, but also the qualities that make for conscientious conduct and stable and efficient social organization. These effects were clearly marked in the barbarians who overran the Roman Empire. The Germanic tribes were perhaps more pugnacious and possessed of the military virtues in a higher degree than any other people that has existed before or since. They were the most terrible enemies, as Julius Caesar found; they could never be subdued because they fought not merely to gain any specific ends, but because they loved fighting, that is, because they were innately pugnacious. Their religion and the character of their gods reflected their devotion to war; centuries of Christianity have failed to eradicate this quality, and the smallest differences of opinion and belief continue to furnish the pretexts for fresh combats. Mr. Kidd argues strongly that it is the social qualities developed by this process of military group-selection which, more than anything else, have enabled these peoples to build up a new civilization on the ruins of the Roman Empire and to carry on the progress of social organization and of civilization to the point it has now reached.

These important social effects of the pugnacious instinct seem to be forcibly illustrated by a comparison of the peoples of Europe with those of India and of China, two areas comparable with it in extent, in density of settled population, and in age of civilization. In neither of these areas has there been a similar perennial conflict of societies. In both of them, the mass of the people has been subjected for long ages to the rule of dominant castes which have established themselves in successive invasions from the central plateau of Asia, that great breeding ground of warlike nomadic hordes. The result in both cases is the same. The bulk of the people are deficient in the pugnacious instinct; they are patient and long-suffering, have no taste for war, and, in China especially, they despise the military virtues. At the same time they seem to be deficient in those social qualities which may be summed up under the one word "conscientiousness" and which are the cement of societies and essential factors of their progressive integration. Accordingly, in the societies formed by these peoples, the parts hang but loosely together—they are but partially integrated and loosely organized. Among these peoples Buddhism, the religion of peace, found a congenial home, and its precepts have governed the practice of great masses of men in a very real manner which contrasts strongly with the formal acceptance and practical neglect of the peaceful precepts of their religion that have always characterized the Christian peoples of Western Europe.

In this connection it is interesting to compare the Japanese with the Chinese

[7] Benjamin Kidd, *Principles of Western Civilization* (New York: Grosset & Dunlap, 1907), p. 156: "The ruling fact which stands clearly out in regarding this movement of peoples as a whole, is that it must have represented a process of military selection, probably the most sustained, prolonged, and culminating in character that the race has ever undergone."

people. Whether the strain of Malayan blood in the Japanese has endowed them from the first with a stronger instinct of pugnacity than their cousins the Chinese, it is impossible to say. But it is certain that the people, in spite of the fact that they have long recognized in their emperor a common spiritual head of the empire, have been until very recently divided into numerous clans that have been almost constantly at war with one another, society being organized on a military system not unlike that of feudal Europe. Hence the profession of the soldier has continued to be held in the highest honor, and the fighting qualities, as well as the specifically social qualities of the people, have been brought to a very high level.

In Japan, also, Buddhism has long been firmly established, but, as with Christianity in Europe, its preaching of peace has never been practically accepted by the mass of the people; the old ancestor worship has continued to flourish side by side with it and now, on the accentuation of the warlike spirit induced by contact with the outside world, seems to be pushing the religion of peace into the background.

In addition to this important role in the evolution of the moral qualities, the pugnacious instinct has exerted a more direct and hardly less important influence in the life of societies.

We have seen how this instinct is operative in the emotion of revenge and in moral indignation. These two emotions have played leading parts in the growth and maintenance of every system of criminal law and every code of punishment, for, however widely authors may differ as to the spirit in which punishment should be administered, there can be no doubt that it was originally retributive and that it still retains something of this character even in the most highly civilized societies. The administration of criminal law is, then, the organized and regulated expression of the anger of society, modified and softened in various degrees by the desire that punishment may reform the wrongdoer and deter others from similar actions.

Though with the progress of civilization, the public administration of justice has encroached more and more on the sphere of operation of the anger of individuals as a power restraining offenses of all kinds, yet, in the matter of offenses against the person, individual anger remains as a latent threat whose influence is by no means negligible in the regulation of manners, as we see most clearly in those countries in which the practice of dueling is not yet obsolete. And in the nursery and the school, righteous anger will always have a great and proper part to play in the training of the individual for his life in society.

It was suggested . . . that emulation is rooted in an instinct which was evolved in the human mind by a process of differentiation from the instinct of pugnacity. However that may be, it seems clear that this impulse is distinct from both the combative and the self-assertive impulses; and just as, according to our supposition, the emulative impulse has acquired in the course of the evolution of the human mind an increasing importance, so in the life of societies it tends gradually to take the place of the instinct of pugnacity, as a force making for the development of social life and organization.

It is among the peoples of Western Europe, who, as we have seen, have been molded by a prolonged and severe process of military selection, that the emulative impulse is most active. With us it supplies the zest and determines the forms of almost all our games and recreations, and Prof. [William] James is guilty of picturesque exaggeration only when he says "nine-tenths of the work of our world is done by it." Our educational system is founded upon it; it is the social force underlying a great deal of strenuous exertion; to it we owe in a great measure even our science, our literature, and our art; for it is a strong, perhaps an essential, element of ambition, that last infirmity of noble minds, in which it operates through, and under the direction of, a highly developed social self-consciousness.

The emulative impulse tends to assert itself in an ever-widening sphere of social life, encroaching more and more upon the sphere of the combative impulse and supplanting it more and more as a prime mover of both individuals and societies. This tendency brings with it a very important change in the conditions of social evolution. Whereas the combative impulse leads to the destruction of the individuals and societies that are least capable of self-defense, the emulative impulse does not directly lead to the extermination of individuals or societies. It is, rather, compatible with a tender solicitude for their continued existence; the millionaire who, prompted by this impulse, has succeeded in appropriating a proportion of the wealth of the community vastly in excess of his deserts may spend a part of it on free libraries, hospitals, or soup kitchens. In fact, the natural tendency of the emulative impulse is to preserve, rather than to destroy, defeated competitors; for their regards bring a fuller satisfaction to the impulse, and the exploitation of their labor by the successful rival is the natural issue of competition. Therefore, as emulation replaces pugnacity within any society, it tends to put a stop to natural selection of individuals within that society so that the evolution of human nature becomes increasingly dependent on group-selection. And, if international emulation should completely supplant international pugnacity, group-selection also will be rendered very much less effective. To this stage the most highly civilized communities are tending, in accordance with the law that the collective mind follows in the steps of evolution of the individual mind at a great interval of time. There are unmistakable signs that the pugnacity of nations is being supplanted by emulation; that warfare is being replaced by industrial and intellectual rivalry; that wars between civilized nations, which are replacing the mortal conflicts between individuals and between societies dominated by the spirit of pugnacity, are tending to become mere incidents of their commercial and industrial rivalry, being undertaken to secure markets or sources of supply of raw material which shall bring industrial or commercial advantage to their possessor.

The tendency of emulation to replace pugnacity is, then, a tendency to bring to an end what has been an important, probably the most important, factor of progressive evolution of human nature, namely, the selection of the fit and the extermination of the less fit (among both individuals and societies) resulting from their conflicts with one another.[8]

[8] The attempt now being made to found a science and an art of eugenics owes its importance largely to this tendency.

◄◄◄ ►►►

D. O. HEBB & W. R. THOMPSON

*Emotion and Society**

THE CONDITIONS OF FEAR AND HOSTILITY

. . . The social determinants of fear and hostility are very complex. If the reader does not find this conclusion new and startling, we can say it another way. The problem of social motivation is apt to be taken too lightly with too much of the reversed-panacea approach—the idea that all our social troubles stem from economic pressure, *or* Oedipus difficulties, *or* frustration, or some other single source. Fix whichever one it is that makes the trouble, and all will be well. A main object here is to show that the infrahuman animal has a more complicated set of motivations than is allowed to man by these one-shot pre-scriptions.

Some of our conclusions . . . will be quite obvious ones: frustration is not a sufficient statement of the causes of aggression; the unknown as such may cause fear; man, who so often avoids pain and effort, also goes to some trouble to expose himself to threat of pain and to situations demanding effort. These things are common knowledge. But they are not common knowledge in psy-chology, and we must remind the reader that everyone knows a lot of things that are not true. One necessary task for scientific psychology is to sort out,

* Reprinted in part from D. O. Hebb and W. R. Thompson, "The Social Significance of Animal Studies," chap. 15, in Gardner Lindzey, ed., *Handbook of Social Psychology*, Vol. I, by permission of the publisher (Copyright 1954, Addison-Wesley Publishing Co., Reading, Mass.).

among the obvious facts of human nature, the true from the untrue, the useful ideas from the useless. The reason for preferring simpler theories of human action is not that anyone thinks that the facts are really simple, but that it is too easy to postulate explanatory entities whenever the going gets hard. Which are the fertile postulates? Which are really needed to account for the facts? It is especially necessary to be careful when a discrepancy between fact and theory is found only at the human level in the adult subject, because of the multifarious and uncontrolled experiences that occur during the long period of human growth, together with the special effects of verbal learning. So it will not be new if we conclude from the animal data that man is hostile to strangers; this is "known" already, but the need for taking theoretical account of it is clearer if its phylogenetic development can be traced and when related behavior can be demonstrated in lower animals, in more controlled conditions, and without the contaminating influence of language.

Chimpanzee Fears and Aggressions

Fear of innocuous objects is very common in the chimpanzee, even though these objects are not associated with some more primitive cause of avoidance. The diary records of the Yerkes Laboratories contain a great many references to unexplained fears of a particular person; some piece of apparatus or part of it; rope of a particular size, color, and texture but not of other ropes; a biscuit in which a worm is found; a vegetable of a peculiar shape; and so on. There are great individual differences, of course, but as a group the adult chimpanzees are markedly subject to such fears. Köhler's observation of panic at sight of small animal models such as a toy donkey is well known.[1] A chance observation, made with a clay model of a chimpanzee head, extended the range of objects known to have such effects.[2] The clay model, reasonably lifelike in proportions but about half life size, produced extreme panic in nearly half the thirty-two adults to whom it was shown and very marked signs of fear in most of the rest. An actual head preserved in formalin had the same effects and so had a very lifelike colored model of a human head from a display dummy.

An attempt to deal with such facts theoretically [3] is not too satisfactory in certain respects, but the line of reasoning suggested a relationship to human emotional disturbance at sight of a mutilated body and fear of the dead, and so the following observations were also made. These are cited in full because of the socially significant aggressions that were elicited along with the fear. A dead chimpanzee was not available for experiment, but anesthetized ones were.

[1] Wolfgang Köhler, *The Mentality of Apes* (2nd ed.; New York: Harcourt, Brace, 1927).
[2] D. O. Hebb, "On the Nature of Fear," *Psychological Review*, LIII (1946), 259–276.
[3] *Idem*, *The Organization of Behavior* (New York: Wiley, 1949).

Aug. 15, 1943. Mars, a young animal who had been anesthetized by nembutal, in order to make physical measurements, was carried out and shown to four of the adults, Jack, Dick, Don, and Dita. The first three of these were markedly excited (Dita less so) and Don attempted to attack. *Aug. 17.* Mars, anesthetized again, was laid on the ground in the infants' enclosure, with his fellow youngsters. One of them, Art, was persistently aggressive, biting and hitting the inert animal, who had to be rescued. Mars was then carried to the cages of some of the adults. Nana and Helene showed interest but no emotional excitement; Don was excited, with hair erect, and somewhat aggressive in manner; Dina and Bula manifested a nonspecific excitation, with hair erect; Wendy's hair was erect, she did not seem as excited, but she came close and remained; and Josie (as it happened Mars' mother, from whom he had been separated early) manifested an apparent mixture of aggression and fear—she was very excited, ran inside when Mars was first brought near, then attacked him through the cage-wire. Her hair was erect throughout.

Since the sight of an anesthetized infant being carried by one of the staff was common, the observations above were later repeated with an anesthetized adult. *Feb. 11, 1945.* Don, under nembutal, was wheeled on a handcart up to the cages of nine other adults. Ami, Nira, and Vera showed fear, and Dina and Bokar did also but then followed this by a show of aggression at a distance; Kambi showed generalized excitation and screaming only; Frank, with hair erect, spat at the anesthetized Don; Pan first avoided, then attacked through the cage-wire; and Lia, with general excitation but not avoidance, also attacked. (The youngsters in the infants' enclosure were afraid, one very much so, and all showed signs of marked excitation.)

Now let us look at the chimpanzees' aggressions as they occur in more ordinary circumstances, in the form of teasing, jealousy, anger, or chronic malice.

The motivation for teasing is often strong. It seems certain that the chimpanzee gets satisfaction simply from the discomfiture of the human being who is startled and frightened or angered by a sudden screaming attack on the cage-wire nearest him or on being squirted with water. Certainly the animal goes to considerable trouble to achieve such results, in spite of being often punished for it and getting no other reward than seeing the effects of the act. Other chimpanzees are teased as well as human beings, as Köhler noted.[4] Deliberate planning is involved, with an evident expectancy of the end effects of the behavior. "Teasing" is too mild a word for some attacks that seemed to be made only for the sake of others' discomfiture (as when Alpha would occasionally yank a handful of hair out of a thoroughly dominated cage-mate, with no provocation), but it is important to note that these minor

[4] *Op. cit.*, pp. 83 ff.

aggressions are not always indications of a desire to do more serious damage if only the victim were within reach. Quite often he *is* within reach or becomes so later without receiving more damage. In the timid-man observations, some of the animals seemed genuinely malicious, but others, after once getting a rise out of the experimenter, became gentle and made no attempt to injure him when he came within reach.

Look next at the causes of anger and their relation to frustration. The usual stimulus to anger is the behavior of a person or another chimpanzee acting in a way that is not desired or failing to act in a desired way. "Desire" is one of the terms proscribed in Watson's revolution, along with images and ideas, not because of its vagueness or trouble in defining it (after all, "learning," "intelligence," and "emotion" were retained), but because such terms were thought to be entirely subjective and anthropomorphic in their reference. We can now see that they are much better treated as referring to intervening variables, postulated processes, either with man or animal. As such, they are more-or-less suitable for use in an objective psychology. They are still vague, but the fault is not in the way the terms are defined but in our theoretical conceptions, which will not be made any better just by using new terms. If one is really serious about stating the conditions in which anger occurs, a reference to desire or some equivalent is necessary.

To speak of "frustration" instead does not avoid the necessity, for it is clear that it is a desire or an expectancy that is frustrated. By some writers, of course, the term "frustration" has been used to emphasize the complexity and importance of internal representative processes in a Freudian or near-Freudian way.[5] With this we have no quarrel. But some writers have seemed to feel that the reference to frustration is a means of simplifying the problem and that it avoids the need of postulating conceptual processes. Others have pointed out that this will not work for man.[6] The evidence seems even clearer for the chimpanzee.

When a female chimpanzee in heat is introduced into the next cage, the male seeing her gets up and comes as close as he can, until he is stopped by intervening cage-wire. At this time he shows no anger, although a goal-directed response, strongly motivated, has been interrupted. But anger becomes highly predictable if the male is first led to expect, by the caretaker's actions, that he will be admitted to the female's cage and then is not. It is the expectancy that gives the physical barrier its effect. In other situations, one can only say that the chimpanzee is angry because he does not *like* what another is doing. No

[5] Saul Rosenzweig, "An Outline of Frustration Theory," in J. McV. Hunt, ed., *Personality and the Behavior Disorders* (New York: Ronald Press, 1944), I, 379–388.
[6] S. S. Sargeant, "Reaction to Frustration—A Critique and Hypothesis," *Psychological Review*, LV (1948), 108–114; Peter McKellar, "Provocation to Anger and the Development of Attitudes of Hostility," *British Journal of Psychology*, XL (1950), 104–114.

goal-directed response is interrupted, and a physical barrier has nothing to do with the cause of anger (although it may prevent the effects of the anger from being visited on its object).

Thus Pan had a temper tantrum at the sight of two experimenters taking a vaginal smear from a female in heat in another cage. Mimi was driven to paroxysms of rage by the two inmates of the next cage, who would wait until her back was turned and then spring screaming at the intervening cage-wire, repeatedly startling her. Bokar was almost as much infuriated by Dick's spitting water at him, even when he was not hit. Köhler has noted that noisemaking and social disturbance as such may be a cause of anger for a chimpanzee just as for man.[7] The diaries of the Yerkes Laboratories likewise record a number of instances in which a noisy temper tantrum by one animal has led another to attack him. We have . . . noted the anger of the chimpanzee at another's begging, even as he yields and hands over food. Defining the frustration in such cases of anger will present difficulty unless it is frankly incorporated in a theory of thought so that frustration can be treated as some sort of conflict with the thought process. With anger, as with fear, the phenomena of emotion point to the intimate relationship of motivation to intellectual processes and the impossibility of treating these things in separate compartments of theory.

The Practical Problems of Social Motivation

It is reasonable, even desirable, to oversimplify theory in its preliminary stages, as long as one is concerned only with theoretical problems. The idea is that later stages of theory will do justice to the facts if early ones cannot. But it is quite another thing to forget that theory is still in these early stages when one is advising on a practical problem. What is virtue in one endeavor is vice in the other, and the more difficult the problem, the truer this becomes. No other scientist deals with issues of such practical urgency as the social psychologist, and, even though he has recognized the complexity of his problem, the social psychologist may still find it worth while to consider some of the practical implications of the emotional behavior of higher animals and perhaps also to be reminded by the animal data of the practical dangers of tacitly accepting too simple a view of motivation.

This last remark, be it noted, is not a covert attack on the theory of biological rewards (plus conditioning). Although we have probably betrayed our preference for another sort of approach, such as that of Harlow or Maslow, we must point out that biological-reward theory is being greatly elaborated by such recent treatments of secondary reward as those of Meehl and Mac-

[7] *Op. cit.*, p. 293.

Corquodale, Mowrer, and Miller.[8] These discussions imply no simple approach to the problem of social motivation.

In the year 1950 the main explanations of social hostility, as outlined by Katz in a review of the literature, make the hostility learned *or* in some way a product of frustration.[9] Although the difficulties in the way of one or the other of such simplifications have been recognized, the comparative psychologist may point out that the literature reviewed by Katz predicates a view of motivation that on our present knowledge is doubtfully adequate for the laboratory rat and quite inadequate for the dog or chimpanzee, let alone man.

From the practical point of view in this matter, the animal evidence offers good news as well as bad. It complicates the issues theoretically, but some of the complications mean that there may be hope for man as a social animal. On the plus side there is, as we have seen, evidence of a fundamental aptitude in higher animals for friendship and helping others. We do not know just what conditions of rearing foster this altruism, but it should be possible to find out experimentally.

A further plus item is that frustration does not always increase hostility and may even decrease it without evidence of undesirable side effects ("displacement"). Punishing an adult chimpanzee for a misdemeanor like spitting or scratching the caretaker does not usually produce signs of resentment. On one occasion at least, punishment of a young animal for repeated biting led to a strong friendship (diary of Gamma, Yerkes Laboratories, 1935). The reader may be reminded also of the sudden friendliness of Beta and Pati to the bold man, when he promptly answered attack with attack. In animal, as in man, the effect of aggression in some circumstances is *respect* and *liking*. Nissen, in a personal communication, points out that forcing a chimpanzee to do something, or forcibly depriving him of something is as often followed by an increase of friendliness as by a decrease. The friendliness cannot be an effect of the frustration alone; it must depend also on the fact that the frustrater is a rewarder at other times. But with a background of beneficence, the important thing is that deprivation need not decrease good will. Social living and educa-

---

[8] Harry F. Harlow, "Levels of Integration along the Phylogenetic Scale: Learning Aspect," in John H. Rohrer and Muzafer Sherif, eds., *Social Psychology at the Crossroads* (New York: Harper, 1951), pp. 121–144; Abraham H. Maslow, "The Instinctoid Nature of Basic Needs," *Journal of Personality*, XXII (1953), 326–335; Paul E. Meehl and Kenneth MacCorquodale, "A Further Study of Latent Learning in the T-Maze," *Journal of Comparative Physiological Psychology*, XLI (1948), 372–396; *idem*, "Some Methodological Comments Concerning Expectancy Theory," *Psychological Review*, LVIII (1951), 230–233; O. H. Mowrer, *Learning Theory and Personality Dynamics* (New York: Ronald Press, 1950); *idem*, "Motivation," *Annual Review of Psychology*, III (1952), 419–438; and Neal E. Miller, "Learnable Drives and Rewards," in Stanley S. Stevens, ed., *Handbook of Experimental Psychology* (New York: Wiley, 1951), pp. 435–472.

[9] Irving Katz, "Behavioral Interaction in a Herd of Barbary Sheep (*Ammotragus Lervia*)," *Zoologica* (New York), XXXIV (1949), 9–18; he concludes in favor of multiple causation (p. 155).

tion inevitably mean an unending series of frustrations but these, it seems, should not be thought of as always making for hostility.

But the bad news must be reckoned with, too. On the minus side is the evidence that timidity, as such, may incite aggression. Fortunately, this is not always so, and the consistently friendly behavior of some chimpanzees to the timid man justifies some hope concerning primate behavior in this respect. Also in the debit column are the mammal's fear and hostility with strangers, even when no injury has ever been received from a stranger.[10] This has an evident meaning for social problems and so has the combined fear and hostility toward a fellow chimpanzee under anesthesia (if, as it seems, this means that the cause of aggression was the failure of the anesthetized animal to behave in the normal way).

There is also another kind of evidence which has both good and bad implications. It shows, in brief, that mammals seek excitement, and this search has desirable possibilities in society as well as extremely undesirable ones. The animal that is so vulnerable to emotional disturbance nevertheless seeks the situations that produce emotional disturbance in mild degree. There may be difficulty about dealing with this theoretically, but it appears empirically that for any one animal there is an optimal level of fear or frustration.[11] First, the evidence concerning fear: strange surroundings tend to produce emotional disturbance in the rat, but Montgomery and Thompson have shown experimentally that the rat which has the choice of familiar and unfamiliar territory will tend to move toward the unfamiliar—the well-known exploratory drive.[12] Whiting and Mowrer and Berlyne have suggested a connection between fear and investigative tendencies, and the dog that is frightened by a strange object is nevertheless apt to return to look at it again, balanced between closer approach and flight.[13] The same thing can be observed in chimpanzees, and Woodworth and Valentine have described the behavior of young children who ask to be shown again—at a safe distance—the object that has frightened them.[14] Second, concerning frustration: Harlow, Harlow, and Meyer have

---

[10] D. O. Hebb and Austin H. Riesen, "The Genesis of Irrational Fears," *Bulletin of the Canadian Psychological Association*, III (1943), 49–50.

[11] Hebb, *The Organization* . . . , *op. cit.*, pp. 232 ff.

[12] Kay C. Montgomery, "The Relation between Exploratory Behavior and Spontaneous Alternation in the White Rat," *Journal of Comparative Physiological Psychology*, XLIV (1951), 582–589; *idem*, "Exploratory Behavior and Its Relation to Spontaneous Alternation in a Series of Maze Exposures," *Journal of Comparative Physiological Psychology*, XLV (1952), 50–57; W. R. Thompson, "Exploratory Behavior as a Function of Hunger in 'Bright' and 'Dull' Rats," *Journal of Comparative Physiological Psychology*, XLVI (1953), 323–326.

[13] J. W. M. Whiting and O. H. Mowrer, "Habit Progression and Regression—A Laboratory Study of Some Factors Relevant to Human Socialization," *Journal of Comparative Psychology*, XXXVI (1943), 229–253; Daniel E. Berlyne, "Novelty and Curiosity as Determinants of Exploratory Behavior," *British Journal of Psychology*, XLI (1950), 68–80.

[14] Robert S. Woodworth, *Psychology* (New York: Holt, 1921); Charles W. Valentine, "The Innate Bases of Fear," *Journal of Genetic Psychology*, XXXVII (1930), 394–419.

demonstrated the monkey's willingness to expose itself repeatedly to the frustrations inherent in problem-solving, without extrinsic reward.[15] Mahut, working in the McGill laboratory, has shown that the rat which is offered two routes to food, one short and direct, the other via a maze problem, will choose the problem on 20 to 40 per cent of the runs. *Some* of the time even a rat prefers to work for his living.

Such phenomena are, of course, well known in man: in the liking for dangerous sports or roller coasters, where fear is deliberately courted, and in the addiction to bridge or golf or solitaire, vices whose very existence depends on the difficulty of the problems presented and an optimal level of frustration. Once more, when we find such attitudes toward fear and frustration in animals, we have a better basis for supposing that we are dealing with something fundamental if a man prefers skis to the less dangerous snowshoes or when we observe an unashamed love of work (problem-solving and frustration included) in the scientist or in the businessman who cannot retire. Such behavior in man is usually accounted for as a search for prestige, but the animal data make this untenable. It seems much more likely that solving problems and running mild risks are inherently rewarding or, in more general terms, that the animal will always act so as to produce an optimal level of excitation. One explanation has been attempted by Hebb; [16] another, into which the facts on the whole would fit very well, is the treatment by Mowrer of anxiety reduction as a reward (though here one needs to assume that problem-solving is also a cause of anxiety).[17]

The potential social benefits of a liking for work and (in some essential occupations) for taking risks are sufficiently obvious. This is the plus side of the mammal's liking for excitement. But, as the chimpanzee's behavior shows, excitement may be sought in other less desirable ways. The plain fact is that the primate is only too ready to become a troublemaker when things are dull, and we had better stop comforting ourselves with the accurate but insufficient statement that man has no instinct to make war. He also needs no special coaching to discover a taste for "adventure," and some of his adventures may be socially disastrous. Fear or dislike of the strange is not innate, since it depends on certain prior experiences, yet it still does not have to be taught.[18] If, therefore, man is not born with a dislike for those who differ from him in habits or appearance, he can still pick up the dislike with no help or encouragement. Making war is not instinctive; neither, unfortunately, is an aversion to certain forms of excitement that may lead to war.

[15] Harry F. Harlow, Margaret K. Harlow, and Donald R. Meyer, "Learning Motivated by a Manipulation Drive," *Journal of Experimental Psychology*, XL (1950), 228–234.

[16] Hebb, *The Organization* . . . , *op. cit.*

[17] Mowrer, *Learning Theory* . . . , *op. cit.*; *idem*, "Motivation," *op. cit.*

[18] Hebb, "On the Nature . . . ," *op. cit.*

It appears, therefore, that we stand on very slippery ground when we suppose that social harmony is to be had on a negative basis, by minimizing frustration for the growing child and not teaching him bad ideas about others. Suppose we do give the child as much freedom as we can; suppose the adult does see that he is not being injured or threatened by other groups—is there not still a strong presumption that more will be necessary? That the child must be taught somehow to *like* others different from himself, to get *pleasure* from knowing more about them and learning about their unusual ways? In addition to correcting economic injustice, may it not be necessary also to develop, systematically, socially harmless sources of excitation? Poker and bridge and pennant races and bowling alleys and detective stories may have more to do with our social stability than we think. Even today, an economically successful society may require circuses in some form, as well as bread.

Economic factors obviously play a large part in social conflict; it is only too evident that children can learn hostile attitudes from their elders. We must recognize and control these factors for a sound society. But it is equally essential to recognize that there is no scientific basis for asserting that these are the only factors underlying war and race prejudice. We may even doubt that they are ever effective by themselves without the deep-seated tendency to be disturbed emotionally by what is different from ourselves.

A THEORETICAL APPROACH TO HUMAN NATURE AND SOCIETY

We have made some effort in the preceding pages to be economical of theory, using no more than was needed to make a connected story. If we have nevertheless been speculative, we must now become more so. Our purpose in this final section is to offer a theoretical view concerning human emotions which, we believe, casts light on the evolution and structure of society.

Doing so is not outside the scope of the present chapter. The views we set forth derive from the study of animal emotions; and we may remind the reader, if need be, that comparative psychology includes man, regarding him simply as the highest in the animal series. Human culture is unique, but this only makes it the more interesting as a comparative phenomenon. From the comparative point of view it constitutes a special problem.

Man is the most intelligent animal, and the most striking feature of his behavior, comparatively, is an increasing control of the physical environment and the accumulation of "wealth" and wealth-producing skills. But almost equally striking is the progressive modification that has gone on in other aspects of human behavior: broadly speaking, a moral and political development. The economic growth can be treated as the result of a search for comfort by an exceptionally intelligent animal; a unique power of communication, particularly, allows for progressive problem-solving. But the cumulative change in other respects—can this be ascribed to the same source?

Can we derive man's social evolution from his exceptional intellectual characteristics? Perhaps we would also allow him some altruism on occasion, and we must certainly recognize that his powers of learning and communication will perpetuate some mistakes, so that, if we see man as intellectually distinctive only, we need not imply that all his social arrangements are intelligent ones. Even after making these allowances, however, we may ask whether such a simple model of the origins of society would not be significantly improved by recognizing that man also has exceptional emotional characteristics.

We have already proposed that the mammal seeks excitement when things are dull. This by itself makes an important change in the theory of "economic man." That theory can hold only in an impoverished society (in which the level of frustration is already above the optimum) and *not* in an economically successful one. With a general increase in wealth and security, the risky venture may be preferred to the sure thing, the interesting occupation to one that pays well.

But let us now go further. Evidence from species comparison suggests that emotional susceptibility increases with intellectual capacity. Man is the most emotional as well as the most rational animal. But this susceptibility is partly self-concealing: its possessor tends to seek the environment in which a too strong emotion is least likely to occur, the one in which disturbance is nearer the optimal level. In man, this makes for the establishment of "civilized" societies, the chief characteristic of which (at least, until recently) is not that they improve the economic lot of the average member, but that they provide an environment in which the frequency of acute fear, disgust, anger, and jealousy is decreased. The further a society has advanced along this path, the less subject to strong emotion its members must appear. Violent emotional outbursts vanish, the well-bred man becomes the norm, and psychologists who seldom see the strong, acute disturbance (except in young children) begin to think of adult man as typically unemotional. But the susceptibility to the disturbance may still be there and, although concealed, have a major influence on social organization.

Emotionality and Intellect

Such views and their comparative origin will be more intelligible if we see how they were arrived at, in the course of constructing a theory presented elsewhere.[19]

The first aim was relatively modest: to find some way of bringing together the facts of learning, perception, and set or attitude. This, it

[19] *Idem, The Organization . . . , op. cit.*

seemed, might be feasible if one could treat the thought process as a "phase sequence," as a series of events in the brain each of which might be aroused sensorily or centrally, or both.

The principal question was as to the nature of these events in the brain. Existing anatomical evidence, and some of the psychological evidence, led to the conception that each of the series of activities would be the activity of an "assembly" of neural cells. These assemblies would have to be established before overt learning could occur, which seemed to deny the truth of the theory, until von Senden's evidence was recalled.[20] The second main difficulty entailed by such ideas, however, is the one that concerns us more. The assembly as postulated would be rather fragile in its function, easily disturbed or disrupted by unusual sensory conditions. The theory thus arrived at the improbable conclusion that a strange environment would interfere with thinking, or might disorganize it completely.

Then came a freeing hypothesis: suppose the interference with thought to be what we already know as *emotion*, and that it is usually mild. The neurophysiological speculations would permit the disturbance to occur in varying degrees, so let us assume that in mild degree it would not disrupt the phase sequence but only slow it. Slowing the phase sequence would mean that thought would continue, with the same general content, for a longer time. The thing thought about (or perceived) would be by definition more "interesting," more capable of arresting and holding attention. A mild disturbance might thus be positively motivating; and a strong disturbance, even though of the same kind, have opposite effects. Since (as we have seen) the behavioral evidence shows that there are such paradoxical effects of emotional stimulation, these neurophysiological notions seemed to have theoretical possibilities even though they still left much to be accounted for.

If such ideas were to be taken seriously, however, they had a further implication which led, rather deviously, to the present problem. If emotion is in some sense a breakdown of the thought process, it seemed that emotionality would become more marked when thought is more complex. The more elaborate the machinery, the more ways its operation can be disturbed. It seemed therefore that development of a higher level of intelligence would mean an increased vulnerability to emotional disturbance.

When the evidence was examined, some support for this idea appeared. The chimpanzee seems to be more subject to emotional disturbance than the dog, and the dog more so than the rat. There were also hints of an ontogenetic correlation, of increased emotionality with intellectual development from infancy to maturity. Now we come to our problem: adult man should be still more emo-

[20] Marius von Senden, *Raum- und Gestaltauffassung bei operierten Blindgeborenen vor und nach der Operation* (Leipzig: Barth, 1932).

tional than the very emotional chimpanzee and more emotional than the three-year-old child, and he does not seem to be.

But certain aspects of man's social behavior were very suggestive when they were examined from this point of view and led us to the conclusion that the predicted susceptibility exists, that it is a major influence on social evolution, and that it tends to produce societies such as ours, in which it can hardly be detected.

This view depends in part on the phylogenetic correlation. Let us therefore consider it first. There are certain primitive causes of avoidance and aggression that seem to work equally well at all levels of mammalian development: pain stimuli, sudden loud noise, sudden loss of support, restriction of movement by the animal that is used to freedom—all have immediate effects that are comparable in laboratory rat and man. But as we go from rat to man, there is a progressive increase in the range of effective stimuli to avoidance and aggression and in the duration and complexity of the response.

In the rat, for example, there is little need of such a term as "anger" for describing the animal's behavior. A rat is aggressive or he is not, and the aggression has about the same pattern in different circumstances. The same seems true of the dog, although occasionally he shows something that may be homologous with the primate's sulking. But with the chimpanzee, it is essential to distinguish anger from chronic malice if the animal is to be handled safely. The peculiarly human patterns of temper tantrum and sulking occur frequently. The causes of aggression are more varied in the dog than in the rat and far more varied in the chimpanzee than in the dog. Finally, the period of emotional disturbance following a brief stimulation also increases from rat to dog to chimpanzee. (The chimpanzee Fifi, for example, sulked for three weeks over not getting a cup of milk, first showing outright anger, then refusing to accept milk from anyone for a day or so, and continuing for three weeks to refuse it from the one who had denied it to her.)

The phylogenetic development of fear susceptibilities is even clearer. In higher mammals' irrational fears, the motionless object may be nearly as much avoided as the moving one. For a lower form like the rat, avoidance of a strange motionless object may occur but it certainly is not a prominent part of the behavior.[21] The dog falls part way between rat and chimpanzee. Melzack has described fears in the dog which are obviously like those of the chimpanzee, although the disturbance seems less intense.[22] As for man's nearest relatives, the apes, it would take a page or more to list the specific objects and situations that are known to have caused *persistent* fear in the chimpanzee, as

[21] Bradford B. Hudson, "One-Trial Learning in the Domestic Rat," *Genetic Psychology Monographs*, XLI (1950), 99–145.

[22] Ronald Melzack, "Irrational Fears in the Dog," *Canadian Journal of Psychology*, VI (1952), 141–147.

reported in the diaries of the Yerkes Laboratories and in systematic experiments.[23]

When one considers also his manifold angers and hostilities, the chimpanzee at first sight is a bundle of emotional disturbances. This is not really so, of course. Most of the time the chimpanzee is no more angry or afraid than his human caretaker, and frequently less. The thing that one fears, another does not. Some animals are "nervous" or short-tempered, but others are placid. Our point here, however, is that, as one goes from rat to dog to chimpanzee, one finds an increasing variety in the causes of emotional disturbance, an increasing variety of manifestation, and an increasing duration following brief stimulation, all of which is consistent with the idea that susceptibility to emotional disturbance increases with intellectual development.

To this phylogenetic correlation may be added an ontogenetic one. In the observations with anesthetized animals as test objects (described in the preceding section), the frequency and degree of excitation aroused in the half-grown chimpanzees was markedly less than in the full-grown. The clay model of a head hardly got a second glance from the one- and two-year-olds; it absorbed the attention of the five- and six-year-olds but produced no avoidance; in most of the adults it produced strong fear, with some avoidance in all of them. Jacobsen, Jacobsen, and Yoshioka and McCulloch and Haslerud have described the increasing emotional responses of the chimpanzee in the first years of life.[24] For man, Jersild and Holmes have shown a similar increase up to the age of five; [25] they conclude that the trend is thereafter reversed, but we shall try to show that this may indicate not a reduction of emotional susceptibility after five years, but the success of our society in protecting us from most of the situations that would produce fear in older children and adults.

Jones and Jones demonstrated that fear of snakes, at least, is much stronger and more frequent in young adults than in children, none of their subjects having had prior exposure to snakes.[26] This was a cross-sectional study, and a longitudinal observation may be added. Two young children, two years apart in age, were encouraged by a parent to handle snakes and liked to do so whenever they saw and could capture one. But the older at the age of eight, the

[23] Köhler, *op. cit.*; Robert M. Yerkes and Ada W. Yerkes, "Nature and Conditions of Avoidance (Fear) Response in Chimpanzees," *Journal of Comparative Physiological Psychology*, XXI (1936), 53–66; Thomas L. McCulloch and George M. Haslerud, "Affective Responses of an Infant Chimpanzee Reared in Isolation from Its Kind," *Journal of Comparative Physiological Psychology*, XXVIII (1939), 437–445; Hebb, "On the Nature . . . ," *op. cit.*

[24] Carlyle F. Jacobsen, Marian M. Jacobsen, and Joseph G. Yoshioka, "Development of an Infant Chimpanzee during Her First Year," *Comparative Psychology Monographs*, IX (1932), 1–94; McCulloch and Haslerud, *op. cit.*

[25] Arthur T. Jersild and Francis B. Holmes, *Children's Fears* (New York: Teachers College Bureau of Publications, 1935).

[26] H. E. Jones and Mary Cover Jones, "A Study of Fear," *Childhood Education*, V (1928), 136–143.

younger at seven, began to show not a fear, but a dislike, of touching a snake, and this repugnance subsequently became strong in both, still definitely without fear and definitely without any associated injury, in a part of the country where poisonous snakes are never found.

Even without the special theoretical views from which the discussion took off, such phylogenetic and ontogenetic correlations between increasing intellect and increasing emotionality would suggest that thought and emotion are intimately, essentially related. There must be doubt concerning any treatment of emotion as a state or process independent of intellectual processes and having a separate seat in the nervous system. Brainstem theories of emotion, as developed originally by Head and by Cannon and Bard or more recently by Lindsley, do not seem to give enough weight to the evident cortical elements in the fears and angers of the higher animal.[27] These appear in the kind of perception that can cause emotion in the higher animal (including the role of fantasy reported by the human subject), as well as in the correlation with intellectual level that has just been discussed.

Emotion and Society

Such theoretical considerations lead one to expect that adult man will be more subject to emotional disturbance than the young child or subhuman animal. But such an expectation, surely, is nonsensical. At the age of three to four years the child is apt to be plagued by imaginative fears [28] and to plague his parents with his strong dislikes and outbursts of temper. The adult chimpanzee must be treated, in effect, as a wild animal, and as yet no one has been able to domesticate him. Surely it is adult man who is *least* subject to emotional disturbance. The chimpanzee, it seems, is explosive, unreliable, fearful, dangerous; man (normal man, normally reared) is ordinarily quiet, not given to sudden violent attack on others without warning, not forever in fear of this or that harmless object.

Perhaps so, but let us look closer.

First, in most primitive societies it is clear that man has generally found himself ringed around by malignant ghosts and devils, with beneficent spirits in the minority, and has found it constantly necessary to spend time, effort, and wealth to propitiate even the friendly ones. Fellow members of the tribe commonly possess evil powers, and the one who has the evil eye is feared and hated or killed, according to circumstances. For any one of the members to be greatly different from the others in appearance, habits, skills, or tastes would be more than apt to cost him his life. As for an outsider, even of the same race, language, and culture—*any* foreigner is distrusted and feared. He may be a convenient source of trophies (a scalp or an embalmed head to show that one

[27] Donald B. Lindsley, "Emotion," in Stevens, *op. cit.*
[28] Jersild and Holmes, *op. cit.*

is a self-respecting human adult) or alternatively may be captured and brought back whole for torture or ceremonial sacrifice for the edification of the whole tribe.

These are well-established facts of human behavior and not rare exceptions either. However, if they are cited and if one cites also the concentration and slave-labor camps of our own generation, to show that man *is* to be thought of as a wild animal, emotionally unstable and often vicious, the answer one will receive is that these things may happen if people are taught as children to behave in these ways, but that fear, hatred, and cruelty are not inherent in man's nature.

If so, one might wonder at the coincidences that allowed the same teaching to originate in so many parts of the globe.

However, we should make it clear at once that we do not argue that these attitudes are inborn. We do argue that man by birth and maturation has a tremendous emotional susceptibility on the one hand and some need for excitement on the other; that, if these are handled carefully in the growing child, with a highly specialized environment, the results may be most admirable, but that these qualities by themselves, with no teaching from others or in spite of ineffective teaching, may by reaction to other environments produce socially disastrous results.

As far as we have gone, therefore, and thinking of our own suburban milieux as providing exceptional rather than typical examples of human social behavior, we might be justified in considering man not a tame animal but inherently dangerous, to be domesticated only with great pains. Picking a human society at random from all those that have existed, one might say that the risk taken by a stranger entering it—a member of another society also chosen at random—would not be less than that taken by a chimpanzee or a wolf encountering a group of his fellows. It is not wholly fantastic, consequently, to suggest that man is more emotionally excited by what is strange than lower animals are, except after special training.

Perhaps we can go further. Even in ourselves, the civilized, amiable, and admirable part of mankind, well brought up and not constantly in a state of fear, there are signs that this urbanity depends as much on our successfully avoiding disturbing stimulation as on a lowered sensitivity. As already suggested, the capacity for emotional breakdown may be self-concealing, leading the animal to find or create an environment in which the stimuli to excessive emotional response are at a minimum. So effective is our society in this respect that its members—*especially* the well-to-do and educated ones—may not even guess at some of their own potentialities. One usually thinks of education, in the broad sense, as producing a resourceful, emotionally stable adult, without respect to the environment in which these traits are to appear. To some extent this may be true. But education can be seen as being also the means of establishing a protective social environment in which emotional stability is possible.

Perhaps it strengthens the individual against unreasonable fears and rages, but it certainly produces a uniformity of appearance and behavior, reducing the frequency with which the individual member of the society encounters the causes of such emotion. On *this* view, the susceptibility to emotional disturbance may not be decreased. It may in fact be increased. The protective cocoon of uniformity in personal appearance, manners, and social activity generally will make small deviations from custom appear increasingly strange and thus (if the general thesis is sound) increasingly intolerable. The inevitable small deviations from custom will bulk increasingly large, and the members of the society, finding themselves tolerating trivial deviations well, will continue to think of themselves as socially adaptable.

The educated man usually prides himself on his broad-mindedness, his judgment of persons by their essential qualities, and his disregard of the superficial. The college student is, if anything, even more confident of his own contempt for appearances. Now suppose that someone whose appearance only departed significantly from the usual pattern applied for a job as a university instructor. Suppose it is a male who takes the highly reasonable view that women's clothing is more comfortable in the North American summer or a female who decides that long hair is a nuisance and shaves her head bare. Or suppose it is a war casualty whose face is really disfigured by scar tissue, without ears, nose, eyebrows, or orbital ridges, but whose senses, intellect, and speech are unimpaired: what chance would any of these have to get a job? If he got the job, what chance would there be that students would sit in a classroom and listen to him, no matter how wise he were? None of these are major deviations from the usual human appearance. Merely asking these questions of an undergraduate class allows one to observe a curious mixture of uneasiness and incredulity. The degree of uniformity in the social environment is such that one has difficulty even thinking of a really different one. The trivial changes of fashion from one year to the next look big to us, and we flatter ourselves that a man's appearance does not fundamentally affect our behavior toward him.

Similarly, the adult may think that he is not disturbed by strange places, darkness, or solitude, although young children are. As our lives are usually arranged, this belief is so easy to maintain. It is more difficult if one has tried being separated from one's companions in the deep woods at night; reportedly, it is also difficult for those who have suffered solitary confinement.

All this, it seems, casts grave doubt on the idea that man has intrinsically a greater emotional stability than the chimpanzee or other animals. The real difference may be in the protective environment man has created for himself, which he so takes for granted that he becomes unable to see how his stability is achieved and how his behavior would look to someone not used to it.

More clearly than anywhere else, this is seen in taboo phenomena. The travelers of the eighteenth and nineteenth centuries were completely astonished by taboo—something new, quite foreign to their own lives. Scholars now recognize that taboo has always existed in civilized cultures, but even today it seems not to be recognized how complete and typical its manifestations are nor how far-reaching in social effect.

Taboo is relevant to the present discussion in several respects. It was drawn to our attention, in the first place, by observing the chimpanzee's response to a chimpanzee or human head (described earlier). This reminded us of the equally puzzling human response to the sight of a major operation or autopsy, so the further observations were made with an apparently dead (i.e., anesthetized) chimpanzee as test object. The ambivalence of the behavior this aroused then recalled Freud's emphasis on the puzzling ambivalence of some primitive taboos: the object may be simultaneously regarded with reverence and as dangerous or contaminating.[29] It seems to be thought that in more enlightened societies such anomalies have disappeared. Any remnants of taboo in our own society are thought of simply as "moral prohibitions." Our taboos are thus regarded as purely negative and more or less based on rational attitudes. But with the chimpanzee's behavior as a starting point and with the question in mind whether man is really as free of susceptibility to irrational emotion as he seems, we found something different.

Consider first a relatively mild taboo, on the word "God." Although the taboo has become much less strong in recent years, its ambivalence is still beautifully clear. The word (a) has a reverent use and (b) is also on occasion described literally as a "dirty word," for using which one of the writers some time ago (about 1910) had his mouth washed out with soap. The lexicographer need not be puzzled to find modern examples to illustrate the double meaning of the Latin *sacer*.

A much more powerful taboo on the dead human body is equally ambivalent. Be reverent to the dead, speak in whispers and make no jokes at the funeral service, and, if you are male, remove your hat. There are still remnants of the Middle Ages and Renaissance prohibition against cutting up the human body, shown in the difficulty of getting bodies for medical-school teaching or permission for autopsy. Dissection violates the sanctity of the dead. But in opposition to such reverence, the corpse is also contaminating, unpleasant, disgusting; disgust may be expressed, for example, at a report that relatives have kissed the dead man after preparation for burial. In general, members of this society are rarely exposed to dead bodies, except in war or disaster, and they tend to be ashamed of their emotional sensitivity thereto, so it is hard to produce formal evidence of the repugnance. An undergraduate class of 198 persons, including some nurses and some veterans, was polled to find out how many had encountered a dead body. Thirty-seven had never seen a corpse in any circumstances; 91 had seen one only after it was prepared for burial—a

[29] Sigmund Freud, *Totem and Taboo*, trans. A. A. Brill (London: Routledge, 1919).

total of 65 per cent who had either not seen a corpse or who had seen one only in the ritualized procedure that rigidly limits exposure to it. These statistics show clearly that society, for some reason, protects its members from something about the dead body, and, if there should still be some doubt that this is the emotional disturbance that the body arouses, the reader can get the evidence for himself if he will obtain a human head from the dissecting room and try to carry it home openly in the subway.

Sex taboos are multifarious, but some of them clearly show the ambivalence we are discussing. On the one hand, marriage is holy; on the other, unsanctified sexual activity is—once more—"dirty," contaminating, filthy. We read with amusement and incredulity of the behavior of the primitive people who put to death those who violate a taboo; but the death sentence for rape and the prison sentence for the bigamist or seller of pictures of sexual congress is exactly in the same class, for it does not have to be shown that physical or psychological harm has been done to anyone, only that the taboo is violated.

That there is a double standard of morals is the old way of saying that as a sex object the human female has a stronger taboo than the male. For the ambivalence of taboos, it is significant that the swing from one extreme to the other is greater with the female than the male: her virginity is more sacred than the male's (which is apt to be a source of derision, except when the male in question is under another taboo, of the clergy), and she is more degraded *and dangerous or contaminating to others* when the taboo has been flagrantly broken. Observe also that young men have been known to say, and even on credible report to feel, that they are "not worthy" of some young woman or other; the converse point of view is notably rare.

The only apparent way of accounting for these ambivalences is to suppose that the taboo object is, in the first place, simply a very exciting one and that this emotional arousal in some circumstances tends to be channeled into one motor outlet (e.g., aggression), in other circumstances another outlet (e.g., fawning or abasement). This implies that there might be individual differences in response to the same object, just as there must be differences in what is exciting to different individuals. It is, of course, evident socially that the growing child left to himself would develop his own set of taboos. "Moral education" has as one of its main objectives to establish uniformity: uniformity of taboo, but more broadly a uniformity of emotional sensitivity.

If all persons could be given the same emotional attitudes, including a fear of acting in a way that arouses emotion too strongly in others, internal social conflict would disappear if at the same time the society is economically successful and provides its members with comfort and safety. This is the direction, it seems, in which society tends to move, up to the point at which the moral prohibition reduces provocative behavior below the optimal level. This level itself varies, of course, with individuals according to past experience, which means that society will never reach complete uniformity. There will always be a tendency to "test the limits" of the social code; the result in some cases will anger or horrify too many members of society, and the testing will be suppressed. In other cases, however, the tester will elicit a degree of response that is acceptable, and the innovation will be socially perpetuated.

We may see human society, therefore, as conditioned primarily by the avoidance of the too strong emotional disturbance. In the first place, this may be the action of "economic man": the search for wealth in the form of shelter and safety. Primitive man is likely to have more than enough emotional disturbance imposed on him by insufficient control of his physical environment. But an equally important determinant of early society is a means of controlling man's own behavior as a source of emotional disturbance. This influence may have definitely uneconomic results, even at an early stage in the development.

If thus we consider man as distinctive not only intellectually but also emotionally, a more adequate picture of human society emerges. Although we have oversimplified, even our account does not make it a simple picture of enforced conformity and avoidance of fear- and rage-provoking stimulation. There are, also, the search for the optimal level of arousal and individual differences of emotional susceptibility. Our society, as well, has a long way to go before it can be supposed to have reached the maximal degree of conformity. But it does not seem to have been recognized how consistently our society has moved in the direction of arranging that its members act so as not to excite their fellows beyond a certain point. When the strong excitation is not avoided, it is aroused under carefully specified conditions only (marriage, law court, and prizefighting are examples) in which the sexual arousal, fear, or anger aroused in one does not spread uncontrolled to others. Producing a low-level chronic excitation in others, such as fear of losing a job or not passing an examination, is not frowned on; but the hypothetical civilized man, the goal at which approved social education aims, does not, except in the special circumstances referred to, act so as to produce acute, strong sexual arousal, jealousy, anger, or fear. He does not display disgusting objects openly; he is equally careful not to get into situations in which his own emotions make a display of him.

Our social arrangements fall short of this admirable goal, but they have, on the whole, achieved in some segments of this society a remarkable success in avoiding the causes of strong emotional arousal in ordinary life. This result seems quite unpredictable from the assumption that man is in himself a relatively unemotional animal, distinctive mainly by his intellect. It does become intelligible if man has a manifold susceptibility to emotional disturbance; if he tends to avoid actions that lead to strong emotion and if one of the causes of emotion is the sight of it in others; and if the gradual establishment of conformity makes things become exciting which would otherwise not be so, because of their strangeness.

Man is a rational, unemotional animal as long as there is nothing to disturb his emotions. Also, the causes of strong emotion are few, as we usually consider them; for all we take account of are the causes that *do* operate in a society the main function of which may be to control and limit strong emotion, and we are almost incapable of thinking of an environment that differs from the social and physical one in which we live and which we have so carefully tailored to our needs. The animal evidence shows that the altruism and friendship so prominent in Homo sapiens are fundamental to his nature: if we are to learn how to foster such attitudes, we must recognize and provide the kind of protective social environment in which it is possible for them to develop.

Psychoanalytic Perspectives

It was suggested earlier that with a broader scope psychology became hospitable to ideas from psychoanalysis. It is interesting to note that some psychiatrists and psychoanalysts have been equally concerned with incorporating into their thinking some of the more systematic considerations so much a part of formal psychology. One psychiatrist who has been concerned with this issue is Harry Stack Sullivan. He points out that psychiatry and psychoanalysis really involve three different dimensions and three different definitions.

The first of these is what Sullivan calls the "conglomerate of ideas and impressions, of magic, mysticism, and information, of conceits and vagaries, of conceptions and misconceptions, and of empty verbalisms." Sullivan then states, "This second definition sets up psychiatry as an art, namely, the art of observing and perhaps influencing the course of mental disorders." Sullivan concludes:

> The third definition of psychiatry, which is the one relevant here, may be approached by considering it as an expanding science concerned with the kinds of events or processes in which the psychiatrist participates while being an observant psychiatrist. . . . The events which contribute information for the development of psychiatry and psychiatric theory are events in which the psychiatrist participates; they are not events that he looks at from atop ivory towers. But of all the actions or operations in which the psychiatrist participates as a psychiatrist, the ones which are

scientifically important are those which are accompanied by conceptual schematizations or intelligent formulations which are communicable.[1]

These various definitions not only illuminate Sullivan's position as a thoughtful person defining his scientific discipline, but they also symbolize the breadth and variability to be found in the following selections.

Sigmund Freud's letter to Albert Einstein continues in the evolutionary tradition of James and McDougall. Freud was indeed the participant observer with and of his clinical patients that Sullivan proposes as his model. From this body of clinical material pertaining to sexuality and aggression, Freud proposes to comment on group behavior. Freud states that war, a social phenomenon, and aggression, a personal phenomenon, are different manifestations of the same drive system. As individuals have evolved and now have a balance between life and death forces within their psyches, societies which are aggregates of such individuals also are going through an evolution of their own. Freud insists on the necessity of our understanding the evolution of society with the same care that the clinician employs when he unravels the history of an individual.

> Here is the way in which I see it. The cultural development of mankind (some, I know, prefer to call it civilization) has been in progress since immemorial antiquity. To this *processus* we owe all that is best in our composition, but also much that makes for human suffering. Its origins and causes are obscure, its issue is uncertain, but some of its characteristics are easy to perceive. It well may lead to the extinction of mankind, for it impairs the sexual function in more than one respect, and even today the uncivilized races and the backward classes of all nations are multiplying more rapidly than the cultured elements. This process may, perhaps, be likened to the effect of domestication on certain animals—it clearly involves physical changes of structure—but the view that cultural development is an organic process of this order has not yet become generally familiar. The psychic changes which accompany this process of cultural change are striking and not to be gainsaid. They consist in the progressive rejection of instinctive ends and a scaling down of instinctive reactions.

Durbin and Bowlby represent in their paper those who accept psychoanalytic theory as a heuristic device which can generate research hypotheses and, as Sullivan has already suggested, thus make the observation of certain phenomena more systematic. The key to their thinking is found in this comment.

> We have now completed our survey of the causes of aggression in human beings. We have suggested that there is no substantial difference

[1] H. S. Sullivan, *The Interpersonal Theory of Psychiatry* (New York: W. W. Norton & Co., 1953), pp. 13–14.

in behavior, that adults are just as cruel—or more so—just as aggressive, just as destructive, as any group of animals or monkeys. The only difference in our view is one of psychological and intellectual mechanism. The causes of simple aggression—possessiveness, strangeness, frustration— are common to adults and simpler creatures. But a repressive discipline drives the simple aggression underground—to speak in metaphors—and it appears in disguised forms. These transformations are chiefly those of displacement and projection. These mechanisms have as their immediate motive the reduction of anxiety and the resolution of the conflicts of ambivalence and guilt. They result in the typical form of adult aggressiveness—aggressive personal relations of all kinds—but above all in group aggression: party conflict, civil war, wars of religion, and international war. The group life gives sanction to personal aggressiveness. The mobilization of transformed aggression gives destructive power to groups. Aggression takes on its social form.

The major difference in this position and the initial statement of Freud is that the critical matter is not man's instinctive attributes, but rather his capacity to use the mechanisms of projection and displacement. The paradox of this is that projection, a useful defense mechanism of the ego which may help preserve self-esteem, can through extreme distortion destroy the individual.

Sullivan's paper represents a different point of view. Sullivan sees man's anxieties and fears deriving largely from his inability under certain conditions to communicate. The lack of communication and its resultant anxiety can lead to terror-ridden distortions; one way, granted an extremely dangerous one, by which these feelings can be resolved is by the *counterphobic* reaction. One strikes out at that which one cannot understand, that which is different, or that with which one cannot establish communication.

The extension of psychiatric theory beyond the confines of the familiar into the world of "foreigners" whose ways of life are alien to us calls for a sharp discrimination between fear and the various manifestations of anxiety and self-system activity, especially those of irrational dislikes, aversions, and revulsions, and today so widespread distrust of others.

Current theory makes hate the characteristic of interpersonal situations in which the people concerned recurrently and frequently provoke anxiety in each other, yet cannot break up the situation because of some conjunctive forces which hold them together. If the conjunctive force acts entirely outside of awareness, uncanny fascination, with moments of revulsion or loathing, may appear. If the integrating forces are not very strong [and] if the situation is not very important, the milder manifestations of more-or-less concealed, actually unjustified, dislike and distrust are shown. The "actually unjustified" means that a consensually valid statement of adequate grounds for the dislike or distrust cannot be formulated. The unpleasant emotion arises from something more than what either person could readily come to know about the situation. . . .

Every constructive effort of the psychiatrist today is a strategy of inter-personal field operations which (a) seeks to map the areas of disjunctive force that block the efficient collaboration of the patient and others and (b) seeks to expand the patient's awareness so that this unnecessary blockage can be brought to an end.

For a psychiatry of peoples, we must follow the selfsame strategy applied to significant groupings of people—families, communities, political entities, regional organizations, world blocs—and seek to map the interventions of disjunctive force which block the integration of the group with other groups in pursuit of the common welfare and seek out the characteristics of each group's culture or subculture and the methods used to impose it on the young, which perpetuate the restrictions of freedom for constructive growth.

A point of view that embraces many of the ideas implicit in these three papers is found in the work of Erik H. Erikson. Erikson sees war arising as a consequence of profound social ambiguities. War is an alternative of a "totalistic" nature to the more difficult task of achieving personal wholeness.

Psychoanalysis has amply demonstrated the fact that the individual develops an amnesia concerning crucial childhood experiences; there is good reason to suspect that this individual amnesia is paralleled by a universal blind spot in the interpretation of history, a tendency to overlook the fateful function of childhood in the fabric of society. . . .

To say it with one sentence: When the human being, because of accidental or developmental shifts, loses an essential wholeness, he restructures himself and the world by taking recourse to what we may call "totalism."

Erikson accepts the general Freudian notion of personality development, although he does not subscribe to Freud's theory of the organic evolution of society. The telling issue that Erikson raises is that the ambiguities and unresolved stresses found in rapidly changing societies may drive individuals to accept totalistic or authoritarian notions which in turn can lead to an acceptance of war as a desirable alternative.

The paper by Levinson subjects some of these ideas of Erikson and others about the genesis of authoritarianism to the scrutiny of research.

The individual's approach to the external, social world will in significant degree reflect his approach to himself—his self-conceptions, character traits, modes of dealing with inner conflict, and the like. A corollary hypothesis in the present case is that *an autocratic approach to problems*

*of social organization will most often be found within an authoritarian
personality structure.*

This hypothesis can be derived from an analysis of the psychological
qualities that are directly represented in nationalism and related viewpoints. Such characteristics as punitiveness, stereotypy, fear of moral
contamination, submission to powerful authority, and exaggerated fear
of weakness—in their extreme form, features of authoritarian personality
—make recurrent appearances in nationalistic thought. . . .

It would appear that the "functionality" of ideology for the person—
the degree to which his social views are imbedded in and serve to maintain other aspects of his personality—will vary with the person and with
the social setting. One individual holds a nationalistic outlook in part
because the images and relationships it portrays reflect so well his unconscious fantasies; the ideology is deeply gratifying and anxiety-binding.
Another individual holds a roughly similar outlook on the basis of a more
superficial acceptance of what is given in his social environment; in this
case, personality factors may play a relatively incidental role in the formation and maintenance of ideology.

The variety of issues raised by these papers suggests both the stimulating
and at times frustrating complexities found presently in personality theory.
The ideas of Freud, although provocative, seem somewhat dated and superficial
when contrasted with the penetrating analyses of Durbin and Bowlby and Levinson. Social evolutionary theories based on psychiatry seem somewhat fore-
shortened when contrasted with the interpersonal and social thinking of Sullivan and Erikson. This increase in precision of expression, the opening of new
strategies for research, new relationships between disciplines, may be one of
our best hopes for future peace.

◄◄◄ ►►►

SIGMUND FREUD

Why War? *

In the summer of 1932 the League of Nations International Institute of Intellectual Cooperation proposed that Professor Einstein should invite a person, chosen by himself, to a frank exchange of views on any problem which Professor Einstein might select. The problem chosen was: Is there any way of delivering mankind from the menace of war?

Professor Freud's answer to the points raised in Professor Einstein's letter is given below, and my thanks and acknowledgments are due to the International Institute of Intellectual Cooperation for its permission to print Professor Freud's letter here—Ed.

VIENNA, SEPTEMBER 1932

DEAR PROFESSOR EINSTEIN,

When I learned of your intention to invite me to a mutual exchange of views upon a subject which not only interested you personally but seemed deserving, too, of public interest, I cordially assented. I expected you to choose a problem lying on the borderland of the knowable, as it stands today, a theme which each of us, physicist and psychologist, might approach from his own angle, to

---

* ("Open Letter Series," Vol. II [Paris: League of Nations International Institute of Intellectual Cooperation, 1933].) Unpublished correspondence between Messrs. Albert Einstein and Sigmund Freud. Translated from the original German by Stuart Gilbert. Reprinted from Sigmund Freud, *Collected Papers* (New York: Basic Books, 1959), Vol. 5, by permission of the publisher (Copyright 1959, Basic Books, New York).

meet at last on common ground, though setting out from different premises. Thus the question which you put me—what is to be done to rid mankind of the war menace?—took me by surprise. And, next, I was dumbfounded by the thought of my (of *our*, I almost wrote) incompetence, for this struck me as being a matter of practical politics, the statesman's proper study. But then I realized that you did not raise the question in your capacity of scientist or physicist, but as a lover of his fellow men, who responded to the call of the League of Nations much as Fridtjof Nansen, the polar explorer, took on himself the task of succoring homeless and starving victims of the World War. And, next, I reminded myself that I was not being called on to formulate practical proposals, but, rather, to explain how this question of preventing wars strikes a psychologist.

But here, too, you have stated the gist of the matter in your letter—and taken the wind out of my sails! Still, I will gladly follow in your wake and content myself with endorsing your conclusions, which, however, I propose to amplify to the best of my knowledge or surmise.

You begin with the relations between might and right, and this is assuredly the proper starting point for our inquiry. But, for the term "might," I would substitute a tougher and more telling word: "violence." In right and violence we have today an obvious antinomy. It is easy to prove that one has evolved from the other and, when we go back to origins and examine primitive conditions, the solution of the problem follows easily enough. I must crave your indulgence if in what follows I speak of well-known, admitted facts as though they were new data; the context necessitates this method.

Conflicts of interest between man and man are resolved, in principle, by the recourse to violence. It is the same in the animal kingdom, from which man cannot claim exclusion; nevertheless, men are also prone to conflicts of opinion, touching, on occasion, the loftiest peaks of abstract thought, which seem to call for settlement by quite another method. This refinement is, however, a late development. To start with, brute force was the factor which, in small communities, decided points of ownership and the question which man's will was to prevail. Very soon physical force was implemented, then replaced, by the use of various adjuncts; he proved the victor whose weapon was the better or handled the more skilfully. Now, for the first time, with the coming of weapons, superior brains began to oust brute force, but the object of the conflict remained the same: one party was to be constrained, by the injury done him or impairment of his strength, to retract a claim or a refusal. This end is most effectively gained when the opponent is definitively put out of action—in other words, is killed. This procedure has two advantages; the enemy cannot renew hostilities, and, second, his fate deters others from following his example. Moreover, the slaughter of a foe gratifies an instinctive craving—a point to which we shall revert hereafter. However, another consideration may be set off against this will to kill: the possibility of using an enemy for servile tasks if his spirit be broken and his life spared. Here violence finds an outlet not in slaughter but in subjugation. Hence springs the practice of giving quarter; but the victor, having from now on to reckon with the craving for revenge that rankles in his victim, forfeits to some extent his personal security.

Thus, under primitive conditions, it is superior force—brute violence or violence backed by arms—that lords it everywhere. We know that in the course of evolution this state of things was modified, a path was traced that led away from violence to law. But what was this path? Surely it issued from a single verity: that the superiority of one strong man can be overborne by an alliance of many weaklings, that *l'union fait la force*. Brute force is overcome by union, the allied might of scattered units makes good its right against the isolated giant. Thus we may define "right" (i.e., law) as the might of a community. Yet it, too, is nothing else than violence, quick to attack whatever individual stands in its path, and it employs the selfsame methods, follows like ends, with but one difference; it is the communal, not individual, violence that has its way. But, for the transition from crude violence to the reign of law, a certain psychological condition must first obtain. The union of the majority must be stable and enduring. If its sole *raison d'être* be the discomfiture of some overweening individual and, after his downfall, it be dissolved, it leads to nothing. Some other man, trusting to his superior power, will seek to reinstate the rule of violence, and the cycle will repeat itself unendingly. Thus the union of the people must be permanent and well organized; it must enact rules to meet the risk of possible revolts, must set up machinery ensuring that its rules—the laws—are observed and that such acts of violence as the laws demand are duly carried out. This recognition of a community of interests engenders among the members of the group a sentiment of unity and fraternal solidarity which constitutes its real strength.

So far I have set out what seems to me the kernel of the matter: the suppression of brute force by the transfer of power to a larger combination, founded on the community of sentiments linking up its members. All the rest is mere tautology and glosses. Now, the position is simple enough so long as the community consists of a number of equipollent individuals. The laws of such a group can determine to what extent the individual must forfeit his personal freedom, the right of using personal force as an instrument of violence, to ensure the safety of the group. But such a combination is only theoretically possible; in practice the situation is always complicated by the fact that, from the outset, the group includes elements of unequal power, men and women, elders and children, and, very soon, as a result of war and conquest, victors and the vanquished—that is, masters and slaves—as well. From this time on the common law takes notice of these inequalities of power, laws are made by and for the rulers, giving the servile classes fewer rights. Thenceforward there exist within the state two factors making for legal instability, but legislative

evolution, too: first, the attempts by members of the ruling class to set themselves above the law's restrictions and, second, the constant struggle of the
ruled to extend their rights and see each gain embodied in the code, replacing
legal disabilities by equal laws for all. The second of these tendencies will be
particularly marked when there takes place a positive mutation of the balance
of power within the community, the frequent outcome of certain historical conditions. In such cases the laws may gradually be adjusted to the changed conditions or (as more usually ensues) the ruling class is loath to reckon with the
new developments, the result being insurrections and civil wars, a period when
law is in abeyance and force once more the arbiter, followed by a new regime
of law. There is another factor of constitutional change, which operates in a
wholly pacific manner, namely, the cultural evolution of the mass of the community; this factor, however, is of a different order and can only be dealt
with later.

Thus we see that, even within the group itself, the exercise of violence cannot be avoided when conflicting interests are at stake. But the common needs
and habits of men who live in fellowship under the same sky favor a speedy
issue of such conflicts and, this being so, the possibilities of peaceful solutions
make steady progress. Yet the most casual glance at world history will show
an unending series of conflicts between one community and another or a group
of others, between large and smaller units, between cities, countries, races,
tribes and kingdoms, almost all of which were settled by the ordeal of war.
Such wars end either in pillage or in conquest and its fruits, the downfall of
the loser. No single all-embracing judgment can be passed on these wars of
aggrandizement. Some, like the war between the Mongols and the Turks, have
led to unmitigated misery; others, however, have furthered the transition from
violence to law, since they brought larger units into being, within whose limits
a recourse to violence was banned and a new regime determined all disputes.
Thus the Roman conquests brought that boon, the *Pax Romana,* to the Mediterranean lands. The French kings' lust for aggrandizement created a new
France, flourishing in peace and unity. Paradoxical as it sounds, we must
admit that warfare well might serve to pave the way to that unbroken peace
we so desire, for it is war that brings vast empires into being, within whose
frontiers all warfare is proscribed by a strong central power. In practice, however, this end is not attained, for as a rule the fruits of victory are but short-
lived, the new-created unit falls asunder once again, generally because there
can be no true cohesion between the parts that violence has welded. Hitherto,
moreover, such conquests have only led to aggregations which, for all their
magnitude, had limits, and disputes between these units could be resolved only
by recourse to arms. For humanity at large the sole result of all these military
enterprises was that, instead of frequent not to say incessant little wars, they
had now to face great wars which, for all they came less often, were so much
the more destructive.

Regarding the world of today the same conclusion holds good, and you, too, have reached it, though by a shorter path. There is but one sure way of ending war, and that is the establishment, by common consent, of a central control which shall have the last word in every conflict of interests. For this, two things are needed: first, the creation of such a supreme court of judicature; second, its investment with adequate executive force. Unless this second requirement be fulfilled, the first is unavailing. Obviously the League of Nations, acting as a supreme court, fulfills the first condition; it does not fulfill the second. It has no force at its disposal and can only get it if the members of the new body, its constituent nations, furnish it. And, as things are, this is a forlorn hope. Still we should be taking a very shortsighted view of the League of Nations were we to ignore the fact that here is an experiment the like of which has rarely—never before, perhaps, on such a scale—been attempted in the course of history. It is an attempt to acquire the authority (in other words, coercive influence), which hitherto reposed exclusively on the possession of power, by calling into play certain idealistic attitudes of mind. We have seen that there are two factors of cohesion in a community: violent compulsion and ties of sentiment ("identifications," in technical parlance) between the members of the group. If one of these factors becomes inoperative, the other may still suffice to hold the group together. Obviously such notions as these can only be significant when they are the expression of a deeply rooted sense of unity, shared by all. It is necessary, therefore, to gauge the efficacy of such sentiments. History tells us that, on occasion, they have been effective. For example, the Panhellenic conception, the Greeks' awareness of superiority over their barbarian neighbors, which found expression in the amphictyonies, the oracles, and games, was strong enough to humanize the methods of warfare as between Greeks, though inevitably it failed to prevent conflicts between different elements of the Hellenic race or even to deter a city or group of cities from joining forces with their racial foe, the Persians, for the discomfiture of a rival. The solidarity of Christendom in the Renaissance age was no more effective, despite its vast authority, in hindering Christian nations, large and small alike, from calling in the sultan to their aid. And, in our times, we look in vain for some such unifying notion whose authority would be unquestioned. It is all too clear that the nationalistic ideas, paramount today in every country, operate in quite a contrary direction. There are some who hold that the Bolshevist conceptions may make an end of war, but, as things are, that goal lies very far away and, perhaps, could only be attained after a spell of brutal internecine warfare. Thus it would seem that any effort to replace brute force by the might of an ideal is, under present conditions, doomed to fail. Our logic is at fault if we ignore the fact that right is founded on brute force and even today needs violence to maintain it.

I now can comment on another of your statements. You are amazed that it is so easy to infect men with the war fever, and you surmise that man has in him

an active instinct for hatred and destruction, amenable to such stimulations. I entirely agree with you. I believe in the existence of this instinct and have been recently at pains to study its manifestations. In this connection may I set out a fragment of that knowledge of the instincts, which we psychoanalysts, after so many tentative essays and gropings in the dark, have compassed? We assume that human instincts are of two kinds: those that conserve and unify, which we call "erotic" (in the meaning Plato gives to *eros* in his *Symposium*) or else "sexual" (explicitly extending the popular connotation of "sex"); and, second, the instincts to destroy and kill, which we assimilate as the aggressive or destructive instincts. These are, as you perceive, the well-known opposites, love and hate, transformed into theoretical entities; they are, perhaps, another aspect of those eternal polarities, attraction and repulsion, which fall within your province. But we must be chary of passing overhastily to the notions of good and evil. Each of these instincts is every whit as indispensable as its opposite, and all the phenomena of life derive from their activity, whether they work in concert or in opposition. It seems that an instinct of either category can operate but rarely in isolation; it is always blended ("alloyed," as we say) with a certain dosage of its opposite, which modifies its aim or even, in certain circumstances, is a prime condition of its attainment. Thus the instinct of self-preservation is certainly of an erotic nature, but to gain its ends this very instinct necessitates aggressive action. In the same way the love instinct, when directed to a specific object, calls for an admixture of the acquisitive instinct if it is to enter into effective possession of that object. It is the difficulty of isolating the two kinds of instinct in their manifestations that has so long prevented us from recognizing them.

If you travel with me a little further on this road, you will find that human affairs are complicated in yet another way. Only exceptionally does an action follow on the stimulus of a single instinct, which is per se a blend of *eros* and destructiveness. As a rule several motives of similar composition concur to bring about the act. This fact was duly noted by a colleague of yours, Prof. Georg C. Lichtenberg, sometime professor of physics at Göttingen; he was perhaps even more eminent as a psychologist than as a physical scientist. He evolved the notion of a "compass-card of motives" and wrote: "The efficient motives impelling man to act can be classified like the 32 Winds, and described in the same manner; for example, *Food-Food-Fame* or *Fame-Fame-Food.*" Thus, when a nation is summoned to engage in war, a whole gamut of human motives may respond to this appeal; high and low motives, some openly avowed, others slurred over. The lust for aggression and destruction is certainly included; the innumerable cruelties of history and man's daily life confirm its prevalence and strength. The stimulation of these destructive impulses by appeals to idealism and the erotic instinct naturally facilitates their release. Musing on the atrocities recorded on history's page, we feel that the ideal motive has often served as a camouflage for the lust of destruction;

sometimes, as with the cruelties of the Inquisition, it seems that, while the ideal motives occupied the foreground of consciousness, they drew their strength from the destructive instincts submerged in the unconscious. Both interpretations are feasible.

You are interested, I know, in the prevention of war, not in our theories, and I keep this fact in mind. Yet I would like to dwell a little longer on this destructive instinct which is seldom given the attention that its importance warrants. With the least of speculative efforts we are led to conclude that this instinct functions in every living being, striving to work its ruin and reduce life to its primal state of inert matter. Indeed it might well be called the "death instinct," whereas the erotic instincts vouch for the struggle to live on. The death instinct becomes an impulse to destruction when, with the aid of certain organs, it directs its action outward, against external objects. The living being, that is to say, defends its own existence by destroying foreign bodies. But, in one of its activities, the death instinct is operative *within* the living being, and we have sought to trace back a number of normal and pathological phenomena to this *introversion* of the destructive instinct. We have even committed the heresy of explaining the origin of human conscience by some such "turning inward" of the aggressive impulse. Obviously when this internal tendency operates on too large a scale, it is no trivial matter, rather a positively morbid state of things; whereas the diversion of the destructive impulse toward the external world must have beneficial effects. Here is then the biological justification for all those vile, pernicious propensities which we now are combating. We can but own that they are really more akin to nature than this our stand against them, which, in fact, remains to be accounted for.

All this may give you the impression that our theories amount to a species of mythology and a gloomy one at that! But does not every natural science lead ultimately to this—a sort of mythology? Is it otherwise today with your physical science?

The upshot of these observations, as bearing on the subject in hand, is that there is no likelihood of our being able to suppress humanity's aggressive tendencies. In some happy corners of the earth, they say, where nature brings forth abundantly whatever man desires, there flourish races whose lives go gently by, unknowing of aggression or constraint. This I can hardly credit; I would like further details about these happy folk. The Bolshevists, too, aspire to do away with human aggressiveness by ensuring the satisfaction of material needs and enforcing equality between man and man. To me this hope seems vain. Meanwhile they busily perfect their armaments, and their hatred of outsiders is not the least of the factors of cohesion amongst themselves. In any case, as you too have observed, complete suppression of man's aggressive tendencies is not in issue; what we may try is to divert it into a channel other than that of warfare.

From our "mythology" of the instincts, we may easily deduce a formula for an indirect method of eliminating war. If the propensity for war be due to the destructive instinct, we have always its counteragent, *eros,* to our hand. All that produces ties of sentiment between man and man must serve us as war's antidote. These ties are of two kinds. First, such relations as those toward a beloved object, void though they be of sexual intent. The psychoanalyst need feel no compunction in mentioning "love" in this connection; religion uses the same language: Love thy neighbor as thyself. A pious injunction easy to enounce, but hard to carry out! The other bond of sentiment is by way of identification. All that brings out the significant resemblances between men calls into play this feeling of community, identification, whereon is founded, in large measure, the whole edifice of human society.

In your strictures on the abuse of authority, I find another suggestion for an indirect attack on the war impulse. That men are divided into leaders and the led is but another manifestation of their inborn and irremediable inequality. The second class constitutes the vast majority; they need a high command to make decisions for them, to which decisions they usually bow without demur. In this context we would point out that men should be at greater pains than heretofore to form a superior class of independent thinkers, unamenable to intimidation and fervent in the quest of truth, whose function it would be to guide the masses dependent on their lead. There is no need to point out how little the rule of politicians and the church's ban on liberty of thought encourage such a new creation. The ideal conditions would obviously be found in a community where every man subordinated his instinctive life to the dictates of reason. Nothing less than this could bring about so thorough and so durable a union between men, even if this involved the severance of mutual ties of sentiment. But surely such a hope is utterly Utopian, as things are. The other indirect methods of preventing war are certainly more feasible, but entail no quick results. They conjure up an ugly picture of mills which grind so slowly that, before the flour is ready, men are dead of hunger.

As you see, little good comes of consulting a theoretician, aloof from worldly contacts, on practical and urgent problems! Better it were to tackle each successive crisis with means that we have ready to our hands. However, I would like to deal with a question which, though it is not mooted in your letter, interests me greatly. Why do we, you and I and many another, protest so vehemently against war, instead of just accepting it as another of life's odious importunities? For it seems a natural thing enough, biologically sound and practically unavoidable. I trust you will not be shocked by my raising such a question. For the better conduct of an inquiry it may be well to don a mask of feigned aloofness. The answer to my query may run as follows: Because every man has a right over his own life, and war destroys lives that were full of promise; it forces the individual into situations that shame his manhood, obliging him to murder fellow men, against his will; it ravages material amenities, the fruits of human toil, and much besides. Moreover, wars, as now conducted, afford no scope for acts of heroism according to the old ideals, and, given the high perfection of modern arms, war today would mean the sheer extermination of one of the combatants, if not of both. This is so true, so obvious, that we can but wonder why the conduct of war is not banned by general consent. Doubtless either of the points I have just made is open to debate. It may be asked if the community, in its turn, cannot claim a right over the individual lives of its members. Moreover, all forms of war cannot be indiscriminately condemned; so long as there are nations and empires, each prepared callously to exterminate its rival, all alike must be equipped for war. But we will not dwell on any of these problems; they lie outside the debate to which you have invited me. I pass on to another point, the basis, as it strikes me, of our common hatred of war. It is this: we cannot do otherwise than hate it. Pacifists we are, since our organic nature wills us thus to be. Hence it comes easy to us to find arguments that justify our standpoint.

This point, however, calls for elucidation. Here is the way in which I see it. The cultural development of mankind (some, I know, prefer to call it civilization) has been in progress since immemorial antiquity. To this *processus* we owe all that is best in our composition, but also much that makes for human suffering. Its origins and causes are obscure, its issue is uncertain, but some of its characteristics are easy to perceive. It well may lead to the extinction of mankind, for it impairs the sexual function in more than one respect, and even today the uncivilized races and the backward classes of all nations are multiplying more rapidly than the cultured elements. This process may, perhaps, be likened to the effect of domestication on certain animals—it clearly involves physical changes of structure—but the view that cultural development is an organic process of this order has not yet become generally familiar. The psychic changes which accompany this process of cultural change are striking and not to be gainsaid. They consist in the progressive rejection of instinctive ends and a scaling down of instinctive reactions. Sensations which delighted our forefathers have become neutral or unbearable to us; and, if our ethical and aesthetic ideals have undergone a change, the causes of this are ultimately organic. On the psychological side two of the most important phenomena of culture are, first, a strengthening of the intellect, which tends to master our instinctive life, and, second, an introversion of the aggressive impulse, with all its consequent benefits and perils. Now war runs most emphatically counter to the psychic disposition imposed on us by the growth of culture; we are therefore bound to resent war, to find it utterly intolerable. With pacifists like us it is not merely an intellectual and affective repulsion, but a constitutional intolerance, an idiosyncrasy in its most drastic form. And it would seem that the aesthetic ignominies of warfare play almost as large a part in this repugnance as war's atrocities.

How long have we to wait before the rest of men turn pacifist? Impossible to say, and yet perhaps our hope that these two factors—man's cultural disposition and a well-founded dread of the form that future wars will take—may serve to put an end to war in the near future, is not chimerical. But by what ways or byways this will come about, we cannot guess. Meanwhile we may rest on the assurance that whatever makes for cultural development is working also against war.

With kindest regards and, should this exposé prove a disappointment to you, my sincere regrets,

Yours,
SIGMUND FREUD

◄◄◄ ►►►

E. F. M. DURBIN & JOHN BOWLBY

Personal Aggressiveness and War *

The purpose of this article is to examine the bearing of some recent biological and psychological work upon the theories of the cause of war.

The authors hold that war—or organized fighting between large groups of adult human beings—must be regarded as one species of a larger genus, the genus of *fighting*. Fighting is plainly a common, indeed a universal, form of human behavior. It extends beyond the borders of humanity into the types of mammals most closely related in the evolutionary classification to the common ancestors of man and other apes. Wars between groups within the nation and between nations are obvious and important examples of this type of behavior. Since this is so, it must of necessity follow that the simplest and most general causes of war are only to be found in the causes of fighting, just as the simplest and most general causes of falling downstairs are to be found in the causes of falling down.

Such a simple thesis could hardly be expected to contain any important conclusion. Yet if the causes of war are to be found in their simplest form only in phenomena more widely dispersed in space and time than comparatively recent forms of political and economic organization, like the nation-state and the capitalist system, it must surely follow that theories tracing the cause of war either to capitalism or nationalism can only at the best contain part of the

* Reprinted from E. F. M. Durbin *et al.*, *War and Democracy*, Part I, pp. 3–31, by permission of the publisher (Copyright 1938, Kegan Paul, Tench, Trubner, & Co., Ltd., London).

truth. Nevertheless, it is theories of this kind that are fashionable in the current discussions of the cause of war.

We shall revert at length to the bearing of our own views upon these theories. In the meantime, it is our primary task to examine some of the evidence recently collected on the extent and causes of fighting. The procedure that we propose to follow is to summarize and analyze the descriptive work that has been done upon fighting among apes, children, and civilized adults . . . and to use the conclusions to be derived from that work in the argument of this article. The empirical evidence that is available is far from complete, but we think that it is more than sufficient to sustain a number of most important conclusions about the effective causes of war.

Fighting, as we have already pointed out, is a form of behavior widely distributed through history and nature. It occurs in the form of group conflict throughout recorded time. It takes place spasmodically between individuals in civilized countries. It occurs among primitives, among children, and among apes. Whether one looks back through time or downward to simpler forms of social organization, it is a common practice for individuals or groups to seek to change their environment by force and for other individuals and groups to meet force with force.

But fighting, or the appeal to force, while universal in distribution, is not continuous in time. The most warlike groups and the most aggressive individuals spend considerable periods in peaceful toleration of, and positive cooperation with, other animals or persons. Most organized communities have enjoyed longer periods of peace than of war. The greater part of human activity—of man-hours—is spent, not in war, but in peaceful cooperation. The scientific problem is, therefore, twofold—why is there peaceful cooperation, and why does peaceful cooperation sometimes break down into war? The practical problem—at least, for lovers of peace—is how peaceful cooperation is to be preserved against the universal tendency exhibited in history for it to degenerate into war.

PEACEFUL COOPERATION

What, then, are the simplest causes of peaceful cooperation? Here it is necessary to distinguish between groups with and without "government"—that is, an apparatus of force constructed with the conscious and explicit purpose of preserving peace within the group. Clearly, the existence of a powerful organization taking action to preserve peace itself constitutes a strong and immediate cause for the appearance of peace.[1] We shall be concerned with the con-

[1] We feel unable to accept Dr. Glover's rather casual rejection of instruments of government and collective security as a means of preserving peace. (See Glover, *The Dangers of Being Human.*) We feel that he does not appreciate the strength of the will to cooperate expressed in them. . . .

sequence of this obvious point at the end of this article. For the moment, however, we are interested in a prior and more fundamental question. What are the causes of peace in a group without government or any effective machinery for the restraint of fighting? Why do animals cooperate in the absence of any agent powerful enough to prevent them from fighting?

Now a survey of the life of mammals in general, and of apes and men in particular, suggests that the causes of peace in the absence of government are, for the extrafamilial group,[2] of three main kinds:

The obvious, most important, and overwhelming advantage to be derived from peace lies in the division of labor and the possibility of thus achieving purposes desired by the individual but obtainable only by active cooperation with others. This is so plain in the case of adult human society that the point is scarcely worth elaborating. The whole of the difference in the variety of satisfactions open to the individual in isolation and the same person in the active membership of a peaceful society measures the advantages to be derived from continuous cooperation between adults. The extent of cooperation in any groups other than adult human societies is, of course, much more limited. But groups of children cooperate in simple tasks and in games that require a specialization of function between the individual members of the group. And there is some evidence to suggest that apes exhibit still simpler forms of cooperation and that even mammals who hunt and live in herds develop simple differentiation of function for various common purposes of defense or attack.[3]

Cooperation extends enormously the opportunities for life and satisfaction within groups that have developed it. It is reasonable to presume that these advantages are also *causes* of cooperation, since many of the results of cooperation are of survival value. In any case, few persons would wish to deny that the sovereign advantages of cooperation are for adult human beings one of the main causes of voluntary peace.

In the case of apes, there is also evidence that satisfaction is found in the mere presence of others of the same species. Whether this satisfaction is exclusively sexual—that is, whether the advantage lies in the possibility of varied relations with the opposite sex—there is not sufficient evidence to determine. Insofar as it is sexual, such gregariousness may easily become a source of conflict within the group. This we shall see in a moment. But insofar as pleasure

2 We have not concerned ourselves with the reasons for peace within the family (a) because it leads at once to the rather different question of the nature of sexual and familial ties; (b) because the family usually exhibits the phenomenon of patriarchal and matriarchal authority.

3 This last point is not universally conceded by the students of animal behavior. Apes appear to scratch each other, and some herds of herbivores seem to maintain a system of outposts and sentries. But it has been denied that these phenomena can be compared with the purposive cooperation found in human society. The conflict of view could only be resolved by further investigation.

is felt in the mere presence of other members of the group, there is a force binding those members together in peace.

The counterpart of the primitive sociability of the apes in children and adult human beings is obvious. Its relationship to sexual promiscuity remains as obscure in human beings as in apes, but the existence of a pleasure felt in the presence of human company could scarcely be denied. Sociability is therefore an independent cause for the existence and stability of society.[4]

The reasons for cooperation so far mentioned are all self-regarding advantages. They derive their importance from the existence of kinds of individual satisfaction that can only be obtained with the aid of others. We do not, however, suppose that self-regarding ends are the sole causes of peaceful cooperation. We think it obvious that in the development of the child there is to be traced the emergence of an interest in others for their own sakes, a gradual but growing recognition of the rights of others to the kinds of advantage desired by oneself and finally, in the fully developed personal relationships of friendship and love, the positive desire for the loved one's happiness as a good for oneself. From reflection and logic this care for the good of others can make the common good a personal end. The existence of a general desire for the common good is clearly a force making for peace in adult society. But its power will only extend as far as the idea of the common good extends. If the common good is only felt to reach to the limits of a racial or a geographic or a social group, there will be no force in this recognition of the common good within the group to prevent the use of force outside and on behalf of it.

All this is very important, but it is also very obvious. It is indeed the commonplace of pacifist literature. It is never difficult to find reasons for peaceful cooperation. And with such overwhelming advantages in its favor, the real problem is why peace so frequently degenerates into fighting. It is consequently much more in the study of the actual breakdown of peaceful cooperation among apes and children and grown-up people that recent descriptive work has brought new light. The work that we think to be of greatest interest falls into two parts. There is first the careful work of observation that has been carried out by Dr. Zuckermann on apes and on children by Dr. Susan Isaacs. This does much to throw into clear perspective the most primitive causes for aggression and fighting in the absence of government. The second clue to the puzzle is to be found, in our opinion, in the mass of descriptive material laid bare by the anthropologist and in the case papers of patients treated by the therapeutic technique of psychoanalysis. We, therefore, propose to distinguish in our brief survey between the simple causes and forms of aggressive behavior common to apes and to human beings, on the one hand, and the more complicated forms exhibited by human beings alone, on the other. For an account of the complications added by the faculties of the adult human mind,

[4] We feel it unnecessary to argue the obscure and rather formal controversy as to whether there is a specific "herd instinct."

we shall offer a brief and necessarily controversial interpretation of the significance of the anthropological and psychoanalytical evidence as to the origins of personal and group aggressiveness.

THE SIMPLER CAUSES OF FIGHTING

The evidence taken from the observation of the behavior of apes and children suggests that there are three clearly separable groups of simple causes for the outbreak of fighting and the exhibition of aggressiveness by individuals.

One of the most common causes of fighting among both children and apes was over the *possession* of external objects. The disputed ownership of any desired object—food, clothes, toys, females, and the affection of others—was sufficient ground for an appeal to force. On Monkey Hill disputes over females were responsible for the death of thirty out of thirty-three females. Two points are of particular interest to notice about these fights for possession.

In the first place they are often carried to such an extreme that they end in the complete destruction of the objects of common desire. Toys are torn to pieces. Females are literally torn limb from limb. So overriding is the aggression once it has begun that it not only overflows all reasonable boundaries of selfishness but utterly destroys the object for which the struggle began and even the self for whose advantage the struggle was undertaken.

In the second place it is observable, at least in children, that the object for whose possession aggression is started may sometimes be desired by one person only or merely because it is desired by someone else. There were many cases observed by Dr. Isaacs where toys and other objects which had been discarded as useless were violently defended by their owners when they became the object of some other child's desire.[5] The grounds of possessiveness may, therefore, be irrational in the sense that they are derived from inconsistent judgments of value. Whether sensible or irrational, contests over possession are commonly the occasion for the most ruthless use of force among children and apes.

One of the commonest kinds of object arousing possessive desire is the notice, good will, affection, and service of other members of the group. Among children one of the commonest causes of quarreling was "jealousy"— the desire for the exclusive possession of the interest and affection of someone else, particularly the adults in charge of the children. This form of behavior is sometimes classified as a separate cause of conflict under the name of "rivalry" or "jealousy." But, in point of fact, it seems to us that it is only one variety of

[5] This finds an interesting echo in the greater world of politics. Nations will often maintain that certain colonial territories are of no advantage to them, and yet bitterly resist any proposal to hand them over to other countries; or rich people, arguing that riches do not bless the rich, angrily resent any suggestion that they should be transferred to the poor.

possessiveness. The object of desire is not a material object—that is the only difference. The object is the interest and affection of other persons. What is wanted, however, is the exclusive right to that interest and affection—a property in emotions instead of in things. As subjective emotions and as causes of conflict, jealousy and rivalry are fundamentally similar to the desire for the uninterrupted possession of toys or food. Indeed, very often the persons, property which is desired, are the sources of toys and food.

Possessiveness is, then, in all its forms a common cause of fighting. If we are to look behind the mere facts of behavior for an explanation of this phenomenon, a teleological cause is not far to seek. The exclusive right to objects of desire is a clear and simple advantage to the possessor of it. It carries with it the certainty and continuity of satisfaction. Where there is only one claimant to a good, frustration and the possibility of loss is reduced to a minimum. It is, therefore, obvious that, if the ends of the self are the only recognized ends, the whole powers of the agent, including the fullest use of his available force, will be used to establish and defend exclusive rights to possession.[6]

Another cause of aggression closely allied to possessiveness is the tendency for children and apes greatly to resent the *intrusion of a stranger* into their group. A new child in the class may be laughed at, isolated, and disliked and even set upon and pinched and bullied. A new monkey may be poked and bitten to death. It is interesting to note that it is only strangeness within a similarity of species that is resented. Monkeys do not mind being joined by a goat or a rat. Children do not object when animals are introduced to the group. Indeed, such novelties are often welcomed. But when monkeys meet a new monkey or children a strange child, aggression often occurs. This suggests strongly that the reason for the aggression is fundamentally possessiveness. The competition of the newcomers is feared. The present members of the group feel that there will be more rivals for the food or the attention of the adults.

Finally, another common source of fighting among children is a failure or *frustration* in their own activity. A child will be prevented either by natural causes such as bad weather or illness or by the opposition of some adult from doing something he wishes to do at a given moment—sail his boat or ride the bicycle. The child may also frustrate itself by failing, through lack of skill or strength, to complete successfully some desired activity. Such a child will then in the ordinary sense become "naughty." He will be in a bad or surly temper. And, what is of interest from our point of view, the child will indulge in aggression—attacking and fighting other children or adults. Sometimes the object of aggression will simply be the cause of frustration, a straightforward

6 This teleological rationalism does not explain the phenomenon of what we have termed irrational possessiveness. Our own explanation of the fact that a child will fight merely to possess objects because they are wanted by others is that the child in question begins to suspect that, just because someone else wants the discarded object, he must have been mistaken in supposing that it was worthless. But evidence on this point is not available.

reaction. The child will kick or hit the nurse who forbids the sailing of his boat. But sometimes—indeed, frequently—the person or thing that suffers the aggression is quite irrelevant and innocent of offense. The angry child will stamp the ground or box the ears of another child when neither the ground nor the child attacked is even remotely connected with the irritation or frustration.

Of course, this kind of behavior is so common that everyone feels it to be obvious and to constitute no serious scientific problem. That a small boy should pull his sister's hair because it is raining does not appear to the ordinary unreflecting person to be an occasion for solemn scientific inquiry. He is, as we should all say, "in a bad temper." Yet it is not, in fact, really obvious either why revenge should be taken on entirely innocent objects, since no good to the aggressor can come of it, or why children being miserable should seek to make others miserable also. It is just a fact of human behavior that cannot really be deduced from any general principle of reason. But it is, as we shall see, of very great importance for our purpose. It shows how it is possible, at the simplest and most primitive level, for aggression and fighting to spring from an entirely irrelevant and partially hidden cause. Fighting to possess a desired object is straightforward and rational, however disastrous its consequences, compared with fighting that occurs because, in a different and unrelated activity, some frustration has barred the road to pleasure. The importance of this possibility for an understanding of group conflict must already be obvious.

These are the three simplest separate categories of cause we are able to observe in the evidence. One further point, however, remains to be made about the character of the fighting that occurs among apes. It is a marked characteristic of this fighting that, once it has broken out anywhere, it spreads with great rapidity throughout the group and draws into conflict individuals who had no part in the first quarrel and appear to have no immediate interest whatever in the outcome of the original dispute. Fighting is infectious in the highest degree. Why? It is not easy to find an answer. Whether it is that the apes who are not immediately involved feel that some advantage for themselves can be snatched from the confusion following upon the rupture of social equilibrium or whether real advantages are involved that escape the observation of the onlooker is not at present determined. Or it may be that the infectiousness of fighting is irrational in the same way that the irrelevant expression of aggression due to frustration is irrational. Whatever the explanation, the fact remains that fighting spreads without apparent cause or justification—that "every dog joins a fight," in other and older words. This excitability and the attraction which fighting may possess for its own sake are likely to be a source of great instability in any society. It is one of the most dangerous parts of our animal inheritance.

So much for the simpler forms of aggression. It is now time to consider the light thrown by anthropological and psychoanalytic evidence upon the behavior of adult human beings.

THE FURTHER CAUSES OF AGGRESSIVE BEHAVIOR

So far the material from which we have sought illumination has been derived from the simple behavior of children and apes. We must now consider more complicated behavior. There are, as we have already pointed out, at least two relevant studies—anthropology and the case histories recorded by psychoanalysts. The present authors have most unfortunately not been able, through lack of time and assistance, to survey the vast mass of anthropological material in detail, but even such a slight study as they have been able to make suffices to show the very great importance of other causes of fighting among primitive peoples.

Before we begin this task it is necessary to make one preliminary and simple observation about the nature of adult aggression in general. It is of first importance to realize that, as far as aggressiveness and fighting are concerned, there is no noticeable improvement in the *behavior* of adults compared with that of the most savage animals and children. If anything, it is more ruthless. The recent history of Europe establishes this conclusion with horrible insistence. There is no form of behavior too ruthless, too brutal, too cruel for adult men and women to use against each other. Torture is becoming normal again; the knuckle-duster and the whip, other more refined instruments of flagellation, and the armory of mental pain are the commonplace instruments of prisons and concentration camps from Japan to Spain. Men and women have been shot down without trial, soaked in petrol and burned to death, beaten to unrecognizable masses of flesh and bone, hanged by the hair and hands until they die, starved and tortured with fear and hope during the "reigns of terror" that have accompanied and succeeded the civil wars in Russia, Italy, Poland, Austria, Germany, and Spain. Cruelty knows no boundary of party or creed. It wears every kind of shirt. And over all of us there hangs, perpetual and menacing, the fear of war. No group of animals could be more aggressive or more ruthless in their aggression than the adult members of the human race.

Are there then no differences between the aggression of more primitive beings and that of adult men? We suggest that there are only two differences. In the first place the aggression of adults is normally a group activity. Murder and assault are restricted to a small criminal minority. Adults kill and torture each other only when organized into political parties or economic classes or religious denominations or nation-states. A moral distinction is always made between the individual killing for himself and the same individual killing for some real or supposed group interest. In the second place, the adult powers of imagination and reason are brought to the service of the aggressive intention. Apes and children, when they fight, simply fight. Men and women first construct towering systems of theology and religion, complex analyses of racial character and class structure, or moralities of group life and virility before they kill one another. Thus they fight for Protestantism or Mohammedanism, for the emancipation of the world proletariat or for the salvation of the Nordic culture, for nation or for king. Men will die like flies for theories and exterminate each other with every instrument of destruction for abstractions.

The differences of *behavior* are therefore not substantial. The form is the same, the results are the same. Group fighting is even more destructive than individual fighting. A machine gun or a bomb is no less lethal because its use can be shown to be a necessity of the class war or noble because it brings the light of Italian civilization to the Abyssinian peoples. Now it might be argued that there is no continuity of character between the wars of civilized people and fighting of the simpler orders. We cannot, however, see any reason for supposing so. Indeed, the only question of interest appears to us to lie in the matter of causation. Are the causes exactly the same, or are they changed in any important way by the greater powers and complexity of the adult human mind?

We are therefore brought back to the question: What are the causes of aggressiveness in adult human beings? We would maintain that anthropology and psychoanalysis suggest a number of ways in which the powers of the human mind change and add to the causes of aggression. There appear to be at least three different mechanisms discernible in the material of these two sciences.

ANIMISM

The first and most obvious of these is the cause of war revealed so very plainly by the study of primitive intergroup conflict. It consists in the universal tendency to attribute all events in the world to the deliberate activity of human or parahuman *will*. All happenings, whether natural and inevitable, or human and voluntary, are attributed to the will of some being either human or anthropomorphically divine. If a thunderstorm occurs or a hurricane visits a village or a man is killed by a tiger, the evil is attributed either to the magic of a neighboring tribe or the ill will of demons and gods. In the same way, good fortune, however natural, is attributed to the deliberate intention of some other being. This universal tendency in the human mind is termed "animism."

It is certain that this imaginative tendency on the part of human beings leads to war. It is obvious why it should. If evil is attributed to the direct malice of neighboring and opposing groups, the only possible protection against further evil lies in the destruction of the source of ill will. It is, however, of great importance whether the supposed enemy is human or supernatural. If it is spiritual, the natural reply will be placatory sacrifices or the harmless ritual of beating or burning or making war upon the evil spirit. . . . But if the supposed author of evil is not supernatural but human, the results are neither harmless nor amusing. If the typhoon is attributed to the magic of neighboring peoples or of dissident minorities within the tribe, then the destruction of the enemy, root and branch, is the only safe course. Hence after a thunderstorm or an accident the restless fears and hatred of the tribe will find expression in a primitive war against neighboring tribes or the stamping out of some hapless group of victims within it. Enemies without and traitors within must be exterminated.

We think it difficult to exaggerate the frequency and importance of this cause of fighting in human societies of all degrees of civilization. It is a universal tendency among the simpler people of all nations to attribute evil to some person or group of persons. It is present everywhere in party politics. Every evil is loaded upon political opponents. Socialists attribute all disasters, whether economic or political, to capitalists or the capitalist class. Conservatives think it obvious that the last uncontrollable and world-wide depression in trade was due to the bad government of the Socialists in this country. Other movements find different and more peculiar scapegoats in the bankers or the Jews or the Russians. In each case what is noticeable and dangerous is that a vast power and a deep malignity is attributed to the inimical group. The supposed malignity is often purely illusory. The attributed power transcends all reality. When the open conflict of party politics is suppressed by an authoritarian regime, the tendency is exaggerated rather than reduced. Some unfortunate minority within the group—the Jews or the kulaks—become the source of all evil, the scapegoat of all disaster. Or an overwhelming hatred is conceived for another nation. Out of these real terrors and derivative hatreds merciless persecutions and international wars are likely to spring.

We shall go on to show that the sources of aggression among human beings are much more complicated than either the simple causes operating in animals or this common habit of attributing everything to some human agency. Yet it should be obvious that much of the behavior of large groups can be explained by the categories of cause we have already discussed. Possessiveness, frustration, animism are potent causes of conflict between groups—whether parties, classes, or states. After we have discussed the complex history of aggression within the individual we shall have reason to revert to these simpler forms of behavior. It seems probable that the complex character of the civilized individual undergoes a degeneration or simplification into simpler forms and simpler reactions when he is caught up into and expresses himself through the unity of the group. The behavior of the group is, in an important sense, simpler and more direct than the behavior of the individual. But in the meantime we must consider the light thrown by psychoanalysis upon the history and development of aggressive impulses in the civilized adult.

THE TRANSFORMATION OF AGGRESSIVE IMPULSES—
DISPLACEMENT AND PROJECTION

What light does psychoanalytic evidence throw upon the problem of adult aggression? It is, of course, impossible to consider at all adequately the mass of material and theory comprised in the work of this school of psychology. . . . All that we can attempt at this point is a brief account of the main conclusions—as they appear to us—of the evidence. It is scarcely necessary to point out that our views are only one interpretation of the data, and, although we think our interpretation to be the most accurate, it could only be verified by the kind of practical test that we suggest at the end of this article.

We suggest tentatively therefore that the evidence of psychoanalysis justifies the following conclusions:

That the *primary* causes of aggression (and of peaceful cooperation) are identical with those of children and apes. The character of the id—or complex of instinctive impulses—does not change materially as the individual grows older. The same sources of satisfaction—food, warmth, love, society—are desired and the same sources of conflict—desire for exclusive possession of the sources of satisfaction or aggression arising from a sense of frustration—are present. But in the life of most children there is a controlling or warping influence present in a varying degree, that of *authority*. The child is denied for various reasons—good or bad—an open and uninterrupted access to the means of its satisfaction. It is denied the breast or bottle, the toy or the company of adults, at the time or to the extent that it wishes. The evidence seems overwhelming that such frustration leads to a violent reaction of fear, hatred, and aggression. The child cries or screams or bites or kicks. We are not for the moment concerned with the question whether this frustration is desirable or not. We are simply concerned with its results. The result is "bad temper" or "naughtiness"—a resentment of frustration. This original resentment and the aggression to which it leads we would call "simple aggression."

Further development turns, in our view, upon the way in which this simple aggression is treated. The statistically normal method of treatment is, we suggest, further frustration or *punishment*. The child is slapped or beaten or subjected to moral instruction—taught that its behavior is wrong or wicked. Again we are not concerned with the question of the rightness or wrongness of this procedure, but only with its consequences. We suggest that the result of punishment is to present the child with a radical conflict—either he must control the expression of his simple aggression or suffer the punishment and the loss of love that simple aggression in a regime of discipline necessarily entails.

This conflict in the child is in our view an important source of aggressive-

ness in the adult. The conflict itself is a conflict between a fundamental tendency to resent frustration and the fear of punishment or, what is just as important, the fear of the loss of love. To the child the parent is both the source
of satisfaction and the source of frustration.[7] To express aggression is to
endanger the life of the goose that lays the golden eggs. Not to express simple
aggression toward original objects is the task that faces the child. Now one
result of the child's attempt to resolve the conflict is called "repression." [8] Much
has been written about the nature and consequences of repression. The hypothesis of the existence and independent functioning of an unconscious mind
has been elaborated to explain the analytical evidence, and a whole literature
of theory has been built upon this idea. We are not here primarily concerned
with psychoanalytic theory, and we feel that the main contributions of the
evidence to an understanding of the sources of aggressiveness can be explained
quite simply. The overwhelming fact established by the evidence is that aggression, however deeply hidden or disguised, does not disappear. It appears later
and in other forms. It is not destroyed. It is safe to conclude from the evidence
that it cannot be destroyed. Whether we conceive simple aggression stimulated
by frustration as a quantity of energy that has to be released somewhere or
whether we imagine that a secret and unconscious character is formed that is
aggressive although the superficial character is peaceful or whether we simply
suppose that a certain kind of character is formed, peaceful in certain directions
and aggressive in others, is a matter of comparative indifference and mainly of
terminology. The fundamental fact is that the punishment of simple aggression
results in the appearance of aggression in other forms. The boy, instead of striking his father whom he fears, strikes a smaller boy whom he does not fear. Disguised aggression has made the boy into a bully. The girl who dares not scream
at her mother grows up to hate other women. Again a character has been
formed by a simple aggressiveness that has been controlled but not destroyed.
And in the same way revolutionaries who hate ordered government; nationalists who hate foreign peoples; individuals who hate bankers, Jews, or their
political opponents may be exhibiting characteristics that have been formed
by the suppression of simple aggression in their childhood education.[9] These

[7] Throughout this article we use the term "parent" to refer to the person or persons, whoever it may be, who are responsible for looking after the child—whether they are in fact
parents or nurses or aunts or teachers.

[8] The tendency to aggression is not the only thing that may be repressed. Certain other
impulses that are punished or condemned by adults or repudiated by the child himself may
also be repressed. Much psychoanalytic evidence and theory is concerned with the repression of these other impulses—particularly the sexual impulses.

[9] We are not for a moment suggesting either (a) that logical and objective cases cannot
be argued in favor of revolutions, wars, and persecutions, or (b) that the positive valuation
of such things as justice, liberty, and other social values may not reasonably involve a hatred
of their opposites. We are only suggesting that the repression of simple aggression may
result in these forms of hatred. The objective cases of these schools of thought are in every
case different in kind from the personal and subjective elements in their supporters' view
of them.

aggressive aspects of adult character and the aggressiveness to which they lead we call "transformed aggression." It is the displaced and unrecognized fruit of suppressed simple aggression.

The second great contribution of psychoanalytic evidence is to show the kind of transformations that simple aggression undergoes as the adult faculties develop. The fundamental problem of the child is, as we have seen, a double one: that of self-control and of *ambivalence*. In order to escape punishment, the child must prevent its aggressive impulses from appearing—it must control its natural aggression. But this is not the whole of the problem. The parent has become for the child the object of two incompatible emotions—love and hatred. As a source of satisfaction and companionship, the parent is greatly beloved. As a source of frustration and punishment, the parent is greatly feared and hated. The evidence demonstrates overwhelmingly that such a double attitude to one person puts a terrible emotional strain upon the child. In the growth and development of character a number of imaginative and intellectual efforts are made to alleviate or avoid the severity of this internal conflict.

One other aspect of the subjective life must be mentioned before we examine the processes by which internal strain or anxiety is reduced to a minimum— and that is the question of *moral judgment*. We are not at this juncture concerned with the theories of the origin of what the moralist calls the conscience and the psychoanalyst the superego. It is obvious that persons are deeply influenced in their behavior and their feeling by what they think they ought to do and ought to be—their sense of duty. We think it also clear from the evidence of psychoanalysis that the content of this moral sense—the total of the things a man feels to be his duty—is made up partly of objective moral judgments and partly of compulsions arising from the teaching and discipline of childhood.[10] The moral sense is neither wholly rational nor wholly subjective and irrational. It is partly the one and partly the other. But whatever the origin of the moral sense, there is conclusive evidence that it can become the source of immense burdens of shame and guilt, both to the child and to the adult. Again we think that the available evidence demonstrates beyond question that such guilt in the adult is composed partly of a sensible consciousness of moral failure, partly of an irrational fear of punishment derived from the experiences and wild imagination of childhood, and partly of a half-conscious recognition of the dangerous aggressive impulses within himself. All these elements combine to make a considerable burden of guilt—acknowledged or unacknowledged—for most individuals, a burden that rises to intolerable levels for depressed and suicidal subjects.

There is, then, much support in the empirical work of character psychology for the theological doctrine of a "man divided against himself." Not only do

[10] And partly of the remnants of the exaggerated and fantastic moral judgments of the child.

we both love and hate the same people, but we are divided into an impulsive and appetitive character only part of which we acknowledge, on the one hand, and a stern and inescapable sense of duty which is often partially unrecognized, on the other. These divisions of our being are at war with each other and are responsible for much of the unhappiness of individual life and are the direct source of the universal phenomenon of *morbid anxiety*.

It is to reduce anxiety and guilt to a minimum and to resolve the conflict of ambivalence that the major psychological mechanisms are developed. These are of two kinds—*displacement* and *projection:* both of them are frequently used for the expression of transformed aggression.

Displacement

This is perhaps the simplest mechanism of all. Several examples of it have already been cited. It is extremely common in political and social affairs. It consists in the transference of fear or hatred or love from the true historical object to a secondary object. The secondary object may be loved or hated for its own sake, but to the sensible degree of feeling is added an intensity derived from the transference to it of irrelevant passion. The child is thwarted by its father and then bullies a smaller child. The father is reprimanded by his employer of whom he is afraid and then is angry with his son. A girl both loves and feels jealous of her mother. To deal with this situation she may direct her loving feelings toward her schoolmistress and feel free to hate her mother more completely. A boy may hate his father through familial discipline and grow up to hate all authority and government. He would be a revolutionary under any regime. Children who both love and hate their parents grow up to love their own country blindly and uncritically and to hate foreign countries with equal blindness and unreason. They have succeeded in displacing their opposite emotions to different objects.

The tendency to identify the self with the community is so common as to be obvious.[11] The transference of the predominant feelings of childhood from parents to the organs of political life—to the state and the parties in it—is almost universal. Hence the importance of symbolical figureheads and governors, kings, and *Führers*. Hence the fanaticism and violence of political life. Hence the comparative weakness of reason and moderation in political affairs.

The advantage to the individual of these displacements or transferences of emotion from their historically relevant objects should be obvious. In the first place the confusion and strain of the ambivalent relation are often resolved.

[11] Nor is such an identification by any means wholly unreasonable. After all, the communities in which we are brought up have entered into us and made us what we are. It is natural that we should feel that what happens to them happens also to us more personally than they really do.

Instead of both loving and hating the mother, it is possible to love the school-mistress and to hate more freely—however secretly—the person who was originally both loved and hated with equal intensity. Instead of both loving and hating the same adults it is possible to love the nation or the Communist Party with pure devotion and hate the Germans or the capitalist class with frenzy. In either case the world of emotional objects is redeemed from its original chaos—simplicity and order are restored to it. Action and purposive life is possible again.[12] In the second place the displacement is often, indeed usually, toward a safer object. It is safer to kick a smaller boy than to kick one's father. It is safer for the individual to hate the capitalists than to hate his wife or to hate the Russians than to hate his employers. Thus fear and anxiety—though not banished—are reduced. Happiness is increased. Of course, greater safety is not always reached in any objective sense. To join the Communist Party instead of divorcing one's wife may result in imprisonment and even death. To become a patriot may mean early enlistment and a premature grave when the alternative was objectively less dangerous. But unless we are to deny the teleological interpretation of human affairs altogether, it seems obvious that the internal conflicts of fear and guilt are alleviated by displacement. And there is ample direct evidence to support this view.[13]

From our present point of view the importance of this mechanism can scarcely be exaggerated. Adult aggression, as we have seen, is normally carried out in group activity. Political parties make civil war. Churches make religious war. States make international war. These various kinds of groups can attract absolute loyalty and canalize torrents of hatred and murder through the mechanism of displacement. Individuals can throw themselves into the life and work of groups because they find a solution to their own conflicts in them. The stores of explosive violence in the human atom are released by and expressed in group organization. The power of the group for aggression is derived partly from the sensible and objective judgments of men, but chiefly, in our view, by their power to attract to themselves the displaced hatred and destructiveness of their members. Displacement, though not the ultimate cause, is a direct channel of the ultimate causes of war.

[12] When a suitable division of emotion and transference is carried out suddenly the phenomenon of "conversion" often appears. Persons suddenly decide to give all their devotion to the church or party and all their hatred to the "world" or the party's enemies. Conflicts suddenly disappear, and a frustrated and unhappy individual becomes a confident and happy Christian or Communist or National Socialist. Of course, which of these things he becomes is determined by other forces—including the social and historical environment.

[13] It is also important to realize that the displacement may be temporary. Certain displacements of hatred or love involve further conflict and guilt. Thus the boy who transfers his hatred to his father into bullying may feel, after a time, extremely guilty about his cruelty. Members of extreme parties may find themselves involved in blood guilt. Thus displacement, always bringing temporary relief, may lead in vicious circles more and more deeply into conflict toward final breakdown or suicide.

Projection

A second group of mechanisms that are of the greatest importance in understanding individual and social behavior are those of projection. It is not so simple a mechanism as that of displacement, but the psychoanalytic evidence demonstrates that it is of frequent occurrence in social life. The mechanism consists in imagining that other individuals are really like our own unrecognized and unaccepted selves. It is the projection of our own characters upon others.

There are two parts of subjective character that the individual "projects upon" others in this way—two kinds of unrecognized motives of his own that he imagines are animating other people: first, his real but unrecognized impulses and, second, his unrecognized conscience. In the first case we suppose others to be wicked in the ways that we do not admit ourselves to be wicked; in the second we suppose them to be censorious and restrictive in ways that we do not recognize our own superego criticizes and restrains us.

The Projection of Impulse. Examples of the way in which people project upon others the evil that is really in themselves are not far to seek. There are men and women who imagine that everyone's hand is against them, persons who are mean and parsimonious and who assume that everyone else is seeking to swindle them. Persecution manias or paranoia contain, as well as simple animism, an element of this mechanism. In all these cases it seems obvious to us that the individual is either assuming that people will treat him as he wishes to treat them or that he imagines them to be animated by the motives and impulses that are really his own. The miser attributes to others his own impulse to swindle. The paranoid imagines the object of his fears to be animated by his own wicked and destructive passions.

To the authors, most cases of political persecution seem to be of this kind. We have already seen that much of this behavior can be explained in terms of the simplest animism—the tendency to blame some human will for all disasters. But the existence of such a tendency does not explain why persecution continues when no disaster is present or threatening. And yet they do continue after all reasonable and unreasonable occasion has passed. Almost all authoritarian regimes treasure a pet object of persecution indefinitely. The National Socialists persecute the Communists and the Jews; the Bolsheviks persecute the Trotskyists and the kulaks. It is commonly said that regimes "need a scapegoat." We suggest that, over and above any objective reasons for persecution —the need for an excuse in case of failure or the desire to crush opposition by fear—and explaining the continuation of persecution long after the objective reasons have lost their force, there is an element of pure projection. The persecuted minorities are made to carry the projected wickedness of the dominant masses. They are truly the scapegoat of the people, not only in the sense that they are hated and despised, but also that they are made literally to bear the "sins of the people." We think it important to realize that the National Socialists seriously believe that the Jews are responsible for national degradation, that the Communists seriously believe that the kulaks threatened the regime, and they believe these things against all evidence because they have successfully projected upon these groups so much of the disruptive elements within themselves. The hated minorities are genuinely thought to be the cause of disruption because they have become the external symbol of internal wickedness.

The advantage of this mechanism is again obvious. It reduces anxiety to force the enemy outside the gate of one's soul. It is better to hate other people for meanness and to bear the fear of their ill will than to hate oneself for being miserly. To see wickedness in others, though terrifying, is better than to be divided against oneself. It avoids the terrible burden of guilt.

Its importance for the understanding of group aggressiveness is also plain. If it is possible to project upon other groups all the evil within the group, then, as in the case of simple animism, the forces of hatred and fear against the external group will grow more and more intense. If Communists can persuade themselves that all aggressiveness and cruelty are with the Fascists and Fascists that all treachery and destructiveness are with the Communists, then civil war can be fought with better will and greater ferocity on both sides. If Englishmen owning a quarter of the world can feel that all ruthless imperialism is exhibited by Germany and Germany with the most powerful army in Europe can feel herself threatened by Russia, then the selfishness of the one group and the aggressiveness of the other can be justified without being reduced. Projection is an admirable mechanism for turning the other man into the aggressor, for making hatred appear as a passion for righteousness, for purifying the hate-tormented soul. By this means all war is made into religious war—a crusade for truth and virtue.

The Projection of Conscience. Finally, to complete the story, there is the projection of the conscience. In order to escape the pains of self-condemnation, the individual projects upon others the moral judgments and condemnation of his own heart. This leads to a particular form of paranoia or persecution mania in which persons resent not only the real, but also purely imaginary moral judgments and legal restraints imposed by the state. It is particularly common among the revolutionary opponents of an existing order. Communists exaggerate enormously the degree and deliberateness of capitalist repression. National Socialists in opposition exaggerated absurdly the oppressions of *das System,* both parties, all the while, intending to create a far more repressive system themselves. This projection of internal moral censorship, while of great interest in explaining many of the phenomena of political life, is not of central importance in understanding the causes of international war. Displacement and the projection of impulse are the great channels of transformed aggression. The projection of the superego is chiefly a cause of revolution and civil war.[14]

We have now completed our survey of the causes of aggression in human beings. We have suggested that there is no substantial difference in behavior, that adults are just as cruel—or more so—just as aggressive, just as destructive, as any group of animals or monkeys. The only difference in our view is one of psychological and intellectual mechanism. The causes of simple aggression—possessiveness, strangeness, frustration—are common to adults and simpler creatures. But a repressive discipline drives the simple aggression underground—to speak in metaphors—and it appears in disguised forms. These transformations are chiefly those of displacement and projection. These mechanisms have as their immediate motive the reduction of anxiety and the resolution of the conflicts of ambivalence and guilt. They result in the typical form of adult aggressiveness—aggressive personal relations of all kinds—but above all in group aggression: party conflict, civil war, wars of religion, and international war. The group life gives sanction to personal aggressiveness. The mobilization of transformed aggression gives destructive power to groups. Aggression takes on its social form. And to justify it—to explain the group aggression to the outside world and to the group itself in terms that make it morally acceptable to the members of the group—great structures of intellectual reasoning—theories of history and religion and race—are built up. The impulses are rationalized. The hatred is justified. And it is typical of the complexity of human affairs that something in these theories is always true. But most is false, most of it a mere justification of hatred, a sickening and hypocritical defense of cruelty. This is particularly true of the political persecutions of dictatorships. We must now try to apply the conclusions of this evidence to the theory of the causes of war.

THE THEORY OF WAR

We hold that the evidence summarized above suggests a certain theory of the causes of war. In the absence of government—the organization of force to preserve the peace—we hold that a group of monkeys or children or men can only achieve, at the best, an unstable social equilibrium. It may very well be that an appreciation of the advantages of cooperation and an agreement to continue it will preserve the peace for some time. But underneath there is a powerful and "natural" tendency to resort to force in order to secure the possession of desired objects or to overcome a sense of frustration or to resist

[14] The projection of the superego is a reason for hating and attacking any form of government. If, therefore, the League of Nations or any collective security system became strong, there would then arise, if our theory be true, aggressive revolutionary minorities within the collective system. This is an important point made by Dr. Glover. . . .

the encroachment of strangers or to attack a scapegoat. Fighting and peaceful cooperation are equally "natural" forms of behavior, equally fundamental tendencies in human relations. Peaceful cooperation predominates—there is much more peace than war—but the willingness to fight is so widely distributed in space and time that it must be regarded as a basic pattern of human behavior. The cause of the transition from one to the other is simply when some change in the circumstances of the group alters the balance between the desire for cooperation and the conflicting desire to obtain self-regarding ends by force. New females are introduced into the community of monkeys, food runs short, rain falls, or a new toy is given to a group of children. The pre-existing balance of desires is disturbed. The advantages to be gained by aggression grow greater. Fighting begins and spreads throughout the group. Social equilibrium is destroyed. Of course, we are not arguing that any real advantage is secured by the appeal to force. In the vast majority of cases the parties to a struggle would all be better off had they been able to continue cooperating with each other. All that we wish to insist upon is the universality of the tendency not to think so and the consequent willingness of minorities to fight.

What differences are made to the operation of these primitive forces by the development of more complex societies and cultures? For the moment we are not concerned with the prevention of aggression. To this vital matter we shall return. We are only concerned with the form of its expression. What activities of a developed society influence the form aggression takes? We suggest that there are two such activities—that of education and that of government.

The character of parental and familial control we have already discussed. Insofar as the emotional education of the child throughout human society involves appetitive frustration and insofar as intellectual education develops powers of reasoning and imagination, the forms of aggression change. It is rationalized, explained, and justified. It is displaced and projected. Above all, it is expressed in the life and activities of groups. Religious, economic, and political groups—churches, classes, and parties—release for the individual the aggression he dares not express for himself. And the greatest of all these groups —at least in the modern world—is the state. It is by an identification of the self with the state and by the expression of aggression through it that the individual has in recent times chiefly exhibited his aggressive impulses. Not exclusively so, for religious war and civil war have played an important part, but the great wars and the great loss of life have been in wars between nation-states.

It is natural that it should be so because the nation-state normally succeeds in preventing or controlling all other forms of aggression. The existence of government—with its apparatus of force—enormously increases the penalties of private aggression. Not only does the rationalizing mind and the conscience of mankind condemn private fighting and killing, but the social will to cooperation creates an instrument of force to control and punish any criminal

minority that disturbs the peace. Hence private aggression is not only condemned by the conscience, it is also punished by the law. And so long as the
state maintains supreme power, the same thing is true of all kinds of group
aggression other than its own. Political and racial parties are prevented from
taking the law into their own hands. Tendencies to civil war are successfully
repressed.[15] In such circumstances it is natural, in our view, that transformed
aggression should be chiefly canalized by, and flow unimpeded through, the
state organizations of common endeavor and military adventure. In the service
of the state the rationalized and transferred impulses of men find their last
remaining and freest outlet.

What, then, causes the state to embark on war? We offer two conclusions in
answer to this question. In the first place, as we have already mentioned, the
expression of aggression on a group scale appears to restore to it simplicity
and directness. In the civilized adult the original and simple causes for fighting
are forgotten and overlaid with every kind of excuse and transformation. But
when aggression is made respectable by manifestation through the corporate
will of the group, it resumes much of its amoral simplicity of purpose. Indeed,
positive moral obligation becomes attached to it. Nations will fight for simple
possession, or through hatred due to animism, or because of national frustration, in a direct and shameless way that would be quite impossible for their
individual members. The mutual approval of the members of the group makes
conscienceless aggression possible. Hence states will fight for the same reasons
as children fight. But not only for those things. In the second place states may
fight, in our submission, because of the pressure of transformed aggression
within their members. The members of the state may be so educated, so frustrated, and so unhappy that the burden of internal aggression may become
intolerable. Such peoples—or the dominant groups within them [16]—may constitute in a real sense aggressive nations. They have reached a point at which
war has become a psychological necessity. Ambivalence is so severe, internal
conflict so painful, fear and hatred of the scapegoat so intense, that a resolution of the crisis can only be found in war. In such cases war will be fought
without adequate objective cause. It will have an objective occasion, some

[15] Of course, the state does not always succeed in preventing group aggression within
itself from breaking out. Not only is there occasional rioting, but in recent years democratic
governments have frequently allowed party groups to grow up and make revolutions and
civil war. Civil war or group aggression within the state means the breakdown of internal
sovereignty.

[16] We should mention in this context that we are quite aware that there is much more to
be said on this subject than we have space to say or the learning to write. Large nations are
not simple homogeneous groups. Power in them is divided between many groups and dispersed over a varying proportion of the members of the nation. The analysis of the group
structure within the nation and of the distribution of power among the subgroups is a task
for sociology and sociologists. We are not competent to perform it. We are only concerned
with the type of impulse dominating groups with power, whether those groups are the whole
or only part of the nation.

trifling incident or dispute, but the real effective causes will be elsewhere, within the tormented souls of the members of the aggressor nation. Such national neuroses can exhibit any or all of the general psychological mechanisms that we have already examined—animism, displacement, the projection of impulse, or the projection of conscience. Thus nations will exhibit the aggressiveness typical of apes and also the much more complex and obscure aggressiveness typical of humanity. They will fight because they are disciplined, because they are divided against themselves, because they have constructed mythical enemies and conjured terrors out of the darkness, because they are paranoid or sadistic. The balance of impulse between cooperation and force has been shifted against the advantages of peace.

This, then, is our theory of international war. War occurs because fighting is a fundamental tendency in human things—a form of behavior called forth by certain simple situations in animals, children, human groups, and whole nations. It is a fundamentally pluralistic theory of international war. If the theory is true, then it follows that nations *can* fight only because they are able to release the explosive stores of transformed aggression, but they *do* fight for any of a large number of reasons. They may fight because of simple acquisitiveness or simple frustration or a simple fear of strangers. They may fight because of displaced hatred or projected hates or fears. There is no single all-embracing cause—no single villain of the piece, no institution nor idea that is wholly to blame. In this sense the theory stands in marked contrast to almost all accepted theories of the day. . . . [Now] one or two further comments . . . in explanation of the theory here defended.

In the first place it should be obvious to the reader that in one sense the theory is nothing more than enlightened common sense. It is no overwhelming novelty to show that war is a common form of human behavior. It resembles the familiar doctrine that "to fight is only human nature." The authors wish to emphasize this. They wish to make no claims to great originality. The value of the evidence here gathered together is simply that it shows the grounds upon which, and the form in which, such a common-sense theory can be held. It seeks to describe in greater detail the kinds of situation that call forth the impulses to aggression. It traces the causes of simple aggression in individuals and follows it through the disguised forms it exhibits in them into its social manifestations. It shows how and why war is a chronic disease of the social organism. It fills out a simple theory with detail and reason. It throws doubt upon all other theories. That is all.

In the second place, it will be as well to say something of the other reasons given by human beings for a willingness to fight in aggressive wars.[17] They fall into two groups. There are first the reasons given by those who defend war as a political institution. It is claimed by such people that war permits and de-

---

[17] We are distinguishing here between aggressive wars and police "wars"—or the use of force to protect peace and ensure law.

mands the display in a marked degree of certain fundamental human virtues—
virility, courage, loyalty, a care for the common good. It has further been suggested to us that this fact, or the belief that this is a fact, is one of the common
reasons why individuals are prepared to fight. Now it is obvious that the bare
statement that war gives an opportunity for the display of certain personal
virtues is true. Moreover, the statement is plainly a most important part of the
stock in trade of militarist propaganda. But that does not carry us far in assessing the effectiveness of this argument in making people willing to fight. It is
a commonplace of moral teaching throughout the history of civilization that
these virtues can be displayed equally well in peaceful competition and peaceful cooperation. It is a platitude to point out that courage, loyalty, and virility
are required as much by the arts of peace as by the arts of war. Pioneer navigation on the sea or in the air, dangerous occupations of social value, demand
courage and comradeship of the highest order. The problem is not why the
virtues of strength attract and compel human endeavor, but why the exercise
of these virtues in the work of destruction and death makes so wide an appeal.
The appeal of adventure is intelligible, but why the appeal of killing? We suggest that, while the desire for a life of strength and virtue is no doubt a sub-
sidiary cause of the willingness to fight, it is impossible to deny that the
peculiar sensitiveness of people to the propaganda of war must be attributed
to the existence of an underlying willingness to kill. No other explanation
seems to us to account for the ease with which courage and virility can be
associated with war.

Then, similarly, it has been suggested to us that the mere desire for change
and movement on the part of most individuals is an independent cause of a
willingness to fight. Most people, it is suggested, are discontented with their
lot in greater or less degree. They are conscious of frustration, disappointment, and even despair. A war is an opportunity to start again, to see new
things, and to escape from old chains. There is no question that there is a
great deal in this—that many persons are released by war from situations in
which they are bored or unhappy. They have, in that sense, a reasonable
motive for welcoming war. But is that all that there is to be said? We hardly
think so. Does anyone suppose that any kind of general disturbance would
be equally welcome? An earthquake that struck half England would stir up
enough excitement to release and change the lives of most of its inhabitants.
Does anyone really suppose that such a disaster would awaken the passions
of exaltation and enthusiasm that are so frequently evoked by war? It seems
to us absurd to suppose so. It is not the fact of a general disturbance that
excites men, but the kind of disturbance in which hatred and destruction may
run and be glorified. It is not the excitement of change, but the excitement of
blood, that fills the streets with cheering crowds and sends the first—though
not the last—regiments into war with trumpets. People are less sensible and

more savage than these rational theories of the willingness to fight seems to suppose.

But in the third place, let us at once make clear that there is nothing in the least alarmist or defeatist in the theory here advanced. We do not hold, nor think it possible to hold, that, because war is a chronic social disease, it is necessarily an incurable disease. Not only have we emphasized throughout this article that the forces making for peaceful cooperation have been more powerful in history than the forces making for war, but we have not yet considered the implications of our evidence for the theory of the *cure* of war—the therapeutic as distinct from the causal problem. . . . All that it is necessary to do at this stage is to repeat and emphasize these three points:

Far more of the time and vitality of any nation has been absorbed in past history by the activities of peaceful cooperation than by war. The impulses to peace are therefore more powerful than the impulses to war. Hence the problem—how can they be further strengthened?

The governments of states have been successful in preserving comparative peace within their countries for centuries at a time. Is it not possible, then, that the expression of aggression can be permanently prevented or controlled by government?

We have only argued that the social and educational environments of the past have in fact produced certain "quantities" of aggression. Is it possible that different societies and different educations might produce less?

◄◄◄ ►►►

HARRY STACK SULLIVAN

Toward a Psychiatry of Peoples *

Psychiatry has come to mean something to a great many people, but, for our purpose, it must be defined. There is a meaning of psychiatry which makes it an art or body of empirical practices pertaining to the treatment or prevention of mental disorder. This meaning of psychiatry is irrelevant here. Psychiatry, as here to be discussed, is a science and its related technology. The science of psychiatry has been nurtured by work with the mentally ailing, has grown in the milieu of hospital and clinic, but is no more a science of mental illness than geography is a science of Western Europe.

The mentally ill are particular instances of people living among others in localities of more-or-less uniform culture. The science that has grown from preoccupation with these mentally disordered ways of living has naturally to become a science of living under the conditions which prevail in the given social order. I believe that this statement is simply axiomatic, but it does not imply that a particular psychiatric scientist need concern himself with any and all aspects of man's life in society.

* This chapter is mainly taken from "Towards a Psychiatry of Peoples," *Psychiatry*, XI (1948), 105–116. Beginning with the section headed "Whence the Urgency?" there appears an excerpt from "Remobilization for Enduring Peace and Social Progress," *Psychiatry*, X (1947), 239–252, p. 244. Most of the chapter has also been reprinted in Hadley Cantril, ed., *Tensions That Cause Wars* (Champaign: University of Illinois Press, 1950). Reprinted from Harry Stack Sullivan, *The Interpersonal Theory of Psychiatry*, chap. 22 (New York: W. W. Norton Co., 1953) by permission of the publisher (Copyright 1953, by the William Alanson White Psychiatric Foundation).

A physicist may usefully concentrate his scientific efforts on particular aspects of the phenomena anciently called light. His results, so far as they are good physics, will be meaningful throughout physics. They may be more richly meaningful in, for example, the region of wave motion than in that of gravitation, but here one may recall the confirmation of Einstein's anticipation that light would be found to "bend" in traversing a gravitational field.

The general science of psychiatry seems to me to cover much the same field as that which is studied by social psychology, because scientific psychiatry has to be defined as the study of interpersonal relations, and this in the end calls for the use of the kind of conceptual framework that we now call field theory. From such a standpoint, personality is taken to be hypothetical. That which can be studied is the pattern of processes which characterize the interaction of personalities in particular recurrent situations or fields which "include" the observer. Since any one participant observer can study but a finite number of these situations or fields, which, in turn, will be anything but representative of the whole variegated world of human life, not all of the personality of the observer will be revealed, and "what he comes to know about himself" will always be somewhat incomplete and variously contingent on poorly defined or actually unnoticed factors. Generalizations which he can make about "the other fellow" cannot but be even more incomplete and contingent.

The observer, the instrument used in assembling the data of psychiatry, is, then, seen to be an only imperfectly understood tool, some of the results of the use of which may be quite misleading. This conclusion might be taken to forbid any effort toward developing a scientific psychiatry, much less a psychiatry of everyone everywhere in the world. It certainly forbids any conceit about the present state of psychiatry, but one may well notice that every science has been—and, less obviously, still is—in the same position. One may note, also, that ignorance of the principles of the internal-combustion engine has not prevented the expert driving of automobiles, although it might prove costly to anyone who substituted a high explosive for gasoline fuel because he was in a hurry.

Bear with me now in an attempt to outline a position in general psychiatry from which I shall presently undertake to make some temporarily valid generalizations of world scope. What anyone can observe and analyze becomes ultimately a matter of tensions and energy transformations, many of the latter being obvious actions, but many others of which are obscure activities that go on, as we say, in the mind.

What anyone can discover by investigating his past is that the patterns of tensions and energy transformations which make up his living are, to a truly astonishing extent, matters of his education for living in a particular expected society. If he is clever, he can also notice inadequacies in his educators' expectations; he finds that he is not any too well prepared for living in the groups in which he has come to be involved.

If he is philosophically inclined and historic-minded, he is apt to conclude that this very element of being ill prepared has characterized people in every period of expanding world contacts and ensuing accelerated social change.

If he is interested in psychiatry, he is almost certain to come to consider the role of foresight in determining the adequacy and appropriateness of the energy transformations, his overt and covert activity, with respect to the actual demands of the situations in which he finds himself involved with significant others.

I touch here on what I believe is the most remarkable of human characteristics, the importance exercised by often but vaguely formulated aspirations, anticipations, and expectations which can be summed up in the term foresight, the manifest influence of which makes the near future a thoroughly real factor in explaining human events. I hope that you will resist the idea that something clearly teleological is being introduced here: I am saying that, *circumstances not interfering*, man the person lives with his past, the present, and the neighboring future all clearly relevant in explaining his thought and action and [that] the near future is influential to a degree nowhere else remotely approached among the species of the living.

Note that I have said "circumstances not interfering." It is from study of the interferences which reduce or otherwise modify the functional activity of foresight that a great deal of light has been thrown on the nature of man as revealed in his doings with others.

We assume that all biological tensions arise from the course of events inside and/or outside the gross spatial limits of the organism. Human tensions are no exception to this, but one of their congeries—one very important kind of tension—ensues from a kind of events the experiencing of which is almost unique to the human being.

With this single important exception, tensions can be regarded as needs for particular energy transformations which will dissipate the tension, often with an accompanying change of mental state, a change of awareness to which we can apply the general term satisfaction.

Thus the particular tension the felt component of which we call hunger is pleasantly satisfied by activity which includes the taking of food. Our hunger is *not* the tension, the tension is not merely a mental state, a phenomenon within awareness, nor is it entirely within us in any simple space-time sense. But for practical purposes, I may usually trust this particular once familiar mental state to coincide perfectly with my need for food, and make up my mind to eat or decide to go to dinner or entertain within awareness some other "thought" which sounds as if something quite powerful named "I" is directing something else—"myself"—to do something about my being hungry, with reasonable certainty that I shall feel more comfortable when the performance has been finished.

Whatever pomp and circumstance may go on in one's head, the need for food reaches into the past in which it has arisen and on the basis of which its felt component can be said to have meaning, and it reaches into the future in which its tension can be foreseen to have been relieved by appropriate action in proper circumstances.

We share most, if not all, of this large congeries of recurrent needs with a good many other species of the living—even including our recurrent need for contact with others, often felt as loneliness, which is paralleled in the gregarious animals.

The single other great congeries of recurrent tensions, some grasp on the nature of which is simply fundamental to understanding human life, is probably restricted to man and some of the creatures which he has domesticated. It arises not from the impact of physicochemical and biological events directly connected with keeping alive and reproducing the species, but from the impact of people. The felt component of any of this congeries of tensions includes the experience of anxiety; action which avoids or relieves any of these tensions is experienced as continued or enhanced self-respect or self-esteem, significantly different from what is ordinarily meant by self-satisfaction. All the factors entering into the vicissitudes of self-esteem, excepting only man's innate capacity for being anxious, are wholly a matter of past experience with people, the given interpersonal situation, and foresight of what will happen.

There is nothing I can conceive in the way of interpersonal action about which one could not be trained to be anxious, so that, if such an action is foreseen, one feels anxious and, if it occurs, one's self-esteem is reduced. The realm of this congeries of tensions is the area of one's training for life at the hands of significant others and of how much or little one has been able to synthesize out of these training experiences.

One cannot be trained by others in advance of certain biological events, namely, the maturation of appropriate capabilities of man the underlying animal. Training efforts exerted before this time are undergone as something very different from what was intended and, if they have any effect, exert thoroughly unfortunate influence on the future development of the victims.[1] This biologically ordained serial maturation of capabilities underlies the currently entertained scheme of stages in human development [infancy, childhood, the juvenile era, preadolescence, early adolescence, and late adolescence to maturity]. . . . Let me discuss the implication of the idea of developmental stages. When, and only when, maturation of capacities has occurred, experience of a valuable kind can occur. *If it does not occur,* if experience is definitely unsuited to providing competence for living with others at this particular level of development, the probabilities of future adequate and appro-

---

[1] They generally contribute to the not-me component of personality, the source of the tension in interpersonal fields elsewhere described as the experience of uncanny emotions —awe, dread, loathing, and horror—felt components of the most strongly disjunctive force of which we have knowledge.

priate interpersonal relations are definitely *and specifically* reduced. The reduction of probability is specifically related to the forms of competence which are customarily developed under favorable circumstances in the course of this particular stage.

Seen from this viewpoint, not the earlier stages only, but each and every stage, is equally important in its own right in the unfolding of possibilities for interpersonal relations, in the progression from birth toward mature competence for life in a fully human world. It is often true that severe warp incurred, say, in childhood interferes so seriously with the course of events in the succeeding juvenile era that the constructive effects of living with compeers and under school and other nonfamily authorities are meager. It also happens, and not infrequently, that quite serious warp from childhood is all but corrected by good fortune early in the juvenile era so that its residual traces are observable only under circumstances of intense emotion, severe fatigue, anoxemia, hypoglycemia, or alcoholic and related decerebration.[2]

In the course of intensive guided psychotherapy, one may observe, in many instances, a condensed, relatively vicarious remedying of deficiencies in developmental experience, and this seems to be a successful way of consolidating favorable change in the patient's interpersonal relations.

Thus unremedied misfortune in the preadolescent phase leaves one at a lifelong disadvantage in dealing with important strangers of the same sex. *When this pattern of discomfort has been made clear* by participant observation "with" the patient, the latter will often develop a belated, transient preadolescence. Some previously guarded contact will deepen into a very warm friendship; the satisfactions and security of the "buddy" become overwhelmingly important to the patient, and his current activities are largely directed to promoting them. At the same time, any strong motivation in the patient-physician relationship is in abeyance, as if he had lost any particular interest in the work. Then, presently, the "outside" attachment loses intensity, and a favorably changed patient is again at work with the psychiatrist, tracking down the ramifications of the disability from which he is now recovering.

This illustrates the meaning of isophilic in my triad: the autophilic, the isophilic, and the heterophilic are those persons, respectively, who can manifest in their interpersonal relations the pattern of field forces properly called love for no one, for a person of one's own sex, or for persons of one's own and of the other sex. The ability to love is a factor in the patterning of genital, sexual behavior, but it is only one of three factors which must be considered in order to make sense of what goes on in that connection. In this culture, many people show the ability to love in advance of the occurrence of puberty. Many others have yet to evolve the ability to love long after a relatively active sexual life of one kind or another has been established.

---

2 Even in these "reduced" states, the peculiarities of interpersonal relations can sometimes be seen to be a movement as if to remedy ancient deficiencies of experience.

Much more important for my present purpose is the import of the illustration as an example of "curative" processes in interpersonal fields. It is from prolonged consideration of psychotherapeutic "successes" and "failures"— and of possibilities for increasing the proportion and speeding the achievement of the former—that I have come to feel sure that we may depend on everyone's drive toward more adequate and appropriate ways of living; in a word, toward improved mental health *if* an improved ability to foresee the future can offer a fair prospect of becoming contented. That "if" is a big one when one has been "out of life" for years in a hospital for the mentally disordered, when one is advanced in years, or when the prospect appears to entail giving up sources of prestige and income which one's current, however troubled, life is providing.

The often great difficulty encountered in achieving improved ability to live with significant others is considered to arise, then, not from a deficiency of tendency but from something else, something which manifests itself as an equilibrating factor in living, whether the living be fortunate or unfortunate— namely, the extensive organization of experience within personality which I have called the self-system.

I think it will suffice for my present purpose to say that anything which would seriously disturb the equilibrium, any event which tends to bring about a basic change in an established pattern of dealing with others, sets up the tension of anxiety and calls out activities for its relief. This tension and the activities required for its reduction or relief—which we call security operations because they can be said to be addressed to maintaining a feeling of safety in the esteem reflected to one from the other person concerned—always interfere with whatever other tensions and energy transformations they happen to coincide with.

This in no way denies the usefulness of security operations. They are often quite successful in protecting one's self-esteem. Without them, life in an increasingly incoherent social organization would be exceedingly difficult or impossible for most people. We, the people of these United States, in particular, would quite certainly exterminate ourselves before we could devise and disseminate adequate substitutes for our now ubiquitous security processes.

Let us be very clear about the fact that anxiety and security operations are an absolutely necessary part of human life as long as the past is more important in preparing the young for life than is the reasonably foreseeable future.

But for all their indispensable utility to each and every one of us in these days, security operations are a powerful brake on personal and on human progress—as I can perhaps indicate by referring to a particular one of them which is very frequently to be observed.

I shall use as an example the process called selective inattention, something very different indeed from mere negligent oversight. By selective inattention we fail to recognize the actual import of a good many things we see, hear, think, do, and say, not because there is anything the matter with our zones of interaction with others, but because the process of inferential analysis is opposed by the self-system. Clear recognition of the implications of matters to which we are selectively inattentive would call for basic change in an established pattern of dealing with the sort of interpersonal situation concerned, would make us either more, or, in some cases, less, competent, but in any case *different* from the way we now conceive ourself to be. Good observation and analysis of a mass of incidents selectively overlooked would expand the self-system, which usually controls the contents of awareness and the scope of the referential processes that are fully useful in communicating with others. The ever iterated miracle of selective inattention explains the faith we have in unnumbered prejudicial verbalisms, "rationalizations," about ourself and others and half explains the characterization of the Bourbon as one who never forgets anything and never learns anything.

While there is some reason to believe that a sufficient degree of novelty will always call out a disjunctive force the felt component of which we know as fear, a very great many otherwise illuminating observations, of by no means intimidating novelty and difference, fail entirely to inform us about the world we live in because of the equilibrating influence of the self-system—the tree that all too frequently reflects the way the twig was bent in the developmental years.

The extension of psychiatric theory beyond the confines of the familiar into the world of "foreigners" whose ways of life are alien to us calls for a sharp discrimination between fear and the various manifestations of anxiety and self-system activity, especially those of irrational dislikes, aversions, and revulsions, and the so widespread distrust of others today.

Current theory makes hate the characteristic of interpersonal situations in which the people concerned recurrently and frequently provoke anxiety in each other, yet cannot break up the situation because of some conjunctive forces which hold them together. If the conjunctive force acts entirely outside of awareness, uncanny fascination, with moments of revulsion or loathing, may appear. If the integrating forces are not very strong [and] if the situation is not very important, the milder manifestations of more-or-less concealed, actually unjustified, dislike and distrust are shown. The "actually unjustified" means that a consensually valid statement of adequate grounds for the dislike or distrust cannot be formulated. The unpleasant emotion arises from something more than what either person could readily come to know about the situation.

Let me illustrate the meaning of these terms by some thoroughly crude examples. A couple make what certainly is a marriage of great convenience. Friends of each notice with increasing discomfort that husband and wife seem more and more bent on humiliating each other in the presence of the friends. This illustrates an increasingly hateful integration.

A mother, taking over the care of her first-born from the nurse, is greatly upset, feels faint, looks pale, trembles severely, and is bathed with perspiration on first encountering soiled diapers. She is undergoing the uncanny variant on the much more commonplace disgust, either of which is mostly a matter of her training for life.

Another mother discovers her fifteen-month-old child holding his obviously excited genital. She is filled with a shuddering emotion not unrelated to the fascination *and* horror many people encounter when first thinking about witches' sabbaths, voodoo rites, or other folk encounters with personified sexual evil. Parenthetically, the infant by empathy is filled with the most primitive anxiety, almost as paralyzing and as uninformative as a blow on the head from a hammer; but, if the mother's reaction does not change by virtue of habituation or insight, he will gradually catch on to enough of what happens to come to the juvenile era a person who shows primitive genital phobia—a more-or-less contentless aversion to action or thought about touching himself in the perineum, often with a lively, if unwelcome, hope that he may be touched by others and perhaps touch them in turn, after which actual experience he would come to dislike and avoid them or, more unhappily, suffer recurrent deeply disturbing revulsion after each of a series of conflictful repetitions.

I can perhaps now proceed to the thesis of this paper—namely, that, while no one can now be adequately equipped for a greatly significant inquiry into the fundamental facts of life of everyone everywhere, there are many possibilities of greatly constructive efforts in this direction if, and only if, instead of plunging into the field recklessly hoping for the best, one prefaces one's attempt with a careful survey of one's assets and liabilities for participant observation.

Every constructive effort of the psychiatrist today is a strategy of interpersonal field operations which (a) seeks to map the areas of disjunctive force that block the efficient collaboration of the patient and others and (b) seeks to expand the patient's awareness so that this unnecessary blockage can be brought to an end.

For a psychiatry of peoples, we must follow the selfsame strategy applied to significant groupings of people—families, communities, political entities, regional organizations, world blocs—and seek to map the interventions of disjunctive force which block the integration of the group with other groups in pursuit of the common welfare and seek out the characteristics of each group's culture or subculture and the methods used to impose it on the young, which perpetuate the restrictions of freedom for constructive growth.

The master tactics for a psychiatrist's work with a handicapped person consist in (a) elucidating the actual situations in which unfortunate action is currently shown repeatedly so that the disorder pattern may become clear; (b) discovering the less obvious ramifications of this inadequate and inappropriate way of life throughout other phases of the present and the near future, including the doctor-patient relationship and the patient's expectations about it; and (c) with the problem of inadequate development now clearly formulated, utilizing his human abilities to explore its origins in his experience with significant people of the past.

It must be noted that an identical distortion of living common to doctor and patient makes this type of inquiry, at the best, very difficult. Neither is able to see the troublesome patterns, and both are inclined to relate the difficulties to the unhappy peculiarities of the other people concerned in their less fortunate interpersonal relations. Each respects the parallel limitation in the other, and their mutual effort is apt to be concentrated on irrelevant or immaterial problems until they both become more discouraged or still more firmly deceived about life.

For a psychiatry of peoples, these tactical requirements of good therapy—which is also good research—have to be expanded into (a) a preliminary discovery of the actual major patterns of tensions and energy transformations which characterize more adequate and appropriate living in that group; this is a background for noticing the exceptions—the incidents of mental disorder among these folk—uninformed study of which would be misleading; (b) a parallel development of skill at rectifying the effects of limitations in our own developmental background in order (c) that it may become possible to observe better the factors that actually resist any tendency to extend the integrations of our subject persons, so that they would include representatives of other groups relatively alien to them—a pilot test of which is the integration with ourself; and (d) thus to find real problems in the foresight of intergroup living which can be tracked down to their origins in our subject people's education for life.

There is good reason to believe that all this is not impossible. These world psychiatric inquiries are not at bottom particularly different from the already mentioned, all too common instances where doctor and patient suffer approximately the same disorders in living. Let me say a word about the way in which one may proceed to reduce the handicap of such a situation, at the same time pointing to the answer to an oft-heard question: "What can I do to help myself?"

My conception of anxiety is in point here. While we may be unaware, at least temporarily, of milder degrees of any one of the other tensions connected with living, we are never unaware of anxiety at the very time that it occurs. The awareness can be, and very often is, fleeting, especially when an appropriate security operation is called out. The awareness can be most variously characterized from person to person, even from incident to incident, excepting only that it is always unpleasant. At the moment that anxiety occurs, one becomes aware of something unpleasant; but whether this seems to be a mere realization that all is not going so well or a noticing of some disturbance in the activity or postural tone in one of the zones of interaction—a change in one's facial expression or in one's voice, as examples—a feeling of tightening up in some group of skeletal muscles, a disturbance of the action of one's heart, a discomfort in one's belly, a realization that one has begun to sweat, as I say, whether it be one of these or yet another variety of symptoms, one is always at least momentarily aware that one has become uncomfortable or more acutely uncomfortable, as the case may be.

No matter what may have followed upon this awareness of diminished feeling of well-being, there was the awareness. It best serves in ordinary interpersonal relations to pay as little attention to it as one can, and to forget it. But if one is intent on refining oneself as an instrument of participant observation, it is necessary to pay the greatest attention, at least retrospectively, to these fleeting movements of anxiety. They are the telltales which show increased activity of the self-system in the interpersonal field of the moment concerned.

They mark the point in the course of events at which something disjunctive, something that tends to pull away from the other fellow, has first appeared or has suddenly increased. They signal a change from relatively uncomplicated movement toward a presumptively common goal to a protecting of one's self-esteem, with a definite complicating of the interpersonal action.

To the extent that one can retrospectively observe the exact situation in which one's anxiety was called out, one may be able to infer the corresponding pattern of difficulty in dealing with others. As these patterns are usually a matter of past training or its absence, detecting them is seldom an easy matter, but, I repeat, it is by no means impossible—unless there is an actual dissociation in one's personality system, in which case there will be prohibitively great difficulty in recalling anything significant about the actual situation which evoked the anxiety.

Two things more remain to be said about this, shall I say, self-observation of disjunctive processes in interpersonal relations.

Anxiety appears not only as awareness of itself but also in the experience of some complex "emotions" into which it has been elaborated by specific early training. I cannot say what all these are, but I can use names for a few of them which should open the mind to their nature: embarrassment, shame, humiliation, guilt, and chagrin. The circumstances under which these unpleasant emotions occur are particularly hard to observe accurately and to subject to the retrospective analysis which is apt to be most rewarding.

A group of security operations born of experience which has gone into the development of these complex unpleasant emotions is equally hard for one to observe and analyze. These are the movements of thought and the actions by which we, as it were, impute to, or seek to provoke in, the other fellow feelings like embarrassment, shame, humiliation, guilt, or chagrin. It is peculiarly difficult to observe retrospectively and to subject to analysis the exact circumstances under which we are moved to act as if the other person "should be ashamed of himself," is "stupid," or is guilty of anything from a breach of good taste to a mortal sin. These interpersonal movements which put the other fellow at a disadvantage on the basis of a low relative personal worth are extremely troublesome elements in living and very great handicaps to investigating strange people.

Disparaging and derogatory thought and action that make one feel "better" than the other person concerned, that expand one's self-esteem, as it were, at his cost, are always to be suspected of arising from anxiety. These processes are far removed from a judicious inquiry into one's relative personal skill in living. They do not reflect a good use of observation and analysis but rather indicate a low self-esteem in the person who uses them. The quicker one comes to a low opinion of another, other things being equal, the poorer is one's secret view of one's own worth in the field of the disparagement.

It is rather easy to correct interferences in participant observation of another which arise from one's true superiorities to him. It is quite otherwise with the baleful effects of one's secret doubts and uncertainties. We are apt to be most severely critical of others when they are thought to be showing an instance of something of which we ourselves are secretly ashamed, and which we hope we are concealing.

This must suffice as an indication of the more pervasive of the often unnoticed interferences with participant observation with representatives of somewhat unfamiliar background. I need scarcely discuss the role of linguistic difficulties or that of sheer ignorance of the culture patterns to which remarks make reference. These latter are actually only somewhat more striking instances of similar interferences in getting acquainted with any stranger.

Progress toward a psychiatry of peoples is to be expected from efforts expended along two lines of investigation: (a) an improving grasp on the significant patterns—and on the pattern of patterns—of living around the world and (b) the uncovering of significant details in the sundry courses of personality development by which the people of each different social organization come to manifest more-or-less adequate and appropriate behavior in their given social setting.

Each of these lines of investigation is a necessary supplement to the other. The first, which may be taken to pertain more to the interests and techniques of the cultural anthropologist, cannot be pushed very far, very securely, without data from the second. The second can scarcely produce meaningful data unless it is informed by the provisional hypotheses of the former. The two provide indispensable checks upon each other without which neither can proceed noticeably without running into increasing uncertainty.

The theory of interpersonal relations lays great stress on the method of participant observation and relegates data obtained by other methods to, at most, a secondary importance. This, in turn, implies that skill in the face-to-face, or person-to-person, psychiatric interview is of fundamental importance.

While the value of interchange by use of the mediate channels of communication—correspondence, publications, radio, speaking films—may be very great, especially if the people concerned have already become fairly well acquainted with each other as a result of previous face-to-face exchange, it must be remembered that communication in the psychiatric interview is by no means solely a matter of exchanging verbal contexts, but is rather the development of an exquisitely complex pattern of field processes which *imply* important conclusions about the people concerned.

This is scarcely the place for a discussion of current views about what one can learn about the theory and practice of psychiatric interviewing; I wish chiefly to emphasize the *instrumental* character of the interviewing psychiatrist and the critical importance of his being free to observe—and subsequently analyze—as many as possible of his performances as a dynamic center in the field patterns that make up the interview.

Everything that can be said about good psychiatric interviewing is relevant to the directly interpersonal aspects of any work in the direction of a psychiatry of peoples. Every safeguard useful in avoiding erroneous conclusions about the other fellow becomes newly important when the barriers of linguistic and other cultural uncertainties are in the way.

Inquiries into the alien ways of educating the young must be oriented with close regard to biological time as it is reflected in the serial maturation of capacities, to social time as it is reflected in the series of formulable expectations concerning what the young will know how to behave about from stage to stage of their development and to the exact chronology of presumptively educative efforts brought to bear on the young.

The spread of variations in each of these three fields is of great importance in understanding the people and their relationships, which make up any community. Consider, for example, the effect of delayed puberty on the adequacy and appropriateness of subsequent behavior in many a youth in any of our urban areas. Consider, again, the effects on the living of the outstandingly bright boy from a small town when he enters a great metropolitan university. And, finally, consider the probable effects of early training in venereal prophylaxis in contrast with that of suppression of information in this field.

It is by virtue of an ever better grasp on the significant patterns in these series of events that we help patients to help themselves, at the same time becoming better and better informed about the factors which govern the possibilities of interpersonal action. To the extent that we have useful approximations to an understanding of the actual processes of personality development which have ensued in the people with whom we deal, we become able to make sense of what seems to be going on. This must be the case, whether one is a stranger in Malaya or host to a visiting Malay.

In a world in which time is of the essence, in which we can scarcely defer great constructive changes until we shall have raised a new generation to political power, the most searching scrutiny of the dynamics of favorable change in personality becomes utterly imperative. Even if time were not of the essence, the imperative would be much the same, for we cannot jump a generation and *training for life as it is becoming* begins in, and reaches very far forward from, the primary group of the home. The less of parents' work that has to be corrected, the quicker man moves ahead. The surer our aid to parents in preparing their young for life, the more geometrically expanding will be the resulting good to the greater number.

I think it is no longer wise or expedient to talk and think *as if* the great majority of chronologically adult people, here or elsewhere, will ever become well informed about a great deal that is acutely vitally important to them.

I think that we must recognize explicitly that universal literacy and complete freedom of information in themselves offer no solution to any of the imperative problems of the times. . . . Freedom of information is meaningless unless it is used for a purpose, namely, to promote the peace and well-being of humanity.

Can anyone who is experienced in dealing with others doubt that it is ever so much easier to replace one prejudice with another than it is to bring about informed judgment? Do we not actually have this in mind when we express ourselves to the so-called laity? Or perhaps better put: *should* we not have this in mind? Consider, for instance, the effects, detectable even in some psychiatrists' homes, of disseminating information about the evil effects of parental mismanagement. Some considerable number of parents now suffer such uncertainty about frustrating and fixating and making dependent and the like that they themselves need psychiatric help and their offspring will certainly require it. We do not seem to have done too good a job of public education in this vital area. Perhaps our information was not adequate; perhaps, on the other hand, it was not so bad but we used it badly.

I hold that it is self-evident that a very great many chronologically adult people must act on faith with respect to almost every field of living. The great hope for the future lies not in attempting to change this fact but in so reducing the effectiveness of certain vicious elements in current faiths that the young who grow up under the influence of these elders will have much greater freedom to observe and to understand and to foresee correctly than had their parents and teachers and the others under whose authority their abilities for interpersonal relations were molded.

The achievement of this exceedingly desirable goal is anything but easy and foolproof. The thinking out of constructive, functionally coherent revisions of any one of the major cultures of the world, so that the personal imperatives which derive from it—whether in the obscure, very early inculcated patterns of conscience or the subsequently acquired, less recondite patterns of acceptable rationalizations and potent verbalisms—shall be less restrictive on understanding and more permissive of social progress; that, truly, is a task to which unnumbered groups of the skillful may well apply themselves.

There will remain the intimidating task of implementing the better once it shall have been designed, but, for the first time in the history of man, there is world-wide, if often most unhappy, realization of the necessity and at the same time a set of administrative agencies clearly charged with the responsibility. I say to you with the utmost seriousness of which I am capable that this is no time to excuse yourself from paying the debt you and yours owe the social order with some such facile verbalism as, "Nothing will come of it; it can't be done." Begin, and let it be said of you, if there is any more history, that you labored nobly in the measure of man in the twentieth century of the scientific, Western world.

◄◄◄ ►►►

ERIK H. ERIKSON

Wholeness and Totality *

A glance at the list of the participants in this conference narrows the area
within which I can contribute a statement to that of childhood. All men begin
as children: does this commonly shared fact contribute significantly to what
is universal in totalitarianism?

Since I am primarily a clinician, I must also draw on psychopathology for
suggestions concerning some of the puzzling features in the emergence of a
totalitarian orientation.

I

Works on history, society, and morality usually contain little reference in
the text, and none in the index, to the simple fact that all individuals are born
of mothers, that everybody was once a child, that people and peoples begin in
their nurseries, and that society consists of individuals in the process of developing from children into parents. To most scholars, childhood seems to belong
to the field of social work rather than to that of social science, to the aspirations of do-gooders rather than to those of thinkers. Yet man is characterized

* Reprinted from Erik H. Erikson, "Wholeness and Totality—A Psychiatric Contribution," pp. 156–171, Carl J. Friedrich, ed., *Totalitarianism* (Cambridge: Harvard University
Press, 1954) by permission of the publisher (Copyright 1954, by the President and Fellows
of Harvard College).

by a long biological childhood, and civilization tends to make psychological childhood ever longer because man must have time to learn how to learn; all his high specialization and all his intricate capabilities of coordination and reflection are contingent upon his prolonged dependence. And only as a dependent does man develop conscience, that dependence on himself which makes him, in turn, dependable; for only when thoroughly dependable with regard to a number of fundamental values can he become independent and teach and develop tradition. But this dependability carries within it the ambiguity of its roots in a slow developmental process which leads from extreme helplessness to a high sense of freedom.

Modern anthropology, following suggestions derived from psychopathology, is studying the ways in which societies "intuitively" develop child-training systems designed not only to keep the small individual alive and well but also to ensure, through him and in him, a continuation of tradition and a preservation of his society's uniqueness. But it is becoming equally clear that the polarity adult-child is the first in the inventory of existential oppositions (male-female being the second) which makes man exploitable and induces him to exploit. The child's proclivity for feeling powerless, deserted, ashamed, and guilty in relation to those on whom he depends is universally utilized to the point of exploitation. The result is that adult man remains irrationally preoccupied with anxieties and suspicions which center in such questions as who is bigger or better and who can do what to whom. The contribution of man's extended childhood to the development of his capabilities and to his capacity for sympathy and faith is well known, but often too exclusively known; it is necessary to acquire deeper insight into the earliest consequences of the potential exploitation of childhood. By psychological exploitation I mean the misuse of a divided function in such a way that one of the partners is impaired in the development of his potentialities—with the result that impotent rage is stored up where energy should be free for productive transformation.

To those who accept all this, it must seem reasonable enough, then, that childhood should be represented at this conference on totalitarianism, so that we may begin to do away with this "oversight" concerning the fateful importance of childhood. Yet it must be said that this oversight does not seem to be an accidental one, and therefore not one so easily corrected. Psychoanalysis has amply demonstrated the fact that the individual develops an amnesia concerning crucial childhood experiences; there is good reason to suspect that this individual amnesia is paralleled by a universal blind spot in the interpretation of history, a tendency to overlook the fateful function of childhood in the fabric of society. Maybe moral man and rational man, having fought so hard to make man's moral and reasonable image absolute and irreversible, refuses to see how each man must begin with the beginning and thus, ever again, develop the potentiality for undoing human accomplishments with infantile compulsions and irrational impulses. It is as if we were dealing here with a deep-seated superstition that rational and practical man would lose his single-minded stamina if he ever turned back to meet the Medusa of childhood anxiety to face again. Here a formidable personal equation imposes itself on all attempts to put the fact of childhood in its proper perspective. Yet, if man would understand this fact, maybe he could manage to become less childish in some respects and remain more childlike in others.

It is probably a result of the long undisputed existence of the universal blind spot discussed here that the sudden emergence in our time of insights into the relationship of childhood, neurosis, and personality in human life have tended to develop another, a compensatory loss of perspective; I mean the tendency on the part of psychologists and psychopathologists to explain societal phenomena (such as totalitarianism) by equating them with specific infantile or adolescent stages, with mental disturbances, or with particular "character structures" (personal or national). From the personological approach, suggestive generalizations have emerged, for example, in regard to certain analogies between patterns of child-rearing, ways of conceptualizing the world, and inclinations toward political creeds. This approach, however, has contributed little to the all-important question, namely, under what conditions the energy invested in given patterns of thought and action becomes available for relevant political indoctrination and for effective mass action. The second, psychopathological approach in turn has led to insights, some of which will be presented in the bulk of this paper, yet it has weakened its case by diagnostic name-calling, designating peoples and people actively or passively involved in totalitarian revolutions as either pathological or immature human beings. Man can be many things on many levels, and history does not always permit him that unification of defined creed, conscious attitude, and pragmatic action which we in the Protestant world have come to demand of a "balanced" or at any rate a "logical" human being.

What follows, then, is not an attempt at fixing the origin or cause of totalitarianism in the fact of childhood or in particular forms of childhood, nor shall I treat it as a transient affliction or localized epidemic. I begin with the assumption that totalitarianism is based on universal human potentialities and is thus related to all the aspects of human nature, wholesome and pathological, adult and infantile, individual and societal. Totalitarianism has often been a near reality; it has merely waited for "its" historical moment. The properties of this moment (for example, the advance of technology) . . . [and the] historical factors . . . I am not unmindful [of], although I must neglect them: I mean the varieties of conditions which give rise to the idea of the total state as a fanatic anticipation, which realize it in well-timed revolutionary acts, and which maintain it through the realities of power and terror. Only such historical perspective can give the proper measure of the different degrees and kinds of ideological involvement on the part of the many types that make up a totalitarian state: fanatic apostles and the shrewd revolutionaries; lonely leaders and oligarchic cliques; obedient bureaucrats and efficient managers, soldiers, engineers; sincere believers and sadistic exploiters; willing followers, apathetic toilers, and paralyzed opponents; unnerved victims and bewildered would-be and could-be victims.

The means at my disposal in my present work permit me to attempt a contribution only to one of the more basic, and yet often less tangible, factors in all of these historical stages and individual functions, namely, the psychological prerequisites of a totalitarian ideology.

II

I can now return to my initial question and try to focus on that something in the nature of childhood which may throw light on man's inclination, under certain conditions, to undergo what the Germans call *Umschaltung* and *Gleichschaltung*, that sudden total realignment and, as it were, coalignment, which accompany conversion to the totalitarian conviction that the state may and must have absolute power over the minds as well as the lives and the fortunes of its citizens.

We discern in normal and abnormal histories, and in occasional transitory states not commonly considered psychopathological, sudden transitions from a balanced "wholeness" of experience and behavior to states of feeling and acting "totally." The most dramatic examples of such total realignment are, of course, to be found on the borderline of pathology. As one young man said to me, smilingly, in looking back on his tendency to withdraw: "I was a majority of one"—by which he meant that, having chosen to be totally alone, he was the universe and thus more than mankind. A young woman spoke, in the same vein, of her "right to oneliness." Yet such solipsism is neither restricted to pathology nor to adult life. Already early in childhood a child's healthy alternation between waking or sleeping, for example, may suddenly turn into a total avoidance of sleep or an over-all sleepiness; a child's happy alternation between sociability and aloneness may turn into an anxious or furious insistence on his mother's total presence or a blank refusal to show awareness of her proximity; many a mother is deeply disturbed when she notices, at her return from a sudden but not so lengthy absence, that her small child has blandly "forgotten" her. Total dependence or total independence may, temporarily or lastingly, become states which are not amenable to normal degrees of alternation, or total goodness or badness may suddenly appear as states seemingly beyond reach of parents who may actually prefer a child who is reasonably good but by all means also a little bad. Such total realignments occur as transitory phases at significant stages of infantile development; they remain a potentiality in the adult, and they may accompany the outbreak of a mental disturbance.

As for the coalignment with an object or a person, we are all familiar with the small child's fetishes, which, sometimes in the form of bedraggled dolls, become the subject of his elder's disdain and yet remain his total and exclusive token of security and comfort. Later, violent loves and hates and sudden conversions and aversions share with the child's fetishism and fears such factors as the exclusive focusing of a set of (friendly or unfriendly) affects on one person or idea, the primitivization of all affects thus focused, and a Utopian (or cataclysmic) expectation of a total gain or a total loss to come from this focus.

Finally we may point to a well-known example of a split of such original unification. In the change that comes over married couples who have decided on a divorce, the sudden transformation of what seemed a reasonably wholesome twoness into two totalities can be rather awesome (as one soon finds out if he tries to remain friends with both).

While such realignments may seem to appear suddenly, they develop slowly. Only uncommonly aware and brave people know about themselves what psychoanalysis reveals in others and particularly in patients—namely, how strong and systematic are man's *proclivities and potentialities for total realignments,* often barely hidden behind one-sided predilections and convictions, and how much energy is employed in inner defenses against a threatening total reorientation in which black may turn into white and vice versa. Only the affect released in sudden conversions and in sudden aversions testifies to the quantity of this energy. Equally revealing is the much described and much deplored, yet therapeutically useful, tendency of even the most enlightened and best-informed patients of psychiatry to develop a "transference" and to become, as it were, violently dependent on their therapists—and this either with predominantly positive or negative feelings—a sobering demonstration of the tendency for totalization which ill fits the intellectual contempt for fellow humans dependent on cosmologies and deities, monarchies and ideologies. At any rate, we have learned to understand such realignments as readjustments on a more primitive level, made necessary by increased anxieties, especially of infantile origin, and called forth by acute life crises. To mark them as pathological and thus as "bad" helps neither to understand nor to overcome them; to chart a purposeful course of action toward them, one must understand their inner rationale, their psycho-logic.

In giving these examples, I have used the terms "wholeness" and "totality." Both mean entireness, yet let me underscore their differences. Wholeness seems to connote an assembly of parts, even quite diversified parts, that enter into fruitful association and organization. This concept is most strikingly expressed in such terms as wholeheartedness, wholemindedness, wholesomeness, and the like. As a *Gestalt,* then, wholeness emphasizes a sound, organic, progressive mutuality between diversified functions and parts within an entirety, the boundaries of which are open and fluent. Totality, on the contrary, evokes a

Gestalt in which an absolute boundary is emphasized: given a certain arbitrary delineation, nothing that belongs inside must be left outside, nothing that must be outside can be tolerated inside. A totality is as absolutely inclusive as it is utterly exclusive—whether or not the category to be made absolute is a logical one and whether or not the parts really have, so to speak, a yearning for one another.

It is, then, the psychological need for a totality without further choice or alternation, even if it implies the abandonment of a much desired wholeness, which I would invite you to consider. To say it with one sentence: When the human being, because of accidental or developmental shifts, loses an essential wholeness, he restructures himself and the world by taking recourse to what we may call "totalism." It would be wise to abstain from considering this a merely regressive or infantile mechanism. It is an alternate, if more primitive, way of dealing with experience and thus has, at least in transitory states, a certain adjustment and survival value. It belongs to normal psychology. Any possible psychiatric inquiry is restricted to these questions: Can the transient means of emergency adjustment be prevented from becoming fixed ends? Can totalism reverse itself when the emergency is over? Can its elements be resynthesized in a wholeness which is then possible?

In the individual it is the inner institution, called by Freud the ego, which has the task of mastering experience and of guiding action in such a way that a certain wholesome synthesis is, ever again, created between the diverse and conflicting stages and aspects of life—between immediate impressions and associated memories, between impelling wishes and compelling demands, between the most private and the most public aspects of existence. To do its job, the ego develops modes of synthesis as well as screening methods and mechanisms of defense. As it matures through the constant interaction of maturational forces and environmental influences, a certain duality develops between higher levels of integration (which permit a greater tolerance of tension and of diversity) and lower levels of integration where totalities and conformities must help to preserve a sense of security. The study of those fusions and diffusions which—on the individual level—make for a successful wholeness or an attempted totality thus belongs to the realm of psychoanalytic ego-psychology. Here I can do no more than point to this field of study.[1]

III

The ego's beginnings are difficult to assess, but, as far as we know, it emerges gradually out of a stage when "wholeness" is a matter of physi-

[1] See the papers of Heinz Hartmann, Ernst Kris, and David Rapaport, and others in D. Rapaport, ed., *The Organization and Pathology of Thought* (New York: Columbia University Press, 1951).

ological equilibration, maintained through the mutuality between the baby's need to get and the mother's need to give. The mother, of course, is not only a parturient creature but also a member of a family and society. She, in turn, must feel a certain wholesome relation between her biological role and the values of her community. Only thus can she communicate to the baby, in the unmistakable language of somatic communication, that the baby may trust her, the world—and himself. Only a "whole" society can vouchsafe to the infant (through the mother) an inner conviction that all the diffuse somatic experiences (from the first search for breath to the disruptions of the teething stage) and all the confusing social cues of early life can be balanced by a sense of continuity and sameness which gradually unites the inner and outer worlds. The ontological source of faith and hope which thus emerges I have called a "sense of basic trust"; it is the first and basic wholeness, for it seems to imply that the inside and the outside can be experienced as an interrelated goodness. Basic mistrust, then, is the sum of all those diffuse experiences which are not somehow successfully balanced by the experience of integration. One cannot know what happens in a baby, but overwhelming clinical evidence indicates that early mistrust is accompanied by an experience of "total" rage, with fantasies of the total domination of the sources of pleasure and provision and that such fantasies, and such rages live on in the individual and are revived in extreme states and situations.

In fact, every basic conflict of childhood lives on, in some form, in the adult. The earliest steps are preserved in the deepest layers. Every tired human being may regress temporarily to partial mistrust whenever the world of his expectations has been shaken to the core. Yet social institutions seem to provide the individual with continuing collective reassurances in regard to such anxieties as have accrued from the steps and layers of his infantile past. There can be no question but that it is organized religion which systematizes and socializes the first and deepest conflict in life: it combines the dim images of each individual's prehistoric providers into collective images of superhuman providers; it makes comprehensible the vague subject matter contained in basic mistrust by giving it a metaphysical reality in the form of tangible evil; and it offers to man by way of rituals a periodic collective restitution of that basic trust which in mature adults ripens to a combination of faith and realism. In prayer man assures a superhuman power that (in spite of everything) he has remained trustworthy and asks for a sign that he now may also continue to trust his deity. In primitive life, which deals with one segment of nature and develops a collective magic, the supernatural providers of food and fortune are often treated as though they were angry if not malicious parents who needed to be appeased by prayer and self-torture. Higher forms of religion and ritual equally clearly address themselves to the nostalgic remnant in each individual of his expulsion from the paradise of wholeness which once gave liberal provision, but which, alas, was lost, leaving forever an undefinable sense of evil division, potential malevolence, and deep nostalgia. Religion restores, at regular intervals and through rituals significantly connected with the important crises of the life cycle and the turning points of the yearly cycle, a new sense of wholeness, of things rebound. But, as is the case with all such endeavors, that which was to be banished beyond the periphery is apt to reappear in the center. Much cruel, cold, and exclusive totalness has dominated some phases of the history of religion. One may well ask in what way the idea of a universe totally embraced by one god and his dogma prepared mankind for the idea of one state as well as for that of one mankind, for there can be no doubt but that, in periods of transition, a total realignment can ensure progress to an eventual greater wholeness, as well as a fixation on totalistic means.

Today no derision on the part of the careless unbeliever and no punitive fervor on the part of the dogmatist can deny the staggering fact that much of mankind finds itself without a living religion such as gave wholeness of existence to the tool man in his productive dealings with nature and to the trading man in his gainful exchange of goods in an expanding world market. How deeply worried self-made man is in his need to feel safe in his man-made world can be seen from the deep inroad which an unconscious identification with the machine (comparable to the magic identification of primitive man with his principal prey) has made on the Western concept of human nature in general and on a kind of automatized and depersonalized child-training in particular. The desperate need to function smoothly and cleanly, without friction, sputtering, or smoke, has attached itself to the ideas of personal happiness, of governmental perfection, and even of salvation. Sometimes one feels a strange totalism creeping up in those naïve initiators who expect a new wholeness to come from the process of technological development in and by itself, just as in times not so distant the millennium was to emerge from the unfailing wisdom of nature, from the mysterious self-balance of the market, or from the inner sanctity of wealth. Machines, of course, can be made more attractive and more comfortable as they become more practical; the question is where that deep sense of specific goodness will come from which man needs in his relation to his principal source and technique of production in order to permit himself to be human in a reasonably familiar universe. Unanswered, this need will continue to increase a deep and widespread basic mistrust which, in areas overcome with all too sudden changes in historical and economic perspective, contributes to a readiness for a totalitarian and authoritarian delusion of wholeness, ready-made with one leader at the head of one party, one ideology giving a simple rationale to all of nature and of history, one categorical enemy of production to be destroyed by one centralized agency of justice—and the steady diversion to outer enemies of the impotent rage stored up within.

It must be remembered here, however, that at least one of the systems which we call totalitarianisms, Soviet Communism, was born from an ideology which envisages beyond all revolutions a final wholeness of a society, freed from the interference of an armed state and of the class structure which necessitated it. In this vision, the total revolution and the totalitarian superstate is only a state to end all states; it will abolish itself by becoming dormant, leaving in the final wholeness of a stateless democracy nothing to be administered except "things . . . and processes of production." . . . However, we must not lose sight of those young peoples (and their young people) on the periphery of both the Soviet world and ours, who are in need of a common belief in this period of common technological change.

IV

I shall not outline here the implications of each of the successive childhood stages for the ideology of totalitarianism. The original alternative of a "whole" solution in the form of basic trust and a total solution in the form of basic mistrust, which we related to the matter of faith, is followed on each step by analogous alternatives, each, in turn, related to one of the basic human institutions.[2] Only in passing do I wish to make reference here to that aspect of infantile development which in the psychoanalytic literature on totalitarianism has received the greatest, if not an exclusive, emphasis: I mean that infantile period (around the age of five) when the child gets ready to develop not only a more goal-directed and rebellious initiative, but also a more organized conscience. The wholesome child of three or four enjoys an unsurpassed sense of autonomous wholeness which leads to great dreams of glory and achievement and, if preserved, outbalances a sense of doubt and a sense of shame. It is then that the child suddenly faces episodes of fear and guilt, evidences of a more organized conscience, an inner governor who has quietly assumed a central position and who, now that the little human being has learned to enjoy the wholeness of being a separate being and to envisage excessive conquests (Oedipus complex), tries to divide him against himself.

The guardian of conscience is, according to Freud, the superego, which is superimposed on the ego like an inner governor, or, one might say, an inner governor-general, who now represents the outer authorities, limiting the goals as well as the means of initiative. One could develop this analogy. While originally imposed by a foreign king, this governor-general now makes himself independent, using native troops (and their methods) to combat native insurrection. The superego thus comes to reflect not only the sternness of the demands and limitations imposed, but also the relative crudeness of the in-

2 To enumerate those which will not be discussed here, there is the sense of autonomy versus the sense of shame and the sense of doubt (related to ideas of Justice), there is the sense of initiative versus the sense of guilt (related to the ethos of production), and the sense of workmanship versus the sense of inferiority (related to techniques of production).

fantile stage during which they were imposed. Thus human conscience, even while serving common ideals, retains a certain primitivity. Historically, a relationship has been emphasized between the father God of the Western world, the absolute power of crowned heads, the absolute power of fathers over their children, on the one hand, and on the other, the cruelly categoric attitude employed by a strict conscience against the self, which is thus exposed to irrational guilt feelings and to moral masochism. There seems no doubt but that the Judaeo-Christian and feudal world has exploited man's proclivity for guilt. Psychologically, however, an assumption of a direct ratio of outer and inner pressure would be too simple. For, to spoil a child, or even be merely tolerant with him, does not necessarily make his conscience more considerate of himself; only a combination of true tolerance (born of maturity) and of firmness (born of integrated ethics) can guide an infantile process which otherwise, in one way or another, becomes one of the main sources of human exploitation.

This inner split, then, is the second great inducement (separation from the mother was the first) to "total" solutions in life, which are based on the simple and yet so fateful proposition that nothing is more unbearable than the vague tension of guiltiness. In transitory states or in lasting personality formations, individuals often try to overcome this vagueness by becoming totally good or totally bad—solutions which betray their totalistic nature in that the totally good may learn to be cruelly stern *ad majorem Dei gloriam,* while the totally bad may develop quite rigid loyalties to leaders and cliques. It is obvious that authoritarian propaganda addresses itself to this conflict by inviting man, collectively and unashamedly, to project total badness on whatever inner or outer "enemy" can be created by state decree and appointed as totally sub-human and verminlike while the obedient adherent may feel totally good as a member of a nation, a race, or a class blessed by history.

I shall now proceed from this relatively better-known fact to considerations pertaining to the end of childhood and to what seems to me the third, and more immediately political, crisis of wholeness.

V

Young people must become whole people in their own right, and this during a developmental stage characterized by a diversity of changes in physical growth, in genital maturation, and in social awareness. The wholeness to be achieved at this stage I have called a "sense of inner identity." [3] The young person, in order to experience wholeness, must feel a progressive continuity be-

[3] The following parallels parts of my paper "On the Sense of Inner Identity," in *Health and Human Relations* (proceedings of an international conference at Hiddesen, Germany) (New York: Blakiston).

tween that which he has come to be during the long years of childhood and that which he promises to become in the anticipated future, between that which he conceives himself to be and that which he perceives others to see in him and to expect of him. Individually speaking, identity includes, but is more than the sum of, all the successive identifications of those earlier years when the child wanted to be, and often was forced to become, like the people he depended on. Identity is a unique product, which now meets a crisis to be solved only in new identifications with age-mates and with leader figures outside of the family. The adolescent search for a new and yet a reliable identity can perhaps best be seen in the persistent endeavor to define, to overdefine, and to redefine oneself and each other in often ruthless comparison, while the search for reliable alignments can be seen in the restless testing of the newest in possibilities and the oldest in values. Where the resulting self-definition, for personal or for collective reasons, becomes too difficult, a sense of role diffusion results: the youth counterpoints rather than synthesizes his sexual, ethnic, occupational, and typological alternatives and is often driven to decide definitely and totally for one side or the other.

Here society has the function of guiding and narrowing the individual's choices. Primitive societies have always taken this function most seriously; their puberty rites replace a horror of undefinedness (dramatized by rituals) with a defined sacrifice and a sacred badge. Advancing civilization has found other more spiritual means of confirming the right life plan. Yet youth has always found ways of reviving more primitive initiations to membership in exclusive cliques, gangs, or fraternities. In America, where youth on the whole is free of primitive traditionalism, of punitive paternalism, and of standardization through state measures, nevertheless a spontaneous self-standardization has developed which makes seemingly senseless and constantly changing styles of clothing and ways of gesturing and speaking absolutely mandatory for insiders. For the most part this is good-natured business, full of mutual support of an other-directed kind, but occasionally cruel to nonconformists and of course quite unmindful of the tradition of individualism which it pretends to extol.

Let me once more refer to individual pathology. The necessity of finding, at least temporarily, a total stamp and standard at this time is so great that youth often prefers to find and to adopt a negative identity rather than none at all. In further pursuit of the old solution of total badness, a youth sometimes prefers to be nothing, and that totally, to remaining a contradictory bundle of identity fragments. Even in individual disturbances, usually called prepsychotic or psychopathic or otherwise diagnosed in line with adult psychopathology, an almost willful *Umschaltung* to a negative identity (and its roots in past and present) can be studied. On a somewhat larger scale, an analogous turn toward a negative identity prevails in the delinquent (addictive, homosexual) youth of our large cities, where conditions of economic, ethnic, and religious marginality provide poor bases for any kind of positive identity. If such negative identities are accepted as a youth's natural and final identity by teachers, by judges, and by psychiatrists, he not infrequently invests his pride as well as his need for total orientation in becoming exactly what the careless community expects him to become. Similarly, many young Americans from marginal and authoritarian backgrounds find temporary refuge in radical groups in which an otherwise unmanageable rebellion and diffusion receives the stamp of universal righteousness within a black-and-white ideology. Some, of course, mean it, but many are merely drifting into such association.

It must be realized, then, that only a firm sense of inner identity marks the end of youth and is a condition for further and truly individual maturation. In outbalancing the inner remnants of the original inequalities of childhood (and in outbalancing the dominance of the superego) a positive sense of identity permits the individual to forego irrational self-repudiation (the total prejudice against themselves which characterizes severe neurotics) as well as an irrational hate of otherness. Such identity, however, depends on the support which the young individual receives from the collective sense of identity characterizing the social groups significant to him—his class, his nation, his culture.[4] Where historical and technological developments severely encroach upon deeply rooted or strongly emerging identities (i.e., agrarian, feudal, patrician) on a large scale, youth feels endangered, individually and collectively, whereupon it becomes ready to support doctrines offering a total immersion in a synthetic identity (extreme nationalism, racism, or class consciousness) and a collective condemnation of a totally stereotyped enemy of the new identity. The fear of loss of identity which fosters such indoctrination contributes significantly to that mixture of righteousness and criminality which, under totalitarian conditions, becomes available for organized terror and for the establishment of major industries of extermination. Since conditions undermining a sense of identity also fixate older individuals on adolescent alternatives, a great number of adults fall in line or are paralyzed in their resistance. My final suggestion, then, is that the study of this third major crisis of wholeness, at the very end of childhood and youth, reveals an additional potentiality for totalism which seems to be of significance in the emergence of new collective identities in our time. Totalitarian regimes everywhere emphasize that youth *is* the wave of the future—and this in countries where youth is left high and

---

[4] It will be seen that in individuals as well as in groups, I prefer to speak of a "sense of identity" rather than of a "character structure" or "basic character." In nations, too, our clinical concepts would lead me to concentrate on the conditions and experiences which heighten or endanger a national sense of identity, rather than on a static national character. A clinical introduction to this subject is offered in my book, *Childhood and Society* (W. W. Norton & Co., 1950). Here it is important to remember that each identity cultivates its own sense of freedom—wherefore a people rarely understands what makes other peoples feel free. This fact is amply exploited by totalitarian propaganda and underestimated in the Western world.

dry by the ebbing wave of the past. A better understanding of this may help us to offer alternatives of guidance and support, instead of our present inclination to disdain or to forbid, in feeble attempts to out-totalize the totalitarians. . . .

To have the courage of one's diversity is a sign of wholeness, in individuals and in civilizations. In our civilization, it is not easy to discern whether or not, and in what respects, wider and firmer identities promise to meet all the diversities, dissonances, and relativities which emerge as we ourselves evolve a new world-image—an image which encompasses all of mankind and extends to the very core of matter as well as of mind. As we orient ourselves, we may well reassess more planfully the resources of wholeness, as well as the mechanisms of totalism which are reborn with each generation.

◄◄◄ ►►►

DANIEL J. LEVINSON

*Authoritarian Personality and Foreign Policy**

Attempts to understand the foreign policy of particular nations or the course of international relations generally have traditionally been guided almost entirely by historical-sociological points of view. The chief focuses of analysis have been in the realms of power politics, geopolitics, national economic interests, and the like. Recently, we have seen a growing interest in the role of psychological factors in international relations.[1] This interest stems in part from the recognition of irrationality in foreign-policy viewpoints. However, it would seem overly narrow to limit our psychological concern to the problem of irrationality. The thesis of this paper is that every foreign-policy orientation, whatever its degree of rationality and constructiveness, has, to an appreciable extent, a psychological foundation in the personalities of its adherents. This is

* This is a revision of a paper presented at a symposium on international tensions at the 1951 convention of the American Psychological Association. I am indebted to Drs. Gordon W. Allport, Alex Inkeles, and Robert W. White for their critical comments on the initial version. This study was supported by a grant from the Laboratory of Social Relations, Harvard University. Reprinted from Daniel J. Levinson, "Authoritarian Personality and Foreign Policy," in *Journal of Conflict Resolution,* I (1957), 37–47, by permission of the publisher.
   [1] Gabriel Almond, *The American People and Foreign Policy* (New York: Harcourt, Brace & World, 1950); George F. Kennan, "The Illusion of Security," *Atlantic Monthly,* August, 1954, pp. 31–34; Otto Klineberg, *Tensions Affecting International Understanding* (Social Science Research Council Bulletin No. 62 [New York: Social Science Research Council, 1950]).

not to say that foreign policy is purely an individual matter or merely a reflection of intrapersonal dynamics. I would argue, rather, for the development of a sociopsychological approach, one that gives due recognition to individual (and modal) personality while yet taking account of broader social forces.

My aim here is to consider certain psychological factors in various foreign-policy orientations within the United States. Specifically, I wish to consider some of the ways in which psychological processes, operating in large numbers of individuals, influence the degree of support given to various foreign-policy orientations. Although the present analysis is limited to the United States, its guiding principles can be applied to other nations as well.

In the analysis of the total process of formation, implementation, and change of foreign policy, there are several focal points which can be studied independently, though each must ultimately be understood in relation to the others. First, we may focus on the processes by which basic policy decisions are made and the determinants of various high-level policy orientations. Subjects of study would include "top" State Department meetings, foreign ministers' conferences, meetings of United Nations bodies, and the like. A second focus might be on the production and distribution of foreign-policy ideology in forms intended for mass consumption and having the purpose of justifying or opposing specific policy stands. The most obvious subject of study here is the mass media of communication, which provide the most potent means for the widespread distribution of ideology. Third, we may study the consumption of foreign-policy ideology, that is, the various ways in which individuals selectively assimilate the diverse viewpoints with which they are constantly bombarded. This part of the total process—what might be considered the "public opinion" aspect—is the chief concern of this paper.

NATIONALISM AND INTERNATIONALISM AS
IDEOLOGICAL ORIENTATIONS

The study of American foreign-policy orientations is complicated from the start by the fact that the American people tend, for the most part, to be relatively unsophisticated about and only partially involved in foreign-policy issues. There is, of course, a keen interest in the more dramatic events, such as the Korean War, the conscription bills, and the periodic American-Russian flare-ups. Nevertheless, we are relatively unconcerned and uninformed about the less dramatic but equally significant issues such as UN policy, the Point Four program, and the like. Historical and current sociological reasons for this are not hard to find: America has only recently come of age internationally; the understanding of international relations requires an ability and a readiness to think in terms of institutional abstractions to which Americans are only just getting accustomed; our newspapers and other communications media tend to perpetuate the existing confusion and ideological immaturity.

However, despite the relative lack of crystallized viewpoints, there does seem to exist a variety of general policy orientations or approaches. For certain purposes the existing foreign-policy orientations can be grouped along a continuum between two opposing extremes—nationalism and internationalism: in the center are the middle-of-the-road viewpoints, which represent constructive synthesis, compromise, or ambivalent shifting between the nationalist and internationalist extremes; in one direction we have increasing degrees of internationalism and in the other direction increasing degrees of nationalism.

To say that nationalism-internationalism is one dimension of foreign-policy ideology is not, of course, to say that this is the only dimension or in all contexts the most significant one. There are, clearly, numerous forms of nationalism and internationalism, and there may well be important similarities among those who hold extreme views at opposite ends of the continuum. Moreover, in certain newly industrializing countries, such as India, Israel, and Burma, we may find conjointly in many individuals a fierce emphasis on national sovereignty and a broadly internationalistic (collaborative, multilateral, pro-UN) ideology. Certain modifications of the present analysis would no doubt be required for its extension to these and other social contexts. This analysis applies most directly to the United States at mid-century as a period in which "extremists" are few and moderation prevails in virtually all ideological domains. The prototypic forms of nationalism and internationalism, as they are conceived to exist within this social context, may be briefly delineated; a fuller exposition is given elsewhere.[2]

Nationalism may be seen as a facet of a broader ethnocentric orientation. It is, so to speak, ethnocentric thinking in the sphere of international relations. Like other forms of ethnocentrism, it is based on a rigid and pervasive distinction between ingroups and outgroups. The primary ingroup in this case is the American nation; all other nations are potential outgroups, the focal outgroups at any given time being those nations whose aims are seen, rightly or wrongly, as different from ours. The American nation as a symbol is glorified and idealized; it is regarded as superior to other nations in all important respects. Great emphasis is placed on such concepts as national honor and national sovereignty. Other nations are seen as inferior, envious, and threatening. At the worst, they are likely to attack us; at best, they seek alliances only to pursue their own selfish aims and to "play us for a sucker." Ethnocentric ideas about human nature rationalize a belief in the inevitability of war. "Human nature being what it is, and other 'races' being what they are," so the reasoning goes, "some nation is bound to attack us sooner or later." Given

[2] T. W. Adorno, Else Frenkel-Brunswik, Daniel J. Levinson, and R. Nevitt Sanford, *The Authoritarian Personality* (New York: Harper & Bros., 1950); Daniel J. Levinson, "An Approach to the Theory and Measurement of Ethnocentrism," *American Political Science Review*, XLIX (1955), 173–190.

this "jungle" conception of international relations, our best policy is to be militarily the strongest of all nations so that none will dare attack us.

Perhaps the two main forms that American nationalism has taken are isolationism and imperialism, though the two often go together. The guiding image of isolationism has been that of Fortress America; its aim is a nation which is militarily impregnable and culturally isolated. Imperialism, on the other hand, is prepared to make foreign alliances and commitments, and it frequently uses internationalist terminology. Its aim, however, is the kind of American Century in which the development and reconstruction of other nations can proceed only on terms set by us, for our supposed economic and strategic advantage. Isolationism and imperialism sometimes merge into a single approach as the lines of American military defense are conceived to move outward into Europe and Asia and as we extend support to all governments, whatever their character, in exchange for military support.

An especially dramatic image exemplifying a nationalistic conception of the world situation has been provided by J. Robert Oppenheimer and discussed by Walter Lippmann.[3] The image is that of the United States and the Soviet Union as "two scorpions in a bottle—each capable of killing the other but only at the risk of his own life." Lippmann suggests that this image gives "a radically false picture of the atomic situation and it is an unmistakable symptom of a dangerous American neurosis." Its falseness lies, as Lippmann points out, in its neglect of the other nations that are so directly involved in the course of world events. In conceiving of American-Soviet relations primarily in military terms and in focusing chiefly on questions of self-defense and enemy annihilation, those who adopt this image fail to utilize existing possibilities of diplomacy, alliance, and negotiation toward constructive cooperation. To say, as Lippmann does, that this orientation is a "neurotic" one is to imply more than that it is false or harmful. A neurotic outlook reflects the activation, perhaps by a highly stressful social environment, of character traits, unconscious anxieties, and reality-distorting modes of ego defense that are of long standing in the individual personality. Without becoming preoccupied with the issue of neurosis as such, I shall turn shortly to a consideration of the inner psychological bases of this conception of world affairs.

It is difficult to formulate a generic conception of internationalism that will hold for the great variety of ideologies falling under this rubric. One common characteristic is the wish to minimize the barriers now existing between nations and to promote full exchange—of ideas, commodities, cultural ways—among all nations. Either military activity is rejected entirely (pacifism), or, more commonly, it is accepted as a last resort after all other means of settling disputes have been used. Great emphasis is placed on the reduction of national sovereignty and on the establishment of an international organization like the

[3] Column, *Boston Globe*, October 7, 1953.

UN. Moreover, the UN is conceived of not merely as a means of settling disputes but, more important, as a mechanism for the economic and cultural development of all nations. This approach does not necessarily assume that there will be no conflict between nations, in either the near or the distant future, but it does assume that conflict, when it does occur, can be dealt with in a nondestructive, nonautocratic manner.

From the point of view of modern social science, the basic tenets of internationalism are presumably more rational—more soundly based on our knowledge of history, social organization, and human nature—than are those of nationalism. It would be unwise, however—and it is certainly not my intent—to regard internationalism as having a monopoly on truth and goodness. Its hopefulness regarding the long-range possibilities of world peace often leads to a naïve optimism concerning what can be achieved in the short run. The dislike of force may lead to unrealistic military policies. And, more generally, the social effectiveness of internationalism or any other ideology is influenced (and often impaired) to a high degree by the individual personalities and organizational policies of its adherents. My concern here is with the nature and the sociopsychological determinants of these viewpoints rather than with their rationality or effectiveness.

Given these admittedly sketchy and incomplete formulations of nationalism and internationalism, let me turn to my central problems: How can we assess nationalism and internationalism as generalized orientations in the individual? What sociopsychological differences are there, if any, between those who stand at opposite ends of this foreign-policy continuum? In what sense can we speak of psychological determinants of foreign-policy ideology?

THE MEASUREMENT OF
NATIONALISM AND INTERNATIONALISM

I shall attempt a partial answer to these questions on the basis of work reported in *The Authoritarian Personality*,[4] as well as a more recent study of my own. Two opinion-attitude scales were developed, at different times, to provide a measure of nationalism that might then be correlated with measures of other psychological and sociological variables. The construction of both scales was guided by the conceptions of nationalism and internationalism just presented. The first scale, developed during the war years, expressed nationalistic ideas concerning the inevitability of war, the importance of militarization, the restriction of immigration, the punishment of conscientious objectors, and so on.[5]

In 1951 I developed a second Internationalism-Nationalism Scale, dealing

[4] *Op. cit.*
[5] *Ibid.*; Levinson, "An Approach . . . ," *op. cit.*

TABLE 1

The Internationalism-Nationalism (IN) Scale

ITEM*		MEAN†	D.P.‡
1	We need more leaders like MacArthur, who have the morals and the strength to put our national honor above appeasement	3.1	4.2
2	If it weren't for Russia and her satellites, the world would be headed toward peace and prosperity by now	3.4	3.5
3*	In the long run, it would be to our best interest as a nation to spend less money for military purposes and more money for education, housing, and other social improvements	2.6	2.2
4	The immigration of foreigners to this country should be kept down so that we can provide for Americans first	3.4	3.8
5	The only way peace can be maintained is to keep America so powerful and well armed that no other nation will dare to attack us	3.2	4.1
6*	Our best policy in China would be to forget about Chiang Kai-shek and to work for a coalition between the Communists and the "center" parties	4.8	3.1
7	If the United Nations doesn't show more signs of getting tough with Russia soon, America must be prepared to carry on the fight by itself	3.4	3.3
8	While we should give military aid to countries which are prepared to fight our enemies, we ought to cut down on foreign economic help, or else the other countries will just play us for a sucker	3.3	3.2
9	In these troubled times, if we are to be strong and united against our common enemy, we must have more laws and safeguards against the spreading of dangerous ideas	3.0	3.8
10*	One main trouble with American foreign policy today is that there is too much concern with military force and too little concern with political negotiation and economic reconstruction	3.0	2.4
11	In view of America's moral and material superiority, it is only right that we should have the biggest say in deciding United Nations policy	2.4	2.8
12	The first principle of our foreign policy should be to join forces with any country, even if it is not very democratic, just as long as it is strongly anti-Communist	2.8	2.4

* Items marked with an asterisk take an "internationalist" position as here defined; the others represent a "nationalist" position.
† Responses are scored on a 1–7 scale; 7 points are given for strong agreement on the nationalistic items and for strong disagreement on the internationalistic items (see Adorno *et al., op. cit.*).
‡ The "D.P." is the "discriminatory power" of an item, i.e., its ability to discriminate between high and low scorers on the total scale. It is obtained by subtracting the item mean earned by the low group (bottom quarter of the total-scale distribution) from the mean of the high group (top quarter). All D.P.'s are significantly greater than zero (at beyond the 1 per-cent level of confidence).

with then current controversial issues.[6] This scale is presented in Table 1. Its twelve items cover a variety of problems relating to our role in the UN, emphasis on military versus economic aid to other countries, our choice of allies in the cold war, and so on. For example: "We need more leaders like MacArthur, who have the morals and the strength to put our national honor above appeasement" (Item 1). Item 9 was included because it seemed that the current attack

[6] I wish to thank Lora W. Heims and Paul E. Sapir for their assistance in various phases of this study.

on freedom of thought was an aspect of the nationalistic orientation: "In these troubled times, if we are to be strong and united against our common enemy, we must have more laws and safeguards against the spreading of dangerous ideas." Item 10 represents a presumably internationalist viewpoint: "One main trouble with American foreign policy today is that there is too much concern with military force and too little concern with political negotiation and economic reconstruction."

The scale was administered and scored in the same manner as those presented in *The Authoritarian Personality* research.[7] Subjects were allowed three degrees of agreement $(+1, +2, +3)$ and three degrees of disagreement with each item. The items were scored on a 1–7 scale, the higher scores being given for agreement with "nationalistic" items and for disagreement with "internationalistic" items. The subject's total-scale score is his mean item score multiplied by 10. The possible range of scores is thus 10–70 points, with a hypothetical mid-point at 40.

This Internationalism-Nationalism (IN) Scale was administered in 1951 to two classes in education and one in social relations at the Harvard University summer session. The eighty-four subjects included some college undergraduates, a few graduate students in education, and a considerable number of persons in teaching and related community work. This sample is thus somewhat more diversified than the usual college sample, but it shows some homogeneity in the direction of high educational level and moderate income. On the IN Scale it earned a mean of 31.8 (slightly on the "internationalist" side of the mid-point), an S.D. of 12.5, and a range of 10–64. There were, in other words, wide individual differences in scale scores.

The reliability and internal consistency of the IN Scale were relatively high. The split-half reliability for the total sample was .86; the test-retest correlation for one of the education classes retested after six weeks was .90. Internal consistency was assessed by the discriminatory power (D.P.) technique.[8] Item means and D.P.'s are presented in Table 1. An item's D.P. indicates its ability to discriminate between high and low scores (top and bottom quarters) on the total scale. All twelve of the items discriminate adequately (beyond the 1 percent level); no items had to be rejected on this ground. Thus each item may be said to represent an aspect of a broader ideological pattern, though some items are more central than others in the sense of reflecting more of the unifying core. A reading of the most discriminating items—Nos. 1, 4, 5, and 9— gives perhaps the clearest indication of the diversity in literal content, as well as the unity in underlying theme, within this ideological domain. The scale properties indicate that most persons are relatively (though by no means entirely) consistent in taking either a nationalist or an internationalist posi-

7 *Op. cit.*
8 *Ibid.*; Rensis Likert, "A Technique for the Measurement of Attitudes," *Archives of Psychology*, CLX (1932), 1–55.

tion in the sense noted above and individuals can be ranked with fair accuracy along a nationalist-internationalist continuum.

SOCIOPSYCHOLOGICAL CORRELATES OF
NATIONALISM AND INTERNATIONALISM

There is a gradually accumulating body of evidence concerning the kinds of personal characteristics that tend to be associated with preference for a strongly nationalistic viewpoint. In briefly defining nationalism, I suggested that it is a facet of a broader ethnocentric approach in which the distinction between ingroups and outgroups plays a central part. A derivative hypothesis is that those who tend most strongly to fear and derogate other nations will exhibit similar beliefs and feelings about various intranational groups, such as Negroes, Jews, foreigners, lower socioeconomic groupings, and the like. This hypothesis was supported in our original research [9] by correlations averaging about .7 between nationalism and other sections of the Ethnocentrism (E) Scale, as well as by interview material. In my 1951 study, the IN Scale correlated .77 with a sixteen-item E Scale derived from the earlier form. Findings such as these support the view that extreme nationalism is a form of pseudopatriotism. Although nationalists glorify America as a symbol, they are inclined to regard most of the American population as an alien outgroup. They are activated, it would seem, less by love of Americans and their heritage than by a sense of hostility and anxiety regarding other nations and "outsiders" generally. Internationalists, being under less compulsion either to glorify their own nation or to condemn others, show a more genuine attachment to their cultural traditions.

Nationalists and internationalists show characteristic differences in ideology spheres apparently far removed from foreign policy and intergroup relations. Nationalism is associated, for example, with an autocratic orientation toward child-rearing, husband-wife relations, and other aspects of family life. Nationalists are inclined to conceive of the family in hierarchical terms. They regard the husband as properly dominant over the wife, the parents as strong authorities requiring obedience and respect above all from their children. They tend to be moralistic and disciplinarian in their child-rearing methods and to be guided by rigidly conventionalized definitions of masculinity and femininity. Evidence in this direction was obtained in the analysis of clinical interviews of high- versus low-scoring subjects on the Ethnocentrism Scale.[10] The Traditional Family Ideology (TFI) Scale was developed specifically to measure this pattern of thought. Correlations of .6–.7 between this scale and the E Scale

[9] Adorno et al., op. cit.
[10] Ibid., especially chapters by Adorno and by Frenkel-Brunswik.

were obtained in several samples.[11] In the 1951 study described above, I obtained a correlation of .65 between the IN and the TFI scales. These findings are consistent with the earlier formulations of Reich, Fromm, Erikson, and Dicks and others writing on nationalism in various European countries.[12]

Again, nationalism is associated with certain patterns of religious ideology, notably those that may be characterized as fundamentalistic or conventionalistic. In these religious orientations God is regarded as a kind of power figure who rewards the virtuous and punishes the sinful and who can be directly appealed to or ingratiated. Great emphasis is placed on the efficacy of ritual, and the precepts of the ingroup religious authority are taken literally and unquestioningly. The Religious Conventionalism Scale, developed by Lichtenberg and the author to measure this outlook, correlated .52 with the IN Scale. Slightly lower correlations, of the order of .3–.4, have been obtained between various measures of nationalism and of politicoeconomic conservatism; for example, in the sample described above, the IN Scale correlated .34 with a variant of the Politico-Economic Conservatism Scale reported by Adorno *et al.*

These and related findings provide substantial evidence that foreign-policy orientation is part of a broader ideological context. Nationalism appears most commonly within an autocratic approach to the social world. This approach embraces not only the domain of international relations but the individual's views concerning religion, family, politics, and other aspects of social life as well.

What are the sources of this complex ideological patterning? The sources are to be found, no doubt, both within the individual and in his social environment. With regard to intraindividual sources, I would speak for the following postulate: The individual's approach to the external, social world will in significant degree reflect his approach to himself—his self-conceptions, character traits, modes of dealing with inner conflict, and the like.[13] A corollary hypothesis in the present case is that *an autocratic approach to problems of social organization will most often be found within an authoritarian personality structure.*

This hypothesis can be derived from an analysis of the psychological qualities that are directly represented in nationalism and related viewpoints.[14] Such characteristics as punitiveness, stereotypy, fear of moral contamination, submission to powerful authority, and exaggerated fear of weakness—in their

[11] D. J. Levinson and Phyllis E. Huffman, "Traditional Family Ideology and Its Relation to Personality," *Journal of Personality*, XXIII (1955), 251–273.

[12] Wilhelm Reich, *The Mass Psychology of Fascism* (New York: Orgone Institute Press, 1946); Erich Fromm, *Escape from Freedom* (New York: Farrar & Rinehart, 1941); Erik H. Erikson, "Hitler's Imagery and German Youth," *Psychiatry*, V (1942), 475–493; Henry V. Dicks, "Personality Traits and National Socialist Ideology," *Human Relations*, III (1950), 111–154.

[13] D. J. Levinson, "Idea Systems in the Individual and Society," in G. Vollschan and W. Hirsch, eds., *Explorations in Social Change* (Boston: Houghton Mifflin Co., 1964).

[14] Adorno *et al., op. cit.*; Erikson, *op. cit.*; Levinson, "An Approach . . . ," *op. cit.*

extreme form, features of authoritarian personality—make recurrent appearances in nationalistic thought. However, adequate testing of this hypothesis requires the independent assessment of personality variables in persons supporting various ideological positions. Various types of empirical work have been carried out along these lines, no one of them fully conclusive but each contributing to the general picture. Among the more directly relevant studies are Erikson's analysis of *Mein Kampf* and Dicks's work on German prisoners of war and Russian *émigrés*.[15]

In *The Authoritarian Personality*, personality variables were assessed by means of clinical interviews, projective techniques, and more structured devices. The so-called F Scale, developed in this research, gives a quantitative, though crude, measure of authoritarianism that can be applied in survey-type studies. Correlations of the order of .5–.7 were obtained between the F Scale and the Ethnocentrism Scale in a variety of samples. In the study of the IN Scale, described earlier, a twelve-item F Scale (Form FERPT) correlated .60 with IN. Similar findings have been obtained with a smaller number of F- and IN-type items in a series of nationwide samples surveyed during the period 1948–1952 by the Survey Research Center, University of Michigan.[16] Lane found, for example, that in 1952 a significantly larger proportion of authoritarians than of equalitarians (by the criterion of the F score) preferred to deal with the Korean crisis either by pulling out of Korea altogether or by bombing Manchuria and China; the equalitarians more often preferred a policy of working toward a peaceful settlement. The general conclusion that seems warranted by the various clinical, survey, and other studies is that personal authoritarianism constitutes an important inner source (though by no means the only source) of the disposition toward nationalism and related ideologies.

In addition to their anchorage in the personality, ideologies are developed, utilized, and to various degrees altered in response to diverse social influences. What a man believes depends in large part on the ideological opportunities and demands presented by a variety of membership groups and reference groups. Thus in the 1951 study of the IN Scale, as in many similar studies, various political and religious groupings were found to differ in their average degree of nationalism. The Republicans had a significantly higher (more nationalistic) mean IN score than the Democrats or the independents, the group means being 39.3, 30.6, and 28.6, respectively. With regard to religious

[15] Erikson, *op. cit.*; Dicks, *op. cit.*; *idem*, "Observations on Contemporary Russian Behaviour," *Human Relations*, V (1952), 111–175.

[16] Significant relationships between brief measures of authoritarianism and nationalism have been found as well in a study of seven Western European nations. The study was carried out by the Organization for Comparative Social Research; this particular analysis was made by Stein Rokkan, Arthur Couch, and the author and will be published in the near future. Cf. Morris Janowitz and Dwaine Marvick, "Authoritarianism and Political Behavior," *Public Opinion Quarterly*, XVII (1953), 185–201; and Robert E. Lane, "Political Personality and Electoral Choice," *American Political Science Review*, XLIX (1955), 173–190.

grouping, the Catholics had an IN mean of 38.7; the Protestants a mean of 32.8; the Jews, 30.1; and those with no affiliation, 21.2. In the case of religious attendance (regardless of affiliation), those who attend services weekly had an IN mean of 36.2; those who attend occasionally, 30.9; and the nonattenders, 25.3. Findings of this sort have been obtained in a large number of surveys which used various types of items and scales. It should be noted, however, that, while these and other groupings show significant differences in *average* score, the degree of individual variation within every major grouping is large indeed. An individual's membership in a particular social group does not, in itself, provide a very adequate basis for prediction of his outlook.

In attempting to generalize from the foregoing research, it should be kept in mind that the samples used have for the most part represented limited sections of the national population, namely, the more highly educated, the urban, the "middle class." Relationships among ideology, personality, and social context have been less intensively studied in the case of the less educated, the very poor and the wealthy, and those in rural and other regions farther removed from university centers. Lubell, for example, has pointed out that the strongest isolationist vote over the years has been registered in counties that are predominantly German/American and/or Catholic and/or rural in composition.[17] It remains for further research to determine whether the widespread isolationist sentiment in these areas is a direct function of tradition and social pressure or whether personal authoritarianism is an equally important factor in facilitating the acceptance of isolationist doctrine. Evidence of gross differences in authoritarianism (F score) in various social strata (distinguished by class, education, and age) has been given by Janowitz and Marvick.[18]

It would appear that the "functionality" of ideology for the person—the degree to which his social views are imbedded in and serve to maintain other aspects of his personality—will vary with the person and with the social setting.[19] One individual holds a nationalistic outlook in part because the images and relationships it portrays reflect so well his unconscious fantasies; the ideology is deeply gratifying and anxiety-binding. Another individual holds a roughly similar outlook on the basis of a more superficial acceptance of what is given in his social environment; in this case, personality factors may play a relatively incidental role in the formation and maintenance of ideology.

One of the major systematic questions in the study of ideology is this: What are the conditions that maximize the role of personality as a determinant of ideology formation? I shall mention two such conditions: first, that his society presents the individual with a reasonable degree of *choice*, that is, with a range of legitimized ideological alternatives from which to select, and, second, that

[17] Samuel Lubell, "The Politics of Revenge," *Harper's Magazine*, April 1, 1956.
[18] *Op. cit.*
[19] Gordon W. Allport, *The Nature of Prejudice* (Cambridge, Mass.: Addison-Wesley Press, 1954) ; Levinson, "Idea Systems . . . ," *op. cit.*

the individual be *personally involved* in ideological issues. In other words, the greater the degree of choice and the greater the involvement in choosing, the more heavily will the person's ideology be influenced by deep-lying personality characteristics.

Given a reasonable degree of choice and involvement, the following types of influence of personality on ideology are found.

(a) *Receptivity.* Each individual is receptive to only a limited number of the total range of available ideologies.

(b) *Immanence.* A person's freely verbalized ideology, with regard to foreign policy, religion, or whatever, can be viewed as a personal document. Like other personal documents, it will be found to express in its thematic and formal qualities many of the person's central personality characteristics. Personality is to varying degrees immanent in ideology.

(c) *Relative consistency.* A person's ideology regarding various social issues (foreign policy, the family, and so on) will show consistency not necessarily in a logical sense but in the sense that similar values, conflicts, and the like will be reflected throughout.

NATIONALISM, INTERNATIONALISM, AND MODAL PERSONALITY PATTERNS

I should like to conclude by mentioning briefly a few implications of the foregoing theory and data for the analysis of American national character and American foreign policy.[20] The classic descriptions of American character by de Tocqueville, Bryce, and others have brought out two sharply contrasting sides. On the one hand, they find such traits as anxious conformism, emphasis on socially defined success, a tendency to escape into the crowd rather than to look within, an emphasis on work over leisure, on quantity over quality, on varied activity rather than deep experience. On the other hand, however, they find genuine humanitarianism, capacity for self-awareness, aesthetic sensitivity, readiness to identify with the underdog, and the like. The former traits have been shown in various studies to characterize authoritarian personalities, while the latter traits characterize equalitarian personalities. There are, of course, many Americans who possess both types of characteristics and who maintain various forms of compromise or conflictful balance between them. However, if the accumulated research has any validity, there are also many individuals who have predominantly one or the other character structure and its associated ideological orientations.

According to this conception, American character can be schematically

[20] For a more general discussion, see Almond, *op. cit.*, and Alex Inkeles and Daniel J. Levinson, "National Character: The Study of Modal Personality and Sociocultural Systems," in Gardner Lindzey, ed., *Handbook of Social Psychology* (Cambridge, Mass.: Addison-Wesley Press, 1954).

represented as falling along a trimodal distribution, the modes representing authoritarian, equalitarian, and in between patterns. The last mode is conceived as a composite of the first two, and each mode contains numerous subvariants. Like all typologies, this one needs to be applied with discrimination; for certain purposes, other bases of analysis will be more useful.

There is one analysis of American history and mentality which exemplifies this approach without benefit—or hindrance—of current technical jargon. It is V. L. Parrington's monumental work, *Main Currents in American Thought*.[21] In Parrington's view—and he documents it well—a major dynamic in America's intellectual and institutional history has been the conflict, partially synthesized but never fully resolved, between authoritarian and equalitarian conceptions of man and society. He finds evidence for this dialectic in the European intellectual traditions transplanted in America by the colonists; in the development of our political, economic, and religious systems; in our artistic and scientific endeavors.

The recurrent conflict so well described by Parrington has never been more dramatically evident than in our present ideas and policies concerning international relations. Both domestic and international conditions have conspired to intensify our anxieties and with them our authoritarian trends. The decline of capitalism in other nations, the rapid rise of Soviet Russia as a world power, the growth of revolutionary anticapitalist movements in the industrially undeveloped nations, the threat of total destruction by atomic warfare, the fear of depression and mass unemployment if war production is curtailed—these and other factors have operated to intensify our nationalistic-chauvinistic potentialities, which are further reinforced and given ideological form by nationalistic leaders in politics, in the mass media, and in other strategic positions.

Similar conclusions, stemming from a somewhat different theoretical and observational base, have been expressed by G. F. Kennan. In 1954, speaking of the widespread tendency to regard "total military security" as the foundation of American foreign policy, he pointed out:

> . . . It is precisely these subjective factors—factors relating to the state of mind of many of our own people—rather than the external circumstances, that seem to constitute the most alarming component of our situation. It is such things as the lack of flexibility in outlook, the stubborn complacency about ourselves and our society, the frequent compulsion to extremism, the persistent demand for absolute solutions, the unwillingness to accept the normal long-term hazards and inconveniences of power —it is these things in the American character that give added gravity to a situation which would in any case be grave enough.[22]

---

[21] Vernon L. Parrington, *Main Currents in American Thought* (3 vols.; New York: Harcourt, Brace & Co., 1943).

[22] *Op. cit.*, p. 32.

One symptom of the trend toward authoritarianism is the rapid decrease in ideological choice now available to the general population. The relative standardization of ideology in the press, as well as the intimidation of teachers, government employees, writers, and others, have led toward an artificial homogenizing of public opinion. This process is dangerous not merely because of the threat to civil liberties and intellectual freedom but also because it goes hand in hand with pressures toward nationalism in our foreign policy. For these and other reasons, our inner predispositions toward internationalism are hindered from achieving full ideological expression.

I have perhaps seemed to underestimate the strength of equalitarian forces in the present social scene. However, in this period, when almost any form of ideological deviance may be called "subversive," it is to be kept in mind that American character has its authoritarian as well as its democratic side. It is unrealistic and, ultimately, dangerous to make the casual assumption that America will *necessarily* constitute a democratic force in world affairs and that our foreign policy will automatically be such as to reduce international tensions. The kind of world role that America plays will depend in no small part on our ability to create the conditions under which our underlying equalitarian potentials can become ideologically and institutionally kinetic.

Social Learning and Intergroup Relations

The selections which make up this group of readings have symbolic as well as explicit relevance. All of these authors are psychologists, American by birth, and trained for the most part in American universities. All made substantial contributions to the psychology of learning and to social psychology between the years 1930 and 1950. Further, by their concern with learning and social behavior, they epitomize that peculiar substratum of philosophical conviction which typifies American psychology: a concern with empirical research and a faith—sophisticated, to be sure, but nonetheless a faith—in the perfectibility of man. As Ernest Hilgard has remarked, many are of the opinion that psychology in America is equivalent to the psychology of learning—a concern with how the individual learns to live in the social group and to master his environment.

Mark May, for many years director of the Yale Institute of Human Relations, once characterized the point of view of that group toward the science of human behavior as follows:

> It proposes that those who work with the principles of learning (psychologists, social psychologists) cannot evolve a theory of social behavior without understanding the social order which sets the conditions for human learning. Conversely, technicians in the social sciences must consent to take some account of the principles governing that long learning experience which fits any individual for participation in the social order.

From psychology, then, are derived the fundamental principles of learning and from social science its prime conditions. Sooner or later the twain must meet.[1]

May remarked at another time that a theory of behavior should combine the rigor of the learning laboratory with the depth insights of psychoanalysis and the breadth of cultural anthropology. The effect of the Institute on its students and on its programs of research in social behavior nationally cannot be overestimated.

It is not surprising, then, that May sees war primarily as a matter of the learning an individual internalizes which tends toward the expression of aggressive behavior rather than toward peace.

Learning to fight and to hate involves much more than learning to box, to duel, or to participate in other forms of ingroup violence. Systematic education for aggressive warfare in ancient Sparta or in modern Germany includes, besides physical education in games and contests, universal compulsory military training; the inculcation of certain attitudes, prejudices, beliefs; and devotion to leaders and ideals. The whole purpose and direction of such education is toward group aggression. . . .

The development of a peace group requires more than the mere discovery that life in organized society is preferable to that of a hermit. There must be a pattern of social organization and rules of human relations which guarantee insofar as possible that all members of a group may reap the maximum benefits from social interaction with each other and with other groups. By definition a peace group is one in which there is a minimum amount of physical violence among the members.

Parallel to this position is that of Edward C. Tolman, long professor of psychology at the University of California. Tolman, like May, is concerned with a science of behavior which has its roots in work with animals in the laboratory. Like May, further, he is convinced that extrapolations may be made from the psychology of learning to social psychology. Tolman's complex system-making, employing not only careful logic but also an extensive experimental program, although differing in detail, is as symbolic of the American approach as is that of May.

It is interesting in Tolman to see a revision or restatement of the ideas of James and McDougall. Tolman sees, for example, a switch from personal aggression to group aggression:

[T]he dammed-up hostility against the parent or superior may, through the dynamisms of identification with the group and of projection onto others, be converted primarily into hostile behavior toward outsiders,

[1] Neal E. Miller and John Dollard, *Social Learning and Imitation* (New Haven: Yale University Press, 1941), p. viii.

with the accompanying feeling (due to the projection) that it is the latter, the outsiders, who are the really guilty ones. This is the setup in what I would call "neurotically motivated war." The evidence for such neurotic components in the prosecution of a war are, I believe, all around us. We observe it in our friends and in ourselves as well as most definitely in the Nazis and the Japanese.

In addition, Tolman, like Freud and McDougall, sees the need for a revision of the social system, a revision which will make war obsolete by the presence of a new character type. Tolman speaks not of the motive of emulation but rather the creation of a new myth and a new ideology:

> What then can we hope for? My answer is that, if we can but combine the emphasis upon the biological drives with a moderate amount of self-assertion and a large amount of collectivity and add to this easy identification with parents, we shall arrive at a new and this time truly workable myth—a myth that in reality would save the world from its horrors. I shall call this the myth of the "psychologically adjusted man."

The work of Gordon W. Allport is many sided. It presents a sophisticated synthesis of many ideas which range from Freud to learning theory.

> It is not necessary to accept Freud's somewhat involved theory of anti-Semitism to recognize that man's hostile impulses themselves are subtle and are capable of much strange channeling. . . .
> For our purpose it is enough to note that channeling of hostility in the directions of war or racial and religious prejudice is an authentic possibility. Strange crystallizations take place around the myths available in our folklore. Originally, of course, these myths were created and maintained by like-minded individuals who felt a need to project their personal conflicts outward. In this way Jews became the mythological cause of people's inner unrest; Communists (or capitalists) became a threat to their very existence. The legend adopted by the individual is available to him in his culture and is often forced on him by his parents, teachers, or leaders.

In this statement Allport as a personality theorist is not only dealing with an issue but representing a point of view. To some extent this same point of view is found in the thinking of Tolman and May. It will be noted that May makes an allusion to Sparta and Germany, that Tolman talks about the Nazis and the Japanese, and that Allport alludes to the problem of ethnic prejudice. These allusions reveal an important aspect of how the social psychologist arrives at his point of view concerning war. Over and above the fundamental concern with the issue of learning, all of these writers in one way or another are concerned with the equation that exists between intergroup relations and war. The dynamics that are behind race prejudice are fundamentally the same dynamics which on a larger scale lead to war. Allport, thus, as a personality theorist, is dealing with some complex issues. For example, his comment on the problem of personal expectation and its relationship to war—even when viewed out of context from the rest of his article—is a brilliant contribution in its own right.

These three social psychologists come to the same general conclusion. War is a real danger because of man's biological heritage of aggression. War, on the other hand, can be avoided if the conditions for learning in the society can be changed. After this has been achieved, peaceful uses for energies presently channeled into aggression and destruction may be found.

MARK A. MAY

*War, Peace, and Social Learning**

Man's biological nature is neither good nor bad, aggressive nor submissive, warlike nor peaceful, but neutral in these respects. He is capable of developing in either direction depending on what he is compelled to learn by his environment and by his culture. It is a mistake to assume that he can learn war more easily than peace. His learning machinery is not prejudiced, as is sometimes thought, toward the acquirement of bad habits. The bias is in his social environment. People who have found by experience that life flows more smoothly, that happiness is more abundant, that their wants and needs are better met by friendly than by hostile relations with others, are far more strongly predisposed to settle disputes, both domestic and foreign, by peaceful means. If an individual is consistently rewarded more for cooperative behavior and friendly relations with other individuals or groups than for competitive behavior and antagonistic relations, he will acquire habits and attitudes that favor peace. But even these do not guarantee peace, as we shall see later.

If, on the other hand, man's environment and his culture are organized so that fighting is more rewarding than peaceful pursuits, he will acquire habits of aggression and attitudes of hostility. People who have found that they can be happier and can satisfy their wants and needs better by war than by peace will, by habit, be more predisposed to fight. Such people are inclined to justify and glorify war and give it a high rank in their system of moral and religious

* Reprinted from Mark A. May, *A Social Psychology of War and Peace*, chap. 2, pp. 20–31, by permission of the publisher (Copyright 1943, Yale University Press, New Haven).

values. The procedures which have proved successful in satisfying man's wants and in meeting his needs are most highly prized and sanctioned by him. Around these his moral and religious values become organized. If man is more aggressive and warlike than he is peaceful, it is to be attributed not to perverseness in his nature or even to original sin, but rather to the fact that life, as he has been compelled to live it, has been such as to reward pugnaciousness and the use of force more than other forms of adaptive behavior. . . .

Man's beliefs, opinions, habits, and especially his emotional attitudes of love and hate are influenced far more by what he is taught by his fellow men, particularly by his parents and elders, than by his physical surroundings. It may be true, as some social scientists have insisted, that the body of customs, manners, morals, and other factors which go to make up culture is in large part determined over a long period of years by such physical factors as climate, food supply, seasons, rainfall, and the like. Be that as it may, our interest is not in the evolution of societies or cultures but rather in their impact on the learning of present populations. [My] main thesis [here] . . . is that the conditions which determine social attitudes and opinions, particularly those that are involved in war or peace, are in large part products of social conditioning, although their origins may have been determined by geographical and ecological factors.

WAR IS NOT A HUMAN INSTINCT

It is recognized that this view stands in opposition to the traditional one which stresses the importance of the biological and constitutional factors in human behavior and implies that a national crisis provides the stimulation that evokes latent but powerful unlearned tendencies to self-preservation. Those who maintain this position point to an array of biological facts concerning the struggle for existence, violent competition among animals, and to the important fact that man himself is a fighting animal. Given the proper stimulus situation, he will always fight and fight well without much, if any, previous education in the process.

The view advanced here does not deny that large segments of the behavior of animals and some unknown fraction of that of adult humans are unlearned. The fact that some animals and young children will bite, claw, kick, and attack when provoked, without previous education in what they are doing, does not force us to the conclusion that the aggressive acts of adult humans are unlearned. The important fact about the biological background of war is the inverse correlation between instinct and learning.[1] Toward the bottom of the

[1] The word "learning" is used here and throughout . . . not in the narrow sense of "scholarship," but in the broader sense of "experience."

evolutionary scale are animals possessing a maximum of instinctive or un-learned responses to their environments and a minimum capacity to learn. At the top of the scale stands man with a minimum number of fixed innate modes of response (such as reflexes), with a maximum power of learning, and with a relatively long period of infancy and parental dependency during which much important education takes place. The general rule seems to be, although there are exceptions, that, as one goes up the evolutionary scale, there is a decrease in the number of fixed innate modes of response and an increase in learning capacity accompanied by an increase in the length of the period of dependency. Nature has been very kind to man. Instead of giving him an innate equip-ment of habits of defense and offense that are suited to life in a particular environment, she has given him a far more precious heritage—a capacity to learn how best to protect himself and to satisfy his needs in any land environ-ment that this planet affords.

The conventional attempts to understand the aggressive behavior of man in terms of the instinctive behavior of lower animals stress only one of the two threads that hold together the evolutionary series. Man is linked to the lower animals not only because he has certain instincts in common with them but also because they have a certain amount of learning capacity in common with him. If man's aggressive behavior seems to resemble that of lower animals, one cannot be sure whether the similarity is due to common instincts or to com-mon products of experience. We know for a fact that most mammals can be taught to fight or not to fight under quite varied conditions. They differ from man mainly in the limits of what they can learn and the speed with which learning takes place. Man's learning ability is so much greater than that of any other animal that it would be surprising if he had not outstripped them in devising techniques for inflicting punishment on others when it suits his needs to do so. Men not only learn when it is best to fight or not to fight, whom to fight and whom to appease, how to fight and how not to; but they also learn whom, when, and how to hate. The roots of aggressive war are more likely to be found by the study of what humans *learn* than by a study of what animals *do*. However, much can be found out concerning the basic principles of learn-ing from studies of the conditions and the extent to which various species of animals *can be taught* to be aggressive or submissive as individuals or in groups.

It is not the purpose here to present a catalogue of social habits and atti-tudes that are involved in antagonistic and peaceful human relations. As illus-trations, four types of social learning have been selected which seem to figure prominently in war and peace. They are learning to hate and to fight, to fear and to escape, to love and to defend, and to follow leaders. An effort will be made to show how these social habits and attitudes are acquired under the conditions provided by our society and how they are mobilized in times of war.

WAR REQUIRES NEW LEARNING

Modern total warfare requires not only the assembly and reorganization of existing skills and motives but also the achievement of many new ones. War presents new problems and new dilemmas. It often happens that old ways are unsuited to the problems and new methods must be found. This is partially true of military tactics. It has already been proved that the tactics which won the last war will not win this one. People who can easily throw off old habits and quickly acquire new ones have a great advantage in modern warfare. Modern weapons such as airplanes and tanks require the development of new military skills. These are superimposed on existing skills of driving automobiles and handling machinery but go far beyond to new heights of technical competence.

Civilians as well as soldiers are required to learn new habits and abandon old ones. Workers in defense industries must learn to change their work–play–sleep habits. Most people in our society have acquired habits of work, play, sleep, in that order. Social institutions in which these function are organized to maintain this sequence. But in wartime these institutions change so that individuals who are on a shift which runs from 3:00 P.M. to midnight cannot very well play after they have quit work for the reason that the nation is not organized for play between the hours of midnight and 6:00 A.M. This is, of course, but one of many instances in which new learning is required.

LEARNING REQUIRES MOTIVATION

One of the first conditions of learning is that the individual must want something which he does not have or want to rid himself of something which he does have. When in want or in need, humans and animals act. Some wants and needs are innate and are called primary drives. Among these are hunger, thirst, sex, extreme heat and cold, fatigue, and pain. Others are acquired and are called secondary drives. Among these are the appetites and aversions; likes and dislikes; the craving for money, prestige, fame, and honor. The secondary drives which figure most prominently in war are hatred, anxiety, love for country, sense of duty, and craving for leadership. These are based on habits which we shall call love habits, hate habits, fear habits, duty habits, and so on. The strength of an acquired drive depends on the strength of the habits on which it is based. The emotions of patriotism, for example, are based on habits of love for country. The degree of patriotic fervor that an individual is capable of experiencing in a national crisis depends in part on how well he has learned to love his country and also on how quickly he can acquire such habits in war-

time. In like manner, the degree of hatred that an individual is capable of feeling toward the enemy depends on the strength of his existing habits of hatred
toward people who are called enemies.

Learning takes place when an individual is acting under the compulsion of
a drive and when no one of his existing habits will fulfill his needs or satisfy
his wants. He is thus forced to try out new modes of response. If he finds a
satisfactory solution to his problem, that act or series of acts is reinforced. On
future occasions and under similar circumstances he will repeat these acts.
They are learned because they were successful and satisfying. . . .

The bare essentials of the process are drive, cue, response, and reward.
Miller and Dollard have summed it up by saying that, in order to learn, "one
must *want* something, *notice* something, *do* something and *get* something." [2]

HABITS OF PEACE USED IN WAR

Most of the attitudes, skills, and knowledge which are assembled for war
were learned for peaceful purposes. Conversely, many of the new habits
acquired for fighting a war are useful later in peace pursuits. It would be a
mistake to assume that war and peace demand habits that stand in opposition
to each other. Many of the habits and attitudes of peace and defense can be
used for offense. For example, most people learn to fear and to hate gangsters
and criminals. These attitudes stand ready for application to outside enemies
who appear in the role of criminals. Were it not for the fact that many of the
skills and attitudes acquired for peace may be used for war also, nations
which do not deliberately educate for war would be tremendously handicapped
in times of national crisis. It is bad enough to be caught without an adequate
armed force, but it would be infinitely worse to be wanting in basic skills and
social attitudes.

Learning to fight and to hate involves much more than learning to box, to
duel, or to participate in other forms of ingroup violence. Systematic education for aggressive warfare in ancient Sparta or in modern Germany includes,
besides physical education in games and contests, universal compulsory military training; the inculcation of certain attitudes, prejudices, beliefs; and
devotion to leaders and ideals. The whole purpose and direction of such education is toward group aggression.

THE HABIT OF AGGRESSION

Aggressive mass movements may be understood in terms of how people
with certain habits, attitudes, beliefs, and expectations react to changes in their

2 Neal E. Miller and John Dollard, *Social Learning and Imitation* (New Haven: Yale
University Press, 1941), p. 2.

social environment. Individuals who have been accustomed to expect a high standard of living, efficiency from government and its leaders, a measure of economic security and social prestige, are more frustrated when deprived of these things than are those who have never enjoyed them. One of the psychological conditions which favors group aggression is a wide gap between levels of achievement and those of aspiration. A group that has relatively little and wants much will employ aggression as a means to the achievement of its ends provided its members have learned that aggression pays. On the other hand, if a group has learned that aggression does not pay, at least in the type of situation that is confronting it, some other technique for achieving its ends will be employed or the ends will be renounced.

An aggressive social group is not necessarily one whose members are aggressive toward each other. Indeed, the opposite is more likely to be the case. Most groups place a heavy taboo on ingroup aggression, whereby assaults on each other are punishable by law. It is quite possible, therefore, for individuals to acquire habits of peaceful living with each other and at the same time be very warlike in their relations with outgroups. It is easier to follow a general rule such as "do not attack any other individual or group unless you are threatened or attacked first." Such a rule applies equally well to behavior between members of a group and between one group and another. It is a rule which most individuals in modern civilized societies have learned. It explains why it is that, in modern times at least, aggressor nations justify their behavior on the ground of self-defense.

CREATING CONDITIONS FOR LEARNING PEACEFUL LIVING

. . . The history of civilization plainly shows that the evolution of peace has been a slow process of social learning. The family is supposed to be the first and oldest peace group. For purposes of defense and for the promotion of other mutual interests, two or more families joined and became a clan, clans united into tribes, tribes into nations, and some nations have been forged into empires. The typical modern peace group is, of course, the independent state or nation. States, however, sometimes form alliances and maintain friendly relations for long periods of time, thereby becoming an effective peace group.

In order for a peace group to be created, man must first discover that the net gains and mutual benefits from living together in organized groups are greater than those to be derived from a solitary existence. This discovery was made long ago in respect to the family, clan, tribe, city, and nation. It is yet a matter of debate whether the formation of larger international peace groups would result in greater mutual benefits to all who might be included in them.

The development of a peace group requires more than the mere discovery that life in organized society is preferable to that of a hermit. There must be a pattern of social organization and rules of human relations which guarantee insofar as possible that all members of a group may reap the maximum benefits from social interaction with each other and with other groups. By definition a peace group is one in which there is the minimum amount of physical violence among the members. Antagonisms, hostilities, and conflicts are held in check by customs, laws, and rules which are enforced in part by duly constituted authorities and in part by inner compulsions of loyalties and the sense of social responsibility. Peace between groups as well as within a group is maintained by the joint action of external authority and social attitudes of tolerance and good will.

The maintenance of peaceful relations by inner authority is much preferred to that of external force provided, of course, that conscience is on the side of law and order, which is usually the case. The process of socialization of children and the induction of new adult members into a group is mainly a matter of the inculcation of habits, attitudes, and loyalties which reflect the customs, ideals, beliefs, and laws of the group. There is ordinarily a close parallel between the external authority of a group and the inner controls of conduct.

Peace groups expand by natural increases in population, by voluntary combinations of groups, and by conquest. Except in cases of slavery, new recruits may become participant members and gain the status of citizens by observing the rules of conduct and by acquiring a set of habits and attitudes that is consistent with the ways of life of the group. The expansion of a peace group is therefore not merely a matter of adding new members but of educating them in the culture of the group. It is education in the broad sense of social conditioning, which is the central process by means of which a group grows and at the same time maintains a historical continuity.

To those who look forward to the ultimate union of all people in one large peace group, it must be said that this goal can be approached only as fast as the conditions are provided for learning loyalties and responsibilities to larger and larger groups. It is, of course, possible for an individual to acquire tolerance, good will, and even a sense of responsibility toward members of other nations. Such education is undoubtedly favorable to the maintenance of peace between groups that are politically and culturally independent of each other. But intercultural education can be carried further and made much more effective *after* the groups concerned have been amalgamated into a single political unit. As each individual becomes aware of membership in a larger group and conscious of the benefits of such membership, he will tend to identify more and more with other members as friends, comrades, and fellow citizens.

The most effective education for citizenship in a larger political unit cannot occur until the unit has first been created. The initial step by which sovereign states may be united into larger political units is by far the most difficult one.

Historically it has been achieved in many ways, one of which is by conquest. There are, however, instances in which groups have voluntarily come together to form a larger and better union. The motives back of such moves are usually the powerful ones of desire for greater security against invasion or the achievement of mutual economic benefits that are obvious to all. Powerful motivations are required to overcome resistances which stem from unwillingness to recognize the possibilities of higher taxes, lower standards of living, or the reluctance to change allegiances and loyalties, and from the ever-present inertia to change. Many people stubbornly refuse to adopt a new invention or to accept a social reform, especially if, by so doing, they are required to change their habits. The public resistance to the adoption of a calendar better suited to modern life is a case in point. There is considerable concern at the moment as to how the peoples of the earth may be convinced of the importance of creating larger peace groups after this war [World War II]. It is hoped that the forces of education and enlightenment are working in the direction of persuading people to try as an experiment some plan of international relations that at least holds promise of preventing future wars.

It often happens that people learn to accept and enjoy new arrangements that had previously appeared undesirable. Daylight saving time is an example. When it was instituted as an emergency measure during World War I, there was considerable doubt about it and some outspoken opposition to it. But many people learned to like it, particularly city dwellers who continued it during the summer months in the years that followed the war. Farmers, however, still opposed it. It remains to be seen whether they, too, will learn to like it during this war. Vaccination against smallpox is another illustration. Gradually and over a considerable period of time, people have learned of its benefits and are more and more inclined to accept it voluntarily. Some even demand it for themselves and their children. Once the conditions for learning a new technique or way of life have been created, the forces of habit and education can do their work. They may work for or against the new plan depending on the net satisfactions that are derived from it.

This raises a question for those who will plan the peace to follow this war. How much weight should be given to the immediate acceptability of a plan by those who are to live under it and how much to possibilities that a more ideal plan might become acceptable if given a fair trial? There is danger that something less than a plan that might eventually win acceptance for itself will be instituted on the ground that immediate acceptability is the most important consideration. It is hoped that the possibilities of education will be fully considered and that a plan will be adopted that provides for its own improvement as experience with it reveals its strength and weakness. . . .

EDWARD C. TOLMAN

Drives toward War*

We turn, now, to a further consideration of the channels laid down by learn-ing and the psychological dynamisms through which the energy from the biological drives becomes converted into the social techniques and ultimately into various types of final behavior. The biological drives are fundamental and subserved by the social techniques. When, therefore, these drives are frus-trated—when, that is, there is some shortage of or interference with their direct biological goals, such as food, sex, water, caresses, toys, etc.—the social tech-niques as ways of overcoming such shortages (or interferences) are resorted to. And it is the processes of learning and of the dynamisms which act in these instances as channels to steer (or convert) the energy from the frustrated

* Reprinted from Edward C. Tolman, *Drives toward War*, chaps. 5–6 by permission of the publisher (Copyright 1942, D. Appleton-Century-Crofts, Inc., New York). The editors also gratefully acknowledge the permission of the *Journal of Mammalogy* to reprint the quotation from "The Self-Mutilation of a Male *Macacus Rhesus* Monkey," by Otto L. Tinklepaugh, IX (1928); the permission of the *Journal of Comparative Physiological Psy-chology* to reprint the quotation from "Sexual Behavior of Free Ranging Rhesus Monkeys (*Macaca mulatta*)," by C. R. Carpenter, XXXIII (1942); the permission of Harper and Brothers and the author to reprint the quotation from *Public Opinion and the Individual* by Gardner Murphy and Rensis Likert (New York: Harper & Bros., 1938); the permission of the *Journal of Genetic Psychology*, XLIX (1936), 192, to reprint the quotation by Abraham H. Maslow; and the permission of the Yale University Press to reprint the quotation from *Becoming a Kwoma* by John W. M. Whiting (New Haven: Yale University Press, 1941).

drives into the particular techniques and resultant behaviors. Figure 1 indicates in diagrammatic form those varieties of these conversion [1] channels which are of principal interest to us in our discussion of the determiners of war.

The biological drives are seen at the top of the figure. They provide all the basic energy. When frustrated, they are shown as giving rise, first, though the

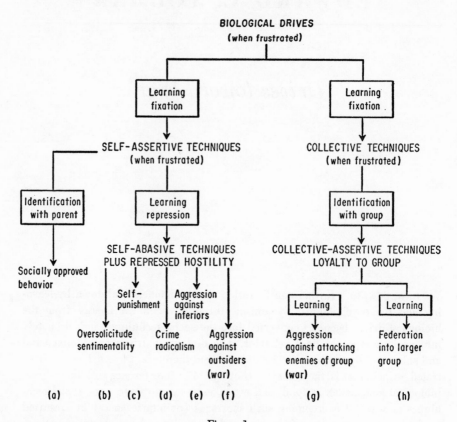

Figure 1

processes of learning and fixation (as indicated by the arrows) either to the self-assertive techniques, on the one hand, or to the collective techniques, on the other. Thus the individual may learn, in a trial-and-error, instrumental fashion, that to be self-assertive is a successful method for getting more of a limited (or interfered with) supply of a biological goal such as food, sex, water, toys, etc., or he may learn that group-collective behavior is a still

[1] It should be noted that the term "conversion" is not used here in the strictly psycho-analytical sense. In strict Freudian terminology "conversion" means the transformation of the energy of the libido primarily into bodily symptoms, such, for example, as a limb paraly-sis or a sensory anesthesia. We are using the word in a broader sense.

more successful technique. Or he may learn to adopt sometimes the one type of technique and sometimes the other, depending upon the particular environmental circumstances.[2]

And the dynamism of fixation may also operate in the sense that, after learning in the given setup has once taken place, then the learned self-assertive or collective techniques may become unduly fixated so that the individual persists in them even in situations in which they are no longer useful. Thus we get an individual who will persist in being self-assertive even though he no longer achieves anything by it or one who persists in trying to be collective although the others in the group have ceased to cooperate and have begun to "do him dirt."

As to which of the two main techniques—the self-assertive or the collective —is generally the more useful, it may be suggested (in passing) that under the conditions of modern technology, in which an economy of scarcity is being replaced by one of abundance, the collective techniques are becoming ever more necessary and probably need special encouragement. And it appears as if (given our culture to date) the collective techniques were relatively the more difficult to acquire. In other words, either as a result of our culture or of our heredity, most men, as we now know them in Western civilization, seem to have a stronger propensity to be self-assertive than to be collective. Collectivity in us is a tender flower that needs special watering.

Look, now, further down on the left of the diagram. Let us consider, in short, the case of an individual, a child, who has adopted self-assertive techniques. He has become bumptious and demanding. Let us assume, further, that the parent or other adult has had enough and has clamped down on this self-assertive bumptiousness. The child's self-assertion is, in short, frustrated. What, then, will happen? There are a number of alternatives.

One thing the child can do is to "identify" with the parent or other adult (see extreme left of Figure 1). This will then direct his self-assertion into socially approved attacks upon relatively objective problems. Taking as his model the parent (or other adult), he does the sort of thing which they and others approve. This seems a relatively ideal outcome as far as mental health in the individual and the stability of the society are concerned.

Such identification is not always achieved, however. That is, instead of producing identification, the reproofs and admonitions of the parent may lead through learning and repression to the appearance of self-abasive techniques. The individual discovers (learns) that by being self-abasive he reduces the punishment meted out to him by the parent or other more dominant individual. He learns that self-abasement is a way of avoiding the direct biological sufferances which come from punishments and reproofs and that it is also a technique for achieving some few direct crumbs from his master's

[2] Also it is supposed that his relative readiness for the one type of technique or the other may be in part determined also by hereditary predispositions as well as by learning.

table. It is to be emphasized further, however, that the individual becomes thus self-abasive only at the cost of accompanying repression. He dams up and represses his hostility against his parents or the other more dominant individuals. And this repressed hostility then tends to come out later in a variety of indirect ways. In Figure 1 five such indirect ways—(b), (c), (d), (e), and (f)—with their resultant final behaviors have been indicated along the bottom.

Each of these different alternative outcomes is brought about, however, through its own relatively special dynamisms or set of dynamisms, and in Figure 2 we have expanded this portion of our diagram to indicate these respective dynamisms.

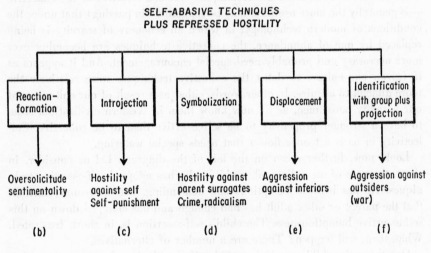

Figure 2

First (see left of Figure 2), the dynamism of reaction-formation may come into play. That is, the repressed aggressions may express themselves as a neurotic sort of compulsion for just the reverse sort of behavior. Instead of being aggressive, the individual becomes overtly oversolicitous or generally sentimental. A pacifist or a worker for the prevention of cruelty to animals is undoubtedly impelled in some part by such converted aggressions. Because of his dammed-up repressed hostilities, the individual becomes oversolicitous and tender.

The dynamism of introjection may also operate. In this case, the hostility against the parent may, through the dynamism of introjection, be converted and turned back into hostility against the self. The individual goes in for self-punishment. Instances of self-punishment have been observed even in monkeys. Let me cite two examples.

The first is found in a series of observations made by O. L. Tinklepaugh in the University of California laboratory. He describes the case of a young male (*Macacus rhesus*) monkey, Cupid, who had lived from the age of six months to that of about three years with an older female, Psyche, of a somewhat different species. Cupid developed a strong sexual attachment to Psyche. After, however, some two and a half years of their being together, the experimenter sought to "condition" Cupid to a new younger female, Topsy, of Cupid's own immediate species. At first he was extremely hostile and would attack Topsy violently whenever she was put into his cage. It was only after several weeks of having them live in adjoining cages and taking them out for walks side by side on two leashes that Cupid finally ceased his attacks upon Topsy and initiated sexual responses instead. The two were then left together for five days. After this five-day period Topsy was removed, and Psyche returned to Cupid's cage for two weeks. He apparently readjusted to Psyche without difficulty. When these two weeks were up, Psyche was again removed and Topsy reintroduced. I quote from the author's own account:

> Cupid mounted Topsy and was about to copulate with her, when he jumped away from her and began biting his hind feet much as he had formerly done in play. This behavior was noted several times during the first three days the two monkeys were reunited. On none of these occasions was Cupid seen to complete the sex act. On the fourth day he was discovered with his hind feet rather badly lacerated. To facilitate examination . . . he was led from his cage by the doorway leading into the area between it and the nearby cage now containing Psyche and Eva [another young female]. . . . Psyche, who had seemed to be much upset by Topsy's presence in Cupid's cage, was now on the side of her cage shrieking threateningly. . . . Suddenly, and with no previous signs of anger or particular emotion, Cupid lurched to the end of his chain and began to bite himself. In a few seconds he tore huge jagged rents in his already lacerated legs. . . . In all there were twenty . . . lacerations in his body, and of that number only one was in close proximity to his genitals.[3]

The second example of what looks like similar self-punishment in a monkey is to be found in a brief note by C. R. Carpenter. He writes:

> A large, vicious adult male Macaque (unknown species) observed in Chiengmai, Thailand, had developed a kind of stereotyped *masochistic* response. The animal has been raised from infancy in captivity and, when observed, was heavily chained. He was beaten when he showed signs of attacking his keepers. When approached closely or threatened, he would clinch his left hind foot with his hands and then bite it vigorously as if

---

[3] O. L. Tinklepaugh, "The Self-Mutilation of a Male *Macacus Rhesus* Monkey," *Journal of Mammalogy*, IX (1928), 298.

to tear it in shreds as an expression of frustrated aggression. Although the foot was swollen, the skin was not broken.[4]

Now, whether or not such cases are true instances of self-punishment in monkeys, it is certainly true that human beings go in for self-punishment. Karl A. Menninger has collected a surprising number of examples from the daily news and still more, of course, from the clinic.[5] Suicides, neurotic invalidism, alcoholism, many types of accidents, and so on all often turn out to be expressions of an unconscious need for self-punishment. And this self-castigation seems to be one of the ways in which the early repressed hostility against the parents may come (through introjection) to express itself.[6]

Still a third way in which, in the case of self-abasement, the dammed-up hostility against parent or adult or some other more dominant individual may express itself is through being converted by the dynamism of symbolization into hostility against symbolic surrogates for parent or other frustrating agent.

Two typical expressions of this hostility against parent surrogates seem to be crime and radicalism. Psychoanalytical studies of some twenty young male criminals carried out by Franz Alexander and William Healy showed that a large amount of their criminal behavior was an unconscious "taking it out" on society where society was a symbolic surrogate for the parents, who the individual felt had been especially cruel and unfair to him in childhood.[7] And a questionnaire study of adult criminals by Ruth Tolman also indicated that to a surprising degree these adult criminals even consciously tended to identify society with the father and in attacking society felt that they were "getting even" with their fathers.[8]

Radicalism, also, is probably to a considerable extent an expression of the early hostility against the parents. This is not, of course, the whole story. In the modern world between World War I and World War II, in which a general disillusionment reigned, merely to be literate has meant among the young to be radical. Let me quote in this connection the pertinent remarks of Gardner Murphy and Rensis Likert:

[4] C. R. Carpenter, "Sexual Behavior of Free Ranging Rhesus Monkeys (*Macaca mulatta*)," *Journal of Comparative Psychology*, XXXIII (1942), 153.

[5] Karl A. Menninger, *Man against Himself* (New York: Harcourt Brace & Co., 1938).

[6] Freud was so impressed by this destructiveness against the self that he made it primary and called it the death instinct. Aggression against others was for him a secondary phenomenon in which the death instinct—normally directed against the self—became reoriented outward against others. The present writer, on the other hand, is assuming that aggression, hostility, destructiveness, or whatever one wants to call it, is normally evoked by outer frustrating agents and only indirectly and somewhat abnormally becomes introjected and directed against the self.

[7] Franz Alexander and William Healy, *Roots of Crime* (New York: Alfred A. Knopf, 1935).

[8] R. S. Tolman, "Differences between Two Groups of Adult Criminals," *Genetic Psychology Monographs*, XX, No. 3 (1938).

Why, then, is the bookish man more radical? The answer lies in the study of the modern temper. The whole whirl of the first third of the twentieth century is definitely a radical whirl, and this is particularly true of the post-war period. To be bookish in this era has meant to steep one-self in the disillusioned gropings of post-war thinkers, most of whom, from philosophers to lyricists, are clearly "radical" in the everyday sense of striving to find a new base for the relations between men. One might theoretically be bookish and take it out in reading Homer or Thomas Aquinas; but anyone in contact with modern students knows that they have done no such thing. To be ignorant of Homer among such men is unfortunate, but it is merely a venial sin; to be found ignorant of Shaw or O'Neill or Dos Passos is a mortal sin, which immediately removes one from the number of the truly literate. The literary groups to which these men belong, the day-by-day conversations in which they train one another to think and to feel, are full of the modern doubt and disquietude, and, even more frequently, of the modern challenge and rebellion. To be bookish today is to be radical. . . .

This is our theory, and it is nothing more; but it is supported by many straws of evidence.[9]

In contrast, however, to this statement by Murphy and Likert we do find in the life history of such an earlier radical as Emma Goldman an explicit sug-gestion that her own radicalism was a protest against the cruelties which had been meted out to her in her childhood.[10]

Again, it would appear that dammed-up hostility against the frustrating parents or other superior individuals may also find expression by means of the dynamism of displacement in the form of hostility, or aggression, against inferiors. A. H. Maslow reports this sort of outlet in monkeys. He studied care-fully a group of six. As a result of pairing each monkey with every other, he learned the dominant status of each in relation to all the others. Then he observed what happened when groups of three were formed. I quote:

(1) Punishment is handed down. When the overlord asserts dominance over his immediate inferior in any way, this latter animal is impelled to assert dominance over *his* inferior by bullying, mounting, etc. (2) The middle animal (C) is made more pugnacious generally with respect to the subordinate animal (K) by the introduction of an overlord (R), even though he (C) was not very pugnacious when alone with K. (3) The middle animal seems to tend to ally himself with the overlord, and seems to prefer his company to that of his inferior. They tend to form a contact

[9] Gardner Murphy and Rensis Likert, *Public Opinion and the Individual* (New York: Harper & Bros., 1938), pp. 107–108. Reprinted by permission.
[10] Emma Goldman, *Living My Life* (New York: Alfred A. Knopf, 1931), I, especially 58–61, 66–69.

group and act to some extent as a unit. (4) The middle animal, rather than the overlord, tends to initiate the bullying of and fighting with the subordinate animal, even though the overlord may join in. (5) If one animal attacks another, the outsider will join with the attacker rather than with the attacked animal. (6) All these considerations seem to justify calling the subordinate animal the "scapegoat animal."

The anomalous middle position thus takes on a certain character of its own. While we should not anthropomorphize about the motivation of this behavior, we can at least point out that the net result of all these activities is (1) to protect the middle animal from the aggression of the overlord, and (2) to allow him to keep the highest possible dominance status.[11]

Such hierarchies in which "middle" individuals "take" it from their superiors but "hand it down" to their inferiors is, of course, characteristic of the fascist setups, and of the relations between the poor whites and the Negroes in our own South.

Finally, the dammed-up hostility against the parent or superior may, through the dynamisms of identification with the group and of projection onto others, be converted primarily into hostile behavior toward outsiders, with the accompanying feeling (due to the projection) that it is the latter, the outsiders, who are the really guilty ones. This is the setup in what I would call "neurotically motivated war." The evidence for such neurotic components in the prosecution of a war is, I believe, all around us. We observe it in our friends and in ourselves as well as most definitely in the Nazis and the Japanese. But as more objective, less prejudiced evidence, let me cite a recent anthropological account. J. W. M. Whiting, in his book *Becoming a Kwoma* (a New Guinea tribe), describes a pretty instance:

One day War and Kar were working on this garden [a jointly owned one] with their wives. War returned to the hamlet. . . . He gave his own wife orders to weed a certain portion of the garden before he returned the next afternoon. When he returned he found the work not yet done. He asked his wife for an explanation, and she said that she had been possessed by a ghost the night before. . . . Kar's wife said that this was not the explanation at all. The real reason why the work was undone, she said, was that the woman had spent the morning in the bushes with Kar. War became furious at this, knocked his wife down with his fist, and threatened to spear his brother Kar. . . . War's wife . . . returned in a fury to the hamlet, packed her things, took her young daughter by the hand and left before War returned. . . . When War returned that evening and found his wife gone, he was even more angry than before. . . . The next day

11 A. H. Maslow, *Journal of Genetic Psychology*, XLIX (1936), 192.

he traced her to Yelagu, a neighboring tribe. . . . He took three spears and set out alone to bring back his runaway wife. Someone warned the Yelagu that he was coming, so that when he arrived there was only a cripple left in the village. War demanded where his wife had gone, but the cripple either could not or would not tell him and offered him a dog and some shell money if War would spare his life. War demanded more money, took it and the dog, and returned home.

The next evening War called his friends together. He distributed the dog meat among them, told them what had happened, and suggested that they go on a head-hunting raid against the Yelagu. He argued that it was a very small tribe and that they were all cowards. . . . Most of those present thought that it was a good idea, but several objected on the grounds that Yelagu was too near Ambunti, the government post. . . . They said that it would be much safer to attack Sowal, a tribe far in the swamp. . . .

For two weeks there was a great deal of discussion. . . . The other men of the tribe, meanwhile, had been swayed by the argument that there was considerable danger of punishment from the whites if Yelagu were attacked, whereas Sowal involved much less danger. It was also reported that high water had driven the Sowal out of their central village, and that they were living on knolls in small isolated groups that would be particularly vulnerable. The pressure of these arguments finally forced War to give up his idea of attacking Yelagu, and he threw his weight into planning for the Sowal raid. . . .

War and some of the older men of the hamlet began to incite the young men to go on the raid. He told them that this was their chance to become big men. . . .

Finally, all the men of the subtribe and some from neighboring tribes met one night at the house tamberan near War's house. . . . It was decided to send a scout ahead to discover the lay of the land. . . .

The next day the scout returned to say that the road to Sowal was impassable. The water was so high that it was impossible to walk there, but it was not high enough to go with a canoe. The raid was therefore called off. I think that if it had not been for many who . . . feared punishment from the whites, a way would have been found and the raid carried out.[12]

This account illustrates neatly the fact that an originally private and direct frustration of the individual "War" and of the younger men who had not yet taken a head came to be drained off into a general hostility against a quite

[12] J. W. M. Whiting, *Becoming a Kwoma* (New Haven: Yale University Press, 1941), pp. 165 ff.

innocent outside tribe, the Sowal. If War and the others had actually carried through their attack upon the Sowal, it would have been a beautiful case of what I would call a neurotically motivated war.

So much for suggestions as to some of the ways in which the hostilities consequent upon frustration of self-assertion may come out. The analysis is not to be conceived of as being by any means final or complete. There are undoubtedly still other ways in which aggressions may express themselves and the different alternatives shown are not to be thought of as mutually exclusive. Further, the indication as to which dynamism or dynamisms plays the more important role in any case is largely a matter of emphasis. All might be called cases of displacement, and symbolization is also undoubtedly involved in all and not merely in crime and radicalism.

Let us return now to our earlier Figure 1. We see there that the original frustration of the biological drives may result not only in self-assertive techniques, but also in collective techniques. And we see also that, when the collective techniques are frustrated by an attack from the outside upon any of the individuals in the group, then through the dynamism of identification with the group there results the group-assertive technique or loyalty to the group; and this, we now note further, may result in either (g) an attack upon the enemies of the group or (h) an attempt to federate with opposition groups into some still larger whole. Let us consider each of these alternatives further.

The collective-assertive technique or loyalty to the group may be converted, through instrumental learning, into aggression against the attacking outside group. That is, the members of the given group proceed to repel by battle actual or threatened aggressions from outsiders. This was the behavior of Köhler's chimpanzees who, as we remember, rushed to attack Köhler himself with howls of "moral indignation" when he sought to punish any one of them. In their case, this resulting behavior would seem to have been mediated primarily by instinct (that is, by heredity). But, in the case of human beings, learning presumably plays the major part. Hence, when today the united nations go to war and attempt to counterattack Germany and Japan, this war is, we believe, more a result of the reasonable processes of learning than of mere neuroticism. It is due to the fact that Germany and Japan really *are* attacking us.

It would appear further, however, that group loyalty (that is, the need to preserve the communal life of the group) ought through still additional learning to lead human beings not just to lie back (as has been done since [World War I]) and to wait until they are again attacked or threatened by attack and then to go to battle. Instead, such learning ought to teach them to seek to federate with the various opposing groups before mutual aggressions can again get started. If Germany during the 1920's, when she was really trying to be democratic, had been backed by Britain and France in the League of Nations and if we in the United States had also done our share by joining the

League, then the present debacle [World War II] would most probably have been avoided. We can see how foolish and mutually destructive it is for the tiny Balkan powers to be constantly seeking to attack one another, and we ought to be able to learn that the same thing is equally foolish for the great powers. A war in response to outside aggression does tend to preserve in some measure the communal life of a nation (if God and oil be on her side), but only in some measure. The accompanying losses are today obviously all too great. But forestalling such wars by having previously federated with the opposing groups will preserve the communal life of both groups *in toto*. The simple facts of international living and psychology must sooner or later teach us this.

We have surveyed now all the drive conversions represented in the figure. They constitute, I believe, all the important possibilities which are of particular interest for characterizing different societies and for suggesting the possibilities for a future, less warlike world.

I

. . . Since the beginning of Christianity, Western Europe has been dominated by a series of some four myths as to the nature of man (Drucker's thesis). Each myth consisted in the belief that certain ones only of man's needs were important. If these really important needs could but be satisfied, then universal individual welfare and happiness would, it was believed, result. These myths were, according to Drucker, successively those of spiritual man, of intellectual man, of economic man, and of heroic man. But each of these myths can now be better understood and defined in terms of the drive-conversion diagram just presented in the preceding section.

The myth of spiritual man, which reigned during early Christianity and the Middle Ages, was, it would now appear, the belief that, whereas both the biological drives and the self-assertive techniques are relatively unimportant and may be neglected, the needs of self-abasement and collectivity are essential and basic. The devout Christian sought to humble himself before God and man (self-abasement), to love his neighbor as himself (collectivity), and to deny the flesh (that is, to crucify his biological drives). Actually a considerable number of men in the Middle Ages did, no doubt, succeed in achieving just such patterns of need satisfaction and need denial. But those individuals were probably always in a minority. Medieval society in general certainly never lived up to any such ideal. The Christian princes were far from humble, and so likewise, I believe, were all save their meanest followers. And the few who did succeed in achieving self-abasement and continuous biological sufferances did so only at the cost of tremendous repression. It was the repressed aggressions of the medieval *religieux* which came out, we can now see, in variegated and elaborate forms of self-punishment, in the torture of heretics, and in the aiding and abetting of wars between the temporal powers.

Indeed, as regards war, Christianity seems always to have been particularly unsuccessful in remaining true to its ideals. For, whenever within the Western world a political unity within which group identification has taken place has been threatened (or has felt itself threatened) by outside groups, then the ministers of the gospel, like their communicants, have rushed to preach war and vengeance, not peace and forgiveness. God has ceased overnight to be the all-loving Father who on earth counseled the turning of the other cheek and has become instead a mere tribal deity preaching pillage, murder, and death by bombing.

Next, during the Renaissance, came the myth of intellectual man. This myth, considered in terms of our need-conversion scheme, seems to have asserted the primary importance of but two of the biological drives—the general exploratory (or curiosity) drive and the aesthetic drive. The Renaissance became, that is, tremendously excited about the nature of the world and about art. But in addition, this myth of intellectual man preached the importance of the techniques of self-assertion and minimized those of self-abasement and collectivity. And, finally, it also minimized the importance of any general satisfactions for the masses. The lordly ones of the Renaissance advanced tremendously the intellectual and aesthetic interests of the elite, but they did not produce a society in which their jealousies could be adjudicated, nor did they satisfy the needs of the common people (save, perhaps, aesthetically). They achieved no adequate and general distribution of food and clothing.

Following the Renaissance, as a result of the mercantile and industrial revolutions, there came the myth of economic man. This was the reacknowledgment (the first since pagan days) of the fundamental importance of the biological drives and of the desirability and necessity of their widespread satisfaction. The rising middle classes demanded wealth (that is, biological satisfactions). And their myth of economic man emphasized the self-assertive techniques as the primary way for getting such wealth. The notions of private initiative and *laissez faire* came to the fore. The self-assertive techniques were emphasized at the expense of the collective ones. During the last century, however, there has developed a second subvariety of this myth of economic man— the socialistic one. This socialistic myth declares that the collective techniques (rather than the self-assertive) are the way to achieve the biological satisfactions and that not the middle classes but the proletariat is to take the lead. For the proletariat (so it is assumed) is collective-minded as the bourgeoisie is not. It is a collectivistic rather than a self-assertive economic man which is to be preached and worked for.

Finally, in the fascist countries, there has arisen what Drucker calls the myth of heroic man. This myth puts especial emphasis upon collectivity and upon the collective-assertive techniques (group loyalty). It combines these with simultaneous emphases upon self-assertion and self-abasement—hitched together in tandem fashion. That is, the leaders are to be self-assertive and the followers self-abasive. Finally, the importance of any widespread satisfaction of the biological drives is denied. Erich Fromm, analyzing the situation in Nazi Germany today [1942], describes the resultant personality structure as "authoritarian." [13] Heroic (or authoritarian) man "takes it" from his superiors and "hands it down" to his inferiors. And those at the bottom of this hierarchy are provided with scapegoats in the form of Jews and foreigners. The total result is a closely knit group of fundamentally sadistic-masochistic personalities bound together by intense group loyalty and by common aggressions against "outsiders."

Drucker confined his analysis to Western Europe. In the light of recent events, however, we can now hardly leave out Japan. What, then, is the myth of present-day Japan? It seems to me that it is very close to this same myth of heroic or authoritarian man which today governs Nazi Germany. Again, there is tremendous emphasis upon collectivity. And there is also tremendous self-abasement and repression of aggression. These latter, however, come out more in the form of self-punishment, as indicated by the prevalence of suicides. But the excesses of the Japanese soldiers in China do suggest that there is also a need, just as in Nazi Germany, for letting out some of the dammed-up aggressions in barbarities against outsiders.

What, now, as to the future? Spiritual man, intellectual man, the two subforms of economic man, and heroic man all have failed to bring the desired welfare and happiness of all individuals. The world is suffering as never before. What then can we hope for? My answer is that, if we can but combine the emphasis upon the biological drives with a moderate amount of self-assertion and a large amount of collectivity and add to this easy identification with parents, we shall arrive at a new and this time truly workable myth—a myth that in reality would save the world from its horrors. I shall call this the myth of the "psychologically adjusted man." That is, referring again to our drive-conversion scheme, my doctrine would be that a truly stable and happy society would be brought about, if we could but embody in that society the following six prescriptive principles:

(1) The biological needs are basic and must be satisfied in all individuals.

(2) Both the self-assertive techniques and the collective techniques are instrumentally useful means toward the biological satisfactions, and both are to be accepted as equally appropriate and necessary types of activity.

(3) The self-abasive techniques, because of their accompanying repressed hostilities, which then tend to come out in individually and

[13] Erich Fromm, *Escape from Freedom* (New York: Farrar & Rinehart, Inc., 1941).

socially disruptive activities, are bad. Self-abasement and accompanying repression are to be reduced to a minimum.

(4) Good identifications with parents or other accepted authorities are, on the other hand, to be encouraged.

(5) Group loyalty (the collective-assertive technique) appears to be something to which human beings, like chimpanzees, are tremendously prone. We probably cannot much diminish or obviate such loyalties. We must try instead to redirect them into more useful and less harmful channels. That is,

(6) Instead of permitting such group loyalties to express themselves primarily in wars between nations, we must redirect them into the mere policing of recalcitrant subgroups and into campaigns against hostile nature.[14]

A society which embodied these six prescriptions would be one which lived according to the myth of psychologically adjusted man. And such a society can tend to be brought about, I would suggest, by the development of three main practical devices:

We must evolve an economic order which will abolish too great biological frustrations.

We must invent an educational and social system which encourages and makes possible easy identification with parents or other acceptable authorities.

We must create a supranational state to which individuals, wherever they may be, can become more loyal than they then will be to their narrower national groups.

Let us consider each of these three devices in more detail.

No Too Great Biological Frustrations

The ultimate and basic needs are, as we have insisted, the biological ones: food, shelter, sex, maternity, nurturance, and all the other biological appetites, plus the aversion needs of security from pain, security from blockings, and security from loneliness. These are the basic demands. Any society which does not permit a large measure of their satisfaction in *all* individuals is *ipso facto* bad. First, and most obviously, it is bad because such nonsatisfactions mean a tremendous load of direct biological suffering. And, second, it is likewise bad because such a society also means that many individuals will be

[14] This last is, of course, essentially the notion long since advocated by William James in his *The Moral Equivalent of War* (*supra*).

driven to become too strongly self-assertive. And, when such overassertiveness is frustrated (as it inevitably will be), not all of the resultant hostility can be drained off into acceptable identifications with parents (or other authorities). Much self-abasement with accompanying repressed hostility is bound to occur. And such repressed hostility will then come out in individually and socially disruptive ways, such as sentimentality, self-punishment, crime, cruelty to inferiors, and neurotically motivated war.

But next, we must ask, just how are such frustrations of the biological drives to be prevented? The answer is clear. What we need is to utilize to the limit the modern techniques of production and to add to them a better system of distribution. This points quite frankly in the direction of more socialism (at least more socialism than we have as yet achieved here in America). But, it will be objected, communism will not work. It requires more collectivity of action than human nature is capable of. "Look at the latest reports from Russia. The Soviets have had to reintroduce differences of reward." Yes, but this does not mean that Soviet Russia is not still far more socialistic than we. In short, the new economic order will, I believe, consist in some sort of a compromise between private initiative (self-assertion), which was the virtue of pure capitalism, and the purely collective techniques which would be the virtue of a pure communism.

Not being an economist, I cannot, of course, attempt to depict the actual details. But I would imagine the final economic system as a set of something like state socialisms in which capital and the means of production would be owned by states but in which differential salaries and wages and some spending of profits on local public works would all be used as incentives for maximum individual effort. Russia today seems to be approaching such a system in her method of managing many of her industries and her collective farms. And I expect she will continue in this direction. I see no reason, however, for her reintroducing inherited wealth. Such unearned wealth seems to be nothing but a device for producing irrational handicaps and head starts. Let us hope, then, that Russia will not backslide into that pitfall. Given equal opportunities for schooling, for health services, and for old-age security, inherited wealth appears meaningless, not to say vicious.

Further, just as we may believe that Russia is already approaching a goal of combined self-assertion and collectivity, moving backward from an extreme communism, I believe that we in the United States (and in Britain) are moving forward from our former extreme individualism toward such a combination or compromise. Both sides are approaching a new myth in which the two subvarieties of the myth of economic man will tend to be combined and reconciled. They are approaching, that is, the new and, as I would hold, more adequate myth of the psychologically adjusted man.

Turn now to our second practical device.

Easy Identification with Parents or Other Authorities

In the postwar Utopia which I am envisaging, it will be particularly important that children shall be able to identify (more easily than they often now can) with parents, or other suitable adults. For they will then be able to drain off such frustrated self-assertion as they still have in socially acceptable ways and will not be driven into the self-abasive techniques. However, the factors which will make such easy identifications are by no means now completely known. But it seems probable that one of the difficulties which in our present highly class-structured societies interferes with such easy identifications is that our different professions and occupational callings are too loaded with prestige values. We today are forever trying to force our children into molds which are appropriate not for their capacities and temperamental traits, but only for satisfying our own social strivings. If we can but arrive at a real psychology of individual differences—whereby we can really measure traits, abilities, and capacities—then we can more intelligently help the child to find its own appropriate models to copy and identify with. Further, in such a Utopia as I am envisaging, farmers, laborers, industrial workers, doctors, lawyers, business executives, and so on would all be living close together and forming integrated social units so that every child would be exposed to all the different adult patterns and could more easily come to pick out or identify with that pattern which most truly expressed his own needs and capacities. In any case, it seems obvious today that the energy of too many of our children goes into trying to be like parents whom they are not like or in trying to be unlike parents whom they are like. The psychologically adjusted man will be one who as child and youth achieves good and appropriate identifications.

Finally, let us turn to our third proposed device, which, from the point of view of the present essay, is the most important.

A Supranational Group with Which to Identify

Collective living as well as individual self-assertion is, as we have seen, a fundamental propensity in human beings. And collective living means not merely internal collaboration within the group but also, because of the individual's tendency to identify with the group, a collective assertion of the group against outsiders. When a group is threatened, the component individuals rush to its defense. They behave like Köhler's chimpanzees. Individuals whose ultimate goals are, or should be, their own biological satisfactions voluntarily rush to the front or send their sons, because their group has been attacked or because they have been led by clever leaders into believing that their group has been so attacked or at least that it has been threatened with an attack. And these identifications with and loyalties to the group go very,

very deep. One has only to observe the reactions of all of us since Pearl Harbor to be convinced how fundamental this process is. The new society living by the myth of psychologically adjusted man will not be able to eliminate group identifications and resultant loyalties.

But how then, we may ask, are such group loyalties to be shorn of their present disastrous consequences? My answer is to declare that, as a result of the previous war and of this war [World War I and World War II], we can now see (that is, we can *learn*) that to federate is an alternative and that it is, in fact, the only really successful method of maintaining group existences. We can see that we must develop a group—a community—which is supranational. It must be something with which individuals everywhere all over the world can be made to identify more strongly than they then will identify with their own narrower national groups. This world federation, or superstate, or whatever we may want to call it, must command all our allegiances more strongly than our national states now do. Just as I am now more loyal to the United States than I am to California, so in the future I must be more loyal to this world federation than I am to the United States. And not only I, but you, and the corner grocer, and the American Legionnaire, and the boys who return from this war, and the capitalist who now hates Russia, and the Russian himself who now scorns the "backward" democracies, and the Chinese, and the Hindus, and the Africans, and the Indonesians, and the Germans, and the Italians, and the Japanese—all, all must then be made to adopt this one greater loyalty. All must feel that they belong to one such greater whole. For, if no such whole be consummated, then we may most certainly expect another and more terrible war when a fresh and unwitting generation shall have been raised to fighting age.

I have no abundant faith that actually we and the others will be intelligent enough and good-willed enough, farsighted enough and unselfish enough, to achieve such a world federation, even though it would be the one security for all of us in our private, individual, most biological and selfish ends. But as a psychologist I feel impelled to suggest certain procedures which, it seems to me, could help to make such a world federation arise and live.

These procedures would consist in all possible devices for emphasizing and making dramatic the one larger world whole and giving each of us a sense of belonging to it—techniques, in short, for leading us all into identifying with this bigger group. First, such a world unit must have an appealing name— perhaps world federation will do. Again, it must have an important and geographically well-located governmental seat. This seat must show up bright and important on the map. And there must be handsome and commanding buildings photographs of which can be in every home. The government itself must have a single head or a small executive council (in addition to a legislative assembly and courts and a secretariat). This executive leader or this council must be such as to serve as father surrogate for individuals all over the world. There must also be an official world language in which all official transactions can take place. This world language, in addition to the mere native tongues, must be taught all over the globe. There must be special classes everywhere for the teaching of it and for the dissemination of world information and for developing patriotism to the world government. The children in these classes must rise and salute their world flag and sing their world anthem as they now rise and salute their national flags and sing their national anthems.

Again, there must be a common enemy or common enemies against whom all the world citizens can unite. For a common enemy brings a group together as nothing else can. Such common enemies will be of two sorts: (a) there will be rebellious subgroups which seek to break away, and (b) there will be the enemies presented by nature, both inanimate and human—disease and corruption, malfeasance and ignorance, tempests and earthquakes. These enemies are everywhere, and the youth in our world federation classes all over the globe must study them without fear or prejudice. They must study not only the problems of the opium trade, of the Hindu caste system, and of race riots in Palestine, but also those of American sharecroppers and of California migratory laborers and of our dispossessed Negroes, both North and South.

And, finally, this world federation must have a world army or police force far surpassing any national armies. This army or force must have its own uniforms and songs and glorious exploits. It must attract adventurous youth from all over the world. And in it such youth must enlist or be drafted on absolutely equal terms. It must be both the symbol and the reality of the one unitary power against which no mere national powers shall dare revolt.

All this, I know, is a Utopian dream. One is almost frightened to put it on paper. And yet, dream or no, it or its like must be enforced by the victors of the present conflict if our children and our children's children are not to rise up and curse us—if the dark night of savagery is not once again to descend upon all of humankind.

◄◄◄ ►►►

GORDON W. ALLPORT

*The Role of Expectancy**

The people of the world—the common people themselves—never make war. They are led into war, they fight wars, and they suffer the consequences, but they do not actually make war. Hence when we say that "wars begin in the minds of men" we can mean only that *under certain circumstances leaders can provoke and organize the people of a nation to fight.* Left alone people themselves could not make war.

Having said this we must hasten to admit that circumstances prevailing today make it tragically easy to fabricate a warlike spirit in the minds of men and to instill in them obedience to war-minded leadership.

The crux of the matter lies in the fact that, while most people deplore war, they nonetheless *expect* it to continue. *And what people expect determines their behavior.*

Expectations are themselves a complex matter, only partially conscious and only partially rational. To change warlike expectations to peaceful expectations requires first a careful analysis of the blend of personal and social factors that determine the anticipations of people in the world today.

* Reprinted from Gordon W. Allport, "The Role of Expectancy," pp. 43–78, in Hedley Cantril, ed., *Tensions That Cause Wars,* by permission of the publisher and author (Copyright 1950, University of Illinois Press, Urbana).

TWO EXTREME VIEWS OF AGGRESSIVE NATIONALISM—
BOTH FALLACIOUS

Among attempts to explain national aggressiveness we find two that because of their extreme one-sidedness are wrong. One errs in finding all cause to lie in the idiosyncrasies of the individual, the other in finding all cause to lie in history and in the economic imbalances of world society. We shall later see that expectation of war is a crystallization of both sets of factors.

Those who see the cause of aggressive nationalism in human nature exclusively sometimes say that every person has an instinct of pugnacity. What is more natural, therefore, than for him to rush to war whenever this biological instinct is provoked? Or, even if instincts are left out of the explanation, it is stated that the frustrations of life are so great that anger, hostility, resentment flow in every bosom and [that] one of the inescapable ways in which these strenuous antipathies are expressed is through war. Personal aggression, we are told, becomes displaced upon an external enemy. The enemy becomes a scapegoat and attracts the wrath logically pertinent to the frustrations encountered in our occupation or in our unsatisfactory family life.

The fallacy of this purely personal explanation lies in the fact that, howsoever pugnacious or frustrated an individual may be, he himself lacks the capacity to make organized warfare. He is capable of temper tantrums, also of chronic nagging, biting sarcasm, or personal cruelty, but he alone cannot invade an alien land or drop bombs upon a distant enemy to give vent to his own emotions. Furthermore, whereas national aggressiveness is total—all citizens being involved in offensive and defensive efforts—relatively few of the citizens feel personally hostile toward the enemy. Studies of soldiers in combat show that hate and aggression are less commonly felt than fear, homesickness, and boredom. Few citizens, in an aggressive nation, actually *feel* aggressive. Thus their warlike activity cannot be due solely to their personal motivations.

An interpretation exclusively in terms of personal life, therefore, will not work. How is it with the historical-economic approach (favored, for example, by Marxist thinkers)? Here, too, a fatal one-sidedness is evident. No social system has yet succeeded in abolishing war. Aggressive nationalism has flourished under communism as well as under capitalism, in Christian and in non-Christian countries, among illiterate and literate peoples, under authoritarian and under democratic political structures. True, some nations (e.g., Switzerland) have been relatively successful in avoiding war, and some systems may make the *probability* of aggression greater than other systems. (Fascism, for example, by its very nature, engenders a war-minded leadership.) But to hold that only one type of social system automatically excludes war and that all others automatically engender war is to violate the evidence of history up to the present time.

The Marxist theory of the causes of war overlooks the indispensable role of expectancy. This theory pivots on the alleged impossibility of achieving basic (and needed) reforms in production and ownership without violence, since, it insists, the owners of the tools of production (stereotyped as "monopolistic capitalism") will not relinquish their grasp without violence (stereotyped as "class warfare"). "Monopolistic capitalism," the argument runs, "will not destroy itself, but must be destroyed." This simple and, I fear, warengendering formula, is itself a reflection of dogmatic expectancy. It is not historic inevitability that is here involved but rather two sets of expectancy—one in the have-nots and one in the haves. Both sets of expectancy have to be built up through psychological stimulation. Poor people, history shows, do not automatically resort to warfare to obtain a fairer share of the world's loot. They must first be led to perceive their interests as their leaders perceive them and then must be exhorted and pushed into organized revolt. Similarly, history shows that the owners of the tools of production often yield peacefully to the expanding force of nationalization. In many progressive countries, mines, sugar refineries, banks, factories, transportation are leaving private hands without violence. And it is by no means uncommon for peacefully minded owners in certain capitalistic countries to yield gracefully to an effective partnership with labor. At the same time, of course, apprehension on the part of owners may be crystallized into horror of the "Commies" and, through the aid of private and public propaganda, become set into a rigid expectancy that war alone will safeguard the owner's prerogatives.

Not only does class warfare thus reduce largely to the anticipation of the contending parties, but so, too, do the "imperialistic wars" decried by Communists (and by decent men everywhere). Wars of expansion, of exploitation, or simply of distraction have not been limited to a given (capitalistic) form of social organization. But in point of fact, belligerent sorties have occurred whenever or wherever greedy leaders have succeeded in inducing enough men (usually mercenaries) to carry out their inhuman raids. Highly collectivistic societies have been as guilty of such raiding parties as have the more individualistic societies.

In short, the indispensable condition of war is that people must *expect* war and must prepare for war before, under war-minded leadership, they make war. It is in this sense that "wars begin in the minds of men." We have seen that personal aggressiveness does not itself render war inevitable. It is a contributing cause when people *expect* to vent their emotions in warfare. Similarly the alleged economic causes of war are effective causes only when people think war is a solution to problems of poverty and economic rivalry. Otherwise they are not. What men expect determines their behavior.

PERSONAL FACTORS IN THE EXPECTANCY OF WAR

Expectancy, as I have said, is a complex state of mind. To imply that men anticipate war only in a simple conscious way, as they anticipate the arrival of a commuter train on schedule or a change in weather, would be an over-simplification. The deeper the emotions that are involved, the more uncon-scious and evasive are the determinants of our expectancies. Let us, therefore, look more closely at the personal conditions involved in hostile expectancies.

Some men have an apparently unbounded capacity for bitter hate, prolonged resentments, and envy. Yet paradoxically, men (often the same men) also have an unlimited capacity for love, friendship, and affiliative behavior. No person seems ever to be able to love or to be loved enough to satisfy him. The best psychological thinking in my opinion holds that hate and jealousy result from interference with affiliative relationships. Hate springs from interference with love. Aggressive nationalism, insofar as it entails elements of hate, represents, therefore, in some devious way an interference with man's basic capacity for affiliative living and loyalty.

Such interference takes a complex course of development. The infant, we know, is at first in a friendly, symbiotic relationship with its mother. Anger is likely to surge up in the infant whenever this happy situation is interrupted, perhaps in connection with weaning or when younger brothers or sisters are born. A child who feels thus rejected is likely both to hate and to love the rejecting parent. Since to hate and to love make a bad conflict, the hate may not be recognized. It may be repressed. Outwardly the child lives at peace with his parents, but has a bottled-up resentment that may slip out in unusual ways. It may slip out against the teacher. It may slip out against many other parent figures—policemen, rulers, clergy.

According to this line of thinking, aggression may exist in a personal life, and yet may be almost unrecognized. The individual is ripe for a channelizing of his hatred upon substitute objects. Freud goes so far as to hold that the com-mon feeling of bitterness and hate toward Jews is due to people's resentment toward God himself for demanding so much of us. This hatred, repressed through fear of God, gets displaced upon the Jews who both taught us about God and are commonly accused of killing Christ, the son of God. In a deeper sense we ourselves would like to kill Christ who expects so much of us. Since we deplore this impulse in ourselves, we blame the Jews who, legend tells us, have actually carried it out.

It is not necessary to accept Freud's somewhat involved theory of anti-Semitism to recognize that man's hostile impulses themselves are subtle and are capable of much strange channeling. . . .

For our purpose it is enough to note that channeling of hostility in the directions of war or racial and religious prejudice is an authentic possibility. Strange crystallizations take place around the myths available in our folklore. Originally, of course, these myths were created and maintained by like-minded individuals who felt a need to project their personal conflicts outward. In this way Jews became the mythological cause of people's inner unrest; Communists (or capitalists) became a threat to their very existence. The legend adopted by the individual is available to him in his culture and is often forced on him by his parents, teachers, or leaders.

The dark-skinned races, we hear, are ready to pollute our "blood." Symbolisms and displacements of this sort are legion. The conflicts within our bosoms are personified outward. In the myth we find the mirror image of our own disordered lives. When one can no longer tolerate one's own problems, one often seizes upon the institutional interpretation and legend. After a time, organized hostility comes to seem inevitable. In warfare one may act out symbolically the buried and unrecognized conflicts in one's own private life.

Such an analysis as this—appropriate to *some* people—shows how deeply buried the roots of expectancy of war may lie.

But men differ exceedingly in the causes of aggression in their lives, in the amounts and types of aggression that they have, and in the manners in which it is expressed. Many people are virtually aggressionless. Frustrations, deprivations, and slights to their pride affect them very little. They have serene and benevolent minds even when they deal with individuals who are hotbeds of hatred. No doubt there are genetic factors of temperament involved here that we know little about. But whether, for reasons of inheritance or of training, it is true that some men will readily blame others when things go wrong, they are impulsively extropunitive. On the other hand, many people, when things go wrong, tend to blame themselves. They are intropunitive and refuse to project their own guilt upon others. For all this diversity, it is not difficult to marshal plenty of resentment against a "common enemy" because enough people exist in any society to provide a large nucleus of extropunitive aggressors. All that is needed is to persuade these individuals that a particular enemy is indeed responsible for the vague discomfort in their personal lives.

This line of reasoning must not lead us to the mistaken assumption that within every nation there is a fixed reservoir of hostility stored up in citizens which *must* be released somehow, perhaps through local conflicts, class prejudices, or else through external warfare. Oddly enough, one does not relieve aggression by expressing it in one channel rather than in another. A country with many internal explosions does *not* have fewer external explosions. Studies show the opposite. Those nations and tribes that are aggressive within the group are also aggressive outside, while peaceful social units tend to be peaceful in both their internal and external relations. The Arapesh (though much undernourished) are a placid and peaceful folk at home and abroad. The Dobu are suspicious, vicious, hateful both among themselves and among strangers. Hence, in speaking of the channeling of aggression, we must not commit the steam-boiler-with-multiple-valves fallacy. The fact is that aggression breeds aggression. One comes to *expect* aggression to be a way of solving all problems. Conversely, peaceful relations breed expectancy of peaceful relations. Thus aggression is pretty much of a habit; the more you express it, the more you have of it. It is not enough, therefore, to find a "moral equivalent for war" (a harmless outlet for aggression); it is equally important to change people's false expectancy that an outlet for aggression will automatically bring solutions. If wars were simply a relief from tension, they might conceivably have their justification. But experience shows that not only does one war engender another, but it brings fierce domestic postwar strain and conflict into the nation itself.

It is true that, while a war is actually in progress, a nation often feels united and friendly within its own borders. It is this fact, among others, that leads some theorists to argue that friendly social relations demand a "common enemy." We never feel so firmly cemented with our friends, they say, as when we are united with them in ridiculing, criticizing, or fighting a common opponent.

If a common enemy is needed to guarantee affiliative relations with our allies, is not the vision of one world chimerical? If all nations were friendly, who would be the enemy to cement our internal loyalty? Three answers come to mind: (a) Whether a common enemy is needed in a more advanced stage of human development is not yet known. (b) If such an enemy is needed, may we not point to the ravages of uncontrolled nature, disease, ignorance, as possible enemies that may, if necessary, be personified to satisfy our need for a tangible villain? (c) In the foreseeable future there will certainly be criminals —both domestic and international—as well as dissident outlawed groups against which the globally minded citizens may unite in their wrath. The expectancy of peaceful relations with all men will be at best a gradual achievement.

To sum up: personal aggressiveness exists in large amounts, in devious forms, and plays many unhappy tricks with our own essential longing for friendship, love, and peace. Mental hygiene is profoundly concerned with these ravages of hate, anxiety, envy in the personal life. In complex ways such individual states of mind intrude themselves into international relations. Sometimes the person with unresolved aggression regards war as a good means of evading a family difficulty and gladly follows a call to the colors. Sometimes the person will see in the enemy, with or without some justification, a "cause" of his own misery. Perhaps he merely wishes to submit to a leader, as many Germans submitted to Hitler, in order to escape from the responsibilities of making the difficult decisions of maturity. "Let the leader be my conscience," says such a person. "If the leader himself is disordered in his inner life—a prey to mythical notions and unresolved hatreds—no matter. I shall follow wherever he calls, for I am too weary with my own conflicts to resist him. Decision is too much of a burden for me. Let the leader interpret the political and economic scene. I will follow."

TRADITION AND SYMBOLS AS FACTORS IN EXPECTANCY

Left alone, the distress in each personal life would take so many forms and seek so many solutions that a concerted warlike effort would not occur. But the members of a group are, after all, imbued with common values and sentiments. They "know" from their ancestors that their group is much sinned against, that the boundaries of their land are unjustly narrow. They "know" also that theirs is an inherently superior group, and therefore most deserving.

One important reason why every national and cultural group feels superior is that in its tradition there existed for this group a "golden age"—a time when it was in fact superior in culture, prosperity, science or power, to all surrounding groups. True, this golden age may have been a hundred, a thousand, or two thousand years ago. But at some time or other every cultural group has had some high mark of artistic, material, or intellectual distinction. Motivated by our personal pride, we thus find it easy to identify ourselves with the golden age of our people. What we deserve today we are inclined to estimate by this age of exaltation.

Such ethnocentricism is well-nigh universal among all peoples. Its roots are deep, as deep as our own boundless self-esteem. Expectancy of war grows in part from the latent resentments we hold against other groups who, perhaps centuries ago, violated the rights of our ancestors with whom we now identify ourselves. The fixity of these self-adulating sentiments may be estimated from the ethnocentric tone of much social science. Openly or implicitly, many a social scientist frames his theories and his observations so that his own culture emerges most glamorous and his own nation as sinless. Until social science becomes truly transnational, we must heed the criticism that comes from the sociology of knowledge. We cannot expect too much of ordinary citizens who often follow the myths manufactured by their intellectuals and build their own expectations upon them.

To some youths, war is definitely appealing. It arouses expectations of adventure, novelty, and exalted comradeship. It removes the heavy burden of maturity since in military service one has few important decisions to make. Economic insecurity, family troubles, overbearing or possessive parents are for the time being disposed of. The question has been asked, "Can peace be made equally exciting? Can it possibly provide expectancies as satisfying as the prospect of war?"

This particular question has led to an experiment, now rapidly expanding, with what are commonly called "work service camps." In 1920 a small group of internationally minded volunteers, with the permission of the local authorities, started to clear and reconstruct the land and buildings around Esnes-Verdun. In April, 1921, however, the prefect of the district declared that "recent developments in Franco-German politics" had made it necessary to suppress the work. The first experiment thus ended under duress from aggressive nationalism. But the efforts continued. Particularly in times of local catastrophe, groups of volunteers have been organized to assist in rebuilding regions affected by flood, fire, or avalanche. In the summer of 1948 at least 130 voluntary service camps were flourishing in Europe, principally under the auspices of the Service Civil International. In the United States and in Mexico, under the auspices of the American Friends Service Committee, a score more were under way. Nearly all camps are international in composition; all are designed to obtain collaborative work of mutual service without financial profit to the participants. The tasks have a positive social value, and the labor is not regarded by ordinary paid laborers as offering dangerous competition.

Slight though the impact of such work service camps is when viewed on a world scale, still their appeal and their success indicate that constructive peacetime projects may be to youth both exciting and satisfying. While conscription and military training affect the anticipation of youth in the direction of aggressive nationalism, work service camps affect their anticipations in the direction of internationalism, constructive activity, and friendly human relationships. It is an important part of the purpose of the Service Civil International to persuade governments to accept voluntary service of this order as an alternative to compulsory military training. Of course, this goal has not yet been reached, but the issue has been well drawn: will nations permit youth to have alternative expectations concerning their public duties—expectations entailing international cooperation and constructive service rather than expectations involving preparation for war? The prospect seems Utopian, but I mention it to illustrate the type of decision that nations will be forced to make if they ever become sufficiently enlightened to consider the psychological importance of expectation on the attitudes of youth.

At the present time, not all youth is susceptible to the appeal of work service camps. Many now prefer military service for reasons I have given. But it is now time to extend the opportunities of work camps to those who find this particular set of ideals congenial. As the opportunity becomes more widely extended, the expectations of more and more youth will flow in this direction. Such a period of apprenticeship in international living may someday be taken for granted.

Symbols are an important factor in expectancy. Germans think of themselves as belonging to the land of Beethoven and Goethe; Norwegians preserve the relics of the Vikings and in fantasy share in their fabulous exploits; Greeks do not forget Praxiteles and Demosthenes. Flags, martial music, noble ruins are profoundly significant to the citizen whose security and whose self-esteem are inseparable from the tradition of his people.

Now most symbols are of an exclusively parochial order. They mark off my country from yours, or they mark off my religion from yours, or my caste from yours. World symbols are virtually lacking: no world parks, gardens, universities, and few symbolic world-minded documents. There is no world currency, no genuine world capital. A few fine words have been spoken: the Atlantic Charter, the United Nations Charter, the Preamble to the UNESCO Charter. But these symbols are little known and still fail to rally appreciable loyalty. Just as the diversified egos within a nation cannot be fused into one "we" without the aid of tradition and symbol, so, too, international loyalty cannot be achieved without a common focus of thought and the common uplift that come from symbols of transnational unity.

Our existing national symbols are not necessarily mischievous. A very considerable amount of national loyalty is compatible with world loyalty. But at times these symbols are deliberately employed for war-making purposes by leaders of government and of public opinion. Patriotic phrases repeated over and over in a warlike context will habituate people to the expectation of war. Nationalistic bureaus of "propaganda and enlightenment" deliberately frame the expectancies of men.

When people's minds have become habituated to accepting a designated enemy as a menace, the next step is to set the final expectation that will lead to war. Leaders usually do this with a formulation of national demands. An "ultimatum" is sent to the enemy. When rejected, people feel that now no path other than war is possible.

The psychology of an ultimatum is a momentous matter. Take the case of two individuals. When they meet to discuss their aims and their needs, they have a fair chance of finding a friendly common solution. But when they confront one another with an ultimatum, a fight ensues. If one party yields momentarily under duress, it is only for the purpose of building up his resources for later revenge. So it is with nations in disagreement. Demands and prefabricated solutions usually succeed only in increasing tensions simply because they deny the other fellow a right to participate in matters affecting his own destiny. The price he would pay in loss of pride is too great. He prefers to fight.

Pride of position is the immediate cause of every war. So decisive and final have been the demands made by each national spokesman that to yield ground would be felt humiliating and shameful. Expectancies have become frozen. It is "54–40 or fight." At this point war is indeed inevitable.

It is before this stage is reached that the art of resolving difficulties through the mutual discussion of desires and needs (in place of demands and ultimatums) must be cultivated. The desires and needs of people are seldom incompatible; more often they are parallel and reciprocal, because one nation generally has something to spare that is required by the others. And since all men need and want freedom from destructive poverty, from irrational fear, from debilitating ignorance, it is plainly through joint action that the pathway to a common goal can best be discovered. The prerequisite of peace lies in developing the habit of discussing *needs* and *desires* in place of the present habit of stating arranged solutions.

IGNORANCE AND EXPECTANCY

One of the most important barriers to international understanding is ignorance of the other fellow's intentions and of his way of life.

Ignorance may be of two kinds: (a) simple ignorance of the facts, (b) distortion of facts to accord with one's own motives or with the motives of demagogic leaders who have much to gain from misrepresentation.

Simple ignorance is the easier of these two kinds to repair. Crusades against illiteracy, now under way from Mexico to India and from Nigeria to Siberia, are exciting and gratifying in their results. Psychological studies have shown that an appreciable relationship does exist between a high level of general education and freedom from prejudice. The relationship, however, is far from perfect. We know that even scholars may be intense bigots. Salvation does not lie in schooling alone.

Ignorance due to the distortion of facts is harder to remedy. Some distortions are simple and understandable, though often damaging, as when certain white children recoil from colored people because they look "dirty." One's personal history often creates the emotional ground for a distortion, as in the case of the youth who hated "the Irish" because his rather cruel father happened to be of Irish descent. The most mischievous capacity of the human mind is its impulsive tendency to categorize and endow all members of a particular group with one set of alleged attributes. My cruel father is Irish; therefore, all Irish are cruel.

A hostile image once formed is peculiarly resistant to the onslaught of contrary evidence. An Oxford student is said to have remarked, "I despise all Americans—but I have never met one I didn't like." Thus do tabloid generalizations persist even when every ounce of firsthand experience contradicts them. We know of no remedy for this mental-emotional tabloidism except the inculcation of habits of discriminating perception and critical thought. Systematic training is possible even in the lower schools.

The emotional economy of a group stereotype is easily seen in the image many Americans hold of the Soviet Union. When the Russians were allies of the Americans in wartime, they were readily perceived as courageous, cheerful, progressive, and liberty-loving people. When in the postwar period circumstances had shifted, the image became one of a cruel, oppressed, atheistic, and double-dealing folk. Thus perceived, Russia came to serve as a satisfactory scapegoat—a distant menace capable of explaining many of our frustrations. "Communists" became the symbolic cause of evil at home. Is my employment jeopardized? Blame the Communists. Am I inconvenienced by inflation? Blame the Communistic labor leaders. Are the colleges advocating dangerous internationalism? Oust the Communist professors. A study shows that the dislocations after World War I in America were blamed on a diversity of scapegoats—Bolsheviks, hyphenated Americans, monopolists, the IWW—but that after World War II the image had sharpened—the ubiquitous villain is simply the "Communist."

Now in order for a villain to become common property, communication and propaganda are needed. Unless newspapers, politicians, special pleaders of all kinds join in painting the picture, people will not unite in focusing their diversity of negative emotions upon one clearly identified menace. Expectancy of a new war within twenty-five years increased in America from 40 per cent in August, 1945, to 65 per cent in July, 1946. Further, in this interval, the enemy became clearly identified as Russia. The services of news agencies and public opinion molders were essential to this shift.

Here one asks the reasonable question whether expectancy may not be well rooted in fact. Are there no natural and inevitable wars, provoked by differences in ideology or by intransigence in one party to a dispute? Must expectancies be only a product of designing propagandists or irresponsible leaders and publicists busily watering the seeds of aggression in the individual life?

The answer, I believe, is as follows: While some serious and basic conflicts of interest may be unavoidable, warlike solutions spring always from warlike expectancies and preparation. The confirmed Marxist who sees class warfare (world-wide revolution preceded by imperialistic wars) as inevitable is merely *seeing* them as inevitable. If enough people on both sides of a dispute see the matter in the same way, then of course such wars *become* inevitable. I shall have more to say about defensive wars shortly.

Unfortunately, the images we have of other people are more often condescending or hostile than friendly. Textbooks, legends, traditions, leaders, and mass media of communication conspire to keep them so. The reason, I presume, is that hostile images accord best with people's desires to hold firmly to provincial islands of security. That the world itself is our natural island of security is a conception too spacious for our fragmented lives to grasp. But fortunately even hostile images are susceptible to change. They change when films, radio, newspapers, and textbooks change. They change when people travel not as the average tourist, but as the scientist or serious student travels. They change if people engage as participants in mutual projects of work or recreation. They change when people gain insight into the myth-making process of their own minds as it is manipulated by publicists.

Let me repeat that school knowledge is insufficient. As Sorokin points out, the twentieth century marks the highest educational level in all of human history. At the same time it is immeasurably the bloodiest century in terms of both civil and international wars, in terms of persecution of minorities and criminal violence of all types. Schools are seldom international in their emphasis, but more often, at all hours of the day, din national glories into the minds of children. Even if this were not so, we have before us the all-important fact that intellectual knowledge is not the same thing as emotional knowledge. The sound mind, free from cramping complexes, is the only one able to turn book learning into international understanding. A scholar may be familiar with all ethical systems and himself be the author of an altruistic doctrine of ethics, and yet in his personal life he may be blatantly egoistic, chauvinistic, war-minded. And a man may understand human frailties and the techniques of propaganda, as Goebbels did, and yet use them for injurious purposes.

THE PERSONAL PHILOSOPHY OF LIFE

It is here that moral and religious leaders have a strong point to make. Only when knowledge is deeply rooted in acceptable values does it become socially effective. Moral inclination is still an essential part of the story of war and peace. We note the many-mindedness of people. They are inconsistently peaceful and warlike, alternately democratic and authoritarian in their behavior. They often agree with the peacemaker who passes by and again with the war-maker who follows.

Recent empirical studies have shown an important relationship between one's philosophy of life and the possession of hostility. People who are afraid of life, who say that the world is a hazardous place where men are basically evil and dangerous, are people with much race and religious prejudice. Usually they hate Catholics, Negroes, Jews. Usually they are superpatriotic and find their security only in nationalistic strength and sovereignty. They are generally institution-minded, docile outwardly to parents, traditions. They like fraternities and sororities and find binding security only in their small ingroup attachments. They are peculiarly rigid in their approach to practical problems, even to the solution of simple arithmetical tasks. This pattern of rigidity marks the aggressor personality. It constitutes a belligerent philosophy of life. International and intercultural understanding require a degree of relaxation and peace with oneself that such personalities lack.

A Jesuit priest, a student of mine, studied the amount of prejudice against Negroes within a Catholic parish. Without being told the purpose of the research, a devoted layman was asked to give the names of members whom he would regard as deeply Christian in their faith and in their lives and to give names of other members whom he felt were merely "institutional" Catholics conforming to the rules but not genuinely Christian in respect to their outlook.

Having been selected in this manner, these two groups were then studied by means of a well-framed questionnaire designed to measure anti-Negro feeling. It turned out that the "institutional" Catholics were vastly more bigoted. To them apparently the church was an island of security in a hostile world. Outsiders were objects of distrust. The essential teachings of Christianity had not penetrated into their personalities. They were living their lives rigidly, holding fast to ingroup security, and hating outsiders. Although this particular study did not deal directly with nationalistic sentiments, it strongly suggests that war-mindedness is closely associated with a philosophy of life that is tense, in-groupish, dependent on small platforms of organized security, not daring to embrace the world as a whole within its view.

Thus we have reason to believe that two types of personality-formation are especially likely to be swept into the stream of national aggressiveness. One is the unintegrated, many-minded person, easily controlled through suggestion and momentary appeals by those leaders and publicists who paint the world for him in a particular way. He will see demons where the morning paper puts them. Being unsure of his own values, he will yield to the demagogue, follow the prevailing fashion in blame.

The other type is the individual whose fears are such that he has himself developed a totalitarian character structure. He needs a safety island in his group, his own nation. Beyond the ingroup, he feels helpless. He suspects, rejects, hates the stranger. To him the world is a jungle. Such a person quickly perceives menace in a harmless minority group in his own land or in any foreign power that is pointed out to him as a threat.

We need corresponding studies of the altruistic and world-minded citizen who has no difficulty in enlarging his circles of loyalty. Wendell Willkie was no less of a good Hoosier or good American for embracing the cause of one world. On the basis of evidence available, psychologists are inclined to believe that men are less likely to be swayed into irrational fears and national antag-onisms if they have themselves spent reasonably secure childhood years in an atmosphere where affection prevailed and where high ideals of altruism were not only taught but practiced. But childhood security is undoubtedly only one of the factors making for strong attitudes of trust and relaxation in dealing with one's fellows. We need to know the other factors involved.

THE ROLE OF PARENT AND LEADER IN BUILDING EXPECTANCIES

The child's philosophy of life grows chiefly from seeds planted by parents. Studies show that in general those who mirror the parents' views in respect to religion, politics, and ethics are likely to be bigoted (unless, of course, the parents' views were exceptionally altruistic). The mature and benevolent outlook on life is not likely to be found among those who cling blindly to parental patterns of security. Rebels from the parental viewpoint are, as a matter of fact, more often world-minded.

Yet for better or for worse, parental attitudes are always in some degree adopted. Few parents realize that they are imparting attitudes unsuited to life in a world greatly altered since their childhood. To some degree schools and colleges modify the parental influence, but the content of instruction in schools and colleges, as I have pointed out, likewise is more often parochial than international.

Political leaders and other figures of public importance also play a vital part. If feelings of insecurity prevail, their interpretations of these inward jitters may become decisive factors in our view of the world at large. If I am told by a person having prestige in my eyes that the Jew is threatening my job or that the Negro endangers my sexual prerogatives or that a certain foreign country threatens my preferred way of life, I am likely to accept the interpretation and to prepare myself perhaps for violent action or at least for a future suspicious separation.

Now Marxist thinkers and others insist that leaders are mere incidents in the stream of history. They are not much more than puppets. They, themselves, reflect prevailing tensions and transmit to the individual the dominant ideology. In only a limited sense is this true. Leaders are, of course, subject to their own fears, insecurities, and images just as are their followers. They are influenced by current myths, by their predecessors, and by the prevailing nationalistic tradition. But it is not true that aggressive nationalism can break out without war-minded individuals seated in a position of dominance. The leader is decisive in matters of war and peace precisely because his followers are themselves ambivalent or many-minded. He can play upon the latent hostility or upon the affiliative impulses of his group. It is he who calls the tune.

An important distinction to make in respect to leadership is between what we may call "person-minded" leaders and "object-minded" leaders. The former are mindful of the human factor, of their responsibility to their constituents, and of their constituents' interests. Object-minded leaders are lovers of power who pursue a goal forcibly and heedlessly. To them human beings are mere *things* to be manipulated in the service of a cause. Object-minded leaders often set their eyes on aggressive nationalism and in the course of their activity raise people's expectancies to accord with their own desires. People can be made to see no other way out than war. Along with object-minded leaders, we may, I think, include a great many incompetent leaders in the international field who stumble into war because their position puts demands on them that are too great for their skill in human relations. They quickly reach the point in international dealings where they can engage only in recrimination. Such bunglers drag the people along with them. Their own maladroitness is interpreted by them as villainy on the part of the enemy.

Person-minded leaders are haters of war because they habitually reckon the human consequences. They are also indisposed to utilize propaganda and manipulative techniques, to create false images and oversimplified categories around which to rally their followers. It is incalculably harder to be consistently skillful in advancing the interests of persons than of an aggressive cause. Can person-minded leaders be trained? Modern experiments in social psychology indicate that the possibility exists. Up to now we have allowed leadership to rise in haphazard fashion. It was more-or-less chance whether the leader turned out to be person-minded or object-minded.

Whether the expectations of a population are directed toward war or toward peace, toward arbitration or open break, toward person-centeredness or object-centeredness, depends, then, largely upon the deeds done and the symbols invoked by national leaders. The greatest menace to the world today are leaders in office who regard war as inevitable and thus prepare their people for armed conflict. For by regarding war as inevitable, it becomes inevitable. Expectations determine behavior.

SOCIAL STRUCTURE AND EXPECTANCY OF WAR

I have said that under all known social systems war has flourished. Therefore, I hold, that the differentiating factor between war and peace is not a surface matter of social organization, but rather human factors of expectancy and channelizing of attitude. Personality is so unstable a unit in nature that it can be swayed to national aggression or to international amity. When I maintain that war can be avoided as soon as we learn how to prevent the swaying of expectancies toward warfare, am I overstating the case?

What, for example, about defensive warfare? A peaceful people invaded by a warlike neighbor would normally seize weapons in self-defense. In this case, is not expectation irrelevant? No, in such a case it is *unilateral expectation* that is the cause of war. One side in the conflict regarded attack as a desirable procedure to be used. If war is to be avoided, no single nation can be permitted to have warlike expectations. One war-minded land endangers all others and keeps war-mindedness alive through fear.

Let me revert to the "economic causes" of war so much under discussion today. I do not for a moment hold such causes to be unimportant. Prolonged hunger, especially in the face of plenty, will engender an understandable violence if no other solution is available. Raids and counterraids on surrounding tribes are as old as human history. Often the motives have been hunger, but at times they have also been revenge, desire for excitement, escape from boredom, and personal frustration (channelized by the leader). Economic wars are not the only kinds of war. There are ideological wars, religious wars, wars of envy, wars of boredom.

And, as I have said, certain political systems make expectancy of war almost inevitable while others render this mode of life relatively unpopular and unlikely. The tradition of a culture may exalt martial virtues or condemn the outlay of funds and the exercise of military prowess. Political systems make for war or for peace according to the expectancies they create.

The factor of expectancy is decisive. The wants of men, even acute hunger, do not lead to violence unless people *think* violence is the way to satisfy them. When those that have refuse to yield to the have-nots, they do, of course, increase the expectancy of war and render it a reasonable mode of behavior to the have-nots. To refuse to negotiate is a way of creating expectancy of violence. The proud and unbending kings of France brought on the Revolution by destroying every other alternative in the minds of their subjects.

Organization for war is a peculiarly low-grade form of social organization, even though in modern times it takes elaborate and ingenious forms. Those who have seen how young draftees are herded into camps, given routine tasks to do, drilled in specialties, and discouraged from thinking as integrated personalities recognize the point I am making. Essentially, only the young man's capacity for obedience is played upon, stimulated by patriotic symbols. The process fulfills some momentary function in relieving personal frustration. The war machine is thus a primitive organization of human resources. As a form of social structure it segmentalizes the individual. Whole personalities are not involved. It is for this reason that the aftermath of war usually brings about demoralization, criminality, and shattered personalities.

The way up from this primitive form of social organization is long and hard. We have always had wars because they have been seen as the simplest mode of solving conflicts between groups of people. If wars had not today become so disastrous, we might be tempted to let this easy "solution" of social conflict remain with us. But as it is, we have no alternative but to change mankind's habit of expecting armed conflict to solve its disagreements.

SUMMARY IN TERMS OF WORLD ORGANIZATIONS

Man's moral ideals, as expressed in the great creeds of the human race, are at a fairly high level. But his capacity to profess one thing and act the opposite seems almost unlimited. At the present time he appears completely unable to bring his conduct in line with his expressed ideals.

In this chapter we have seen three principal reasons why this fatal chasm exists:

Men's personalities are seldom well unified. There are anxieties and repressions, unsatisfied wants and unrequited love, shame, guilt, and awe before the unknown. Pressed between two oblivions, man's life is to him mysterious, fearful, yet vaguely beautiful and intensely interesting. Seldom is he able to build a consistent pattern of life that unites his basic desire for love and understanding of the world about him with an underlying feeling of trust for his fellow men. Relatively few personalities are integrated to such an adequate degree and possessed of the required freedom from fear.

This basic ambivalence in life and its confusedness make man a prey to slanderous conceptions of his fellow men. Security is found only within the ingroups, within the family, the church, the tribe, or nation. All else appears hazardous and unknown. Myths exalting the ingroup and legends depicting the menace or inferiority of the outgroup arise. This view of the outgroup often entails an expectancy of armed conflict. Images of the "enemy" seldom correspond to reality both because of people's basic ignorance of facts and because of their tendency to oversimplify the motives and characteristics of the outgroup and thus to justify their inimical sentiments.

Such vaguely hostile expectancies are easily manipulated by warminded leaders or by the incompetent who slip willy-nilly into patterns of nationalism.

For these reasons a state of cynicism results wherein men despair of ever achieving their desire for peace. They expect war—and this expectancy itself brings war.

Only by changing the expectation in both leaders and followers, in parents and in children, shall we eliminate war.

Our perspective on this giant task of attitude change is still limited, and the outlook still discouraging. Yet we find hope in the fact that within the past five years three significant quasi-global organizations have been formed. The function of each in its own area is to alter the mode of human anticipation from one of war to one of peace. The area of activity of these three organizations corresponds well to the three obstacles I have just enumerated.

World Health Organization

The aim of the World Health Organization as stated in its constitution is "the attainment by all peoples of the highest possible level of health." Health is defined as "a state of complete physical, mental and social well-being and not merely the absence of disease or infirmity." Since "mental and social well-being" are included, it is clear that this organization is dedicated to causes of integrated, peaceable personalities capable of handling personal and interpersonal tensions without resort to violence. Mental hygiene, health on the level of personality, is of primary concern to this organization. With improvement in mental health, the number of relaxed, wholesome, internationally minded citizens will increase.

There are, of course, many other agencies existing whose aim is constructive action on this same level. Wise physicians, parents, teachers, psychiatrists, clergy, individually and in their professional organizations, work ceaselessly for the same end.

UNESCO

This organization is dedicated to erecting the "defenses of peace" in the minds of men. In terms of our analysis, the special function of UNESCO is to correct the distorted images that make for war and thus to diminish expectations of war and rationalizations of war. In issuing the [original] volume, UNESCO has endeavored to clarify the forces making for national aggressiveness. In its program of international education and cooperation, it tries to reduce strangeness and strain among the peoples of the world. It facilitates the contributions of schools, of international voluntary work camps, of artists, publicists, and scholars to the process of altering belligerence into friendliness. And UNESCO, of course, represents only one line of constructive effort in this direction. But its international character makes it a particularly significant effort.

The United Nations

At the level of political and economic relations between nations, the UN is dedicated likewise to altering expectancies. It provides a means for making peaceful solutions of conflicts possible. It brings the leaders of nations together. The confidence of people in the efficacy of this activity is still weak. The success of the UN will be guaranteed as soon as the people and their leaders really *expect* it to succeed. Today the great majority of the people of the world have heard of the United Nations and know of its efforts. About two-thirds of the people who know about it in the United States give the UN a good or fair chance of succeeding in its purpose. In other countries the view is less optimistic. In Italy, for example, two-thirds of the people believe its chances are poor. Confidence in the UN is itself the secret key to the prevention of war.

All of these three organizations (and other bodies with analogous functions) are hard at work. Their endeavor in all cases is to build expectancy of peace and to provide machinery for its achievement. That men are hopefully yearning for their success is the first step in acquiring a new expectancy. Yearning, we trust, may gradually turn into confidence. *And when men are fully confident that international organizations can eradicate war, they will then at last succeed in doing so.*

PART II

Studies from Sociology and Anthropology

INTRODUCTION

The late anthropologist Robert Redfield often said that sociology and anthropology represented two traditions engaged in a common task. That task has been interpreted by students of society and culture to be the determination of the order, meaning, and coherence which inform human group life. Men at war are usually acting as part of a collectivity, and social scientists have tried to discuss the conditions under which wars arose in the course of group life. Through accidents of origin and tradition, anthropologists have devoted their efforts to the study of primitive peoples living in isolated places, whereas sociologists have concentrated on the analysis of modern societies. Both enterprises have been profoundly influenced by the theory of evolution, but as the analysis of the causes of war has proven a more salient problem for sociologists, our remarks will be directed mainly to a consideration of the intellectual background of their work.

It was the nineteenth century, which, though relatively peaceful, was a century of many wars, which provided the social, political, and intellectual context for the development of modern anthropology and sociology. The concerns of the most influential thinkers in sociology were frequently directed to an understanding of the conditions fostering social cohesion. The breakdown of consensus and social solidarity under the impact of social change was viewed as a consequence of encroaching urbanism, secularism, industrialism, egalitarianism, and rationalism. This preoccupation was far more characteristic of the French tradition in social thought represented by Saint-Simon, Comte, and ultimately of Durkheim and his school than it was of the German tradition stemming from Hegel. The latter's view of war and conflict was favorable contrasted with that of the early French sociologists. Hegel set the tone for much subsequent German thought on the subject when he declared:

War has the higher meaning that through it, as I have said elsewhere, the ethical health of nations is maintained, since such health does not require the stabilizing of finite arrangements; just as the motion of the winds keeps the sea from the foulness which a constant calm would produce—

so war prevents a corruption of nations which a perpetual, let alone an eternal peace would produce.[1]

His emphasis on conflict as a necessary and desirable element in the evolution of society was carried forward in the thought of Marx and his followers, as well as in the writings of conservative, nationalistic social theorists, and constituted the source for a characteristically German sociology of conflict.

It was social Darwinism which provided unexpected support for both the French and German traditions in the last quarter of the nineteenth century. On one side, it evoked a score of treatises showing that war among men was merely a special case of the universal law which guaranteed "the survival of the fittest." The application of Darwin's ideas to social relations produced a number of highly ingenious efforts to show that the most bloodthirsty doctrines of national, racial, and class aggrandizement and conquest were now legitimized by the findings of modern biological science. The struggles among men were now interpreted as resting on immutable laws of nature in which armed conflict provided the final court of appeal in world history. Attendant philosophies of nationalism, imperialism, military conquest, and authoritarian dictatorship were also deduced from this elusive doctrine.

But the protean character of the doctrine of social Darwinism could give rise to sociological inquiries which stressed completely differing aspects of social life in relation to war. So ambiguous was it that it could seemingly provide the safe harbor of legitimacy for ideas which emphasized consensus and cohesion rather than social conflict in human society. For was it not those societies which were most closely integrated, most cohesive, which were best fitted for the struggle for existence? This notion was taken up by English interpreters of Darwin such as Walter Bagehot in *Physics and Politics*, which first appeared in 1867. Such an interpretation of Darwin, emphasizing the internal solidarity of the groups engaged in struggle, lent itself readily to racist and nationalist elaborations.

The ferocity of this Darwinist rhetoric ultimately gave rise to a countertrend in the form of a critique based on the naturalistic and evolutionary study of animals and men which emphasized mutual aid. Jacques Novicow, Peter Kropotkin, and others pointed out that close study of the animal world revealed considerable evidence that the "struggle for existence" in nature is a struggle carried on by members of different species, not between members of the same species.[2] Within each species, naturalists like Kropotkin were able to show that the success of the group was in large measure a result of the degree of cooperation and mutual aid which its members were able to muster. And

---

[1] Georg Friedrich Hegel, *Philosophy of Right*, § 324.

[2] Jacques Novicow, *La Politique internationale* (Paris: 1896), and *idem, Les Luttes contra sociétés humaines* (Paris: F. Alcan, 1893) ; Peter Kropotkin, *Mutual Aid* (McClure, Phillips & Co., 1902).

the idea of social cohesion as possessing survival value was central to the social theories of such an eminent sociologist as Émile Durkheim, who, following Herbert Spencer, emphasized the evolution of modern society through the growing interdependence fostered by the division of labor and the peaceful differentiation of social groups. Thus Darwinism in a sense helped to sharpen cleavages in social theory which already existed, such as the emphasis on conflict over consensus, and was selectively interpreted as lending support to both sides.

For many late nineteenth-century sociologists whose interest in war took shape in this ideological context, the focus was the study of the role of war in the rise and development of the nation-state.[3] In an organic analogy the nation was conceived as having a natural tendency toward expansion or decline. Viewed against a background of national struggle, this meant that nature itself enjoined a policy of conquest and imperialism. Those nations which fell behind were held to be entering the stage of degeneration and decay. The influence of this theory on the acts of statesmen in the final quarter of the nineteenth century was considerable. In this connection, Darwinism served to rationalize motivations which were at the same time subtle, complex, and extremely primitive. Walt W. Rostow has said of this period:

> . . . Certain non-colonial powers came, as a matter of prestige and style, to desire colonial possessions as a symbol of their coming of age. For example, nothing in the capital markets of the Atlantic world or in their trading patterns justified much ado about colonies, on strictly economic grounds, from, say, 1873 to 1914. A little more could be said for certain colonial positions on military or strategic grounds in the 19th century. But the competition for colonies was conducted for reasons that were unilaterally rational on neither economic nor military grounds; the competition occurred essentially because competitive nationalism was the role of the world arena and colonies were an accepted symbol of status and power within the arena.[4]

At one extreme of the astonishing variety of interpretations of Darwinism were to be found such German apologists for militarism as Friedrich von Bernhardi. Bernhardi echoed Gumplowicz in contending that the results of war provided an infallible verdict on the relative greatness of nations. This

---

[3] In the works of the sociologists Ludwig Gumplowicz and Friedrich Ratzenhofer, a favorable judgment on war was rendered in the light of what was regarded as its historic function in the conflict of races and the forming of national states. Space limitations forbade the inclusion of their writings, characteristic of the early German sociology of conflict. Cf. Gumplowicz, *Der Rassenkampf* (Innsbruck: 1883) and *The Outlines of Sociology*, trans. F. W. Moore (Philadelphia: 1899) ; and Ratzenhofer, *Die Sociologische Erkenntnis* (Leipzig: 1898).

[4] *The Stages of Economic Growth* (London: Cambridge University Press, 1960), pp. 110–111.

judgment was regarded as all the more awesome and impartial for being written in blood. Rather than postulating an unconscious process of evolution through natural selection, which would have at least had the merit of faithfulness to Darwin's theory, such an interpretation (like those of the Socialists) emphasized the active intervention of men in the historical process.

But it was not only among Teutonic philosophers of history that the thunder of Darwinism was heard. Even in the United States the doctrine of a competitive struggle for survival among nations regarded as a law of nature was echoed in the public pronouncements of leading political and intellectual figures.[5] Theodore Roosevelt counseled his countrymen against avoiding imperial responsibilities in Hawaii, Cuba, Puerto Rico, and the Philippines and exhorted them to retain "the great, fighting masterful virtues."

> I preach to you, then, my countrymen, that our country calls not for the life of ease but for the life of strenuous endeavor. The twentieth century looms before us big with the fate of many nations. If we stand idly by, if we seek merely swollen, slothful ease and ignoble peace, if we shrink from the hard contests where men must win at hazard of their lives and at the risk of all they hold dear, then the bolder and stronger peoples will pass us by, and will win for themselves the domination of the world.[6]

It was against this background that the studies of war by American sociologists included here were framed. Though separated by a generation, William Graham Sumner and Robert Ezra Park were both profoundly influential in the history of American sociology. Their somewhat milder interpretations of Darwinism represented an attempt to merge the traditions of German conflict sociology, Anglo-American empiricism, and Spencerian evolutionary theory into a truly scientific sociology. In their writings may already be seen those elements which serve to distinguish their views from the more bellicose Darwinism of Gumplowicz and Ratzenhofer on the one hand and the more detached sociologism of Durkheim on the other. Their contributions thus fall somewhat between the two emphases and approaches in the study of war.

One approach, characteristically German, glorified conflict and struggle in the service of nationalistic or racist militarism or, in the tradition of Marx, emphasized international class conflict. The other, characteristically French and English, best represented perhaps by Durkheim and his school in both sociology and anthropology, emphasized the sources of social cohesion and consensus *within* nations and cultures. The thinkers who emphasized class conflict tended to see war as a result of economic causes, particularly imperial-

[5] See the excellent discussion in Richard Hofstadter, *Social Darwinism in American Thought* (Boston: Beacon, 1955), especially chaps. 8–10.

[6] Theodore Roosevelt, *The Strenuous Life* (1899), cited in Hofstadter, *op. cit.*, p. 180.

ism,[7] whereas students of social cohesion and consensus have tended to focus on the functions of war in maintaining, intensifying, or destroying the pattern of societal relations in primitive cultures or modern nations.

The two divergent traditions in the study of war and conflict may be studied from the standpoint of the social units which were regarded as fundamental to each approach. Thus Marx could visualize a class conflict which crossed national lines and was a truly international movement—obstructed, perhaps, by "false consciousness," but not limited to particular societies.[8] Durkheim, by contrast, presented a sociological theory which emphasized the study of the sources of cohesion in society as a whole rather than as rent by class conflict. Durkheim's work appeared an entire intellectual generation later, when the fatuities of militaristic social Darwinism had already been completely exposed, in the work of Jacques Novicow, for example.

Durkheim used the tools of the sociological empiricist in continuing the quest for the sources of social solidarity in modern society initiated by Saint-Simon and Auguste Comte. He regarded the division of labor, occupational specialization, as the major structural source of solidarity in modern industrial society. In Durkheim's theory, however, is an unstated assumption concerning the larger consensus which united these bundles of solidarity provided by professional and occupational groupings. It is nationalism which provides the social cement for highly differentiated modern societies of which Durkheim wrote. Yet this element remains implicit rather than explicit in his analysis, leaving a logical gap in his theory.

The extent of intellectual indebtedness to social Darwinism of both of the approaches briefly sketched above is striking, though the implicit emphasis on survival and natural selection in modern functionalism has gone largely unnoticed. For there is a sense in which the entire development of modern functionalism in sociology and anthropology may be regarded as an intellectual offshoot of social Darwinism. The suppressed premise in all statements regarding the "function" of an institution or a specific group practice is its survival value. And survival of the fittest through natural selection in the struggle for existence was the keynote of social Darwinism, as it had been in the concepts of natural process of Darwin and Alfred Russell Wallace. These visions were themselves inspired by the work of Thomas Malthus, who presented in his *Essay on Population* the idea of a competitive struggle to the death for mere

[7] Marx's response to *The Origin of Species* was to pronounce it "a basis in natural science for the class struggle in history." Marx to Lasalle, January 16, 1861, cited by Gertrude Himmelfarb, *Darwinism and the Darwinian Revolution* (New York: Doubleday, 1959), p. 398.

[8] In this regard, the classical writings of Lenin, John Hobson, Thorstein Veblen, Joseph Schumpeter, and others constitute a significant aspect of the study of war by social scientists. Space limitations prohibited inclusion of what could easily have been another volume devoted to writings on the economic causes of war.

existence and a dispassionate analysis of the limitation of human population growth through war, disease, and famine. Thus the social scientists like William Graham Sumner, Robert Ezra Park, and even Bronislaw Malinowski had been influenced in their basic conceptions of society by the Darwinist world picture, and their notion of the "social function" of institutions reflects this to a greater or lesser degree in each case.

The essays in this section are limited to the works of sociologists and anthropologists who addressed themselves directly to the question of the causes of war or who asked themselves questions about its social functions. In this regard, there is a curious difference in the generations. Sociologists' interest in the causes of war appears to have been negligible during the past twenty years. With the possible exception of a few sociologists such as Hans Speier and Pitirim Sorokin, Americans in particular seem to have turned their attention elsewhere.[9] Alvin Gouldner, after examining twenty-five textbooks in introductory sociology published between 1945 and 1954, concluded that out of 17,000 pages of material, only 275 dealt with some aspect of the causes or effects of war. "More than half of the texts," reports Professor Gouldner, "dealt with this single most important problem of the modern world in less than ten pages." [10]

There have been many studies of the sociology of the military, notably by Samuel Stouffer and his associates and more recently by Morris Janowitz. But on the whole the neglect of war by contemporary sociologists has only recently begun to show signs of change, for example, in the polemical work of the late C. Wright Mills; of Amitai Etzioni; and of the contributors to the recent volume on *Preventing World War III* [11] and another volume, sponsored by the American Academy of Arts and Sciences, by social scientists on international conflict.[12]

By contrast, anthropologists have evidenced a continual interest in the phenomenon of war among primitive peoples. Some of their contributions may be gleaned from the selected bibliography, as well as from Joseph Schneider's reflective methodological contribution, which is included here. Most anthropologists who have studied war have dealt with the phenomenon in the context of specific ethnographic or comparative studies among relatively small, isolated, preliterate societies. They have tended to avoid the question of the causes of war in more general terms, and thus the contributions of Malinowski and Margaret Mead included here are not typical of anthropological writings on the subject. Rather, the latter tend to focus on the detailed examination of

[9] See Hans Speier, *Social Order and the Risks of War* (New York: Stewart, 1952), and Pitirim Sorokin, *Social and Cultural Dynamics* (4 vols.; New York: American Book Co., 1937), III, especially chap. 11.

[10] Introduction to Émile Durkheim, *Socialism and Saint-Simon* (London: Routledge and Kegan Paul, 1959), p. vii.

[11] Quincy Wright, William Evan, Morton Deutsch, eds. (New York: Simon and Schuster, 1962).

[12] *International Conflict and Behavioral Science* (New York: Basic Books, 1964).

specific practices regarding primitive warfare and the ways in which these are articulated in the social structure. Yet some anthropologists have recently reaffirmed the importance of the study of war and encouraged renewed interest in the subject "because anthropologists, accustomed to viewing phenomena in a cross-cultural, non-ethnocentric evolutionary perspective, have special contributions to make to the study of war." [13]

To sum up: the interest in the causes of war, mirrored in the attention of a previous generation of sociologists and anthropologists, largely represented in our selections, has not continued to the present. It is only now, with the threat of total annihilation through total war, that social scientists appear to be renewing their interests in these questions.

[13] Andrew P. Vayda and Anthony Leeds, "Anthropology and the Study of War," *Anthropologica*, III, No. 2 (1961), 131.

◀◀◀ ▶▶▶

WILLIAM GRAHAM SUMNER

War *

We have heard our political leaders say from time to time that, "War is necessary," "War is a good thing." They were trying to establish a major premise
which would suggest the conclusion, "Therefore let us have a little war now,"
or "It is wise, on general principles, to have a war once in a while." That argument may be taken as the text of the present essay. It has seemed to me worth
while to show from the history of civilization just what war has done and has
not done for the welfare of mankind.

In the eighteenth century it was assumed that the primitive state of mankind
was one of Arcadian peace, joy, and contentment. In the nineteenth century
the assumption went over to the other extreme—that the primitive state was
one of universal warfare. This, like the former notion, is a great exaggeration.
Man in the most primitive and uncivilized state known to us does not practice
war all the time; he dreads it. He might rather be described as a peaceful animal. Real warfare comes with the collisions of more developed societies.

If we turn to facts about the least civilized men, we find proofs that they are
not warlike and do not practice war if they can help it. The Australians have
no idea of conquest or battle. Their fights do not lead to slaughter or spoils or
other consequences of victory.[1] Sometimes a fight takes the form of a friendly
trial of skill with weapons between two parties who, one by one, cast their

---

* Reprinted from William Graham Sumner, *War and Other Essays*, by permission of the
publisher (Copyright 1911, Yale University Press, New Haven).

[1] Edward Curr, *The Australian Race* (Melbourne: J. Ferres, 1886–1887), I, 86.

weapons at each other. Quarrels between tribes are sometimes settled by a single combat between chiefs. "Real fighting rarely takes place unless the women arouse the men," and even then it is only carried on by taunts and wrestling. "The first wound ends the combat." It is often followed by a war of words, hair-pulling, and blows with yam sticks between the women.[2] The Australians have no war because they have no property that is worth pillaging; no tribe has anything to tempt the cupidity of another. They have no political organization, so there can be no war for power.[3] Each group appropriates hunting grounds, and over these war arises only with the increase of population. An Englishman who knew them well said that he knew of serious wounds, but he had known of but one death from their affrays.[4]

Neither are the Papuans of New Guinea warlike in all parts of the island. Like other men on the same grade of civilization, they may be assassins, but they are not warriors, and, if two bodies of them meet in hostility, we are told that "there is a remarkably small death-roll at the end of the battle."[5] Of another group of them we are told that they have no offensive weapons at all, but live without disturbance from neighbors and without care for the future.[6] Their children rarely quarrel at play, and, if they do, it ends in words. We are told that they lack the courage, temper, and concentration of will which would be necessary for a good schoolboy fight. Perhaps the converse would be true: they have no schoolboy fights and therefore have no courage, temper, and concentration of will. We are not astonished to hear that they develop excessive tyranny and cruelty to those who are weaker than themselves, especially to women, and even to their mothers.[7] These people are excessively distrustful of each other, and villages but a little distance apart have very little intercourse. This is attributed in great part to head-hunting and cannibalism. In general they know the limits of their own territory and observe them, but they quarrel about women.[8] The people in German Melanesia are of the same kind; they are cowardly and mean, make raids on each other's land to destroy and plunder when they think they can do it safely, but they will not join battle.[9] On some of the small islands war is entirely unknown.[10]

[2] James Dawson, *Australian Aborigines* (Melbourne: G. Robertson, 1881), p. 77.

[3] Richard Semon, *In the Australian Bush* (London and New York: Macmillan Co., 1899), p. 225.

[4] Robert B. Smyth, *Aborigines of Victoria* (Melbourne: J. Ferres, 1878), I, 156, 160.

[5] Charles W. Abel, *Savage Life in New Guinea*, etc. (London: London Missionary Society, 1902), p. 130.

[6] Maxmillian Krieger, *Neu Guinea* (Berlin: A. Schall, 1899), p. 205.

[7] Joachim Pfeil, *Studien und Beobachtungen aus der Südsee* (Braunschweig: F. Vieweg und Sohn, 1899), p. 23.

[8] Bernard Hagen, *Unter den Papua's*, etc. (Wiesbaden: C. W. Kreidel, 1889), p. 250.

[9] Pfeil, *op. cit.*, p. 125.

[10] Jan Kubary, *Beitrag zur Kenntnis der Núkúoro-oder Monteverde-Inseln*, p. 20; *idem, Ethnographische Beitrag zur Kenntnis des Karolinen Archipels* (Leiden: P. W. M. Trap, 1895), p. 94; Adolf Bastian, *Die mikronesischen Kolonien*, etc. (Berlin: A. Asher, 1899), p. 4.

The Chatham Islanders sometimes quarreled over booty won in pursuing seals or whales, but they had a law that the first drop of blood ended the fight.[11] The Khonds in Madras became insubordinate a few years ago, and a police force was sent against them; they prepared stones to roll down the hill in front of their village, but left the rear unguarded and, when the police entered by the rear, the Khonds protested against the unfairness of this movement after they had taken such precautions in front. The Rengmahs on the Assam Hills attach to the body a tail of wood eighteen inches long, curved upward, which they use to wag defiance at an enemy.[12] Such people evidently could never have had much experience of war. The Mrú on the Chittagong Hills are peaceable, timid, and simple; in a quarrel they do not fight, but call in an exorcist to take the sense of the spirits on the matter.[13]

Livingstone says that the tribes in the interior of South Africa, where no slave trade existed, seldom had any war except about cattle, and some tribes refused to keep cattle in order not to offer temptation. In one case only had he heard of war for any other reason; three brothers, Barolongs, fought over one woman, and their tribe had remained divided, up to the time of writing, into three parties. During his residence in the Bechuana country he never saw unarmed men strike each other. They quarrel with words, but generally both parties burst into a laugh and that ends it.[14] By an exception among the Canary Islanders, the people of Hierro knew no war and had no weapons, although their long leaping poles could be used as such when occasion demanded.[15]

A Spanish priest, writing an account in 1739 of the Aurohuacos of Colombia, says that they have no weapons of offense or defense.[16] If two quarrel, they go out to a big rock or tree, and each with his staff beats the rock or tree with vituperations. The one whose staff breaks first is the victor; then they embrace and return home as friends. Even our American Indians, who appear in our legends to be so bloodthirsty and warlike, always appreciated the blessings of peace. Wampum strings and belts were associated with peace pacts and with prayers for peace.

In contrast with these cases we find others of extreme warlikeness which account for the current idea that primitive men love war and practice it all the time. But if we examine the cases of peacefulness or unwarlikeness which have been cited, we see that only two or three seem to present evidence of Arcadian peace and simplicity, such as, in the imagination of the eighteenth-century

[11] B. Weiss, *Mehr als fünfzig Jahre auf Chatham Island*, p. 18.

[12] *Journal of the Anthropological Institute of Great Britain and Ireland*, XI, p. 197.

[13] Thomas H. Lewin, *Wild Races of South-Eastern India* (London: W. H. Allen & Co., 1870), p. 232.

[14] David Livingstone, *Missionary Travels and Researches in South Africa* (New York: Harpers, 1872), I, 232; II, 503.

[15] *American Anthropologist*, N.S. II, 475.

[16] *Ibid.*, N.S. III, 612.

philosophers, characterized men in a state of nature. Probably if we had fuller knowledge these few instances would be much modified. What we see is that men have always quarreled. The cases which have been selected are some of them also those of people who have been defeated, broken, and cowed down. Another set of examples consists of those in which abstinence from war is due to cowardice, and with it go the vices of cowardice—tyranny and cruelty to the weak. These cases are calculated to delight the hearts of the advocates of strenuosity. What our testimonies have in common is this: they show that we cannot postulate a warlike character or a habit of fighting as a universal or even characteristic trait of primitive man.

When we undertake to talk about primitive society, we should conceive of it as consisting of petty groups scattered separately over a great territory. I speak of groups because I want a term of the widest significance. The group may consist, as it does among Australians and Bushmen, of a man with one or possibly two wives and their children, or it may have a few more members, or it may be a village group as in New Guinea or a tribe or part of a tribe as among our own Indians. It is to be observed that this ultimate unit is a group and not an individual. Every individual excludes every other in the competition of life unless they can by combining together win more out of nature by joint effort than the sum of what they could win separately. This combination is what makes groups and brings about industrial organization. When a man and woman unite in the most elementary group known, they do it for economic reasons, because they can carry on the struggle for existence better together than apart. In time this turns into a kin group, united by blood. This remains undivided as long as its organization gives advantages, but breaks up when it grows too big for the existing economic system. As soon as it breaks, the fractions begin to compete with each other. If by greater culture a higher organization becomes possible, two groups coalesce by intermarriage or conquest, competition gives way to combination again, and the bigger unit enters into competition with other composite units. Thus at all stages throughout the history of civilization, competition and combination forever alternate with each other.

These groups are independent of each other, their size being determined by their mode of life, because the number who can live together economically is limited by the possibilities of the food quest. When a group outgrows this limit, it breaks up and scatters. The fact of former association is long remembered, and there is a bond of kinship and alliance which may at times draw former associates together again for festivals and religious observances, but, after they separate, the tendency is to become entirely independent and to fall under the type just described, that is, scattered groups each with its individuality, yet in a certain neighborhood to each other. Their remoter relationship does not keep them from quarreling and fighting. In the book of Judges we see cases of war between tribes of Israel in spite of the higher bond which united them with each other and separated them from the Gentiles.[17]

All the members of one group are comrades to each other and have a common interest against every other group. If we assume a standpoint in one group, we may call that one the "we group" or the ingroup; then every other group is to us an "others-group" or an outgroup. The sentiment which prevails inside the we-group, between its members, is that of peace and cooperation; the sentiment which prevails inside of a group toward all outsiders is that of hostility and war. These two sentiments are perfectly consistent with each other; in fact, they necessarily complement each other. Let us see why that is so.

War arises from the competition of life, not from the struggle for existence. In the struggle for existence a man is wrestling with nature to extort from her the means of subsistence. It is when two men are striving side by side in the struggle for existence to extort from nature the supplies they need that they come into rivalry, and a collision of interest with each other takes place. This collision may be light and unimportant, if the supplies are large and the number of men small, or it may be harsh and violent, if there are many men striving for a small supply. This collision we call the competition of life. Of course, men are in the competition of life with beasts, reptiles, insects, and plants— in short, with all organic forms; we will, however, confine our attention to men. The greater or less intensity of the competition of life is a fundamental condition of human existence, and the competition arises between those ultimate units groups which I have described. The members of the unit group work together. The Australian or Bushman hunter goes abroad to seek meat food, while the woman stays by the fire at a trysting place with the children and collects plant food. They cooperate in the struggle for existence, and the size of the group is fixed by the number who can work together to the greatest advantage under their mode of life. Such a group, therefore, has a common interest. It must have control of a certain area of land; hence it comes into collision of interest with every other group. The competition of life, therefore, arises between groups not between individuals, and we see that the members of the ingroup are allies and joint partners in one interest while they are brought into antagonism of interest with all outsiders. It is the competition of life, therefore, which makes war, and that is why war always has existed and always will. It is in the conditions of human existence. In the cases which have been cited of nature peoples who have no war, we have heard mention already of division of hunting grounds and of quarrels which arise about them. Wherever there is no war, there we find that there is no crowding, as among the scattered Eskimo, or that, after long fighting, treaties and agreements have

17 *Judges* 12, 20.

been made to cover all relations of interest between the groups. These we call peace pacts, and it is evident that they consist in conventional agreements creating some combination between the groups which are parties to the agreement.

Each group must regard every other as a possible enemy on account of the antagonism of interests, and so it views every other group with suspicion and distrust, although actual hostilities occur only on specific occasion. Every member of another group is a stranger; he may be admitted as a guest, in which case rights and security are granted him, but, if not so admitted, he is an enemy. We can now see why the sentiments of peace and cooperation inside are complementary to sentiments of hostility outside. It is because any group, in order to be strong against an outside enemy, must be well disciplined, harmonious, and peaceful inside; in other words, because discord inside would cause defeat in battle with another group. Therefore the same conditions which made men warlike against outsiders made them yield to the control of chiefs, submit to discipline, obey law, cultivate peace, and create institutions inside. The notion of rights grows up in the ingroup from the usages established there securing peace. There was a double education, at the same time, out of the same facts and relations. It is no paradox at all to say that peace makes war and that war makes peace. There are two codes of morals and two sets of mores, one for comrades inside and the other for strangers outside, and they arise from the same interests. Against outsiders it was meritorious to kill, plunder, practice blood revenge, and to steal women and slaves, but inside none of these things could be allowed because they would produce discord and weakness. Hence, in the ingroup, law (under the forms of custom and taboo) and institutions had to take the place of force. Every group was a peace group inside, and the peace was sanctioned by the ghosts of the ancestors who had handed down the customs and taboos. Against outsiders religion sanctioned and encouraged war, for the ghosts of the ancestors, or the gods, would rejoice to see their posterity and worshipers once more defeat, slay, plunder, and enslave the ancient enemy.

The Eskimos of Bering Strait think it wrong to steal from people in the same village or tribe; a thief is publicly reproached and forced to return the thing stolen. But to steal from an outsider is not wrong unless it brings harm on one's own tribe.[18] Strabo says of the Scythians that they were just and kind to each other, but very savage toward all outsiders.[19] The sentiment of cohesion, internal comradeship, and devotion to the ingroup, which carries with it a sense of superiority to any outgroup and readiness to defend the interests of the ingroup against the outgroup, is technically known as ethnocentrism. It is really the sentiment of patriotism in all its philosophic fullness, that is, both

[18] *Bureau of American Ethnology*, 18, I, 207.
[19] *Ibid.*, pp. 300, 302.

in its rationality and in its extravagant exaggeration. The Mohaves and the Seri of southern California will have no relations of marriage or trade with any other people; they think themselves superior. The Mohaves are wild and barbarous, and the Seri are on a lower grade of civilization than any other tribe in America. Therefore, we see that ethnocentrism has nothing to do with the relative grade of civilization of any people. The Seri think that "the brightest virtue is the shedding of alien blood, while the blackest crime in their calendar is alien conjugal union." [20] Perhaps nine-tenths of all the names given by savage tribes to themselves mean "men," "the only men," or "men of men"; that is, "We are men, the rest are something else." A recent etymology of the word Iroquois makes it mean "I am the real man." [21] In general Indians held that they were a favored race, due to a special creation.[22] Nansen gives a letter written by an Eskimo in 1756 when he heard of the war between England and France.[23] He burst into a rhapsody about Greenland. "Your unfruitfulness makes us happy and saves us from molestation." The writer was surprised that the Christians had not learned better manners amongst the Eskimo, and he proposed to send missionaries to them. A traveler in Formosa says that the Formosans thought foreigners barbarians, "civilization being solely within the dominion of the Celestial Emperor. All the rest of the world—if there was any poor remainder—was benighted, and but the home of 'barbarians,' not 'men.' " [24] This is the language of ethnocentrism; it may be read in the newspapers of any civilized country today.

We find then that there are two sentiments in the minds of the same men at the same time. These have been called militancy and industrialism. The latter term does not seem to be a good one, and it is not apt until we reach high civilization; what we want is a term to express the peace sentiment in antithesis to militancy, but industrialism has obtained currency and it has this much justification even for savage life—that inside the group the needs of life must be provided for by productive labor. Generally that is left to the women, and the men practice militarism.

It would not be possible for neighboring groups to remain really isolated from each other. One has in its territory stone or salt, water or fuel, limited fruits, melons, nuts, fish, or perhaps other natural materials which the others need. They also take wives from each other, generally, but not always. Hence arise treaties of *commercium* and *connubium,* which bring about a middle state of things between war and peace. These treaties are the origin of international law. A comparison of modern municipal and international law will show that

[20] *Ibid.,* 17, I, 11; *American Anthropologist,* N.S. IV, 558.
[21] *American Anthropologist,* N.S. IV, 558.
[22] *Bureau of American Ethnology,* VIII, 36.
[23] Fridtjof Nansen, *Eskimo Life* (London: Longmans, Green and Co., 1893), p. 180.
[24] William A. Pickering, *Pioneering in Formosa* (London: Hurst & Blackett, 1898), p. 136.

the difference between the relations of members of the ingroup with each other and of the groups with each other still exists.

If now we turn back to the question with which I started, whether men began in a state of peace or a state of war, we see the answer. They began with both together. Which preponderated is a question of the intensity of the competition of life at the time. When that competition was intense, war was frequent and fierce, the weaker were exterminated or absorbed by the stronger, the internal discipline of the conquerors became stronger, chiefs got more absolute power, laws became more stringent, religious observances won greater authority, and so the whole societal system was more firmly integrated. On the other hand, when there were no close or powerful neighbors, there was little or no war, the internal organization remained lax and feeble, chiefs had little power, and a societal system scarcely existed.

The four great motives which move men to social activity are hunger, love, vanity, and fear of superior powers. If we search out the causes which have moved men to war, we find them under each of these motives or interests. Men have fought for hunting grounds, for supplies which are locally limited and may be monopolized, for commerce, for slaves, and probably also for human flesh. These motives come under hunger, or the food quest, or more widely under the economic effort to win subsistence. They have fought for and on account of women, which we must put partly under love, although the women were wanted chiefly as laborers and so, along with the slaves, would come under the former head. They have fought to win heads or scalps or other trophies and for honor or dignity or purely for glory; this comes under the operation of vanity. They have fought for blood revenge, to prevent or punish sorcery, and to please their gods; these motives belong under the fear of superior powers. It was reserved for modern civilized men to fight on account of differences of religion, and from this motive the fiercest and most persistent wars have been waged.

Is there anything grand or noble in any of these motives of war? Not a bit. But we must remember that the motives from which men act have nothing at all to do with the consequences of their action. Where will you find in history a case of a great purpose rationally adopted by a great society and carried through to the intended result and then followed by the expected consequences in the way of social advantage? You can find no such thing. Men act from immediate and interested motives like these for which they have waged war, and the consequences come out of the forces which are set loose. The consequences may be advantageous or disadvantageous to men. The story of these acts and consequences makes up human history. So it has been with war. While men were fighting for glory and greed, for revenge and superstition, they were building human society. They were acquiring discipline and cohesion; they were learning cooperation, perseverance, fortitude, and patience. Those are not savage virtues; they are products of education. War forms larger social units and produces states; of the North American Indians, those had the intensest feeling of unity who were the most warlike.[25] The Netherlands form a striking example in modern history of the weakness of a state which is internally divided; the best historian of Dutch civilization tells us that the internal disintegration was always greatest in times of truce or of peace.[26] There can be no doubt that the Germans of today owe their pre-eminence in industry and science to the fact that they are a highly disciplined nation. A Portuguese sociologist says that, "War is the living fountain from which flows the entire society." [27] If we fix our minds on the organic growth and organization of society, this assertion is not exaggerated. An American sociologist says that, "In spite of the countless miseries which follow in its train, war has probably been the highest stimulus to racial progress. It is the most potent excitant known to all the faculties." [28] The great conquests have destroyed what was effete and opened the way for what was viable. What appalls us, however, is the frightful waste of this process of evolution by war—waste of life and waste of capital. It is this waste which has made the evolution of civilization so slow.

Here, then, let us turn back and see how the peace element develops alongside the war element. We shall find that peace rules and peace institutions have been established, from the earliest civilization, even for the relations of groups with each other. House peace is perhaps the simplest form. The nature people very often bury a man under his own fireplace, and from this usage radiate various customs, all of which go to associate the ghosts of the dead with the hearthstone of the living. It follows that quarreling, brawling, or violence near the hearth is an insult to the ghosts. Hence arises a notion of religious sacredness about the hearth, an atmosphere of peace is created, and the women who live in the house and work at the hearth profit by it. The householder has a dignity and prerogative in his house however humble his social position may be; hence the maxim that a man's house is his castle goes back to the beginning of civilization. It may be only a wind shelter, but the ghosts protect it and any stranger, fugitive, suppliant, even an enemy, if admitted, comes under the house protection and hospitality while there. As the house becomes larger and better, the peace taboo extends from the fireplace to the whole house and then to the yard or enclosure. This is the house peace.

If any group which possesses deposits of salt, flintstone fit for implements, pipestone, water supply, or special foods should try to prevent others from having access to the same, all others would join in war against that one until an agreement was made and established by usage. This agreement is either one of peaceful access to natural supplies or one of trade. Tribes also agree to take

[25] *American Anthropologist,* N.S. IV, 279.
[26] C. F. van Duyl, *Overzicht der Beschavingsgeschiedenis van het Nederlandsche Volk,* p. 190.
[27] J. P. Oliveira Martins, *As Raças Humanas,* etc., II, 55.
[28] Daniel G. Brinton, *Races and Peoples* (Philadelphia: D. McKay, 1901), p. 76.

wives from each other. We often have reason to be astonished at the institution-making power of nature men when disagreeable experience has forced them to find relief. The Tubu of the Sahara are warlike and distrustful even of each other to such an extent that they scarcely form a society; even in their villages they quarrel and fight. It is a very noteworthy feature that these people have no notion of rights. It is the ingroup as a peace group which is the school of rights; as we have seen, there can be peace and order inside only by law (using this term in its broadest sense), but a law creates and enforces rights. Now these Tubu have been forced to make a law that inside the village no weapons may be worn, so that here already we find an institutional arrangement to limit warlikeness.[29] When Nachtigal, visiting the Tubu, complained of their ill usage of himself and threatened to go away, they pointed out to him that, as soon as he had left their territory, he would be at their mercy.[30] This shows that even they had an idea of some rights of a guest inside their group as compared with his status outside, when he would be protected by nothing. The Bedouins have the same notion. They are ruthless robbers and murderers, but a guest in the tent is perfectly safe and entitled to their best hospitality. When he leaves it he is fair game, whether enemy, friend, or neighbor.[31]

The west Australians have a usage that any man who has committed a wrong according to their code must submit to a flight of spears from all who think themselves aggrieved, or he must allow a spear to be thrust through his leg or arm. There is a tariff of wounds as penalty for all common crimes.[32] We understand that this is an ingroup usage. It is a common custom in Australia that a man who has stolen a wife from an outgroup must submit to a flight of spears from her group comrades; this is now only a ceremony, but it is a peace institution which has set aside old warfare on account of stolen women. As we have seen, the Australians live in very small groups, but they assemble from time to time in large kin groups for purposes of festivals of a religious character. The kin groups are not peace groups, because they are loose and have no common life.[33] At the assemblies all the sacred objects are brought into the ceremonial ground, but, on account of the danger of quarrels, no display of arms is allowed anywhere near the sacred objects.[34] Bearers of messages from one tribe to another are regarded as under a peace taboo in eastern Australia; women are under a peace taboo and hence are employed as ambas-

---

[29] Gustav Nachtigal, *Sahara und Sudan* (Berlin: Weidmann, 1879–1889), I, 439.

[30] *Ibid.*, I, p. 276.

[31] John Lewis Burckhardt, *Notes on the Bedouins,* etc. (London: Henry Colborn & Richard Bentlet, 1830), p. 90.

[32] George Grey, *Journals of Two Expeditions of Discovery in North-west and Western Australia* (London: T. & W. Boone, 1841), II, 243.

[33] Curr, *op. cit.,* I, p. 69.

[34] Baldwin Spencer and F. J. Gillen, *Native Tribes of Central Australia* (London and New York: Macmillan Co., 1899), p. 135.

sadors to arrange disputes between tribes. After a quarrel there is a corroboree
to make and confirm peace.[35] These usages are institutional. They are positive
rules of an arbitrary character, depending upon agreement and usage, but are
devised to satisfy expediency. In Queensland no fighting at all is allowed at
night in camp; those who want to fight must go outside, and after a fight the
victor must show to his comrades that he had a real grievance. If he does not
convince them of this, they force him to submit to the same mutilation from
his victim that he has inflicted. The women fight with their yam sticks, which
are about four feet long. One woman allows the other to strike her on the head;
the second must then submit to a blow; thus they go on until one does not
want any more.[36] What we have to notice here is that the fight, inside the
group, is under regulations, which fact makes it institutional. The duel is a
similar case of a conventionalized fight in the midst of a peaceful civil order.
In all these cases we see that war is admitted inside of a peace group when
individuals are wronged or offended by comrades, but only in conventionalized
and regulated form, so that it is a kind of lawful war.

We also find war between groups under some regulation and convention-
alization when there is a bond of kinship or religion uniting the two groups.
It appears that this is the origin of the rules of war by which its horrors are
reduced. On the island of Tanna in the New Hebrides the eight thousand inhabitants are divided into two groups, one at each end of the island, and each
group is subdivided into villages. If two villages in the same division fight, as
they often do, the fighting is not intense, and there is no cannibalism; but between the two big divisions there is blood revenge, and, if they fight, there
is no limit to the ferocity, cannibalism being then practiced.[37] On the Mortlock
Islands, when two tribes go to war, each warrior must select as his antagonist
on the other side one who is not in the same kin group with himself.[38] Among
certain Sumatrans, if a man of one village has a grievance against a man of
another, the men of the former go into the fields of the other, where they are
met by the local chief, who asks their errand. They answer that they have
come to destroy the plantation of the man in the village who has injured a man
of theirs. The chief admits that this is just, but proposes to avoid violence; so
he brings to them fruit from the plantation of the offender and, if the offense
was great, he allows them to destroy a certain number of trees on it. They also
burn down the offender's house "ceremonially"—a little hut is built of light
material on his field and with triumphant cries is set on fire by the offended

[35] Robert H. Matthews, "Message Sticks Used by the Aborigines of Australia," *American
Anthropologist*, X, 290; Smyth, *op. cit.*, I, pp. 165, 181; Curr, *op. cit.*, I, p. 92.

[36] Walter E. Roth, *Ethnological Studies among the North-West-Central Queensland
Aborigines* (Brisbane: E. Gregory, 1897), p. 141.

[37] *Australian Association for the Advancement of Science*, 1892, p. 648.

[38] Otto Finsch, *Ethnologische Erfahrungen und Belegstücke aus der Südsee* (Wien:
1888–1891), III, 311.

party. Generally an agreement is reached, but, if not, long hostilities endure between two neighboring villages.[39]

The Christian states have always professed to moderate somewhat the horrors of war when they went to fighting with each other, and so we have laws of war which are good between the states agreeing to them, but not with outsiders. This makes a limited peace group of all the states which unite now to make international law. Let us follow these peace institutions up into higher civilization.

The Scandinavian people spread in small bodies over their territory, and these bodies often engaged in war with each other. They had a common sanctuary at Uppsala at which there were annual festivals. This religious bond kept up a certain sense of national unity, which, however, has never produced national sympathy. At the festivals at Uppsala peace was enforced for the time and place; disputes were settled and fairs held, and there were also feasts and conferences.[40] The Swedes in the thirteenth century formed kin groups which adopted rules of mutual succor and defense.[41] The dwellings of kings also came to have insofar the character of sanctuaries that peace was maintained around them.[42] The ancient Germans maintained by law and severe penalties peace for women as to person and property; the penalties for wrong to a woman varied in the laws of the different German nations, but were two or three times as great as for wrongs to men.[43] The house peace was also very fully developed in German law.[44] The Peace of God was perhaps the most remarkable case in history of a law to establish a time taboo against war and violence. In the tenth century the church tried to curb the robber barons and to protect merchants; the attempts were often repeated with little result, but the Truce of God was at last established in 1041 by the bishop of Arles and the abbot of Cluny, and it won some acceptance throughout France. There was to be no fighting between Wednesday evening and Monday morning; later these limits were changed.[45] No such law was ever obeyed with any precision, and it never became a custom, much less an institution, but it had some influence. As the kings gained real power and prestige in the feudal states, they made the king's peace a great reality; it went with the development of the modern state. The king's peace was a name for a central civil authority which could put down all private war and violations of public order and establish a peace group over a

[39] Christian Snouck-Hurgronje, *The Achehnese* (London: Luzac & Co., 1906).

[40] Erik G. Geijer, *Svenska Folkets, Historia* (Stockholm: P. A. Norstedt & Söner, 1876), I, 12, 112.

[41] Oscar Montelius, *Sveriges Historia* (Stockholm: H. Linnströms förlag, 1877–1881), I, 461.

[42] *Folklore*, XI (1900), p. 285.

[43] Carl Stammler, *Ueber die Stellung der Frauen im alten deutschen Recht* (Berlin: 1877), p. 9.

[44] Eduard Osenbrüggen, *Der Hausfrieden* (Erlangen: Ferdinand Enke, 1887).

[45] Van Duyl, *op. cit.*, p. 110.

great extent of territory within which rights, law, and civil authority should
be secured by competent tribunals. In the Holy Roman Empire of the German
nation the public general peace of the empire was introduced in 1495, but the
emperors never had the means to enforce it, and it did not exist until 1873. We
can see how the king's peace grew by the following case: Canute the Dane
made a law in England that, if any unknown man was found dead, he should
be assumed to be a Dane, and a special tax, called *murdrum,* should be paid
for him to the king. William the Conqueror followed this example, only the
unknown man was assumed to be a Norman; if it could be proved that he was
an Englishman ("proving his Englishry"), then the murderer or the hundred
had nothing to pay to the king but only the legal compensation to the family
of the deceased, if he had one.[46] This means that the king first extended his
peace over his own countrymen by a special penalty on the murder of one of
them, while Englishmen were left only under the old law of composition for
blood revenge; but in time equal protection was extended to all his subjects.
Again, at the time of the Conquest all crimes committed on the roads which ran
through a city (Canterbury, for instance) were crimes against the king's peace
—which also extended one league, three perches, and three feet beyond the
city gate. This means that the high roads which ran through a town were first
brought under the king's peace, and this peace also extended beyond the royal
burgh for an extent which was measured with droll accuracy. What was a
crime elsewhere was a greater crime there, and what was not a crime elsewhere
might be a crime there. King Edmund forbade blood revenge in his burgh; [47]
that is, he delimited an ingroup in which there must be law and an administration of justice by his tribunal. Jews and merchants bought the protection of
the king's peace throughout his realm. From this germ grew up the state as a
peace group and the king's peace as the law of the land; we Americans call it
the peace of the people.

One of the most remarkable examples of a peace group which could be mentioned is the League of the Iroquois which was formed in the sixteenth century; it deserves to be classed here with the peace institutions of civilized
states. This league was a confederation of five, afterward six, tribes of Indians,
to maintain peace. By Indian usage blood revenge was a duty, but the Iroquois
confederation put a stop to this, as between its members, by substituting laws
and civil authority. It was, for its stage, fully as marvelous a production of
statesmanship as are these United States—themselves a great peace confederation. Compared with Algonquins and Sioux the Iroquois were an industrial
society. They tried to force others to join the confederacy—that is, to come
into the peace pact or to make an alliance with it; if they would do neither, war

[46] Frederick A. Inderwick, *The King's Peace* (London: S. Sonnenschoen & Co., 1895),
p. 27.
[47] Frederick W. Maitland, *Domesday Book and Beyond* (Cambridge, Eng.: Cambridge
University Press, 1897), p. 184.

arose, and the outside people were either exterminated or absorbed.[48] Hiawatha was the culture hero to whom the formation of the league was attributed. The constitution was held in memory by strings of wampum, and at annual festivals there were confessions and exhortations. The duties inculcated were those of a warrior toward outsiders and of tribal brotherhood toward insiders. "The duty of living in harmony and peace, of avoiding evil-speaking, of kindness to the orphan, of charity to the needy, and of hospitality to all would be among the prominent topics brought under consideration" at the annual assemblies.[49]

We have now found a peace of the house, of the sanctuary, of religion, of the market, of women, of the popular assembly, and of the king, all of which were legal and institutional checks upon war and an introduction of rational and moral methods in the place of force. Let us see next what has been the relation between religion on the one side and peace or war on the other.

Those who perform the rites of worship toward the same ancestors or the same gods come into the same cult group, but no religion has ever succeeded in making its cult group into a peace group, although they all try to do it. The salutation of members of a cult group to each other is very generally "Peace" or something equivalent. Quakers call themselves "friends" and always have a closer bond to each other than to the outside world. Such a peace group is only an ideal for all who profess the same religion; in most of the great religions down to the seventeenth century, dissenters or heretics were always treated with great severity, because it was thought that they would bring down the wrath of the ghost or the god not only on themselves but also on the whole community. The New England Puritans had this notion that the sins of some would bring down the wrath of God on the whole. Religion has always intensified ethnocentrism; the adherents of a religion always think themselves the chosen people, or else they think that their god is superior to all others, which amounts to the same thing. The Jews looked down upon all non-Jews as Gentiles; the Mohammedans despise all infidels—their attitude toward non-Muslims is one leading to aggression, plunder, and annihilation. The Greeks looked down on all non-Greeks as barbarians, but in their case the sentiment was only partly religious; they themselves were never united by their own religion. In the thirteenth and fourteenth centuries, when Mohammedanism threatened to overwhelm Christendom, Latin Christians were inflamed with greater rage against Greek Christians than against Mohammedans. Nicholas V in 1452 gave to Alfonso V of Portugal authority to subjugate any non-Christians, having in view especially people of the west coast of Africa, and to reduce them to servitude (*illorum personas in servitutem*), which probably did not mean slavery,

<hr/>

[48] Horatio Hale, *The Iroquois Book of Rites* (Philadelphia: D. G. Brinton, 1883), in D. G. Brinton, *Library of Aboriginal American Literature* (Philadelphia: D. G. Brinton, 1882–1890), II, 68, 70, 92; Lewis H. Morgan, *League of the Iroquois* (New York, Dodd, Mead, 1901), p. 91.

[49] *Ibid.*, p. 190; Hale, *op. cit.*, p. 320.

but subjection.[50] The Spaniards and Portuguese of the sixteenth century treated all aborigines with ruthlessness because the aborigines were outside of Christianity and entitled to no rights or consideration. When the American colonies revolted, the English were amazed that the colonists could ally themselves with Frenchmen against the mother country, although the French were Roman Catholics in religion, absolutists in the state, and of an alien nationality. Buddhism is characterized by a pervading peacefulness, but no religion has ever kept its adherents from fighting each other. The instances which have been cited suffice to show that religion has been quite as much a stimulus to war as to peace, and religious wars are proverbial for ruthlessness and ferocity.

Christianity has always contained an ideal of itself as a peace group. The medieval church tried to unite all Christendom into a cult and peace group which should reach over all the disintegration and war of the feudal period. This was the sense of medieval Catholicity. Churches, convents, and ecclesiastical persons were put under a peace taboo. The church, however, at the same time entered into an alliance with the feudal nobles and adopted militant methods; heretics were dealt with as outside the fold. The modern state, as it began to take definite form, entered into a contest with the church for the control of society and for the guardianship of peace because the church had failed to secure peace.

The United States presents us a case quite by itself. We have here a confederated state which is a grand peace group. It occupies the heart of a continent; therefore there can be no question of balance of power here and no need of war preparations such as now impoverish Europe. The United States is a new country with a sparse population and no strong neighbors. Such a state will be a democracy and a republic, and it will be "free" in almost any sense that its people choose. If this state becomes militant, it will be because its people choose to become such; it will be because they think that war and warlikeness are desirable in themselves and are worth going after. On their own continent they need never encounter war on their path of industrial and political development up to any standard which they choose to adopt. It is a very remarkable fact, and one which has had immense influence on the history of civilization, that the land of the globe is divided into two great sections, the mass of Europe, Asia, and Africa on the one side and these two Americas on the other and that one of these worlds remained unknown to the other until only four hundred years ago. We talk a great deal about progress and modern enlightenment and democracy and the happiness of the masses, but very few people seem to know to what a great extent all those things are consequences of the discovery of the New World. As to this matter of war which we are now considering, the fact that the New World is removed to such a distance from the Old World made it possible for men to make a new start here. It was pos-

[50] Odoricus Raynaldus, *Annales Ecclesiasticae* (Lucae: Typis. Venturini, 1738–1746), pp. 18, 423.

sible to break old traditions, to revise institutions, and to think out a new philosophy to fit an infant society at the same time that whatever there was in the inheritance from the Old World which seemed good and available might be kept. It was a marvelous opportunity; to the student of history and human institutions it seems incredible that it ever could have been offered. The men who founded this republic recognized that opportunity and tried to use it. It is we who are now here who have thrown it away; we have decided that, instead of working out the advantages of it by peace, simplicity, domestic happiness, industry, and thrift, we would rather do it in the old way by war and glory, alternate victory and calamity, adventurous enterprises, grand finance, powerful government, and great social contrasts of splendor and misery. Future ages will look back to us with amazement and reproach that we should have made such a choice in the face of such an opportunity and should have entailed on them the consequences—for the opportunity will never come again.

Some illustration of our subject has, however, been furnished by the internal history of our peace group. The aborigines of this continent have never been taken into our peace bond, and our law about them is, consequently, full of inconsistencies. Sometimes they have been treated as comrades in the ingroup, sometimes as an outgroup with which our group was on a footing of hostility. Another question seems to be arising with respect to the Negroes; we have been trying, since the Civil War, to absorb them into our peace bond, but we have not succeeded. They are in it and not of it now, as much as, or more than, in the days of slavery, for the two races live more independently of each other now than they did in those former days. The Southern States do not constitute true societies because they lack unity of interest and sentiment on account of the race difference which divides them. This discord may prove worse and more fatal to the internal integrity of the peace group than such old antagonisms of interest as disturb Ireland, the national antagonisms which agitate Austria-Hungary, or the religious antagonisms which distract Belgium. In short, a state needs to be a true peace group in which there is sufficient concord and sympathy to overcome the antagonisms of nationality, race, class, and so on, and in which are maintained institutions adequate to adjust interests and control passions. Before even the great civilized states have reached this model, there is yet much to be done.

If we look at these facts about peace laws and institutions and the formation of peace groups in connection with the facts previously presented about the causes of war and the taste for war, we see that militancy and peacefulness have existed side by side in human society from the beginning just as they exist now. A peaceful society must be industrial because it must produce instead of plundering; it is for this reason that the industrial type of society is the opposite of the militant type. In any state on the continent of Europe today these two types of societal organization may be seen interwoven with each other and fighting each other. Industrialism builds up; militancy wastes. If a railroad is built, trade and intercourse indicate a line on which it ought to run; military strategy, however, overrules this and requires that it run otherwise. Then all the interests of trade and intercourse must be subjected to constant delay and expense because the line does not conform to them. Not a discovery or invention is made but the war and navy bureaus of all the great nations seize it to see what use can be made of it in war. It is evident that men love war; when two hundred thousand men in the United States volunteer in a month for a war with Spain which appeals to no sense of wrong against their country and to no other strong sentiment of human nature, when their lives are by no means monotonous or destitute of interest, and where life offers chances of wealth and prosperity, the pure love of adventure and war must be strong in our population. Europeans who have to do military service have no such enthusiasm for war as war. The presence of such a sentiment in the midst of the most purely industrial state in the world is a wonderful phenomenon. At the same time the social philosophy of the modern civilized world is saturated with humanitarianism and flabby sentimentalism. The humanitarianism is in the literature; by it the reading public is led to suppose that the world is advancing along some line which they call "progress" toward peace and brotherly love. Nothing could be more mistaken. We read of fist law and constant war in the Middle Ages and think that life must have been full of conflicts and bloodshed then, but modern warfare bears down on the whole population with a frightful weight through all the years of peace. Never, from the day of barbarism down to our own time, has every man in a society been a soldier until now, and the armaments of today are immensely more costly than ever before. There is only one limit possible to the war preparations of a modern European state; that is, the last man and the last dollar it can control. What will come of the mixture of sentimental social philosophy and warlike policy? There is only one thing rationally to be expected, and that is a frightful effusion of blood in revolution and war during the century now opening.

It is said that there are important offsets to all the burden and harm of this exaggerated militancy. That is true. Institutions and customs in human society are never either all good or all bad. We cannot adopt either peacefulness or warlikeness as a sole true philosophy. Military discipline educates; military interest awakens all the powers of men, so that they are eager to win and their ingenuity is quickened to invent new and better weapons. In history the military inventions have led the way and have been afterward applied to industry. Chemical inventions were made in the attempt to produce combinations which would be destructive in war; we owe some of our most useful substances to discoveries which were made in this effort. The skill of artisans has been developed in making weapons, and then that skill has been available for industry. The only big machines which the ancients ever made were battering rams, catapults, and other engines of war. The construction of these things familiarized men with mechanical devices which were capable of universal application.

Gunpowder was discovered in the attempt to rediscover Greek fire; it was a grand invention in military art, but we should never have had our canals, railroads, and other great works without such explosives. Again, we are indebted to the chemical experiments in search of military agents for our friction matches.

War also develops societal organization; it produces political institutions and classes. In the past these institutions and classes have been attended by oppression and by the exploitation of man by man; nevertheless, the more highly organized society has produced gains for all its members, including the oppressed or their posterity. The social exploitation is not essential to the organization, and it may be prevented by better provisions. In long periods of peace the whole societal structure becomes fixed in its adjustments, and the functions all run into routine. Vested interests get an established control; some classes secure privileges and establish precedents, while other classes form habits of acquiescence. Traditions acquire a sacred character and philosophical doctrines are taught in churches and schools which make existing customs seem to be the "eternal order of nature." It becomes impossible to find a standing ground from which to attack abuses and organize reform. Such was the case in France in the eighteenth century. By war new social powers break their way and create a new order. The student is tempted to think that even a great social convulsion is worth all it costs. What other force could break the bonds and open the way? But that is not the correct inference, because war and revolution never produce what is wanted, but only some mixture of the old evils with new ones; what is wanted is a peaceful and rational solution of problems and situations—but that requires great statesmanship and great popular sense and virtue. In the past the work has been done by war and revolution, with haphazard results and great attendant evils. To take an example from our own history: the banking and currency system of the United States, in 1860, was at a deadlock; we owe the national bank system, which was a grand reform of currency and banking, to the Civil War. It is impossible to see how else we could have overcome the vested interests and could have extricated ourselves from our position. It was no purpose of the war to reform the currency, but it gave an incidental opportunity and we had to win from it what we could.

There is another effect of war which is less obvious but more important. During a period of peace, rest, and routine, powers are developed which are in reality societal variations among which a certain societal selection should take place. Here comes in the immense benefit of real liberty, because, if there is real liberty, a natural selection results; but if there is social prejudice, monopoly, privilege, orthodoxy, tradition, popular delusion, or any other restraint on liberty, selection does not occur. War operates a rude and imperfect selection. Our Civil War may serve as an example; think of the public men who were set aside by it and of the others who were brought forward by it and compare them in character and ideas. Think of the doctrines which were set aside as false and of the others which were established as true, also of the constitutional principles which were permanently stamped as heretical or orthodox. As a simple example, compare the position and authority of the president of the United States as it was before and as it has been since the Civil War. The Germans tell of the ruthless and cruel acts of Napoleon in Germany, and all that they say is true, but he did greater services to Germany than any other man who can be mentioned. He tore down the relics of medievalism and set the powers of the nation to some extent free from the fetters of tradition; we do not see what else could have done it. It took another war in 1870 to root out the traditional institutions and make way for the new ones. Of course the whole national life responded to this selection. The Roman state was a selfish and pitiless subjugation of all the rest of mankind. It was built on slavery, it cost inconceivable blood and tears, and it was a grand system of extortion and plunder, but it gave security and peace under which the productive powers of the provinces expanded and grew. The Roman state gave discipline and organization, and it devised institutions; the modern world has inherited societal elements from it which are invaluable. One of the silliest enthusiasms which ever got control of the minds of a great body of men was the Crusades, but the Crusades initiated a breaking up of the stagnation of the Dark Ages and an emancipation of the social forces of Europe. They exerted a selective effect to destroy what was barbaric and deadening and to foster what had new hope in it by furnishing a stimulus to thought and knowledge.

A society needs to have a ferment in it; sometimes an enthusiastic delusion or an adventurous folly answers the purpose. In the modern world the ferment is furnished by economic opportunity and hope of luxury. In other ages it has often been furnished by war. Therefore some social philosophers have maintained that the best course of human affairs is an alternation of peace and war.[51] Some of them also argue that the only unity of the human race which can ever come about must be realized from the survival of the fittest in a war of weapons, in a conflict of usages, and in a rivalry issuing in adaptability to the industrial organization. It is not probable that aborigines will ever in the future be massacred in masses as they have been in the past, but the case is even worse when—like our Indians, for instance—they are set before a fatal dilemma. They cannot any longer live in their old way; they must learn to live by unskilled labor or by the mechanic arts. This, then, is the dilemma: to enter into the civilized industrial organization or to die out. If it had been possible for men to sit still in peace without civilization, they never would have achieved civilization; it is the iron spur of the nature process which has forced them on, and one form of the nature process has been the attack of some men upon others who were weaker than they.

We find, then, that in the past as a matter of fact war has played a great part

[51] Ludwig Gumplowicz, *Grundriss der Sociologie* (Wien: Manz, 1885), p. 125.

in the irrational nature process by which things have come to pass. But the nature processes are frightful; they contain no allowance for the feelings and interests of individuals—for it is only individuals who have feelings and interests. The nature elements never suffer, and they never pity. If we are terrified at the nature processes, there is only one way to escape them; it is the way by which men have always evaded them to some extent; it is by knowledge, by rational methods, and by the arts. The facts which have been presented about the functions of war in the past are not flattering to the human reason or conscience. They seem to show that we are as much indebted for our welfare to base passion as to noble and intelligent endeavor. At the present moment things do not look much better. We talk of civilizing lower races, but we never have done it yet; we have exterminated them. Our devices for civilizing them have been as disastrous to them as our firearms. At the beginning of the twentieth century the great civilized nations are making haste, in the utmost jealousy of each other, to seize upon all the outlying parts of the globe; they are vying with each other in the construction of navies by which each may defend its share against the others. What will happen? As they are preparing for war, they certainly will have war, and their methods of colonization and exploitation will destroy the aborigines. In this way the human race will be civilized—but by the extermination of the uncivilized—unless the men of the twentieth century can devise plans for dealing with aborigines which are better than any which have yet been devised. No one has yet found any way in which two races, far apart in blood and culture, can be amalgamated into one society with satisfaction to both. Plainly, in this matter which lies in the immediate future, the only alternatives to force and bloodshed are more knowledge and more reason.

Shall any statesman, therefore, ever dare to say that it would be well, at a given moment, to have a war, lest the nation fall into the vices of industrialism and the evils of peace? The answer is plainly no. War is never a handy remedy which can be taken up and applied by routine rule. No war which can be avoided is just to the people who have to carry it on, to say nothing of the enemy. War is like other evils; it must be met when it is unavoidable, and such gain as can be got from it must be won. In the forum of reason and deliberation war never can be anything but a makeshift, to be regretted; it is the task of the statesman to find rational means to the same end. A statesman who proposes war as an instrumentality admits his incompetency; a politician who makes use of war as a counter in the game of parties is a criminal.

Can peace be universal? There is no reason to believe it. It is a fallacy to suppose that, by widening the peace group more and more, it can at last embrace all mankind. What happens is that, as it grows bigger, differences, discords, antagonisms, and war begin inside of it on account of the divergence of interests. Since evil passions are a part of human nature and are in all societies all the time, a part of the energy of the society is constantly spent in repressing them. If all nations should resolve to have no armed ships any more, pirates would reappear upon the ocean; the police of the seas must be maintained. We could not dispense with our militia; we have too frequent need of it now. But police defense is not war in the sense in which I have been discussing it. War in the future will be the clash of policies of national vanity and selfishness when they cross each other's path.

If you want war, nourish a doctrine. Doctrines are the most frightful tyrants to which men ever are subject, because doctrines get inside of a man's own reason and betray him against himself. Civilized men have done their fiercest fighting for doctrines. The reconquest of the Holy Sepulcher, "the balance of power," "no universal dominion," "trade follows the flag," "he who holds the land will hold the sea," "the throne and the altar," the revolution, the faith— these are the things for which men have given their lives. What are they all? Nothing but rhetoric and phantasms. Doctrines are always vague; it would ruin a doctrine to define it, because then it could be analyzed, tested, criticized, and verified; but nothing ought to be tolerated which cannot be so tested. Somebody asks you with astonishment and horror whether you do not believe in the Monroe Doctrine. You do not know whether you do or not because you do not know what it is, but you do not dare to say that you do not because you understand that it is one of the things which every good American is bound to believe in. Now when any doctrine arrives at that degree of authority, the name of it is a club which any demagogue may swing over you at any time and apropos of anything. In order to describe a doctrine, we must have recourse to theological language. A doctrine is an article of faith. It is something which you are bound to believe not because you have some rational grounds for believing it true, but because you belong to such and such a church or denomination. The nearest parallel to it in politics is the "reason of state." The most frightful injustice and cruelty which has ever been perpetrated on earth has been due to the reason of state. Jesus Christ was put to death for the reason of state; Pilate said that he found no fault in the accused, but he wanted to keep the Jews quiet and one man crucified more or less was of no consequence. None of these metaphysics ought to be tolerated in a free state. A policy in a state we can understand; for instance, it was the policy of the United States at the end of the eighteenth century to get the free navigation of the Mississippi to its mouth even at the expense of war with Spain. That policy had reason and justice in it; it was founded in our interests; it had positive form and definite scope. A doctrine is an abstract principle; it is necessarily absolute in its scope and abstruse in its terms; it is a metaphysical assertion. It is never true because it is absolute and the affairs of men are all conditioned and relative. The physicists tell us now that there are phenomena which appear to present exceptions to gravitation which can be explained only by conceiving that gravitation requires time to get to work. We are convinced that perpetual motion is absolutely impossible within the world of our experiences, but it now appears that our universe taken as a whole is a case of perpetual motion.

Now, to turn back to politics, just think what an abomination in statecraft an abstract doctrine must be. Any politician or editor can, at any moment, put a new extension on it. The people acquiesce in the doctrine and applaud it because they hear the politicians and editors repeat it, and the politicians and editors repeat it because they think it is popular. So it grows. During the recent difficulty between England and Germany on one side and Venezuela on the other, some newspapers here began to promulgate a new doctrine that no country ought to be allowed to use its naval force to collect private debts. This doctrine would have given us standing ground for interference in that quarrel. That is what it was invented for. Of course it was absurd and ridiculous, and it fell dead unnoticed, but it well showed the danger of having a doctrine lying loose about the house—and one which carries with it big consequences. It may mean anything or nothing at any moment, and no one knows how it will be. You accede to it now within the vague limits of what you suppose it to be; therefore you will have to accede to it tomorrow when the same name is made to cover something which you never have heard or thought of. If you allow a political catchword to go on and grow, you will awaken someday to find it standing over you, the arbiter of your destiny, against which you are powerless, as men are powerless against delusions.

The process by which such catchwords grow is the old popular mythologizing. Your Monroe Doctrine becomes an entity, a being, a lesser kind of divinity, entitled to reverence and possessed of prestige, so that it allows of no discussion or deliberation. The president of the United States talks about the Monroe Doctrine, and he tells us solemnly that it is true and sacred, whatever it is. He even undertakes to give some definition of what he means by it, but the definition which he gives binds nobody, either now or in the future, any more than what Monroe and Adams meant by it binds anybody now not to mean anything else. He says that, on account of the doctrine, whatever it may be, we must have a big navy. In this, at least, he is plainly in the right; if we have the doctrine, we shall need a big navy. The Monroe Doctrine is an exercise of authority by the United States over a controversy between two foreign states if one of them is in America, combined with a refusal of the United States to accept any responsibility in connection with the controversy. That is a position which is sure to bring us into collision with other states, especially because it will touch their vanity or what they call their honor—or it will touch our vanity or what we call our honor, if we should ever find ourselves called upon to back down from it. Therefore it is very true that we must expect to need a big navy if we adhere to the doctrine. What can be more contrary to sound statesmanship and common sense than to put forth an abstract assertion which has no definite relation to any interest of ours now at stake, but which has in it any number of possibilities of producing complications which we cannot foresee, but which are sure to be embarrassing when they arise.

What has just been said suggests a consideration of the popular saying, "In time of peace prepare for war." If you prepare a big army and navy and are all ready for war, it will be easy to go to war; the military and naval men will have a lot of new machines, and they will be eager to see what they can do with them. There is no such thing nowadays as a state of readiness for war. It is a chimera, and the nations which pursue it are falling into an abyss of wasted energy and wealth. When the army is supplied with the latest and best rifles, someone invents a new field gun; then the artillery must be provided with that before we are ready. By the time we get the new gun, somebody has invented a new rifle, and our rival nation is getting that; therefore we must have it—or one a little better. It takes two or three years and several millions to do that. In the meantime somebody proposes a more effective organization which must be introduced; signals, balloons, dogs, bicycles, and every other device and invention must be added, and men must be trained to use them all. There is no state of readiness for war; the notion calls for never-ending sacrifices. It is a fallacy. It is evident that to pursue such a notion with any idea of realizing it would absorb all the resources and activity of the state; this the great European states are now proving by experiment. A wiser rule would be to make up your mind soberly what you want, peace or war, and then to get ready for what you want; for what we prepare for is what we shall get.

◄◄◄ ►►►

ROBERT E. PARK

The Social Function of War *

. . . By making warfare more efficient and more terrible, modern technology
has made war itself our number one social problem. There is a vast literature
on war and peace, but, aside from what has been written about the science and
art of warfare, there is little or nothing in the literature that throws light on
the nature of war or its role and function in the life and natural history of
society. Furthermore, what we have learned about the effects of war, while it
has made peace more desirable, has not made war any less inevitable.

Most of what has been written in recent years in regard to the problem of
war and of peace may be fairly summed up in the vigorous language of Gen.
[William] Sherman's apology for his "march to the sea." "War," said he, "is
hell"—that is to say, it is cruel, barbarous, economically disastrous and politically atavistic, and generally unconscionable. This recognizes the problem
but contributes nothing to its solution. I might add that problems which can
be fairly described only in epithets are notoriously hard to deal with. Insofar
as this is true in the case of war, it seems to be because we have no adequate
working conception of what war is.

The immediate consequences of war are obvious enough, but we do not
know the long-run effect of wars and the preparations for wars upon society
and human nature. It is inevitable that struggles which involve the very exist-

* Reprinted from Robert E. Park, "The Social Function of War," pp. 551–570, *The
American Journal of Sociology*, XLVI (1941), by permission of The University of Chicago
Press.

ence of peoples have had and will continue to have, as long and as often as they are repeated, a profound effect upon the nature of men, their attitudes, and institutions. "Peace," it has been said, "has been the dream of wise men but war has been the history of nations." When, however, we seek to make war the subject of systematic and scientific investigation, we do not seem to have language in which to describe these influences in general terms. We need to ask ourselves: What is war?

We do not know whether to regard war as a natural phenomenon, like an earthquake or a pestilence, or to classify it as a social phenomenon, like a political contest or an elementary form of judicial procedure, like the ancient trial by battle—an institution which may be said to survive at present in Germany and elsewhere in continental Europe in the form of the duello. In short, we do not know whether war is to be conceived as a social institution or as a biological and social process.

Trial by combat seems to have been a peculiar custom of certain German tribes and was imported by them into Western Europe in the course of the Germanic invasions. It was, according to [Edward] Gibbon, first made a legal institution in Burgundy by an edict of King Gundobald in A.D. 501 and was later "propagated and established in all the monarchies of Europe from Sicily to the Baltic." The church and the clergy were, for various reasons, opposed to the institution, and it is recorded that the King, in defending his edict against the objections and complaints of one of his bishops, disposed of the matter finally with this appeal to common sense and the consensus of mankind. "Is it not true," he said, "that the event of national wars and private combats is directed by the judgment of God; and that his providence awards the victory to the juster cause?" [1]

The conception of war as a procedure in which issues that cannot otherwise be adjudicated are decided, if not by force of arms, at least by physical combat, has persisted to the present day in several interesting forms—the strike, for example.[2] Taking account of the changes in the modes of thought which have taken place since Gundobald made his defense of trial by battle, it is interesting and, in a sense, reassuring to note that the conception of war upon which warfare is conducted today is not substantially different from what it was fourteen hundred years ago. [Heinrich von] Treitschke, in his lectures on politics, in which he set forth fully the Prussian conception of war, defined its function in much the same language as King Gundobald. He says: "Between civilized nations also war is the form of litigation by which states make their claims valid. The arguments brought forward in these terrible lawsuits of the nations compel as no arguments in civil suits ever can do."

In illustrating and enforcing his conception of war as an instrument of

---

[1] Edward Gibbon, *The Decline and Fall of the Roman Empire*, III, chap. xxxviii, 331.

[2] E. T. Hiller, *The Strike: A Study in Collective Action* (Chicago, Ill.: University of Chicago Press, 1928).

political policy and a method by which states may, if they can, "make their claims valid," Treitschke reminds his students, to whom these lectures are addressed, that "often as we have tried by theory to convince the small states that Prussia alone can be the leader in Germany, we had to produce the final proof upon the battlefields of Bohemia and the Main."

Treitschke's notion that war may be conceived as a form of litigation between states, whether wholly valid or not, helps to make war intelligible insofar as he seems to identify the role of modern war with that of the ancient custom of trial by battle. "It is important," Treitschke adds, "not to look upon war always as a judgment from God. Its consequences are evanescent but the life of a nation is reckoned in centuries, and the final verdict can be pronounced only after a survey of the whole epoch," a sentence which reminds one of Schiller's famous dicta, "Die Weltgeschichte ist das Weltgericht."

When and how far war may be conceived as a judicial procedure remains a question. While the institution of trial by battle seems to have been based, like war, on a purely nonrational procedure, these contests did, nevertheless, have the character of a judicial procedure insofar as they were duly regulated by custom and sanctioned by tradition.

The same may be said—with some qualifications, to be sure—of war. Even in the little wars of primitive people, intertribal etiquette usually prescribed some formalities for the declaration of war and the conclusion of peace. In the great wars of more civilized peoples, there have always been some accepted rules of warfare, though not always rigidly enforced. The so-called laws of war were mainly designed to lessen the cruelties and hardships of warfare, particularly for the innocent bystanders, namely, the neutrals and civilian populations.[3]

One of the more important actions taken for the regulation of warfare between European peoples was the Declaration of Paris, adopted in 1856 at the close of the Crimean War. This was followed by the Red Cross Convention of 1864, providing for certain immunities for doctors, nurses, and other persons engaged in caring for the sick and wounded.

Not only civilians, however, but military experts and professional soldiers acknowledging that there are "technical limits at which war ought to yield to the requirements of humanity," have from time to time sought to regulate by international understanding the consequences of unrestricted warfare. In 1868 the Russian czar called an international conference composed entirely of military officers and experts to secure an agreement to limit the use of a type of bullet which inflicted needless suffering. The recommendations of this conference were embodied in the Declaration of St. Petersburg, binding the parties to renounce, among other things, the use of "projectiles weighing less than 400 grammes (about 14 ounces) which are explosive or charged with fulminat-

---

3 *Encyclopaedia of the Social Sciences* (New York: Macmillan Co., 1935), XV, 359.

ing or inflammable substance." The Hague conferences of 1899 and 1907 followed, and, as a result of these and other conferences, an elaborate code for the conduct of war was drawn up and adopted. However, in view of the uncertainties of the interpretation and enforcement of these "laws" under actual conditions of warfare, the code was happily supplemented by a proviso in the preamble which provided that, until a more complete system of regulation should be agreed upon, "inhabitants and belligerents should remain under the protection and the rule of the principles of the law of nations, as they result from the usages established among civilized peoples, from the laws of humanity and the dictates of the public conscience." [4]

Since that time warfare, with the rapid advance in the technology of war, has assumed ever vaster proportions and achieved an ever more terrible efficiency. International politics, meantime, has become more realistic and more cynical. Total warfare, so called, is limited neither to the heavens above nor to the waters under the earth, and, with the advent of the new "strategy of treachery and terror," war has invaded the realm of the spirit—the last stronghold of free souls. Under these circumstances a "peace offensive" may be as effective a means of conquest as physical warfare.

Since propaganda has come to be recognized as one of the weapons of warfare, it has, by means of the radio and other forms of communication, not only broken down the last effective barrier dividing nations, but abolished the distinction that once existed between peace and war. William James said [fifty] years ago in an article that sounds as if it had been written yesterday:

> "Peace" in military mouths today is a synonym for "war expected." The word has become a pure provocative, and no government wishing peace sincerely should allow it ever to be printed in a newspaper. Every up-to-date dictionary should say that "peace" and "war" mean the same thing, now *in posse*, now *in actu*. It may even reasonably be said that the intensely sharp competitive *preparation* for war by the nations *is the real war*, permanent, unceasing, and that the battles are only a sort of public verification of the mastery gained during the "peace" intervals. [5]

Under these conditions it is difficult to conceive of war as a form of judicial procedure even as elementary as the ancient trial by battle. It is even doubtful whether it can any longer be regarded, as it once was, as an "institution recognized by international law." [6] This is true in spite of the *German War Book* and other treatises in which the rules of the game have been rigorously defined. [7]

---

[4] *Ibid.*, p. 361.
[5] *The Moral Equivalent of War* (*supra*).
[6] Herman Lutz, "War Guilt," *Encyclopaedia Britannica*, XXIII, 356.
[7] See "Kriegsbrauch im Landkriege," trans. J. H. Morgan, *Encyclopaedia of the Social Sciences, op. cit.*, XV, 361.

War has, in a summary way, settled international disputes but not always in accordance with any recognized principle of justice or necessity inherent in the international situation. Otherwise, each new war as it occurred would have provided a precedent not merely for defining progressively the rules of war-fare but for determining the issues involved in these "terrible lawsuits." As a matter of fact, the precedents do exist. They make up a large part of the subject matter of our histories. But no principle seems to have emerged from them that is likely to enable us to deal with the issues of new wars as they arise. More often, so far from adjudicating international disputes in accordance with some general understanding or tradition, not to say principle, of international law, war has been an innovating and revolutionary force tending to overturn the existing international order and to challenge the tradition and principles upon which that order at any time has rested.

Thus World War II, which began with the assumption that its purpose was to revise the treaties with which World War I was concluded, is now proclaim-ing itself a world revolution. It is no longer, as was once announced, a war to enforce the claims of the have-nots against the haves. It is rather an ideological war—a war to establish a new order based upon a new political philosophy and a new philosophy of life.

This, then, is the interesting but anomalous status which war seems to occupy in the international social order. It is an institution—a political insti-tution—in process, an institution whose function has not been defined, whose structure is not yet fixed in custom and in tradition. Such usages governing the conduct of wars as have grown up and been accepted in the past have, in-deed, tended to legitimatize wars and give them an institutional character. But legitimacy is a characteristic that attaches to something regarding which we know what to expect. We do not know what to expect of war any more.

Considering the manner in which wars are now waged and the definition of total war by Gen. [Erich] Ludendorff,[8] the modern world, whatever it may do in practice, has accepted as an intellectual proposition Prof. George Mead's dictum that war "as a policy for adjudicating national differences is utterly discredited." It is discredited because, as Professor Mead concludes, "if logically pursued it leaves nothing to be adjudicated, not even the enemy nations themselves." [9]

[8] "Every individual in the nation is expected to give his entire strength either at the front or at home, and this he can only do when he realizes that it is an immutable and inviolable truth that war is being waged solely for the existence of the nation. A totalitarian policy must put at the disposal of such a war the strength of the nation and preserve it and only a conformity to the fundamental racial and spiritual laws will succeed in welding nation, conduct of war, and politics into that powerful unity which is the basis of national preservation" (Gen. Erich Ludendorff, *The Nation at War* [London: Hutchinson & Co., 1936], p. 54).

[9] George H. Mead, "National-Mindedness and International-Mindedness," *International Journal of Ethics*, XXXIX, No. 4 (1929), 400–404.

The obvious, if not insuperable, difficulties of bringing war within the limitations of an institutional order where its function would be defined and its excesses controlled have led some students of political society to conceive war in biological rather than in sociological terms and to define its function accordingly as biological rather than social. Thus, Spencer Wilkinson, professor of military science at Oxford University, in an article on war in the *Encyclopaedia Britannica*, introduces the subject with a reference to an observation upon which [Thomas] Malthus based his theory of population and [Charles] Darwin his theory of the origin of the species—namely, the observation that living organisms multiply more rapidly than the food supply and for that reason there is "a perpetual competition among all living creatures, including human beings, for the means of subsistence." Among the higher organisms, certainly in the case of man, competition often assumes the form of conflict. As a matter of fact, animals "are usually equipped with organs of attack and of protection or evasion. On the one hand teeth, tusks, paws, claws, electricity; on the other hand shells, hides, scales and devices for camouflage."

Because he is not only a gregarious animal like sheep, but a social and rational creature as well, man carries on the "struggle for existence," as Darwin described it, not merely by individual competition, but by the conflict of organized groups or societies. Such a conflict between organized groups is war, and the instrument by which wars are carried on are armies.

The author pushes the biological interpretation still further. He conceives the army as itself an organism, "a society within a society." The weapons with which an army fights are—like the claws, paws, and tusks with which the lower animals are equipped—the instruments with which nations and peoples carry on the struggle for existence. So conceived, war becomes a form of natural selection, its function being to determine the survival not so much of individuals as of peoples and of the institutions by means of which nations and peoples carry on their collective life. The conception of war in terms of Darwin's theory of evolution, since it seems to accept war as fatally rooted in the very nature of human relations and of society, has not been accepted by the advocates of international peace. Militarists, on the other hand, even when they make no apologies for it, are likely to regard war as an inevitable incident of international relations, just as conflict has invariably been an incident and an instrument of political action wherever a political society has existed.

[Helmuth] von Moltke, who led the Prussian army in the three wars which brought about the establishment of the Second German Reich, wrote in a letter that has become famous: "Perpetual peace is a dream and not even a happy dream." From other statements one gathers that Moltke conceived of war, as others have before and since, as one of the instruments of God's mysterious providence designed not to settle international disputes but (a) to purge society of a political regime and a social order which were decadent and doomed to destruction and (b) to supersede these with forms more vigorous and fit to live.[10]

The attempt to put war into a biological category goes astray, it seems to me, not so much from a failure to distinguish between the social and biological aspects of wars as from a failure to distinguish between competition and conflict as different aspects of the struggle for existence. As a matter of fact, the existing species have not survived merely because they were "superior" to those that perished, but rather because they were the "fitter," that is, they fitted the niches in the natural economy in which they occur. Thus the first effect of competition has not been to destroy but to distribute the different organisms and species as they have successively appeared in the evolutionary series. It is as if each individual and each species had been condemned to be forever seeking the particular spot in the biosphere where it could live and to survive by reproducing its kind. In turn, this distribution has been one of the instruments for the evolution of new species. The dispersion of the species, their diversification and preservation in all their diversity, as described by the older naturalists and their successors, the plant and animal ecologists, is one of the most fascinating chapters in the story of biological evolution.[11]

Dispersion was facilitated by the fact that competition between organisms of the same species, since they make similar demands on the habitat, is more intense than the competition between organisms of different species. Dispersion is an incident of the food quest. A further consequence of this dispersion has been the formation of associations, like that of the vine and the fig tree, of mutually interdependent species. This interdependence, like that of the predacious animal and its prey, does not necessarily result in the extirpation of either species, but rather in the preservation of both.

It is by competition in the first instance that the dispersion and diversity of organisms are made possible, but it is by competition also that what is called the balance of life is maintained and the diversity of the species is preserved. This mutual interdependence of organisms has been described as the web of life.

Within the limits of a geographical habitat, the interdependence of the species inhabiting it tends to become more intimate and more vital. Such a region in which plants and animals maintain a kind of biological economy is described by ecologists as a "community." This is, however, a community, *nota bene*, without institutions. Such a community is, in fact, a kind of society, since it is composed of individual organisms living together, but it is different from the so-called animal societies, like those of the social insects, in this

[10] See Dr. Georg F. Nicolai, *The Biology of War* (New York: Century Co., 1918), pp. 521–522. Written during World War I and translated from the German by Constance A. Grande and Julian Grande, this volume by a professor of physiology is perhaps the most thoroughgoing criticism of the biological conception of war in the literature of the subject.

[11] See Richard Hesse, *Ecological Animal Geography*, trans. Wairder C. Allee and Karl P. Schmidt (New York: Wiley & Co., 1937).

important respect—it is composed of species which, because they do not interbreed, have no family ties. They have no instincts, as is the case of the social insects, which hold the individual units of the family or of other genetic groups together during the periods of reproduction and of the infancy of the progeny. Animal societies are, after all, merely great families. Communities, as the term is used by ecologists, are associations organized territorially in which the nexus which holds individual organisms of the divergent species together is purely economic. Societies, as the term applies to animals, are associations of individuals genetically related and organized on a familial pattern.

The two fundamental types of association which I have sought to distinguish as they exist among the inferior species—namely, (a) the territorial and ecological or economic and (b) the familial or social—are reproduced, with substantially the same differences, in the interrelations of races and peoples. This is true even though the different races, being of the same species, interbreed freely where the opportunity offers, as organisms of different species do not.

Generally speaking, the type of association that I have called communal—using the word in the sense in which that term is employed in ecology—is identical with that widespread system of relationships which commerce has spun among the peoples of the world, a form of association which is likely to be more intimate and personal among neighbors but more impersonal and less intimate among those who are either wholly unaware of their biotic and economic interdependence or know it only at second hand. This net of economic relationships in which, individually and collectively, races and peoples are ineluctably bound together corresponds in a general way to the web of life in which all living creatures are involved.[12]

On the other hand, within this wide-ranging economy which at the present time extends to the limits of the habitable world, kinship ties and economic relationships are, in human society, further complicated by the existence of

---

[12] "We have studied the forms of life, and we have considered the adaptation of these forms to the exigencies of this or that habitat. In every habitat we find that there is a sort of community or society of organisms not only preying upon but depending upon each other and that certain balance, though often a violently swaying balance, is maintained between the various species so that the community *keeps on*. The particular name given to this subject of vital balances and interchanges is 'Ecology.' 'Economics' is used only for human affairs; ecology is really an extension of economics to the whole world of life. Man is always beginning his investigations too close to himself and finding later that he must extend his basis of inquiry. The science of economics—at first it was called political economy—is a whole century older than ecology. It tries to elucidate the relations of producer, dealer, and consumer in the human community and show how the whole system carries on. Ecology broadens out this inquiry into a general study of the give and take—the effort, accumulation, and consumption in every province of life. Economics, therefore, is merely human ecology; it is the narrow and special study of the ecology of the very extraordinary community in which we live. It might have been a better and brighter science if it had begun biologically" (H. G. Wells, Julian S. Huxley, G. P. Wells, *The Science of Life* [New York: Doubleday, Doran & Co., 1931], III, 1961).

institutions—familial, economic, political, and religious—which do not exist in animal societies.

It is quite possible, as some anthropologists have contended, that primitive man—the genuinely primitive man—being a gregarious creature, may have lived for long periods of time wandering about in the forests in flocks or herds, without formal organization or institutions of any sort. There are, at any rate, in remote corners of the world peoples like the Semangs in the tropical forest of the Malay Peninsula, the Veddas of Ceylon, or the blameless Punan of Borneo whose mode of life is said to approach in its simplicity that of the lower animals. In this age of innocence, where there were no formal social order and no institutions, there were, we are told, no wars.[13] As soon, however, as men came together to carry on any common enterprise under circumstances where it was necessary to preserve discipline and maintain tension over any considerable length of time, some more efficient sort of organization was needed. It was under these circumstances that institutions seem to have come into existence.

Institutions, generally speaking, have had their origins in some collective action—some common enterprise or social movement that required concert and continuity of action over a considerable period of time. The most elementary form which these movements take is undoubtedly that of mass migration. The connection and correlations between mass migration and war in the historical process have been discussed in a . . . volume by Frederick Teggart.[14] Other social movements are those that seek to bring about some sort of reform in the manners or in the economic and political organization of existing society, like the feminist or the prohibition movement. But there are also other movements that aim at more drastic changes, for example, the revolutionary and religious movements initiated by political sects—Fascism, Communism, and Socialism.

All these movements entail a more-or-less consistent collective action over a considerable period of time, but, compared with the changes which are ordinarily described as evolutionary, they are relatively sudden and catastrophic. They are, however, different not merely in degree, but in kind, from those more gradual and evolutionary, sometimes insensible, changes which

13 "The Punan of Borneo are among the most primitive people, culturally speaking, in the world. For untold ages they have lived in the forests of Borneo, well out of the way of the great movements that have swept through the archipelago, carrying culture from India to the East. There is no reason to believe that they had been influenced strongly by any food-producing people until the Kayan and kindred tribes came up into the central watershed on their way toward Sarawak.

"In the Punan we have a food-gathering people of good physique and bright intelligence who have remained comparatively undisturbed and therefore present to us typical conditions among really primitive peoples in general" (see G. Elliot Smith, *Human History* [New York: W. W. Norton & Co., 1929], p. 199).

14 *Rome and China: A Study of Correlations in Historical Events* (Berkeley: University of California Press, 1939).

take place with the slow accumulations of time—changes which are the results of the minor innovations, accommodations, and adaptations of a multitude of individuals who, like these little marine animals (Anthozoa) which build the coral islands, cooperate unconsciously to bring into existence a structure of whose character and dimensions they are hardly conscious.

Such changes as social movements bring about might be characterized as mutations—mutations that are planned and promoted. Social changes that are planned, particularly when they are planned on a grand scale, almost always have consequences that can never quite be foreseen. These consequences, therefore, are very largely just what happens rather than what was planned. Society is so far from being a closed system that one cannot deal with it either as an artifact or as a system of mechanical forces.[15]

Of all the common enterprises and of all the collective actions that men have undertaken, war is undoubtedly the most imposing in the amount and quality of the effort men put forth, the most devastating and revolutionary in its consequences. Into war—a great war, a total war—man puts all that he has: his wealth, his science, his indomitable will, and eventually his very existence. It is certain, therefore, that as far as man has sought to control his destiny by his collective planning and collective action, these titanic contests—the death struggles of superorganisms—have had the most tremendous effects not only upon society and its institutions, but upon man himself, his spirit, his personality, and his terrestrial career. The amount of effort that man puts forth in war, however, as well as the passions and sentiments that these efforts arouse, is due not merely to the fact that man is here competing with other men, but that he is conscious of those with whom he is in competition—not only of their acts, but of their purposes and intentions. Under these circumstances competition becomes conflict; a competitor, an enemy.

[Charles] Cooley, who seems to have been the first to undertake to give an account of competition in sociological terms, says its function is "to assign each individual his place in the social system." He adds that "competition is not necessarily a hostile contention nor even something of which the competing individual is always conscious," since "from our infancy onward throughout life judgments are daily forming regarding us of which we are unaware, but go to determine our careers."

Cooley does not, however, distinguish the very different consequences that ensue (a) when competition is not conscious and (b) when it is, that is, when it is conflict. Competition does indeed determine our place in the economic

---

[15] "Where will you find in history a case of a great purpose rationally adopted by a great society and carried through to the intended result and then followed by the expected consequences in the way of social advantage? You can find no such thing. Men act from immediate and interested motives like these for which they have waged war, and the consequences may be advantageous or disadvantageous to men. The story of these acts and consequences makes up human history" (Albert Galloway Keller and Maurice R. Davie, eds., *Essays of William Graham Sumner* [New Haven: Yale University Press, 1934], p. 148).

system since it assigns us to the job and function we can perform rather than to the one we should choose to perform. But status, whether it is occupational or social—in any of the various senses of that term—gets its peculiar character because it is a result of conscious competition, that is, emulation, personal conflict, war; because, in short, it is the outcome of a struggle not merely for a spot in the sun or for a job, but for recognition and a place in an existing social order.

Gaetano Mosca in his *Elementi di scienza politica*, recently translated under the title of *The Ruling Class*, referring to the attempts to introduce Darwin's doctrine of evolution of the species into the social sciences, declared that its application to social relations is based upon a fundamental confusion, since it identifies "the struggle for existence" which is characteristic of the lower animals with "the struggle for pre-eminence" which is characteristically human and "a constant phenomenon that arises in all human societies, from the most highly civilized down to such as have barely issued from savagery." Incidentally, Mosca points out that conflict, like competition, is not merely a means of biological selection. On the contrary, like competition, it is the principle of organization. Its function is not to destroy, but ultimately to assimilate the vanquished. This involves the imposition upon them of the status of a subject people and, incidentally, the assignment to them of a function in the territorial economy within which the victors are dominant. Mosca's statement is:

> In a struggle between two human societies, the victorious society as a rule fails to annihilate the vanquished society, but subjects it, assimilates it, imposes its own type of civilization upon it. In our day in Europe and America war has no other result than political hegemony for the nation that proves superior in a military sense, or perhaps the seizure of some bit of territory.[16]

Although the struggle for status or, as [Gaetano] Mosca calls it, "the struggle for pre-eminence" is an obvious characteristic of human society, it has by no means diminished or taken the place of the unceasing, if silent, struggle of races and peoples for survival. Comparative studies of vital statistics of different peoples and population groups show that.[17] Rather has the struggle for pre-eminence, as Corrado Gini's demographic investigations indicate, had a profound effect upon biotic competition, "the competition of life," as Sumner calls it. This is a consequence of the fact that every population group tends to die at the top. Pre-eminence as it is achieved by any group or class is accompanied by a declining birth rate in the pre-eminent class. "As a rule," says

[16] G. Mosca, *The Ruling Class*, trans. Hannah D. Kahn, ed. Arthur Livingston (New York and London: McGraw-Hill, 1939), p. 29.

[17] See J. Holmes, *The Negro's Struggle for Survival* (Berkeley: University of California Press, 1937); also Romanzo Adams, *Interracial Marriage in Hawaii: A Study of the Mutually Conditioned Processes of Acculturation and Amalgamation* (New York: Macmillan Co., 1937).

Gini, "the upper classes are less fertile than the middle, and these, as a rule, are less so than the lower classes." [18] The effect of this is "to provoke a current from the middle classes to the upper, and from the lower to the middle" in order to fill the gaps that have been created by the decline of fertility in the upper classes or the decline in birth rate from whatever causes.

These and other considerations to which recent population studies have called attention indicate that the struggle for existence, that is, the competition of life and for space—*Lebensraum,* to use the German expression—whether it takes the form of biotic competition or the more obvious form of struggle for pre-eminence, is a more complicated matter than has been assumed by those who have sought to explain war as an incident of natural selection and the struggle for existence.

From this point of view competition, as distinguished from conflict, appears as an individuating, not to say analytic, process. It tends to dissolve the traditional social order into its individual elements in order that it may bring about a greater specialization and wider division of labor in an ever wider circle of those economically interdependent individuals and groups which constitute the economic community. The communal order, where it exists, is thus an effect of competition. Conflict, on the other hand, tends to bring about an integration and a superordination and subordination of the conflict groups, whether they be familial and tribal in character, as among the simpler peoples, or national, racial, and religious, as among more sophisticated peoples.

These two terms—community and society—employed in this restricted sense, designate two aspects—biological and cultural—of a single entity which presents itself in one aspect as a biotic community, that is, a population occupying a territory, settled in a habitat, and in the other as an institutional and cultural unit, a society organized to act collectively and eventually politically.

However one may finally conceive the role which war has played in the long process of history, it is obvious that its function has not been merely that of an adjudicator of intertribal or international disputes. Rather, these disputes and the wars that grew out of them have provided the occasion and the necessity for an organization of society which, as it evolved, has become immeasurably superior, for the purposes of collective action at least, to the gregariousness of the primitive horde or the animal herd.

The effect of hostility upon the organization and solidarity of the groups in conflict has been frequently noted, but no one has stated it in more memorable terms than William Graham Sumner in his *Folkways,* where, discussing the mechanisms of "we-group" and the "others-group" relationships, he says:

> The relation of comradeship and peace in the we-group and that of hostility and war towards others-groups are correlative to each other. The

[18] Corrado Gini, Shiroshi Nasu, Oliver E. Baker, and Robert Kuczynski, *Population* ("Lectures on the Harris Foundation" [Chicago: University of Chicago Press, 1929]).

exigencies of war with outsiders are what make peace inside, lest internal discord should weaken the we-group for war. These exigencies also make government and law in the in-group, in order to prevent quarrels and enforce discipline. Thus war and peace have reacted on each other and developed each other, one within the group, the other in the intergroup relation. The closer the neighbors, and the stronger they are, the intenser is the warfare, and then the intenser is the internal organization and discipline of each.[19]

In ensuring peace within as its consequence, war has created (a) in the family and in societies organized on a familial pattern a moral solidarity based on personal loyalties and piety and (b) in the state a political institution which has made collective action possible on a scale of which there is no promise in primitive society.[20] The fact that in the division of labor between the sexes man was not only the hunter but the fighter who now and then brought home a strange woman is responsible for putting him at the head of the family. It is probably one reason that, in primitive society, the matriarchate has, in most cases, been succeeded by the patriarchate—a change which Sumner believes may have been the greatest and most revolutionary in history.[21]

It was not merely war, but the lifelong intimacy and dependency of every member of the family on every other, the sense of security in the family circle, and the terror of all that was outside of it, which created the moral solidarity so characteristic of familial society including the clan and the tribe. As soon as man achieved a more-or-less settled existence and began to accumulate property, wars were undertaken for less romantic purposes and for less interesting and more manageable booty. In fact, war became with pastoral peoples not merely an adventure but a vocation. Robbery among many of the Bedouin tribes was considered as legitimate a method of gaining a livelihood as agriculture. [Julius] Lippert refers to it as "Bedouin livelihood."

It happens occasionally today in North Africa that desert tribes come to terms with a settled population whom they have long regarded as their legitimate prey by accepting tribute in lieu of the booty they were accustomed to carry off. In such case it is part of the agreement that the erstwhile marauders become the protectors of their erstwhile victims, holding off other tribesmen

19 (Boston: Ginn & Co., 1906), p. 12; see also Sumner's essay "War" (*supra*).

20 "When for the first time in the history of the world the group of people who happened to be living in Egypt abandoned the nomadic life and began to till the soil they were accomplishing a vastly greater revolution in the affairs of mankind than the mere invention of the crafts of the farmer and the irrigation engineer. They were committing themselves to the much more formidable task of erecting the complicated edifice of civilization and formulating the fantastic doctrine of the state system which has dominated the world ever since" (Smith, *op. cit.*, pp. 252–253).

21 See Sumner, *Folkways* (Boston: Ginn & Co., 1906), pp. 355–356; see also Maurice R. Davie, "War and Women," in his *The Evolution of War: A Study of Its Role in Early Societies* (New Haven: Yale University Press, 1929), pp. 96–102.

who would otherwise plunder them. Sometimes, however, mobile and warlike desert tribes have not been content merely to exact tribute from, but have chosen to make a conquest of, their sedentary neighbors. This, in fact, seems to have been the way in which the state has normally come into existence, that is, by the conquest of an agricultural by a pastoral and nomadic people. Friedrich Ratzel says:

> The war-like character of the nomads is a great factor in the creation of states. It finds expression in the immense nations of Asia controlled by nomad dynasties and nomad armies, such as Persia, ruled by the Turks; China, conquered and governed by the Mongols and Manchus; and in the Mongol and Radjaputa states of India, as well as in the states on the border of the Soudan.[22]

In any case, sociologists and historians who have investigated the subject seem to agree that the state not only had its origin in war, but that its chief business is still, as Dealey says, "to be ready for war and to wage it whenever national safety or national interest demand it." [23]

As states have come into existence by war, it has seemed to certain writers that they are forever condemned to continue their conquests in order to maintain their existence. Nothing is more demoralizing to an army or to a military state than peace, and nations to survive must act. There must always be some great collective enterprise on the national agenda in which all classes can actively participate. "It is not yesterday, tradition, the past, which is the decisive, the determining force in the nation. . . . Nations are made and go on living by having a program for the future." [24]

War has been and still is the greatest, the most strenuous, if no longer the most glorious, enterprise in which nations can engage, and there seems to be, as George Mead has insisted in his reply to William James, no substitute for war. "The age of discussion" has not yet, as Walter Bagehot believed it should and would, superseded the age of war.[25]

What is probably taking place is that the issues in international controversies are being steadily narrowed by the increase of political knowledge, that is, a more searching analysis of international situations and a more realistic conception of the processes involved in the functioning of political societies. Even discussions are more fruitful when they are based on facts. But facts assume the existence of some common assumptions, either implicitly or explicitly accepted by the parties to the discussion. In political controversies they

[22] Quoted by Franz Oppenheimer, *The State: Its History and Development Viewed Sociologically* (Indianapolis: Bobbs-Merrill Co., 1914), p. 54.

[23] See Davie, *op. cit.*, p. 166.

[24] José Ortega y Gasset, *Invertebrate Spain*, trans. Mildred Adams (New York: W. W. Norton Co., 1937), p. 26.

[25] Walter Bagehot, "The Age of Discussion," *Physics and Politics* (New York: D. Appleton, 1904), chap. v.

involve the existence of a common body of tradition and of constitutional—
that is to say, fundamental—understandings by reference to which what was
a datum becomes a fact. In most wars what I have called "constitutional understandings" are involved, as they were, for example, in our War between the
States, as they [were] in . . . World War [II]. In such cases neither discussion nor appeasement is likely to bring a solution. Where no common interest
appears that makes compromise possible, wars seem inevitable. But men like
Mead believe there is, or should be, no such instance, no situation that would
not eventually yield to an intelligent analysis of the facts.[26]

As states brought into existence a society that was organized on the basis of
territory rather than on common race and culture, it was more-or-less inevitable that they should seek to expand their territories. In carrying on their
wars for that purpose, however, they were always seeking a frontier which they
could defend, always seeking to find a boundary behind which the state could
stabilize society and live in peace. But always the frontiers receded as the
armies approached them. A land-hungry population was always moving beyond the established frontiers, and new means of travel and transportation
were constantly extending the area over which it was possible and necessary
to exercise sovereignty in order to maintain peace.

With the organization of the city-state there began, in contrast with the dispersion of peoples characteristic of primitive life, a movement for the coming
together and integration of races and peoples—a tendency which is characteristic of cities and civilized life. The city, as we must remember, has been not
merely the market place and focal center of a constantly expanding trade area
or market. It has been at the same time the seat and center of an expanding
dominion—a dominion and an authority which was invariably dispersed or
relaxed in times of peace but constantly tightened and intensified when the
beacons on the hilltops announced the approach of war. For war and peace
are, as Sumner suggests, so intimately related that one may say that peace
creates the problem that war is required to solve.

While the struggle for possession of the land has provided the occasion for
most international wars, there have been other wars, like the Crusades to gain
possession by Christians of the Holy Sepulcher or the Islamic wars to win the
world for Allah and Mohammed. These so-called holy wars were actually
ideological wars, seeking primarily to propagandize a cult. But all wars, imperialistic wars, that seek to expand the territory of the state always turn out,
as in the case of . . . World War [II], to have an ideological core. They are
wars "to end war," or they are wars to defend the democratic way of life from
the invasions of a collectivistic and totalitarian imperialism.

On the other hand, ideological wars turn out, likewise, to be struggles for
land and living space. This is because, in order to maintain the different ways

26 Mead, *op. cit.*, pp. 355–407.

of life represented by the parties to these conflicts, political control and sovereignty of a territory in which they can survive are indispensable.

What can one say, finally, in regard to the nature of war and its function? Generally speaking, one may say that war is politics. It is, generally speaking, politics in its original, noninstitutional, and nonrational form—a form in which the belligerent states or parties seek by force of arms (a) to extend the territorial limits of their sovereignty and (b) to establish and impose upon the nations and peoples with whom they are in conflict a political and economic order which is in the interest of the dominant party, race, or nation. This gives a new significance to Freeman's statement that "history is past politics" and "politics is present history."

Historically, the function of war has been (a) to extend the area over which it is possible to maintain peace, (b) to create and organize within that area a political power capable of enforcing it, and, finally, at least in most cases, (c) to establish an ideology which rationalizes, and a cult which idealizes and so gains understanding and acceptance for, the new political and social order which the victor has imported or imposed upon the vanquished. This is the way that war settles issues. It is in this sense that one may say with Schiller: "The world's history is the world's judgment" on the acts of men and of nations.

◄◄◄ ►►►

BRONISLAW MALINOWSKI

*An Anthropological Analysis of War**

WAR THROUGH THE AGES

. . . In any symposium of social sciences on war a place might be rightly claimed for anthropology, the study of mankind at large. Obviously the anthropologist must not appear merely as an usher, heralding the advent of war in the perspective of human evolution, still less as the clown of social science, amusing the symposium with anecdotes on cannibalism or head-hunting, on preposterous magical rites or quaint war dances.

Anthropology has done more harm than good in confusing the issue by optimistic messages from the primeval past, depicting human ancestry as living in the golden age of perpetual peace. Even more confusing is the teaching of those who maintain or imply that war is an essential heritage of man, a psychological or biological destiny from which man never will be able to free himself.[1]

* Reprinted from Bronislaw Malinowski, "An Anthropological Analysis of War," pp. 521–550, *The American Journal of Sociology*, XLVI (1941), by permission of The University of Chicago Press.

[1] The view of the primeval pacifism of man is associated with the names of Grafton Elliot Smith, William J. Perry, of Fr. W. Schmidt and the other members of the Vienna school. The studies of Rudolph Holsti, van der Bij, and Gerald C. Wheeler show that the "lowest savages" did not live in a state of "perpetual warfare." This is substantially correct. It does not, however, justify generalizations such as Elliot Smith's: "Natural man . . . is a good-natured fellow, honest and considerate, chaste and peaceful."

The view that war has been, is, and will remain the destiny of mankind has been elab-

There is, however, a legitimate role for the anthropologist. Studying human societies on the widest basis in time perspective and spatial distribution, he should be able to tell us what war really is. Whether war is a cultural phenomenon to be found at the beginnings of evolution, what are its determining causes and its effects, what does it create and what does it destroy—these are questions which belong to the science of man. The forms, the factors, and the forces which define and determine human warfare should, therefore, be analyzed in a correct anthropological theory of war.

All these problems have their practical as well as theoretical bearing. As a member of a symposium on war, inspired by pragmatic as well as philosophical interests, the anthropologist himself must be fully acquainted with the present circumstances of warfare and the practical problems which arise out of our contemporary crisis. There is no time to be wasted on fiddling while Rome burns—or, more correctly, while Rome assists Berlin in burning the world.

Dictated by common sense, indispensable to sound statesmanship, running through abstract and philosophic reflection, persistent in and above the battle cries of entrenched armies and scheming diplomacies, the main problem of today is simple and vital: Shall we abolish war, or must we submit to it by choice or necessity? Is it desirable to have permanent peace, and is this peace possible? If it is possible, how can we implement it successfully? There is obviously a price and a great price to be paid for any fundamental change in the constitution of mankind. Here, clearly, the price to be paid is the surrender of state sovereignty and the subordination of all political units to world-wide control. Whether this is a smaller or greater sacrifice in terms of progress, culture, and personality than the disasters created by war is another problem, the solution of which may be foreshadowed in anthropological arguments.

I think that the task of evaluating war in terms of cultural analysis is today the main duty of the theory of civilization. In democratic countries public opinion must be freed from prejudice and enlightened as regards sound knowledge. The totalitarian states are spending as much energy, foresight, and constructive engineering on the task of indoctrinating the minds of their subjects as in the task of building armaments. Unless we scientifically and ethically rally to the counterpart task, we shall not be able to oppose them. At the same time the full cultural understanding of war in its relation to nationality and state, in its drives and effects, in the price paid and advantages gained, is necessary also for the problem of implementing any fundamental change.

The problem of what war is as a cultural phenomenon naturally falls into the

orated by Selved R. Steinmetz and supported by such anthropological authorities as Sir Arthur Keith and Prof. Ralph Linton. It has been partly accepted, among other leaders in social science, by Dr. James T. Shotwell and Prof. Quincy Wright. A balanced and clear, as well as essentially sound, presentation of the beginnings of warfare and its real determinants is to be found in the article, "War," *Encyclopaedia of the Social Sciences* (New York: Macmillan Co., 1935), XV, 331–342, written by Prof. Alvin Johnson.

constituent issues of the biological determinants of war, its political effects, and its cultural constructiveness. In the following discussion of pugnacity and aggression, we shall see that even preorganized fighting is not a simple reaction of violence determined by the impulse of anger. The first distinction to emerge from this analysis will be between organized and collective fighting as against individual, sporadic, and spontaneous acts of violence—which are the antecedents of homicide, murder, and civic disorder, but not of war. We shall then show that organized fighting has to be fully discussed with reference to its political background. Fights within a community fulfill an entirely different function from intertribal feuds or battles. Even in these latter, however, we will have to distinguish between culturally effective warfare and military operations which do not leave any permanent mark either in terms of diffusion, of evolution, or of any lasting historical aftereffect. From all this will emerge the concept of "war as an armed contest between two independent political units, by means of organized military force, in the pursuit of a tribal or national policy."[2] With this as a minimum definition of war, we shall be able to see how futile and confusing it is to regard primitive brawls, scrimmages, and feuds as genuine antecedents of our present world catastrophe [World War II].

WAR AND HUMAN NATURE

We have, then, first to face the issue of "aggressiveness as instinctual behavior," in other words, of the determination of war by intrinsically biological motives. Such expressions as "War is older than man," "War is inherent in human nature," "War is biologically determined" have either no meaning or they signify that humanity has to conduct wars, even as all men have to breathe, sleep, breed, eat, walk, and evacuate, wherever they live and whatever their civilization. Every schoolboy knows this, and most anthropologists have ignored the facts just mentioned. The study of man has certainly evaded the issue concerning the relation between culture and the biological foundations of human nature.[3]

Put plainly and simply, biological determinism means that in no civilization can the individual organism survive and the community continue without the integral incorporation into culture of such bodily functions as breathing, sleep, rest, excretion, and reproduction. This seems so obvious that it has been constantly overlooked or avowedly omitted from the cultural analyses of human

[2] Cf. my article, "The Deadly Issue," *Atlantic Monthly*, CLIX (December 1936), 659–669.

[3] The above phrases within quotation marks have been taken from current scientific literature concerning war. The theoretical problems of basic human needs and their satisfaction in culture have been fully treated in my article, "Culture," *Encyclopaedia of the Social Sciences* (op. cit., 1936), pp. 621–645, and in an essay, "The Group and the Individual in Functional Analysis," *The American Journal of Sociology*, XLIV (May 1939), 938–964.

behavior. Since, however, the biological activities are in one way determinants of culture and since, in turn, every culture redefines, overdetermines and transmutes many of these biological activities, the actual interrelation and interdependence cannot be left outside anthropological theory. We shall have briefly to define in what sense certain phases of human behavior are biological invariants and then apply our analysis to aggression and pugnacity.

Every human organism experiences at intervals the impulse of hunger. This leads to search for food, then to the intake, that is, the act of eating, which, in its wake, produces satiety. Fatigue demands rest; accumulated fatigue, sleep; both followed by a new state of the organism which the physiologist can define in terms of the conditions of the tissues. The sex impulse, more sporadic in its incidence and surrounded by more elaborate and circumstantial cultural determinants of courtship, sex taboos, and legal rulings, nevertheless leads to a definite joint performance—that of conjugation, which again is followed by a state of temporary quiescence as regards this impulse. Conjugation may start a new biological sequence of events: conception, pregnancy, and childbirth, which must occur regularly within any community if [the community] is to survive and its culture to continue.

In all these simple and "obvious" facts, there are a few theoretical principles of great importance. Culture in all its innumerable varieties redefines the circumstances under which an impulse may occur, and it may in some cases remold the impulse and transform it into a social value. Abstinences and long-drawn fasts may slightly modify the workings of the organism as regards sex and hunger. Vigils and prolonged periods of intensive activity make rest and sleep determined not merely by organic but also by cultural rulings. Even the most regular and apparently purely physiological activity of breathing is linked up with cultural determinants—partly in that housing and sleeping arrangements somewhat condition the amount of oxygen available and the rate of breathing, and partly in that the act of breathing, identified with life itself, has been the prototype of a whole set of practices and beliefs connected with animism. What, however, can never be done in any culture is the full elimination of any of these vital sequences, imposed on each culture by human nature. We can condense our argument into the form of the simple diagram:

IMPULSE → BODILY REACTION → SATISFACTION

We can say that the least variable as regards any cultural influences of the three phases is the central one. The actual intake of air or food, the act of conjugation, and the process of sleep are phenomena which have to be described in terms of anatomy, physiology, biochemistry, and physics. The second important point is that both links—between impulse and bodily reaction and between that and the satisfaction—are as clear-cut physiological and psychological realities as is the bodily reaction itself. In other words, each culture has integrally to incorporate the full vital sequence of the three phases. For each of those tripartite vital sequences is indispensable to the survival of the organism or, in the case of sexual conjugation and pregnancy, to the survival of the community. However complicated and substantial might be the cultural responses to the basic needs of man—responses such as courtship, marriage, and family in relation to sex; economic arrangements within the household, food-producing activities and the tribal or national commissariat in response to hunger—they are in one way biologically determined in that they have to incorporate each integral vital sequence with all its three phases and links between them, intact and complete.

Can we regard pugnacity and aggressiveness and all the other reactions of hostility, hate, and violence as comparable to any vital sequence so far discussed? The answer must be an emphatic negative. Not that the impulse of aggression, violence, or destruction be ever absent from any human group or from the life of any human being. If the activity of breathing be interrupted by accident or a deliberate act of another individual, the immediate reaction to it is a violent struggle to remove the obstacle or to overcome the human act of aggression. Kicking, biting, pushing immediately start; a fight ensues which has to end with the destruction of the suffocated organism or the removal of the obstacle. Take away the food from the hungry child or dog or monkey, and you will provoke immediately strong hostile reactions. Any interference with the progressive course of sexual preliminaries—still more, any interruption of the physiological act—leads in man and animal to a violent fit of anger.

This last point, however, brings us directly to the recognition that the impulse of anger, the hostilities of jealousy, the violence of wounded honor and sexual and emotional possessiveness are as productive of hostility and of fighting, direct or relayed, as is the thwarting in the immediate satisfaction of a biological impulse.

We could sum up these results by saying that the impulse which controls aggression is not primary but derived. It is contingent upon circumstances in which a primary biologically defined impulse is being thwarted. It is also produced in a great variety of nonorganic ways determined by such purely cultural factors as economic ownership, ambition, religious values, privileges of rank, and personal sentiments of attachment, dependence, and authority. Thus to speak even of the *impulse* of pugnacity as biologically determined is incorrect. This becomes even clearer when we recognize, by looking at the above diagram, that the essence of an impulse is to produce a clear and definite bodily reaction, which again produces the satisfaction of the impulse. In human societies, on the contrary, we find that the impulse of anger is in almost every case transformed into chronic states of the human mind or organism—into hate, vindictiveness, permanent attitudes of hostility. That such culturally defined sentiments can lead, and do lead, to acts of violence simply means that acts of violence are culturally, not biologically, determined. Indeed, when we look at the actual cases of violent action—individual or collective and organized—we find that most of them are the result of purely conventional, traditional, and ideological imperatives, which have nothing whatsoever to do with any organically determined state of mind.

It is interesting to find that, when the argument for a biological or psychological determinism of aggressiveness as something inherent in man's animal nature is put forward, examples from prehuman behavior are easy to find. It is easy to show that dogs, apes, baboons, and even birds fight over females, food, spatial or territorial rights. The study of immature children in primitive tribes or in our own nurseries discloses that the argument by violence is very often used and has to be constantly watched over and regulated by adults.[4] This, indeed, might have suggested to any competent observer that the elimination of violence and of aggression, and not its fostering, is the essence of any educational process.

When we are faced with the question where, how, and under what circumstances acts of purely physiological aggression occur among human adults, we come again to an interesting result. Cases of sound, normal people attacking, hurting, or killing one another under the stress of genuine anger do occur, but they are extremely, indeed, negligibly, rare. Think of our own society. You can adduce an indefinite number of cases from a mental hospital. You can also show that within very specialized situations, such as in prisons or concentration camps, in groups cooped up by shipwreck or some other accident, aggression is fairly frequent. Such a catastrophe as a theater on fire or a sinking boat has sometimes, but not always, the effect of producing a fight for life in which people are trampled to death and bones broken through acts of violence determined by panic and fear. There are also cases in every criminal record, primitive or civilized, of homicidal injuries or bruises which occur under outbursts of anger and hatred or a fit of jealousy. We see that "aggressiveness" within the framework of an adult cultural group is found under the headings of "panic," "insanity," "artificial propinquity," or else that it becomes the type of antisocial and anticultural behavior called "crime." It is always part and product of a breakdown of personality or of culture. It is not

---

[4] Cf., for instance, the arguments and factual documentation given in the books by E. F. M. Durbin and John Bowlby, *Personal Aggressiveness and War* (London: K. Paul, Trench, Trubner & Co., 1938), and by Edward Glover, *War, Sadism and Pacifism* (London: G. Allen & Unwin, 1933). Both these books can be taken as examples of the incorrect and insufficient analysis of what aggressiveness really is and of the tendency to confuse the issues by blaming human nature for the present catastrophic incidents of collective, mechanized slaughter, which we like to call World War II. Good examples without faulty interpretation will also be found in John Dollard *et al.*, *Frustration and Aggression* (New Haven: Institute of Human Relations, Yale University, 1939). To my colleagues at this Institute, to Dr. John Dollard and Dr. Neal A. Miller, I am greatly indebted for the benefit derived in discussions on aggressiveness and instinctive behavior. Part of the present argument was read as a paper before the Monday evening group of the Institute, and the suggestions and criticisms of Profs. Mark A. May, Clark L. Hull, and Robert M. Yerkes have been incorporated into this article.

a case of a vital sequence which has to be incorporated into every culture. Even more, since it is a type of impulsive sequence which constantly threatens the normal course of cultural behavior, it has to be and is eliminated.

THE HARNESSING OF AGGRESSION BY CULTURE

Another interesting point in the study of aggression is that, like charity, it begins at home. Think of the examples given above. They all imply direct contact and then the flaring up of anger over immediate issues where divergent interests occur or, among the insane, are imagined to occur. Indeed, the smaller the group engaged in cooperation, united by some common interests, and living day by day with one another, the easier it is for them to be mutually irritated and to flare up in anger. Freud and his followers have demonstrated beyond doubt and cavil that within the smallest group of human cooperation, the family, there frequently arise anger, hatred, and destructive, murderous impulses. Sexual jealousies within the home, grievances over food, service, or other economic interests occur in every primitive or civilized household. I have seen myself Australian aborigines, Papuans, Melanesians, African Bantus, and Mexican Indians turning angry or even flaring into a passion on occasions when they were working together or celebrating feasts or discussing some plans or some issues of their daily life. The actual occurrence, however, of bodily violence is so rare that it becomes statistically negligible. We shall see shortly why this is so.

Those who maintain that natural aggressiveness is a permanent cause of warfare would have to prove that this aggressiveness operates more as between strangers than between members of the same group. The facts taken from ethnographic evidence give an entirely different answer. Tribal strangers are above all eliminated from any contact with one another. Thus the Veddas of Ceylon have arrangements by which they can transact exchange of goods and give symbolic messages to their neighbors—the Tamils and Singhalese—without ever coming face to face with them. The Australian aborigines have an elaborate system of intertribal avoidances. The same applies to such primitive groups as the Punans of Borneo, the Firelanders, and the pygmies of Africa and Malaysia.[5]

[5] Cf. Charles G. and Brenda Z. Seligman, *The Veddas* (Cambridge, Eng.: Cambridge University Press, 1911), and Gerald C. Wheeler, *The Tribe and Intertribal Relations in Australia* (London: J. Murray, 1910). A full ethnographic analysis of factual data cannot be given in this article. The professional anthropologist will be able to assess the documentary evidence of the references. I hope soon to publish a memoir with full ethnographic material in support of the present argument. I am under a great debt of obligation to the cross-cultural survey, organized by Prof. G. P. Murdock at the Institute of Human Relations, Yale University. In this survey evidence concerning war and intertribal relations is fully collected and classified under rubrics 43–44. It is accessible to all students of anthropology. Dr. Stephen W. Reed and Dr. Alfred Métraux have assisted me greatly in discussing the anthropological problems and facts bearing on my approach to war.

Besides the avoidances there are also to be found clear and legalized forms of contact between tribes. In Australia and in New Guinea, all over the Pacific, and in Africa we could find systems of intertribal law which allow one group to visit another, to trade with them, or to collaborate in an enterprise. In some regions an intrusion on the part of a stranger against the rules of intertribal law and breaking through the normal dividing line was dangerous to the intruder. He was liable to be killed or enslaved; at times he served as the *pièce de résistance* in a cannibal repast. In other words, the execution of such a trespasser was determined by tribal law, by the value of his corpse for the tribal kitchen or of his head to the collection of a head-hunting specialist. The behavior of the murderers and of the murdered has, in such cases, obviously nothing to do with the psychology of anger, pugnacity, or physiological aggressiveness. We have to conclude that, contrary to the prevailing theoretical bias, aggression as the raw material of behavior occurs not in the contact between tribal strangers, but within the tribe and within its component cooperative groups.

We have seen already that aggression is a by-product of cooperation. This latter organizes human beings into systems of concerted activities. Such a system—or institution, as we can call it—is the family. A small group of people is united under the contract of marriage. They are concerned with the production, education, and socialization of children. They obey a system of customary law, and they operate conjointly a household—that is, a portion of environment with an apparatus of implements and consumer goods. The clan and the local group, the food-producing team and the industrial workshop, the age grade and the secret society, are one and all systems of concerted activities, each organized into an institution.[6]

Let us try to understand the place of aggressiveness within an institution. There is no doubt at all that, within these short-range cooperative and spatially condensed forms of human organization, genuine aggressiveness will occur more readily and universally than anywhere else. Impulses to beat a wife or husband or to thrash children are personally known to everybody and ethnographically universal. Nor are partners in work or in business ever free of the temptation to take each other by the throat, whether primitive or civilized. The very essence of an institution, however, is that it is built upon the charter of fundamental rules which, on the one hand, clearly define the rights, prerogatives, and duties of all the partners. A whole set of minor and more detailed norms of custom, technique, ethics, and law also clearly and minutely lay down the respective functions as regards type, quantity, and performance in

[6] I have suggested, in the above-mentioned article "Culture," that this concept of institution is, in anthropological analysis, preferable to that of culture complex. This point is more fully elaborated in "The Scientific Approach to the Study of Man," Ruth N. Anshen, ed., *Science and Man* ("Science and Culture Series" [New York: Harcourt, Brace & Co., 1942]), pp. 207–242.

each differential activity. This does not mean that people do not quarrel, argue, or dispute as to whether the performance or prerogatives have not been infringed. It means, first and foremost, that all such disputes are within the universe of legal or quasi-legal discourse. It also means that the dispute can always be referred not to the arbitrament of force, but to the decision of authority.

And here we come upon the fact that the charter—the fundamental customary law—always defines the division of authority in each institution. It also defines the use of force and violence, the regulation of which is, indeed, the very essence of what we call the social organization of an institutionalized group. The patriarchal family supplies the father with the right to rule and even with the implements of violence. Under mother right the father has to submit, to a much larger extent, to the decisions and influences of his wife's family, notably of her brother. Within the institution of the clan, quarrels and dissensions are very stringently proscribed, for the clan in many cultures acts as the unit of legal solidarity. The myth of the perfect harmony of all clansmen, however, had to be exploded.[7] Nevertheless, quarrels within the clan are rapidly and effectively eliminated by the definite, centralized, and organized authority vested in the leaders and the elders. The local group not only has the right to coordinate the activities and the interests of its component households and clans; it also has the means of enforcing its decisions if violence has to be used or prevented. The tribe, as the widest coordinating group, has also its legal charter, and it has often also some executive means for the enforcement of decisions bearing upon quarrels, disputes, and feuds within the group.

It is characteristic once more that most fighting on the primitive level occurs between smaller units of the same cultural group. The members of two families or two clans or two local groups may come to blows. We have instances of such fighting among the Veddas, the Australian aborigines, and other lowest primitives.[8] Such intratribal fighting is always the result of the infraction of tribal law. A member of a clan or a family is killed. A woman is abducted, or an act of adultery committed. Only in the rarest of cases a spontaneous brawl or fight ensues immediately, for there exist rules of tribal law which define the way in which the dispute has to be fought out. The whole type of fighting between families, clans, or local groups is conventional, determined in every detail by beliefs and elements of material culture or by values and agreements. The collective behavior in such fighting, which is characteristic of the primitive level

---

[7] Cf. my *Crime and Custom in Savage Society* (New York: Harcourt, Brace & Co., 1926), among other contributions to this problem.

[8] Perhaps the best and most detailed account of a type of fighting in which one clan functions as a social unit against another is to be found in Lloyd Warner's book on the Murngin, *A Black Civilization* (New York: Harper & Bros., 1937). His evidence shows that such armed disputes, though at times destructive and lethal, are carried out with strict rules over definite issues of clan interests and are concluded in a peace ceremony which re-establishes the order of tribal law after an infraction by one of the clan members. All the data, well assembled and classified, can be easily studied in the cross-cultural survey at Yale.

of lowest savages, is guided at every step and is controlled by factors which can be only studied with reference to the social organization, to customary law, to mythological ideas, as well as to the material apparatus of a primitive culture.[9]

When there is a strong rivalry between two groups and when this leads to a general state of mind—generating frequent outbursts of anger and sentiments of hatred over real divergences of interest—we find an arrangement in which occasional fights are not only allowed, but specially organized, so as to give vent to hostile feelings and re-establish order after the feelings have been overtly expressed. Such occasional tournament fights take sometimes pronouncedly peaceful form. The public songs of insult, by which the Eskimo even up their differences and express hatred, grievances, or hostility, are a well-known example of this. In Central Europe the institution of Sunday afternoon drinking and fighting fulfills the function of an organized and regulated exchange of insults, blows, at times injuries and casualties, in which accumulated resentments of the week are evened up. We have a good description of such regulated fights within the group among the Kiwai Papuans, among the Polynesians, and among the South American Indians.

Anthropological evidence, correctly interpreted, shows, therefore, that there is a complete disjunction between the psychological fact of pugnacity and the cultural determination of feuds and fights. Pugnacity can be transformed through such cultural factors as propaganda, scaremongering, and indoctrination into any possible or even improbable channels. We have seen the change in France: the pugnacity of yesterday has overnight become a lukewarm alliance, and the friendship of the most recent past may, at any moment, flare up into the pugnacity of tomorrow. The raw material of pugnacity does admittedly exist. It is not in any way the biological core of any type of organized violence in the sense in which we found that sex is the core of organized family life, hunger of commissariat, evacuation of sanitary arrangements, or the maintenance of bodily temperature a biological factor around which center cultural adjustments of clothing and housing. Anger and aggressiveness may flare up almost at any moment in the course of organized cooperation. Their incidence decreases with the size of the group. As an impulse, pugnacity is indefinitely plastic. As a type of behavior, fighting can be linked with an indefinitely wide range of cultural motives.

Everywhere, at all levels of development, and in all types of culture, we find that the direct effects of aggressiveness are eliminated by the transformation of pugnacity into collective hatreds, tribal or national policies, which lead to organized, ordered fighting but prevent any physiological reactions of

[9] If space would allow, we could show that witchcraft, which is also an important tool of expressing anger or hatred, is a characteristic substitute mechanism. The use of direct violence is eliminated by translating the reaction of anger into a sentiment of hatred and expressing this not by any fighting or use of force, but by mystical acts of hostility.

anger. Human beings never fight on an extensive scale under the direct influence of an aggressive impulse. They fight and organize for fighting because, through tribal tradition, through teachings of a religious system, or of an aggressive patriotism, they have been indoctrinated with certain cultural values which they are prepared to defend and with certain collective hatreds on which they are ready to assault and kill. Since pugnacity is so widespread, yet indefinitely plastic, the real problem is not whether we can completely eliminate it from human nature, but how we can canalize it so as to make it constructive.

TRIBE-NATION AND TRIBE-STATE

In our study of anthropological evidence insofar as it throws light on modern warfare, we are in search of genuine primitive antecedents of fighting such as occurred in historical times and of fighting as it has become transformed in the modern world wars. The use of violence, clearly, has to receive a fuller sociological treatment. Nationalism and imperialism and even totalitarianism —in my opinion, a phenomenon of cultural pathology—must be supplied with their evolutionary background and their ethnographic antecedents.

We have already seen that, when two clans or two local groups fight with each other within the framework of the same tribal law, we deal with cases of legal mechanisms, but not with antecedents of war. We have to face now the question of how to define, in terms of social organization and of culture, the groups which can legitimately be regarded as pursuing some prototype of international policy, so that their battles can be considered as genuine precursors of warfare.

The concept of tribe and of tribal unity would naturally occur to every anthropologist or student of social science. An ethnographic map of the world shows, on every continent, well-defined boundaries which separate one tribe from the other. The unity of such a tribe consists *de facto* in the homogeneity —at times, identity—of culture. All tribesmen accept the same tradition in mythology, in customary law, in economic values, and in moral principles. They also use similar implements and consume similar goods. They fight and hunt with the same weapons and marry according to the same tribal law and custom. Between the members of such a tribe communication is possible because they have similar artifacts, skills, and elements of knowledge. They also speak the same language—at times, divided by some dialectical varieties—but generally allowing free communication. As a rule, the tribe is endogamous, that is, marriage is permitted within its limits but not outside. Consequently, the kinship system usually welds the whole tribe into a group of related and mutually cooperative, or potentially antagonistic, clans. The tribe in this sense, therefore, is a group of people who conjointly exercise a type of culture. They also transmit this culture in the same language according to similar educational principles, and thus they are the unit through which the culture lives and with which a culture dies.

In the terminology here adopted, we can say that the tribe as a cultural entity can be defined as a federation of partly independent and also coordinated component institutions. One tribe, therefore, differs from the other in the organization of the family, the local groups, the clan, as well as economic, magical, and religious teams. The identity of institutions; their potential cooperation due to community of language, tradition, and law; the interchange of services; and the possibility of joint enterprise on a large scale—these are the factors which make for the unity of a primitive, culturally homogeneous group. This, I submit, is the prototype of what we define today as nationality: a large group, unified by language, tradition, and culture. To the division as we find it between primitive culturally differentiated tribes there correspond today such divisions as between Germans and Poles, Swedes and Norwegians, Italians and French. In our modern world these divisions do not always coincide with the boundaries of the state. Hence, all the contemporary political problems of nationalism, imperialism, the status of minorities, and of irredentist groups are covered by the principle of national self-determination. All such problems hinge obviously on the relation between nation and state.

The principle of political unity or statehood can also be found—on a primitive level—in creating divisions as well as in establishing unity. We know already that authority, as the power to use physical force in the sanctioning of law, exists even at the lowest level of development. We have seen that it is the very essence of the constitution of organized systems of activities, that is, institutions. We have seen that it also functions as the basis for a wider territorial control of the relations between institutions. At the lowest level we found the local group as the widest coordinating unit with political prerogatives. If we were to survey the political conditions at a somewhat higher level of development, we would find in most parts of the world, in Melanesia and Polynesia, in Africa and parts of America, that political power is wielded by much larger regional groups united on the principle of authority and, as a rule, equipped with military organization the duty of which is partly internal policing, partly external defense or aggression. Much of my own field work has been done in the Trobriand Islands, where such politically organized regions were to be found and where a clear prototype of a politically organized state could be seen at work.

We have thus introduced another concept for which the word "tribe" is also used in anthropology. I submit that the distinction between political and cultural units is necessary. To implement it terminologically, I suggest that we coin the two expressions "tribe-nation" and "tribe-state." The tribe-nation is the unit of cultural cooperation. The tribe-state has to be defined in terms of political unity, that is, of centralized authoritative power and the corresponding organization of armed force. It is clear from all that has been said that the tribe-nation is an earlier and more fundamental type of cultural differentiation than the tribe-state. The two do not coincide, for we have many instances of the tribe-state as a subdivision of the tribe-nation. The Maori of New Zealand, the Trobriand Islands, the Zulu before European advent, as well as many North American tribes, could be quoted as examples of this. Among them the tribe-nation embraces many tribe-states. On the other hand, we could adduce from East and West Africa examples in which two or more tribe-nations are united within the same tribe-state. I have in mind the kingdoms of Unyoro and Uganda, such political units as the Masai or the Bemba, all of whom have "subject minorities" within their dominion.[10]

The two principles of statehood and nationality must, therefore, be kept apart in theory, even as they are different in cultural reality. Nevertheless, there has always existed a convergence of the two principles and a tendency toward the coalescence of the two groups—the nation and the state. In Europe this tendency, under the name of nationalism, has made its definite appearance in political aspirations and as a cause of wars and rebellions ever since the French Revolution and the Napoleonic Wars. Its main exponents were Germany, Poland, and Italy, where the disjunction of the two principles had been most pronounced. Many historians regard nationalism in this sense as an entirely new phenomenon of recent European history. In reality nationalism is probably as old as an early appearance of political power. On the one hand, a primitive nation, that is, a tribe carrying a homogeneous culture, is best protected against outside disturbances by being organized into a tribe-state. On the other hand, the strongest tribe-state is the one which coincides with the tribe-nation, since political organization is even under primitive conditions most solidly based on the association with the group who are fully cooperative through the possession of one language, one system of customs and laws, one economic machinery, and one type of military equipment.

WAR AND PRIMITIVE POLITICS

We can now return to the role played by fighting in the early crystallization of statehood and nationality. As a working hypothesis, we might suggest that, once a strong local group developed a military machine, it would use this in the gradual subjugation of its neighbors and extension of its political control. Ethnography supplies us with the evidence that fighting between local groups

[10] Such conditions can clearly be paralleled from the map of historical and even contemporary Europe. Austria-Hungary was a monarchy in which some fourteen or fifteen nationalities were federated. Germany before the Napoleonic Wars was a nation divided into many small states. Italy was also parceled out and partly subject to foreign rule before its unification in 1871. Poland for one hundred and fifty years was a nation partitioned among three large states. Switzerland is a political entity embracing four component nationalities.

of the same culture does exist. It also supplies us with a clear picture of conditions in which fairly extensive political units which form states within a larger nation are in existence. The study of the *status quo* and of fragments of history among the Maori of New Zealand, among several African tribes, as well as all we know about the pre-Columbian history of Mexico and Peru, points to the fact that, once armed military operations start in a region, they tend to the formation of the nation-state. The archaeologist and historian concerned with the Mediterranean world might show that analogous developments produced the Roman state, some of the Greek political units, and the empires of Egypt, Babylonia, Assyria, and Persia. Wars of nationalism, therefore, as a means of unifying under the same administrative rule and providing with the same military machine the naturally homogeneous cultural group, that is, the nation, have always been a powerful force in evolution and history.

Warfare of this type is culturally productive in that it creates a new institution, the nation-state. Obviously, since the political unit extends to embrace the cultural one, both assume a different character. The coordination of any subdivisions of such a group, whether regional or institutional, become standardized and organized. Moreover, a nation-state usually assumes a much more pronounced control over economics and man power, over contributions to the tribal exchequer and public services rendered. It can also enforce its decisions, that is, sanction administrative activities and customary law. It is legitimate, therefore, to regard fighting of this type as a genuine antecedent of certain historical wars. For fighting here functions as an instrument of policy between two tribe-states, and it leads to the formation of larger political groups and, finally, of the tribe-nation.

It is necessary to remember that organized fighting at higher stages of savagery or barbarism does not always present this politically significant character. Most of the fighting at this stage belongs to an interesting, highly complicated, and somewhat exotic type: raids for head-hunting, for cannibal feasts, for victims of human sacrifice to tribal gods. Space does not allow me to enter more fully into the analysis of this type of fighting. Suffice it to say that it is not cognate to warfare, for it is devoid of any political relevancy, nor can it be considered as any systematic pursuit of intertribal policy. Human man-hunting in search of anatomic trophies, the various types of armed body-snatching for cannibalism, actual or mystical, as food for men and food for gods, present a phase of human evolution which can be understood in terms of ambition, thirst for glory, and of mystical systems. In a competent analysis of warfare as a factor in human evolution, they must be kept apart from constructive or organized systems of warfare.[11]

So far we have dealt with fighting organized on political principles and performing a political function, and we have dealt briefly with sportive types of

[11] See my article, "The Deadly Issue," *Atlantic Monthly*, CLVIII (December 1936), 559–569.

human man-hunting. Where does the economic motive enter into our problem? It is conspicuously absent from the earliest types of fighting. Nor are the
reasons difficult to find. Under conditions where portable wealth does not exist,
where food is too perishable and too clumsy to be accumulated and trans-
ported, where slavery is of no value because every individual consumes exactly
as much as he produces, force is a useless implement for the transfer of wealth.
When material booty, human labor, and condensed wealth—that is, precious
metals or stones—become fully available, predatory raids acquire a meaning
and make their appearance. Thus we have to register a new type of fighting:
armed expeditions for loot, slave wars, and large-scale organized robbery. We
could quote examples from East and Southeast Africa, where cattle-raiding
was a lucrative industry associated with war. Among the tribes of northwestern
America, slavery is found perhaps in its simplest type and furnishes one of the
main motives of intertribal feuds. Nomadic tribes who, as organized robber
bands, controlled some of the caravan routes in North Africa and in Asia developed and used their military efficiency for a systematic levy of tribute and
for loot at the expense of their wealthier sedentary, mercantile, or agricultural neighbors.

We have, in the above analysis, made one or two distinctions, perhaps too
sharply, but for the purpose of isolating the principles which lead to the appearance of genuine, purposeful warfare. We have spoken of nationalism as
an early tendency leading to political wars and the formation of primitive
nation-states. We spoke of organized raids carried out under the economic
motive. These types of fighting very often coincide. It is even more important
to realize that nationalism, as the tendency of extending political control to
the full limits of cultural unity, is never a clear-cut phenomenon. Nationalism
seldom stops at the legitimate cultural boundaries of the nation. Whether it be
a Hitler or a Chaka, a Napoleon or an Aztec conqueror, a Genghis Khan or an
Inca ruler, he will readily and naturally overstep the boundaries of his nation.
Nationalism readily turns into imperialism, that is, the tendency of incorporating other nations under the political rule of the military conqueror.

Here we arrive at a new phenomenon which has played an important role in
the development of mankind. Conquest, the integral occupation of another
cultural area by force, combines all the benefits of loot, slavery, and increase
in political power. Conquest is a phenomenon which must have played an
enormous part in the progress of mankind at the stage where, in a parallel
and independent manner, we had the establishment of large agricultural communities and militarily strong nomadic or cattle-raising tribes. From the conditions found in various parts of the ethnographically observable world and
from the records of history, we can retrace and reconstruct the main characteristics of culturally constructive conquest. The best ethnographic areas for this
analysis are to be found among the East African tribes, where we still can
study the symbiosis of invading Hamitic or Nilotic cattle-breeders and nomads

with sedentary agricultural Bantus. Or, we could turn to some parts of West Africa, where we find extensive monarchies in which the sedentary agricultural West African Negroes live under the rule of their Sudanese conquerors. From the New World the histories of the Mexican and Peruvian states embody rich material for this study of conquest.

The most important cultural effect of conquest is an all-round enrichment in national life through a natural division of function between conquerors and conquered and through the development and crystallization of many additional institutions. The conquerors provide the political element; those conquered, as a rule, supply economic efficiency. This also means that the conquerors, in exploiting the subject community, organize a tribal exchequer, institute taxes, but also establish security and communication and thus stimulate industry and commerce. Under the impact of two different cultures, the customary law of each tribe becomes formulated, and often a compound system of codification is drawn up. Religious and scientific ideas are exchanged and cross-fertilize each other.

War as an implement of diffusion and cross-fertilization by conquest assumes, therefore, an important role in evolution and history. Such war, let us not forget, made a very late appearance in human evolution. It could not occur before such high differentiation in types of culture as that of nomadic pastoralism and sedentary agricultural pursuits. No fruits of victory were obtainable in any economic, political, or cultural sense before slavery, loot, or tribute could be effected by violence.

THE CONTRIBUTION OF ANTHROPOLOGY TO THE PROBLEM OF WAR

Glancing back over our previous arguments, we can see that we have arrived at certain theoretical conclusions, new to anthropological theory. It will still be necessary to show where our gains in clarity and definition are related to modern problems.

As regards the theoretical gains, we have shown that war cannot be regarded as a fiat of human destiny in that it could be related to biological needs or immutable psychological drives. All types of fighting are complex cultural responses due not to any direct dictates of an impulse, but to collective forms of sentiment and value. As a mechanism of organized force for the pursuit of national policies, war is slow in evolving. Its incidence depends on the gradual development of military equipment and organization, of the scope for lucrative exploits, of the formation of independent political units.

Taking into account all such factors, we had to establish, within the genus of aggression and use of violence, the following distinctions.

(a) Fighting, private and angry, within a group belongs to the type of breach of custom and law and is the prototype of criminal behavior. It is countered and curbed by the customary law within institutions and between institutions.

(b) Fighting, collective and organized, is a juridical mechanism for the adjustment of differences between constituent groups of the same larger cultural unit. Among the lowest savages these two types are the only forms of armed contest to be found.

(c) Armed raids, as a type of man-hunting sport, for purposes of head-hunting, cannibalism, human sacrifices, and the collection of other trophies.

(d) Warfare as the political expression of early nationalism, that is, the tendency to make the tribe-nation and tribe-state coincide, and thus to form a primitive nation-state.

(e) Military expeditions of organized pillage, slave-raiding, and collective robbery.

(f) Wars between two culturally differentiated groups as an instrument of national policy. This type of fighting, with which war in the fullest sense of the word began, leads to conquest, and, through this, to the creation of full-fledged military and political states, armed for internal control, for defense and aggression. This type of state presents, as a rule, and for the first time in evolution, clear forms of administrative, political, and legal organization. Conquest is also of first-rate importance in the processes of diffusion and evolution.

The types of armed contest listed as (d) and (f), and these two only, are, in form, sociological foundations and, in the occurrence of constructive policy, are comparable with historically defined wars. Every one of the six types here summed up presents an entirely different cultural phase in the development of organized fighting. The neglect to establish the differentiation here introduced has led to grave errors in the application of anthropological principles to general problems concerning the nature of war. The crude short-circuiting—by which our modern imperialisms, national hatreds, and world-wide lust of power have been connected with aggression and pugnacity—is largely the result of not establishing the above distinctions, of disregarding the cultural function of conflict, and of confusing war, as a highly specialized and mechanized phenomenon, with any form of aggression.

We can determine even more precisely the manner in which anthropological evidence, as the background of correct understanding and informed knowledge, can be made to bear on some of our current problems. In general, of course, it is clear that, since our main concern is whether war will destroy our Western civilization or not, the anthropological approach, which insists on considering the cultural context of war, might be helpful.

Especially important in a theoretical discussion of whether war can be controlled and ultimately abolished is the recognition that war is not biologically founded. The fact that its occurrence cannot be traced to the earliest beginnings of human culture is significant. Obviously, if war were necessary to human evolution, if it were something without which human groups have to decay and by which they advance, then war could not be absent from the earliest stages in which the actual birth of cultural realities took place under the greatest strains and against the heaviest odds. A really vital ingredient could not, therefore, be lacking in the composition of primitive humanity struggling to lay down the foundations of further progress.

War, looked at in evolutionary perspective, is always a highly destructive event. Its purpose and *raison d'être* depend on whether it creates greater values than it destroys. Violence is constructive, or at least profitable, only when it can lead to large-scale transfers of wealth and privilege, of ideological outfit, and of moral experience. Thus, humanity had to accumulate a considerable stock of transferable goods, ideas, and principles before the diffusion of those through conquest, and even more, the pooling and the reorganization of economic, political, and spiritual resources could lead to things greater than those which had been destroyed through the agency of fighting.

Our analysis has shown that the work of cultural exercise is associated with one of the two widest groups, the tribe-nation. The work of destroying and also of reconstructing in matters cultural is associated with the tribe-state. Here, once more, it will be clear to every social student that, in giving this ethnographic background to the concepts of state and nation, of nationalism and imperialism, we may have contributed to the theoretical clarification of the corresponding modern facts.

What matters to us today, as ever, is human culture as a whole, in all its varieties, racial and religious, national or affected by regional differentiation of interests and of values. Nationhood in its manifold manifestations, today as always, is the carrier of each culture. The state should be the guardian and the defender of the nation, not its master, still less its destroyer. The Wilsonian principle of self-determination was scientifically, hence morally, justified. It was justified to the extent only that each culture ought to have full scope for its development—that is, every nation ought to be left in peace and freedom. Self-determination was a mistake in that it led to the arming of new nations and more nations, while it ought to have meant only the disarming of dangerous, predatory neighbors. Self-determination can be perfectly well brought about by the abolition of all states rather than by the arming of all nations.

Thus, the general formula which anthropological analysis imposes on sound and enlightened statesmanship is the complete autonomy of each cultural group and the use of force only as a sanction of law within and, in foreign relations, a policing of the world as a whole.

TOTALITARIANISM AND WORLD WARS I AND II
IN THE LIGHT OF ANTHROPOLOGY

Anthropological analysis of modern conditions cannot stop here, however, nor need it remain satisfied with the important but very general statement just formulated. To vindicate its claim of applicability to the savagery of civilization, as well as to the civilizations of savages, it is necessary to go a step or two further and submit the cultural pathology of today, that is, totalitarian systems and World Wars I and II, to a somewhat more detailed and searching analysis.

World war, that is, total war, is, in the light of our anthropological criteria, as distinct from the historical wars up to 1914 as these were different from head-hunting or slave-raiding. The influence of present warfare on culture is so total that it poses the problem whether the integral organization for effective violence—which we call totalitarianism—is compatible with the survival of culture.

Culture, as we know, is exercised in each of its varieties by the cooperative working of partly independent, partly coordinated, institutions within the group, which we defined as the nation. It has been thus exercised and transmitted from the very beginnings of humanity, right through to the beginnings of this century. The foundations of the industrial, liberal, and democratic era which, as I am writing this, still survives in the United States and in a few Latin American countries, were laid on the very same structure of institutional differentiation and coordination by the state, which controlled the development of human civilization as a whole. The principle of totalitarianism, black or red, brown or yellow, has introduced the most radical revolution known in the history of mankind. In its cultural significance it is the transformation of nationhood and all its resources into a lethal, "technocratic" instrument of violence. This becomes a means justified by the end. The end is the acquisition of more power for one state, that is, more scope for organizing violence on a larger scale and for further destructive uses. Thus the end of totalitarianism, insofar as it gradually saps all the resources of culture and destroys its structure, is diametrically opposed and completely incompatible with the constitution of human societies for the normal, peaceful business of producing, maintaining, and transmitting wealth, solidarity, reason, and conscience, all of which are the real indexes and values of civilization.

The war of 1914–1918 was, I submit, different in all fundamentals from the historical wars of constructive conquest. In its technique, in its influence on national life, and also in its reference to the international situation, it became a *total* war. Fighting goes on now not merely on all the frontiers geographically possible; it is waged on land, on sea, and in the air. Modern war makes it impossible to distinguish between the military personnel of an army and the civilians; between military objectives and the cultural portion of national wealth; and the means of production, the monuments, the churches, and the laboratories. Lines of communication; seats of government; centers of industry; and even centers of administrative, legal, and scientific activity are rapidly becoming targets for destruction, as much as garrisons, fortified lines, and airdromes. This development is not only due to the barbarism of a nation or of a dictator. It is inevitable, for it is dictated by the modern technique of violence.

The total character of war, however, goes much further. War has to transform every single cultural activity within a belligerent nation. The family and the school, the factory and the courts of law, are affected so profoundly that their work—the exercise of culture through autonomous self-contained institutions—is temporarily paralyzed or distorted. It is enough to look at the statistics of mobilization in man power, in activity, and in public opinion to realize that at present it has become possible to transform some hundred million human beings into one enormous war machine. And it is obvious that when two war machines of this size are launched against each other, the one with the less perfect and total mobilization is bound to succumb.[12]

The stupendous, almost miraculous, successes of Hitler's Germany have so dazzled the public opinion of neutrals and belligerents alike that some of the real lessons have not yet been learned. In the mingled reaction of horror and

[12] Fuller data illustrating the complete remolding of all national life during war and as preparedness for war will be found in Prof. Willard Waller, *War in the Twentieth Century* (New York: Dryden Press, 1940). The four essays on economy, the state, propaganda and public opinion, and on social institutions in wartime should, in my opinion, be read carefully by all students of the subject. They show that total war completely transforms the substance of modern culture. The reader, pursuing them in the light of our present analysis, may be able to draw even more pointed conclusions, especially in assessing that totalitarianism is nothing but the constitution of the nation on a wartime basis. That this effect of war is not generally understood or appreciated can be seen from the final essay in Professor Waller's volume, in which Dr. Linton, a competent authority upon all matters anthropological, seems to minimize the destructiveness of war and of its profound influence on culture. Speaking of modern war, he affirms that "its uniqueness, especially as regards potentialities for destruction, has been greatly overrated. . . . The principles upon which successful war must be waged have not changed since the dawn of history, while the destructive intent of war has certainly diminished. . . . In Europe . . . still other factors . . . will keep intentional destruction to a minimum. . . . It seems safe to predict . . . that . . . there will be no swift victories against large or powerful nations" (What about France? *op. cit.*, pp. 535–538). Such opinions, and they are by no means exclusive to the writer quoted, show how easy it is to miss the real issue. Even if we admitted that the toll of some twenty million human lives taken by World War I was of no great importance nor yet the fifty million maimed and rendered useless, we would have to assess the disorganization in economic matters, the lack of security as regards wealth and life, and the general debasement of civic and ethical principles. The real issue, however, discussed in the text, is whether the integral influence of preparedness for, and the use of, violence do or do not disorganize the texture of modern civilization.

admiration which followed the *Blitzkrieg* against Poland, the "conquest" of Denmark and Norway, with the implicit subjugation of Sweden, the campaign against the Low Countries, and the shattering collapse of France, many of us had to fight hard against the feeling that, after all, totalitarianism is "a better and bigger" regime than "the decaying demo-plutocracies." Sound anthropological understanding of these facts as cultural phenomena teaches something else. An organized gang of criminals will always gain the upper hand in an armed attack on a bank. The only chance the bank has is not in fighting the gang, but in having a police force to protect it. And the police will be really efficient if it prevents the formation of an armed gang with such instruments of violence at its disposal as would make defense impossible or, at least, costly and destructive. Prepared aggression will always get the better of unprepared defense. Defense must be prepared so as to prevent aggressiveness, rather than fight it.

And here we come to the most important element in the cultural assessment of totalitarianism. Born out of World War I, it was, in principle, nothing less and nothing more than the application of the political techniques developed between 1914 and 1918 as the type of political, economic, educational, and propagandist regime suitable to the carrying out of a major war.

Nazi Germany developed a system of values which could, through the technique of modern propaganda and under the sanction of a perfectly organized police, be made to become the doctrine of the whole nation. The system of values was based on the superiority of one race, of one nation within this race, and of one organized gang within the nation. Such a doctrine, it can be seen easily, is functionally adapted to the creation of highly artificial, but nevertheless effective, sentiments of superiority, aggressiveness, national egoism, and a morality which fits perfectly well into a universal barrack-room drill. Parallel to indoctrination, there had to go the complete reorganization of social life. The family, the municipality, the schools, the courts, the churches, and all institutions of intellectual and artistic production were put directly under the forced and armed control of the state. Never before in humanity has the autonomous working of component institutions been so completely submitted to state control. Never, that is, has the exercise of culture become so completely paralyzed. This means, in terms of individual psychology, that any differential initiative, any formation of independent critical judgment, any building up of public opinion through discussion, controversy, and agreement, has been replaced by a passive acceptance of dictated truths. As regards the social structure of the nation, the control from above has had the effect of replacing spontaneous solidarity between husband and wife, between parents and children, among friends or partners, by a mechanically imposed "spirit of unity" to be accepted regardless of any personal impulse, reasonable judgment, or ruling of conscience.

We know well how the results of individual research, the teaching of the various religions, and the creation of artists have been prescribed, limited, and directed. In religion, notably, we can see that Nazism is trying to substitute its own dogmatic system, its ritual, and its ethics for those of Christianity, as well as for the established ethics of Western civilization and the convictions of scientific judgment.

It is not necessary to inveigh against the totalitarian system; certainly this is not a place for moral indignations or partisan views. Scientific ethics, in any case, must be limited to a clear statement of the consequences of a type of action, whether this be a small-scale enterprise or a world-wide system. The science of man, however, has always the right and the duty to point out what the consequences of a cultural revolution will be. This is the foundation of all applied science. Social science must not be afraid of predicting, anticipating, and developing some ethics of reason. This does not mean that we have the duty or the liberty of condemning certain ends on moral grounds. We can, however, point out, if this is the result of our considered opinion and analysis, that totalitarianism must lead to the destruction of the nation with which it is associated and, later on, to destruction on international scale.

Totalitarianism is an extreme expression in the shift of balance between state and nation. It is extreme because modern means of mechanical mobilization of man power, economic resources, and spiritual values have become so dangerously effective that it is now possible to refashion whole communities—consisting of hundreds of millions—and to change each of them from a nation, exercising, transmitting, and developing culture, into a belligerent machinery supreme in war, but unsuited, perhaps unable, to carry on the national heritage of culture. The German nation, once leading in science and in art, rich in a highly differentiated regional folklore, peasant life, and economic diversity, has now been changed into a large-scale barracks. It would be an important historical task to show how much of Germany's greatness was due to the racial, regional, and traditional differences of its component parts. The progressive extinction of this diversity is the price which Germany as a nation had to pay in order to make Germany the state so powerful. Nationalism in this modern totalitarian form is pernicious because it has become the greatest enemy of the nation itself.

And what is the place of totalitarianism in international policies and politics? It is obvious that humanity is now faced with two alternatives—the final victory, in the long run, of totalitarianism or democracy. No state organized on a peace basis, that is, for the fullest and most effective exercise of civilization, can compete with a state organized for efficiency in war. Nazi victory can be final only if Hitler's nation-state, one and alone, assumes full control of the whole world. If this were probable or even possible, we might well argue that, once humanity is submitted to one conqueror, the conditions of creative and constructive conquest will set in, with the usual beneficent results, obtained at a great price, but finally acceptable.

The possibility of a complete victory of one state does not exist. If Germany wins, she will have at least three more totalitarian powers to reckon with—Italy, Russia, and Japan. When Italy falls out and becomes a mere appendage of Hitlerism, the United States of America may have to enter the ranks of totalitarian countries. For, on the assumption that Great Britain is beaten and absorbed into the German-led totalitarian bloc, as France has become, the United States must continue in isolation. This will mean, again, either embracing totalitarianism or withdrawing into a precarious state of semi-independence in matters political, economic, and cultural. Fortunately, Great Britain is still fighting the battle of liberty and civilization, and, as its habit has always been, it may remain beaten in all battles except the final one.

Totalitarianism, unless it becomes the universal empire of one single power, is not a source of stability but of age-long periodic world wars. Anthropological analysis supports those who believe that war must be abolished. Nationalism, in the sense of a demand for cultural autonomy within each group united by language, tradition, and culture is legitimate and indispensable to the carrying out of the very business of culture. Such cultural autonomy of the component parts of present-day humanity is, or was, the principle of the national life of Switzerland and of the old Austro-Hungarian Empire, of the relations between the powerful United States and its Latin American neighbors, who would be entirely unable to defend their cultural autonomy by force, but enjoy it, with all-round benefits, by the policy of the "good neighbor."

We are now living in a world where fashions come and go and where the soundest ideals and principles are discredited because they are considered to have become worn out or worn too long. This attitude in itself is almost as pernicious as certain germs of totalitarianism. The student of social science ought to fight against it. I would, therefore, reiterate the beliefs which inspired some of the finest thinkers and best fighters of the last war [World War I]. I believe that war can legitimately be fought only to end war. I believe that the future peace of mankind is possible only on a principle of a commonwealth of nations. I believe that, in a humanity still divided by races, cultures, customs, and languages, a full tolerance in racial relations, in the treatment of nationalities and national minorities, and in the respect for the individual is the very mainspring of all progress and the foundation of all stability. The great enemy of today is the sovereign state, even as we find it in democratic commonwealths—certainly as it has developed into the malignant growth of totalitarianism. The real failure of the Wilsonian League of Nations was due to the fact that its very builders refused to pay the price which it obviously imposed. They were not prepared to abrogate one ounce of their national sovereignty, forgetting that this was the very material out of which the League had to be constructed.

Unless we courageously, resolutely, and with due humility take up the principles, the ideals, and the plans which originated at first in America and were also first denounced by this country, we shall not be able to overcome the major disease of our age. This may be called total war, or totalitarianism, or extreme state sovereignty, or injustice in matters racial, religious, and national. It always results in the substitution of force for argument, of oppression for justice, and of crude, dictated mysticism for faith and reason.

MARGARET MEAD

*Warfare Is Only an Invention— Not a Biological Necessity**

Is war a biological necessity, a sociological inevitability, or just a bad invention? Those who argue for the first view endow man with such pugnacious instincts that some outlet in aggressive behavior is necessary if man is to reach full human stature. It was this point of view which lay back of William James's famous essay, "The Moral Equivalent of War" (*supra*), in which he tried to retain the warlike virtues and channel them in new directions. A similar point of view has lain back of the Soviet Union's attempt to make competition between groups rather than between individuals. A basic, competitive, aggressive, warring human nature is assumed, and those who wish to outlaw war or outlaw competitiveness merely try to find new and less socially destructive ways in which these biologically given aspects of man's nature can find expression. Then there are those who take the second view: warfare is the inevitable concomitant of the development of the state, the struggle for land and natural resources of class societies springing not from the nature of man, but from the nature of history. War is nevertheless inevitable unless we change our social system and outlaw classes, the struggle for power, and possessions; and in the event of our success warfare would disappear, as a symptom vanishes when the disease is cured.

One may hold a sort of compromise position between these two extremes; one may claim that all aggression springs from the frustration of man's bio-

* Reprinted from Margaret Mead, "Warfare Is Only an Invention—Not a Biological Necessity," pp. 402–405, *Asia*, XL (1940), by permission of the author.

logically determined drives and that, since all forms of culture are frustrating, it is certain each new generation will be aggressive and the aggression will find its natural and inevitable expression in race war, class war, nationalistic war, and so on. All three of these positions are very popular today among those who think seriously about the problems of war and its possible prevention, but I wish to urge another point of view, less defeatist, perhaps, than the first and third and more accurate than the second: that is, that warfare, by which I mean recognized conflict between two groups *as groups*, in which each group puts an army (even if the army is only fifteen pygmies) into the field to fight and kill, if possible, some of the members of the army of the other group— that warfare of this sort is an invention like any other of the inventions in terms of which we order our lives, such as writing, marriage, cooking our food instead of eating it raw, trial by jury, or burial of the dead, and so on. Some of this list anyone will grant are inventions: trial by jury is confined to very limited portions of the globe; we know that there are tribes that do not bury their dead but instead expose or cremate them; and we know that only part of the human race has had the knowledge of writing as its cultural inheritance. But, whenever a way of doing things is found universally, such as the use of fire or the practice of some form of marriage, we tend to think at once that it is not an invention at all but an attribute of humanity itself. And yet even such universals as marriage and the use of fire are inventions like the rest, very basic ones, inventions which were, perhaps, necessary if human history was to take the turn that it has taken, but nevertheless inventions. At some point in his social development man was undoubtedly without the institution of marriage or the knowledge of the use of fire.

The case for warfare is much clearer because there are peoples even today who have no warfare. Of these the Eskimos are perhaps the most conspicuous examples, but the Lepchas of Sikkim described by Geoffrey Gorer in *Himalayan Village* are as good.[1] Neither of these peoples understands war, not even defensive warfare. The idea of warfare is lacking, and this idea is as essential to really carrying on war as an alphabet or a syllabary is to writing. But, whereas the Lepchas are a gentle, unquarrelsome people, and the advocates of other points of view might argue that they are not full human beings or that they had never been frustrated and so had no aggression to expand in warfare, the Eskimo case gives no such possibility of interpretation. The Eskimos are not a mild and meek people; many of them are turbulent and troublesome. Fights, theft of wives, murder, cannibalism, occur among them—all outbursts of passionate men goaded by desire or intolerable circumstance. Here are men faced with hunger, men faced with loss of their wives, men faced with the threat of extermination by other men, and here are orphan children, growing up miserably with no one to care for them, mocked and neglected by those

[1] G. Gorer, *Himalayan Village* (London: M. Joseph, 1938).

about them. The personality necessary for war, the circumstances necessary to goad men to desperation are present, but there is no war. When a traveling Eskimo entered a settlement, he might have to fight the strongest man in the settlement to establish his position among them, but this was a test of strength and bravery, not war. The idea of warfare, of one *group* organizing against another *group* to maim and wound and kill them was absent. And, without that idea, passions might rage but there was no war.

But, it may be argued, is not this because the Eskimos have such a low and undeveloped form of social organization? They own no land, they move from place to place, camping, it is true, season after season on the same site, but this is not something to fight for as the modern nations of the world fight for land and raw materials. They have no permanent possessions that can be looted, no towns that can be burned. They have no social classes to produce stress and strains within the society which might force it to go to war outside. Does not the absence of war among the Eskimos, while disproving the biological necessity of war, just go to confirm the point that it is the state of development of the society which accounts for war and nothing else?

We find the answer among the pygmy peoples of the Andaman Islands in the Bay of Bengal. The Andamans also represent an exceedingly low level of society; they are a hunting and food-gathering people; they live in tiny hordes without any class stratification; their houses are simpler than the snow houses of the Eskimo. But they knew about warfare. The army might contain only fifteen determined pygmies marching in a straight line, but it was the real thing none the less. Tiny army met tiny army in open battle, blows were exchanged, casualties suffered, and the state of warfare could only be concluded by a peace-making ceremony.

Similarly, among the Australian aborigines, who built no permanent dwellings but wandered from water hole to water hole over their almost desert country, warfare—and rules of "international law"—were highly developed. The student of social evolution will seek in vain for his obvious causes of war, struggle for lands, struggle for power of one group over another, expansion of population, need to divert the minds of a populace restive under tyranny, or even the ambition of a successful leader to enhance his own prestige. All are absent, but warfare as a practice remained, and men engaged in it and killed one another in the course of a war because killing is what is done in wars.

From instances like these it becomes apparent that an inquiry into the causes of war misses the fundamental point as completely as does an insistence upon the biological necessity of war. If a people have an idea of going to war and the idea that war is the way in which certain situations, defined within their society, are to be handled, they will sometimes go to war. If they are a mild and unaggressive people, like the Pueblo Indians, they may limit themselves to defensive warfare, but they will be forced to think in terms of war because there are peoples near them who have warfare as a pattern, and offensive, raiding, pillaging warfare at that. When the pattern of warfare is known, people like the Pueblo Indians will defend themselves, taking advantage of their natural defenses, the mesa village site, and people like the Lepchas, having no natural defenses and no idea of warfare, will merely submit to the invader. But the essential point remains the same. There is a way of behaving which is known to a given people and labeled as an appropriate form of behavior; a bold and warlike people like the Sioux or the Maori may label warfare as desirable as well as possible, a mild people like the Pueblo Indians may label warfare as undesirable, but to the minds of both peoples the possibility of warfare is present. Their thoughts, their hopes, their plans are oriented about this idea—that warfare may be selected as the way to meet some situation.

So simple peoples and civilized peoples, mild peoples and violent, assertive peoples, will all go to war if they have the invention, just as those peoples who have the custom of dueling will have duels and peoples who have the pattern of vendetta will indulge in vendetta. And, conversely, peoples who do not know of dueling will not fight duels, even though their wives are seduced and their daughters ravished; they may on occasion commit murder but they will not fight duels. Cultures which lack the idea of the vendetta will not meet every quarrel in this way. A people can use only the forms it has. So the Balinese have their special way of dealing with a quarrel between two individuals: if the two feel that the causes of quarrel are heavy, they may go and register their quarrel in the temple before the gods, and, making offerings, they may swear never to have anything to do with each other again. . . . But in other societies, although individuals might feel as full of animosity and as unwilling to have any further contact as do the Balinese, they cannot register their quarrel with the gods and go on quietly about their business because registering quarrels with the gods is not an invention of which they know.

Yet, if it be granted that warfare is, after all, an invention, it may nevertheless be an invention that lends itself to certain types of personality, to the exigent needs of autocrats, to the expansionist desires of crowded peoples, to the desire for plunder and rape and loot which is engendered by a dull and frustrating life. What, then, can we say of this congruence between warfare and its uses? If it is a form which fits so well, is not this congruence the essential point? But even here the primitive material causes us to wonder, because there are tribes who go to war merely for glory, having no quarrel with the enemy, suffering from no tyrant within their boundaries, anxious neither for land nor loot nor women, but merely anxious to win prestige which within that tribe has been declared obtainable only by war and without which no young man can hope to win his sweetheart's smile of approval. But if, as was the case with the Bush Negroes of Dutch Guiana, it is artistic ability which is necessary to win a girl's approval, the same young man would have to be carving rather than going out on a war party.

In many parts of the world, war is a game in which the individual can win

counters—counters which bring him prestige in the eyes of his own sex or of
the opposite sex; he plays for these counters as he might, in our society, strive
for a tennis championship. Warfare is a frame for such prestige-seeking merely
because it calls for the display of certain skills and certain virtues; all of these
skills—riding straight, shooting straight, dodging the missiles of the enemy
and sending one's own straight to the mark—can be equally well exercised in
some other framework and, equally, the virtues—endurance, bravery, loyalty,
steadfastness—can be displayed in other contexts. The tie-up between proving
oneself a man and proving this by a success in organized killing is due to a
definition which many societies have made of manliness. And often, even in
those societies which counted success in warfare a proof of human worth,
strange turns were given to the idea, as when the plains Indians gave their
highest awards to the man who touched a live enemy rather than to the man
who brought in a scalp—from a dead enemy—because the latter was less
risky. Warfare is just an invention known to the majority of human societies
by which they permit their young men either to accumulate prestige or avenge
their honor or acquire loot or wives or slaves or sago lands or cattle or appease
the blood lust of their gods or the restless souls of the recently dead. It is just
an invention, older and more widespread than the jury system, but none the
less an invention.

But, once we have said this, have we said anything at all? Despite a few instances, dear to the hearts of controversialists, of the loss of the useful arts,
once an invention is made which proves congruent with human needs or social
forms, it tends to persist. Grant that war is an invention, that it is not a biological necessity nor the outcome of certain special types of social forms, still,
once the invention is made, what are we to do about it? The Indian who had
been subsisting on the buffalo for generations because with his primitive
weapons he could slaughter only a limited number of buffalo did not return
to his primitive weapons when he saw that the white man's more efficient
weapons were exterminating the buffalo. A desire for the white man's cloth
may mortgage the South Sea Islander to the white man's plantation, but he
does not return to making bark cloth, which would have left him free. Once
an invention is known and accepted, men do not easily relinquish it. The
skilled workers may smash the first steam looms which they feel are to be
their undoing, but they accept them in the end, and no movement which has
insisted upon the mere abandonment of usable inventions has ever had much
success. Warfare is here, as part of our thought; the deeds of warriors are
immortalized in the words of our poets, the toys of our children are modeled
upon the weapons of the soldier, the frame of reference within which our
statesmen and our diplomats work always contains war. If we know that it is
not inevitable, that it is due to historical accident that warfare is one of the
ways in which we think of behaving, are we given any hope by that? What
hope is there of persuading nations to abandon war, nations so thoroughly

imbued with the idea that resort to war is, if not actually desirable and noble, at least inevitable whenever certain defined circumstances arise?

In answer to this question I think we might turn to the history of other social inventions, and inventions which must once have seemed as firmly entrenched as warfare. Take the methods of trial which preceded the jury system: ordeal and trial by combat. Unfair, capricious, alien as they are to our feeling today, they were once the only methods open to individuals accused of some offense. The invention of trial by jury gradually replaced these methods until only witches, and finally not even witches, had to resort to the ordeal. And for a long time the jury system seemed the one best and finest method of settling legal disputes, but today new inventions, trial before judges only or before commissions, are replacing the jury system. In each case the old method was replaced by a new social invention. The ordeal did not go out because people thought it unjust or wrong; it went out because a method more congruent with the institutions and feelings of the period was invented. And, if we despair over the way in which war seems such an ingrained habit of most of the human race, we can take comfort from the fact that a poor invention will usually give place to a better invention.

For this, two conditions, at least, are necessary. The people must recognize the defects of the old invention, and someone must make a new one. Propaganda against warfare, documentation of its terrible cost in human suffering and social waste, these prepare the ground by teaching people to feel that warfare is a defective social institution. There is further needed a belief that social invention is possible and the invention of new methods which will render warfare as out of date as the tractor is making the plow, or the motor car the horse and buggy. A form of behavior becomes out of date only when something else takes its place, and, in order to invent forms of behavior which will make war obsolete, it is a first requirement to believe that an invention is possible.

◄◄◄ ►►►

JOSEPH SCHNEIDER

Primitive Warfare: A Methodological Note*

The literature of primitive warfare is acknowledged as being in an unsatisfactory state.[1] There are a number of reasons for this, only one of which will be discussed here, namely, the tendency to classify under primitive war all forms of group-sanctioned violence whether the fighting can properly be called war or not. The fact that blood vengeance is nearly everywhere an attribute of primitive fighting has encouraged the view that fighting within the group cannot be distinguished from fighting between groups. One consequence of this bit of taxonomic indolence is that no criteria are available by which crime and punishment may be distinguished from war. It will, first, be the purpose of this paper to illustrate the practice complained of. Second, it will be argued that whether the fighting reported can be called war depends upon the social unit employed as basic.

Hobhouse, Wheeler, and Ginsberg in their study of the institutions of primitive peoples point out that it is not always easy to

> . . . distinguish between private retaliation when exercised by kinfolk or a body of friends, and a war which is perhaps organized by a leader chosen for the occasion, followed by a body of volunteers. Strictly, we

* Reprinted from Joseph Schneider, "Primitive Warfare: A Methodological Note," pp. 772–777, *American Sociological Review*, XV (1950), by permission of the publisher and author.
[1] W. W. Newcomb, Jr., "A Re-examination of the Causes of Plains Warfare," *American Anthropologist*, LII (July-September 1950), 317–330.

take it that external retaliation means a quarrel exercised by a part of a community only upon members of another community, while war means an operation conducted in the name of the community as a whole. Feuds would thus also be the appropriate name for reprisals exercised by one branch of a community upon another, e.g., as between two clans or two local groups within a tribe. As distinguished from a feud, war implies a certain development of social organization, and is probably not so common at the lowest stages as it becomes higher up.[2]

The distinction made by these authors between war and the feud is unambiguous and would probably be concurred in by students of war as a social institution generally.[3] The literature of anthropology does not, however, in the opinion of these writers, admit the application of this clear-cut differentiation of war and the feud to ethnographic data.[4] Thus, when they came to the task of distinguishing between war and the feud, they found the evidence inadequate. As a result, their statistical compilation of the instances of fighting among several hundred contemporary primitives falls into two categories: (a) wars and feuds; (b) no war.

The same taxonomic difficulties appear in Quincy Wright's treatment of primitive war.[5] Like Hobhouse, Wheeler, and Ginsberg, Wright observes that it is difficult to draw a distinction between "privately initiated external violence sanctioned by the group, such as feuds and head-hunting," and "violence sanctioned by the group as a whole against other human beings external to the group."

> In most cases these two types of activity, which may be denominated, respectively, "reprisals" and "war," can be distinguished. They are, however, closely related, and it seems advisable to include all external, group-sanctioned violence against other human beings in the conception of primitive war.

Excluded from the conception of primitive war is "violence against members of the group sanctioned by that group," that is, crime and punishment.[6] The difference between the feud and war exists in the war practices observed to-

[2] Leonard T. Hobhouse, Gerald C. Wheeler, and Morris Ginsberg, *The Material Culture and Social Institutions of the Simpler Peoples: An Essay in Correlation* (London: Chapman & Hall, 1930), p. 228.

[3] Alvin Johnson, "War," *Encyclopaedia of the Social Sciences* (New York: Macmillan, 1934), XV, 331–341; Bronislaw Malinowski, "The Deadly Issue," *Atlantic Monthly*, CLVIII (December 1936), 559–569; *idem*, "An Anthropological Analysis of War, *supra*; Harry Holbert Turney-High, *Primitive War: Its Practice and Concepts* (Columbia: University of South Carolina Press, 1949), p. 30.

For a different view see Margaret Mead, "Warfare Is Only an Invention—Not a Biological Necessity," *supra*; and Camilla A. Wedgwood, "Some Aspects of Warfare in Melanesia," *Oceania*, I (April 1930), 5–33.

[4] *Ibid.*, pp. 7–8.

[5] *A Study of War* (Chicago: University of Chicago Press, 1942), I, chap. VI.

[6] *Ibid.*, p. 59.

ward a related and normally friendly group and an alien group. "Hostilities of the first type, although group-sanctioned, are usually of the nature of a feud to secure revenge, reprisal, or glory for a particular individual or family within the group." [7]

The principal difference between Wright's treatment of primitive war and that of Hobhouse, Wheeler, and Ginsberg is that the former contends that feuds and war can be distinguished in the literature. The latter hold that the "evidence is often very inadequate for the purpose." [8] Were it not, therefore, for the fact that the tabulations presented by Wright are more detailed, there would be no data readily available to illuminate the problem here under consideration. Wright's use of a fourfold classification makes it possible to discern to some extent the number of cases of feuding among contemporary primitives relative to war.

Table 1 shows the primitives in Wright's data classified by the four types of

TABLE 1

Absolute Number of Cases Practicing Each Type of Warfare in the Data Supplied by Quincy Wright, Classified by Level of Economic Culture *

Level of Economic Culture	DEFENSIVE WAR	SOCIAL WAR	ECONOMIC WAR	POLITICAL WAR	TOTAL
Lower Hunters	5	91	2	—	98
Higher Hunters	11	72	33	—	116
Lower Agriculturists	9	37	14	1	61
Middle Agriculturists	2	98	51	10	161
Higher Agriculturists	1	38	46	25	110
Lower Pastorals	—	8	15	—	23
Higher Pastorals	—	2	13	4	19
TOTAL	28*	346	174	40	588

* *A Study of War, op. cit.,* I, Appendix IX.

warfare and level of economic culture. It will be observed that 64 per cent of all the cases tabulated fall into the combined categories of defensive and social war.[9] Second, among hunters 83 per cent of all the cases fall into these classifications, and none whatsoever into the category of political war. On the other hand, pastoral peoples tend to be warlike in the accepted sense, with agriculturists less so.[10]

[7] *Ibid.,* p. 90.

[8] Hobhouse *et al., op. cit.,* p. 228.

[9] Defensive war includes all peoples without "war in their mores," who have neither military weapons nor organization and do not fight unless attacked. Social war includes fighting for blood revenge, glory, sport, religion, and so on.

[10] John R. Swanton differs from Wright only in arguing "that violence within the tribe in primitive society, or civil wars if you please, cannot be differentiated from wars between group and group." See his *Are Wars Inevitable?* ("Smithsonian Institution War Background Studies," No. 12 [Washington, D. C., 1943]), p. 8.

Wright's readiness to follow Hobhouse, Wheeler, and Ginsberg in grouping under primitive war external retaliation and war leaves unresolved the problem of what criteria may be employed to distinguish crime and punishment or vengeance from war. In cultures where there exist scant forms of public justice, retaliation or self-help is the only means of redress available. Thus, whether one method of redress is called punishment and another war depends upon the social unit of classification employed as basic or primary.[11]

Wright is implicitly aware that warfare is dependent upon a type of social organization not characteristic of primitive cultures. He points out, for example, that peoples organized into clans tend to be least warlike and those integrated into tribal federations most warlike.[12] He also notes, as observed above, that the feud is confined to related peoples normally friendly. But the self-limiting criticisms by which Hobhouse, Wheeler, and Ginsberg suggest a way out of the taxonomically difficult task of distinguishing war and the feud are wanting. One explanation for this lack, possibly, is that the latter deal with war as well as justice, including modes of redress.[13] There is the implication in what these students have to say on justice and related topics that what comes to be called war has not a little to do with the social unit chosen as the basis of classification. Whether, for instance, the clan or the tribe is employed as the social unit has nothing to do with the presence or absence of violence in a group, but it would make some difference what nomenclature would be employed to describe the types of violence observed. If an injured individual and a group of kinsmen from one clan slay a member of another clan within the same tribe for adultery, is that deed to be designated an act of war or a form of primitive penology? An answer to this question is more than an exercise in classificatory ingenuity.

Hobhouse, Wheeler, and Ginsberg point out that sometimes weighty reasons may be adduced for using either the clan or the tribe as the unit of classification. This is notably true of the Australians.

[11] One way out of the difficulty here posed has appeared in the literature on primitive conflict. That way has been to resolve historic warfare into its type parts—for example, formations, leadership, surprise, supply, and so on—and matching them up with the type parts present in primitive fighting. Margaret Mead, op. cit., uses this approach to separate unwarlike primitives from the warlike. On this basis the Andaman Islanders and the Australian aborigines are adjudged warlike because the former use the principle of formations and the latter conclude hostilities with peace ceremonials. Needless to say, external retaliation assumes organized forms and may put to use cultural devices associated with historic warfare.

Turney-High uses the same approach in his Primitive War, op. cit. He does not, however, call primitive fighting true war, largely because fighting among simpler peoples is not a political device. He also remarks that the primitive fighter is not a soldier but a warrior; he will not submit to discipline.

[12] Op. cit., p. 66.
[13] Hobhouse et al., op. cit., pp. 53–67.

When the various groups that compose a tribe live in habitual intercourse with one another, practising intermarriage, owning a common cult, and accepting a common name, we must speak of them as forming, under certain aspects, one society, though they have no common government. We must also bear in mind that under another aspect they form several societies, and in considering our results we must allow both aspects to pass in review.[14]

It is the contention, then, of these students that it is possible to speak of a people as comprising a single society though they have no common government. They also add that this will not always do. Their reasoning is that, if emphasis is placed upon the tribe as the basic social unit, no statement can be made relative to justice within the clan or lesser group. When interest is focused upon the tribe,

> We are too likely to hear nothing of justice within the clan. It is between clans that trouble arises and with this trouble that the code of the tribe is concerned. Such a society therefore is apt to figure . . . as an instance in which self-redress by kinsfolk is the regular method of obtaining justice, for there is no doubt that it is one society, and that self-redress exists as between its constituent parts while of the internal regulation of the parts we hear nothing.[15]

The explanation of how it happens that Hobhouse, Wheeler, and Ginsberg find it expedient to use different units of classification for comparison and tabulation is clear. They are concerned with justice and methods of redress within both the clan and the tribe. Yet it is precisely on these points that the student of primitive warfare has erred. He has confused the limits of the larger society with the lesser units comprised within it and called "the regular method of obtaining justice," that is, "self-redress by kinsfolk," warfare. It is only on these grounds that it is possible to understand how violence between groups comprising one society, though without common government, came to be labeled warfare in the literature of anthropology. Apparently the student of primitive fighting has given less attention to the structure of primitive societies than needful.[16] That does not mean that students of war have not had an uneasy feeling about calling the fighting which occurs among primitives war.

[14] *Op. cit.,* p. 48.

[15] *Ibid.,* pp. 64–65.

[16] H. Ian Hogbin is a distinguished exception to this statement. Where others speak of warfare, he talks about crime and punishment. He views vengeance, ambushment, raids, mass duels, and ceremonial combats as methods of punishment. See his *Experiments in Civilization, The Effects of European Culture on a Native Community of the Solomon Islands* (London: George Routledge and Sons, 1939), chap. III, and *idem,* "Social Reaction to Crime: Law and Morals in the Shouten Islands, New Guinea," *Journal of the Royal Anthropological Institute,* LXVIII, pp. 232–262.

Davie observes that the "native Australians are far from being a warlike race in spite of their frequent affrays. . . . Real war does not exist among the Australians." [17]

It is now clear whether the student of primitive warfare takes the clan or the tribe as the basic social unit is of no small importance in coming to a conclusion respecting what the prevailing forms of collective violence among primitives are to be called. Thus, where clan exogamy is the rule, the student of warfare has no alternative but to recognize the tribe as the basic social unit. An exogamous clan is, in the nature of the case, an incomplete society. Clansmen trace their descent from a common ancestor through either males or females, never both. One consequence of this fact is that the individuals in a clan can seldom, if ever, act together as an independent group. Each clansman is trapped in a system of interlaced and overlapping kinship ties that theoretically ramify out into the several clans that comprise the tribe. Since that is so, a clan cannot be treated as a separate, independent community of common residence capable of making war, however true it may be that the clan always seems to be the unit of social and economic order and the origin of external violence.[18] It is only by first exploring the consanguineous ties of the exogamous clans in an area to the limit where the component groups become a community of common life and residence that it becomes possible to designate those clan clusters capable of making war. Anything less than this reveals a type of social structure breached by internal factions between which organized violence of the kind often called "war" appears.

For example, Murdock describes the quarrels which erupt into violence between Haida clans or villages war, although the individuals who quarrel and fight are related to one another by descent and marriage. The women, who are the peace-makers, are the spouses of the men in one village and the sisters and sibmates of the other. Indeed, the account given of the development of open fighting between the men from two villages illustrates perfectly the observation that clan groups are incomplete societies, incapable of acting as fighting units. In this instance the Haida women are caught up in the divided loyalties and "unpatriotic" behavior which characterizes membership in groups of this kind. When trouble brews, it is they who attempt to mediate the quarrels that arise between villages by going first to one and then to the other, since they enjoy free passage by virtue of their relationship to the males in both clans. It is only when they fail to pacify the angry males and fighting ensues that they align themselves with their husbands.[19]

---

[17] Maurice Rea Davie, *The Evolution of War* (New Haven: Yale University Press, 1926), p. 52. Also see W. I. Thomas, *Primitive Behavior* (New York: McGraw-Hill, 1937), p. 421.

[18] George Peter Murdock, *Social Structure* (New York: Macmillan Co., 1949), p. 73.

[19] *Ibid.*, p. 73. The Haida engage in fighting for plunder, booty, and slaves against the Tlingit, Tsimshian, and Bellabella. Clans in both moieties of several villages unite under a chieftain for purposes of carrying out raids. George Peter Murdock, *Our Primitive Contemporaries* (New York: Macmillan Co., 1934), pp. 241–242.

But the most singular example of this failing appears in William Lloyd Warner's study of Murngin fighting.[20] It is to this exposition that the reader's attention will now be directed.

Warfare is, according to Warner, the most important social activity of the Murngin. But it is clear from the description of the fighting given, as well as of the social system within which the fighting takes place, that the referent is to intratribal conflict and not war. Beginning with the last point first, it is observed that group solidarity even at the clan level is rendered so unstable by the complicated kinship system that the fighting which occurs becomes almost the activity of a single individual.[21] Later on the same point is made with reference to the wergild. The ceremonial termination of a feud would require the participation of all the kin in the repayment, which never happens because of the ramifications of kinship ties.[22]

Warner's exposition is, however, not unambiguous respecting the degree of clan solidarity prevalent among the Murngin. In another instance kinship solidarity is described as so compelling that a single killing may turn an entire region into a battleground.[23] Juxtaposed is the remark that kinship solidarity has also the opposite effect. It tends to limit the scope of fighting and actually prevents it from taking place. Since fighting within the clan is forbidden, the dispersed loyalties of clansmen have the effect of extinguishing any conflict, excepting the ceremonial peace-making fight, that might erupt between clans. Ties of marriage and descent ally different clansmen, thus preventing clans from fighting one another as units as well as mitigating the chances that an aggrieved individual may have in enlisting kinsmen and friends in seeking redress through retaliation.

The clan is the social unit within which violence, short of brawling and wife-beating, does not happen. Also, because of the practice of clan exogamy, fighting does not take place between a man's clan and his wife's or mother's clan. The fighting which occurs is between clans in the same moiety, although fights between individuals from opposite moieties are said to be possible. These fights tend to extinguish themselves because there exists no rivalry for women, a principal reason for interclan conflict.[24] Disputes between clans in opposite moieties are, therefore, likely to be terminated ceremonially. In short, then, the prevailing kinship system among the Murngin is so structured that within the clan there exists some measure of spontaneous order and justice, while between clans there exists a tribal code of collective redress. It is to the practices eventuating from the adherence to this Murngin tribal code that Warner refers when he uses the term warfare.

20 "Murngin Warfare," *Oceania*, I (January-March 1931), 457–494, and *idem, A Black Civilization, A Social Study of an Australian Tribe* (New York: Harper and Bros., 1937).

21 *A Black Civilization, op. cit.*, pp. 156, 168, 190.

22 *Ibid.*, pp. 389, 393.

23 *Ibid.*, p. 156.

24 *Ibid.*, pp. 29, 32–33, 155.

We are not yet finished with the obscurities in Warner's exposition of Murngin fighting. Reference is made several times to tribal warfare among the Murngin,[25] although the tribe is elsewhere described as being almost non-existent, without sovereign authority or capacity to make war.[26] The explanation for these two seeming contradictory statements is not easy to unravel. It appears that what is meant is that the kinship system of the peoples of north-eastern Arnhem Land permits the enlargement of a two-clan feud to a stage where all the clans in the whole area may become involved. That is, of course, possible since intermarriage occurs between individuals belonging to different tribes. If this interpretation is correct, it is not permissible to call such fighting—when it occurs—tribal warfare, but a case where individuals in clans from different tribes are arrayed against one another. It is nowhere stated that all the clans in two tribes are ever arrayed against one another. The kinship system would rule out that kind of union and alignment. It is, therefore, reasonable to infer from Warner's exposition of Murngin "warfare" that all the fighting which occurs is between individuals as clan members. Tribal conflict is utterly out of the question. Indeed, it is asserted that a clan seldom goes to battle as a group, that the clan is politically impotent when it comes to taking positive action.[27]

Murngin fighting cannot be called war. It is a form of penology. The principle underlying Murngin fighting is reciprocity.[28] The killing of a clansman by an outsider demands that the wrong done be paid back to make things even once more. Deaths resulting from interclan rivalries for women lead to blood vengeance. The same principle applies to woman-stealing. Only the return of the woman and a regulated fight to punish the abductor or the killing or wounding of an enemy clansman can even the score. The improper viewing of the totem is similarly regarded as a wrong to be redressed by exacting vengeance. Another encouragement to Murngin fighting is the belief that the spirit of the deceased enters the body of the killer and increases his strength. This belief alone, Warner conjectures, would furnish ample cause for young males eager to become strong and adult to go out and slay an individual from another clan.[29]

The foregoing summary exposition of the fighting among an aboriginal people should make it clear that fighting which occurs among primitives who live in exogamous clans or local residence groups which tend to be exogamous cannot be called war. Attempts to differentiate between historic and primitive warfare by enlarging the scope of the latter term to include privately initiated violence sanctioned by the group against outsiders can only be disapproved.

25 *Ibid.*, pp. 77, 155, 156.
26 *Ibid.*, pp. 9, 35, 77.
27 *Ibid.*, pp. 17, 389.
28 *Ibid.*, pp. 159, 162.
29 *Ibid.*, p. 166.

Such efforts derive from a failure to observe that in primitive societies punishment for wrongdoing tends to take two forms. Within the local group there exists some degree of social discipline or order of a formal nature. Between local groups formal control may be entirely lacking. Redress in such a case is an individual affair and, if the aggrieved individual or his kin make no effort to punish the offender by violent means, nothing is done. What we have here is a matter of crime and punishment within populations where systems of public justice are undeveloped. That is not war.

PART III

War, Liberal Democracy, and Industrial Society

INTRODUCTION

In previous parts of this book the editors have sought to represent the thought of social scientists concerned with the causes of war in its most universal dimensions. For the most part, these social scientists have viewed war in the light of man's psychological and social nature. In this part, however, we wish to draw special attention to the sociological significance of war in the modern age.

Students of society have characteristically analyzed modern war in the context of larger social, political, economic, and technological change. Classic sociological formulations, beginning with Saint-Simon and Comte and culminating with that of Spencer, reprinted here, stressed the contrast between the ethos of a military and of an industrial society. Following Sir Henry Maine, Spencer identified the industrial society with the liberal social order based on contract, as against the ancient and feudal military societies based on ascribed status. The military society represented a more primitive phase in a linear evolutionary progress and ultimately gave way to the industrial society. The idea that modern society was to be progressively pacific is easy to dismiss with a contemptuous air. Raymond Aron gives this theory the close attention it deserves in the final selection. He contrasts the optimism of Comte and Spencer regarding the future of modern society with the tradition of pessimism represented by Spengler and Nietzsche and enlarges our understanding by showing that their differences concerning war are based on differing philosophies of history. Though optimists and pessimists shared an organic theory of society, in Comte and Spencer it was somewhat inconsistently linked with a linear theory of progress, whereas in Spengler the biological analogy took the form of a cyclical theory of society which emphasized the growth and decline of cultures.

Neither Comte nor Spencer visualized a future condition of Western society which featured what Alfred Vagts has called "the militarism of the civilians." [1] Neither anticipated the militarization of industry and the industrialization of

[1] Alfred Vagts, *A History of Militarism* (New York: Meridian, 1959).

the military. Perhaps it is the organic theory of society which should be called into question, for neither Spencer nor Comte could have imagined that military and industrial institutions could mesh into such an effective cultural "fit." Perhaps we have overemphasized the degree to which the elements of a culture must be integrated with one another, or perhaps Comte and Spencer ignored nonindustrial elements which were integral in modern society.

Over a half-century later, the social and political dimensions of the future society were sketched in dark colors by Harold D. Lasswell in a famous essay, "The Garrison State," reprinted here. Since that essay was written another quarter century has elapsed, and we have considerable perspective concerning the relative merits of the various theories; it is left to the reader to determine whether the balance tilts in favor of the optimists or the pessimists.[2]

Among the many developments which help explain the contrast between the views of Spencer and of Lasswell, we have selected one for special attention— the role of the military in the various kinds of social and political order of the modern age. For it is increasingly clear that it is the hallmark of the age that wars are waged by nation-states, and their monopoly of violence is concentrated in the hands of military professionals who direct the energies of vast citizen armies. De Tocqueville's incisive observations, made in the third decade of the nineteenth century, on armies and the role of the military elites in aristocratic and democratic states are presented together with Morris Janowitz's contemporary assessment of some of the same problems. Here the interaction of political, social, and technological elements becomes very complex. The comparison of de Tocqueville and Janowitz also serve to provide perspective concerning the special role of military elites in the liberal democracies, totalitarian states, and many developing nations. With these contributions to political sociology, we arrive at the edge of that political analysis which is essential to the understanding of war in modern society. In preparation for that task, Raymond Aron's essay illuminates the problem of the sociological significance of war in liberal society as viewed from the nineteenth century by contrast with the contemporary outlook.

The sociologist of war has frequently asked the Durkheimian question: What are the sources of social solidarity? Though racism and class conflict are prominent in the history of the past century, it is nationalism that presents itself as fundamental in the analysis of the terrible wars of this modern period. Yet there does not exist a fully developed social psychology or a sociology of nationalism. Sociologists have noted the general loosening of traditional social bonds under the conditions of urban and industrial life, and an interesting hypothesis regarding the relevance of these phenomena for

---

[2] Cf. Harold D. Lasswell, "The Garrison-State Hypothesis Today," in Samuel P. Huntington, ed., *Changing Patterns of Military Politics* (New York: Free Press of Glencoe, 1962).

nationalism and war may be found in "the theory of mass society." [3] The liberating and concomitantly disorganizing influence of liberal society in its impact on traditional social orders in the West, it is held, is responsible for the rise of intense nationalism and the attendant appeals to war.

Nationalistic wars are to be understood as arising under the conditions where older identities of estate, class, region, and religion are eroded by mass society. Nationalism and the nation-state emerge as the only focus for identity for millions of alienated workers and farmers whose conditions of life have been transformed by industrialism. Though claiming only a small share of the national wealth, they could claim a large share of the national glory. Led by militaristic civilians who fused their personal destinies with that of the nation, these individuals found social cohesion in the creation of a new community— the mass citizen army. They provided the sanction of public opinion behind the liberal rhetoric of freedom which became transformed into the doctrine of national self-determination. That doctrine led, as Malinowski has pointed out, "to the arming of new nations and more nations, while it ought to have meant only the disarming of dangerous, predatory neighbors." [4]

The very techniques of that industrialism which had shattered the old order were now applied to military technology. In spite of advances in this field which quickly made the ratio of casualties to combatants the highest in world history,[5] the experience of shared danger helped create a new community of citizen soldiers and a new *mystique* of war among hitherto peaceful literary men in many Western nations. This *mystique* quickly filtered down to the broad masses of the population. The experience of combat was held to involve the creation of a new community—those who fought; at the same time it formed the basis for a new aristocracy—those who survived. Such a community could retain meaning even after the concept of "total war" of the military philosopher and strategist Clausewitz was turned into an actuality by civilian militarists aided by science and industrial techniques.

It is incumbent on the student of war to see the positive aspects of this experience in understanding its appeals. From Oliver Wendell Holmes to Ernest Hemingway the experience of combat has been proclaimed as the most meaningful epiphany in human existence. Of the Spanish Civil War, Hemingway wrote: "It gave you a part in something that you could believe in wholly and completely and in which you felt an absolute brotherhood with the others who were engaged in it." In the hands of Hemingway and other exponents of the strenuous life of the late nineteenth and twentieth centuries, war offered a new

[3] Leon Bramson, *The Political Context of Sociology* (Princeton: Princeton University Press, 1961).

[4] B. Malinowski, "An Anthropological Analysis of War," *supra*.

[5] Pitirim A. Sorokin, *Social and Cultural Dynamics* (4 vols; New York: American Book Co., 1937), III, chap. 11.

opportunity for heroic action, brotherhood, community, dedication, selfless-
ness, order, command, ritual, and aristocracy in an era when all these were
being eroded by bourgeois liberal society.[6] For in the hands of such writers,
war represents the antithesis of the liberal society, as it did also for Spencer.
The question here for the sociologist is whether this ideology is limited in its
appeals to a small group of literary militarists or whether it reflects the deepest feelings in the breasts of ordinary men at all levels of the social structure.
"We are against the comfortable life," said Mussolini, and we must not forget
that he was engaged in a social and political program which had broad popular support. Though many thinkers have recognized the possibilities of war in
fostering social cohesion, few have made systematic efforts to determine the
relative permanence of such bellicose attitudes, their relative strength in different parts of a society, and their functional importance in the national
consensus.[7]

We live in a century which has seen the result of mobilizing "the nation in
arms," but is only now beginning to grasp the lesson provided thereby. Those
who proclaim an end to ideology must reckon with the appeals of a militaristic
totalism for millions of men and women in new nations. Far from representing
an approach to outmoded nineteenth-century realities, the psychology and
sociology of nationalism may reveal the sources of its resurgence among those
sections of humanity who are experiencing the impact of industrial society for
the first time. For many of them this experience is not taking place in a context of political liberalism. It is paradoxical that the flame of nationalistic
passion should be fanned in so many places at the same time that the international basis for the abolition of total war is being contemplated. The student
of war must achieve an understanding of the meaning of nationalistic violence
to contemporary populations if the errors of the past are to be avoided.

    [6] Vagts helps to remind us of the roll call of bourgeois civilians who idealized the mili-
tary, a long line beginning with Thiers and running through "Carlyle, Treitschke, Theodore
Roosevelt, Nietzsche, Barres, Charles Maurras, and Kipling" (*op. cit.*, p. 20). Perhaps most
puzzling of all are the writings of men like Robert Graves (*Goodbye to All That*) and
George Orwell (*Homage to Catalonia*) regarding the experience of war. What are we to
make of the fact that in the autobiographical works of two intellectuals ostensibly opposed
to war we find a covert but unmistakable pro-war message?
    [7] See Stanislaus Andrzejewski, *Military Organization and Society* (London: Routledge
& Kegan Paul, 1954), and Lewis Coser, *The Functions of Social Conflict* (Glencoe, Ill.: Free
Press, 1956), chap. 5.

◄◄◄ ►►►

HERBERT SPENCER

The Military
and the Industrial Society [*]

THE MILITARY TYPE OF SOCIETY

. . . [The way has been] prepared for framing conceptions of the two fundamentally unlike kinds of political organization proper to the militant life and
the industrial life, respectively. It will be instructive here to arrange in
coherent order those traits of the militant type already incidentally marked
and to join with them various dependent traits and . . . [then] to deal in
like manner with the traits of the industrial type.

During social evolution there has habitually been a mingling of the two.
But we shall find that, alike in theory and in fact, it is possible to trace with
due clearness those opposite characters which distinguish them in their respective complete developments. Especially is the nature of the organization
which accompanies chronic militancy capable of being inferred a priori and
proved a posteriori to exist in numerous cases, while the nature of the organization accompanying pure industrialism, of which at present we have little
experience, will be made clear by contrast, and such illustrations as exist of
progress toward it will become recognizable.

Two liabilities to error must be guarded against. We have to deal with
societies compounded and recompounded in various degrees, and we have to
deal with societies which, differing in their stages of culture, have their struc-

* Reprinted from Herbert Spencer, *Principles of Sociology* (New York: D. Appleton &
Co., 1896), II.

tures elaborated to different extents. We shall be misled, therefore, unless our comparisons are such as take account of unlikenesses in size and in civilization. Clearly, characteristics of the military type which admit of being displayed by a vast nation may not admit of being displayed by a horde of savages, though this is equally militant. Moreover, as institutions take long to acquire their finished forms, it is not to be expected that all militant societies will display the organization appropriate to them in its completeness. Rather may we expect that in most cases it will be incompletely displayed.

In face of these difficulties the best course will be to consider, first, what are the several traits which of necessity militancy tends to produce and then to observe how far these traits are conjointly shown in past and present nations distinguished by militancy. Having contemplated the society ideally organized for war, we shall be prepared to recognize in real societies the characters which war has brought about.

For preserving its corporate life, a society is impelled to corporate action, and the preservation of its corporate life is the more probable in proportion as its corporate action is the more complete. For purposes of offense and defense, the forces of individuals have to be combined, and, where every individual contributes his force, the probability of success is greatest. Numbers, natures, and circumstances being equal, it is clear that of two tribes or two larger societies, one of which unites the actions of all its capable members while the other does not, the first will ordinarily be the victor. There must be a habitual survival of communities in which militant cooperation is universal.

This proposition is almost a truism. But it is needful here as a preliminary consciously to recognize the truth that the social structure evolved by chronic militancy is one in which all men fit for fighting act in concert against other societies. Such further actions as they carry on they can carry on separately, but this action they must carry on jointly.

A society's power of self-preservation will be great in proportion as, besides the direct aid of all who can fight, there is given the indirect aid of all who cannot fight. Supposing them otherwise similar, those communities will survive in which the efforts of combatants are in the greatest degree seconded by those of noncombatants. In a purely militant society, therefore, individuals who do not bear arms have to spend their lives in furthering the maintenance of those who do. Whether, as happens at first, the noncombatants are exclusively the women or whether, as happens later, the class includes enslaved captives or whether, as happens later still, it includes serfs, the implication is the same. For if, of two societies equal in other respects, the first wholly subordinates its workers in this way while the workers in the second are allowed to retain for themselves the produce of their labor or more of it than is needed for maintaining them, then in the second [society] the warriors, not otherwise supported or supported less fully than they might else be, will have partially to support themselves and will be so much the less available for war purposes. Hence in the struggle for existence between such societies, it must usually happen that the first will vanquish the second. The social type produced by survival of the fittest will be one in which the fighting part includes all who can bear arms and be trusted with arms, while the remaining part serves simply as a permanent commissariat.

An obvious implication, of a significance to be hereafter pointed out, is that the noncombatant part, occupied in supporting the combatant part, cannot with advantage to the self-preserving power of the society increase beyond the limit at which it efficiently fulfills its purpose. For otherwise some who might be fighters are superfluous workers, and the fighting power of the society is made less than it might be. Hence in the militant type the tendency is for the body of warriors to bear the largest practicable ratio to the body of workers.

Given two societies of which the members are all either warriors or those who supply the needs of warriors and, other things equal, supremacy will be gained by that in which the efforts of all are most effectually combined. In open warfare joint action triumphs over individual action. Military history is a history of the successes of men trained to move and fight in concert.

Not only must there be in the fighting part a combination such that the powers of its units may be concentrated, but there must be a combination of the subservient part with it. If the two are so separated that they can act independently, the needs of the fighting part will not be adequately met. If to be cut off from a temporary base of operations is dangerous, still more dangerous is it to be cut off from the permanent base of operations—namely, that constituted by the body of noncombatants. This has to be so connected with the body of combatants that its services may be fully available. Evidently, therefore, development of the militant type involves a close binding of the society into a whole. As the loose group of savages yields to the solid phalanx, so, other things equal, must the society of which the parts are but feebly held together yield to one in which they are held together by strong bonds.

But in proportion as men are compelled to cooperate, their self-prompted actions are restrained. By as much as the unit becomes merged in the mass, by so much does he lose his individuality as a unit. And this leads us to note the several ways in which evolution of the militant type entails subordination of the citizen.

His life is not his own, but is at the disposal of his society. So long as he remains capable of bearing arms, he has no alternative but to fight when called on, and, where militancy is extreme, he cannot return as a vanquished man under penalty of death.

Of course, with this there goes possession of such liberty only as military obligations allow. He is free to pursue his private ends only when the tribe or nation has no need of him, and, when it has need of him, his actions from hour to hour must conform not to his own will, but to the public will.

So, too, with his property. Whether, as in many cases, what he holds as private he so holds by permission only or whether private ownership is recognized, it remains true that in the last resort he is obliged to surrender whatever is demanded for the community's use.

Briefly, then, under the militant type the individual is owned by the state. While preservation of the society is the primary end, preservation of each member is a secondary end—an end cared for chiefly as subserving the primary end.

Fulfillment of these requirements—that there shall be complete corporate action; that to this end the noncombatant part shall be occupied in providing for the combatant part; that the entire aggregate shall be strongly bound together; and that the units composing it must have their individualities in life, liberty, and property thereby subordinated—presupposes a coercive instrumentality. No such union for corporate action can be achieved without a powerful controlling agency. On remembering the fatal results caused by division of counsels in war or by separation into factions in face of an enemy, we see that chronic militancy tends to develop a despotism since, other things equal, those societies will habitually survive in which, by its aid, the corporate action is made complete.

And this involves a system of centralization. The trait made familiar to us by an army, in which under a commander in chief there are secondary commanders over large masses and under these tertiary ones over smaller masses and so on down to the ultimate divisions, must characterize the social organization at large. A militant society requires a regulative structure of this kind since otherwise its corporate action cannot be made most effectual. Without such grades of governing centers diffused throughout the noncombatant part as well as the combatant part, the entire forces of the aggregate cannot be promptly put forth. Unless the workers are under a control akin to that which the fighters are under, their indirect aid cannot be ensured in full amount and with due quickness.

And this is the form of a society characterized by status—a society the members of which stand one toward another in successive grades of subordination. From the despot down to the slave, all are masters of those below and subjects of those above. The relation of the child to the father, of the father to some superior, and so on up to the absolute head is one in which the individual of lower status is at the mercy of one of higher status.

Otherwise described, the process of militant organization is a process of regimentation which, primarily taking place in the army, secondarily affects the whole community.

The first indication of this we trace in the fact everywhere visible that the military head grows into a civil head—usually at once and, in exceptional cases, at last, if militancy continues. Beginning as leader in war, he becomes ruler in peace, and such regulative policy as he pursues in the one sphere he pursues, so far as conditions permit, in the other. Being, as the noncombatant part is, a permanent commissariat, the principle of graduated subordination is extended to it. Its members come to be directed in a way like that in which the warriors are directed—not literally, since by dispersion of the one and concentration of the other exact parallelism is prevented, but, nevertheless, similarly in principle. Labor is carried on under coercion, and supervision spreads everywhere.

To suppose that a despotic military head, daily maintaining regimental control in conformity with inherited traditions, will not impose on the producing classes a kindred control is to suppose in him sentiments and ideas entirely foreign to his circumstances.

The nature of the militant form of government will be further elucidated on observing that it is both positively regulative and negatively regulative. It does not simply restrain; it also enforces. Besides telling the individual what he shall not do, it tells him what he shall do.

That the government of an army is thus characterized needs no showing. Indeed, commands of the positive kind given to the soldier are more important than those of the negative kind: fighting is done under the one, while order is maintained under the other. But here it chiefly concerns us to note that not only the control of military life, but also the control of civil life, is, under the militant type of government, thus characterized. There are two ways in which the ruling power may deal with the private individual. It may simply limit his activities to those which he can carry on without aggression, direct or indirect, upon others, in which case its action is negatively regulative. Or, besides doing this, it may prescribe the how and the where and the when of his activities— may force him to do things which he would not spontaneously do, may direct in greater or less detail his mode of living—in which case its action is positively regulative. Under the militant type this positively regulative action is widespread and peremptory. The civilian is in a condition as much like that of the soldier as difference of occupation permits.

And this is another way of expressing the truth that the fundamental principle of the militant type is compulsory cooperation. While this is obviously the principle on which the members of the combatant body act, it no less certainly must be the principle acted on throughout the noncombatant body if military efficiency is to be great, since otherwise the aid which the noncombatant body has to furnish cannot be ensured.

That binding together by which the units of a militant society are made into an efficient fighting structure tends to fix the position of each in rank, in occupation, and in locality.

In a graduated regulative organization there is resistance to change from a lower to a higher grade. Such change is made difficult by lack of the possessions needed for filling superior positions, and it is made difficult by the opposition of those who already fill them and can hold inferiors down. Preventing intrusion from below, these transmit their respective places and ranks to their descendants, and, as the principle of inheritance becomes settled, the rigidity of the social structure becomes decided. Only when an "egalitarian despotism" reduces all subjects to the same political status—a condition of decay rather than of development—does the converse state arise.

The principle of inheritance, becoming established in respect of the classes which militancy originates and fixing the general functions of their members from generation to generation, tends eventually to fix also their special functions. Not only do men of the slave classes and the artisan classes succeed to their respective ranks, but they succeed to the particular occupations carried on in them. This, which is a result of the tendency toward regimentation, is ascribable primarily to the fact that a superior, requiring from each kind of worker his particular product, has an interest in replacing him at death by a capable successor, while the worker, prompted to get aid in executing his tasks, has an interest in bringing up a son to his own occupation, the will of the son being powerless against these conspiring interests. Under the system of compulsory cooperation, therefore, the principle of inheritance, spreading through the producing organization, causes a relative rigidity in this also.

A kindred effect is shown in the entailed restraints on movement from place to place. In proportion as the individual is subordinated in life, liberty, and property to his society, it is needful that his whereabouts shall be constantly known. Obviously the relation of the soldier to his officer and of this officer to his superior is such that each must be ever at hand, and, where the militant type is fully developed, the like holds throughout the society. The slave cannot leave his appointed abode; the serf is tied to his allotment; the master is not allowed to absent himself from his locality without leave.

[Thus] the corporate action, the combination, the cohesion, the regimentation, which efficient militancy necessitates, imply a structure which strongly resists change.

A further trait of the militant type, naturally accompanying the last mentioned, is that organizations other than those forming parts of the state organization are wholly or partially repressed. The public combination occupying all fields excludes private combinations.

For the achievement of complete corporate action, there must, as we have seen, be a centralized administration not only throughout the combatant part, but throughout the noncombatant part, and, if there exist unions of citizens which act independently, they insofar diminish the range of this centralized administration. Any structures which are not portions of the state structure serve more or less as limitations to it and stand in the way of the required unlimited subordination. If private combinations are allowed to exist, it will be on condition of submitting to an official regulation such as greatly restrains independent action, and, since private combinations officially regulated are inevitably hindered from doing things not conforming to established routine and are thus debarred from improvement, they cannot habitually thrive and grow. Obviously, indeed, such combinations, based on the principle of voluntary cooperation, are incongruous with social arrangements based on the principle of compulsory cooperation. Hence the militant type is characterized by the absence or comparative rarity of bodies of citizens associated for commercial purposes, for propagating special religious views, for achieving philanthropic ends, and so on.

Private combinations of one kind, however, are congruous with the militant type—the combinations, namely, which are formed for minor defensive or offensive purposes. We have, as examples, those which constitute factions, very general in militant societies; those which belong to the same class as primitive guilds, serving for mutual protection; and those which take the shape of secret societies. Of such bodies it may be noted that they fulfill on a small scale ends like those which the whole society fulfills on a large scale—the ends of self-preservation or aggression or both. And it may be further noted that these small included societies are organized on the same principle as the large including society—the principle of compulsory cooperation. Their governments are coercive—in some cases even to the extent of killing those of their members who are disobedient.

A remaining fact to be set down is that a society of the militant type tends to evolve a self-sufficient sustaining organization. With its political autonomy there goes what we may call an economic autonomy. Evidently, if it carries on frequent wars against surrounding societies, its commercial intercourse with them must be hindered or prevented; exchange of commodities can go on but to a small extent between those who are continually fighting. A militant society must, therefore, to the greatest degree practicable, provide internally the supplies of all articles needful for carrying on the lives of its members. Such an economic state as that which existed during early feudal times, when, as in France, "the castles made almost all the articles used in them," is a state evidently entailed on groups, small or large, which are in constant antagonism with surrounding groups. If there does not already exist within any group so circumstanced an agency for producing some necessary article, inability to obtain it from without will lead to the establishment of an agency for obtaining it within.

Whence it follows that the desire "not to be dependent on foreigners" is one appropriate to the militant type of society. So long as there is constant danger that the supplies of needful things derived from other countries will be cut off by the breaking out of hostilities, it is imperative that there shall be maintained a power of producing these supplies at home and that to this end the required structures shall be maintained. Hence there is a manifest direct relation between militant activities and a protectionist policy. . . .

In three ways, then, we are shown the character of the militant type of social organization. Observe the congruities which comparison of results discloses.

Certain conditions, manifest a priori, have to be fulfilled by a society fitted for preserving itself in presence of antagonist societies. To be in the highest degree efficient, the corporate action needed for preserving the corporate life must be joined in by everyone. Other things equal, the fighting power will be greatest where those who cannot fight labor exclusively to support and help those who can, an evident implication being that the working part shall be no larger than is required for these ends. The efforts of all being utilized directly or indirectly for war will be most effectual when they are most combined, and, besides union among the combatants, there must be such union of the non-combatants with them as renders the aid of these fully and promptly available. To satisfy these requirements, the life, the actions, and the possessions of each individual must be held at the service of the society. This universal service, this combination, and this merging of individual claims presuppose a despotic controlling agency. That the will of the soldier chief may be operative when the aggregate is large, there must be subcenters and sub-subcenters in descending grades through whom orders may be conveyed and enforced both throughout the combatant part and the noncombatant part. As the commander tells the soldier both what he shall not do and what he shall do, so, throughout the militant community at large, the rule is both negatively regulative and positively regulative—it not only restrains, but it directs; the citizen as well as the soldier lives under a system of compulsory cooperation. Development of the militant type involves increasing rigidity since the cohesion, the combination, the subordination, and the regulation to which the units of a society are subjected by it inevitably decrease their ability to change their social positions, their occupations, their localities.

On inspecting sundry societies past and present, large and small, which are or have been characterized in high degrees by militancy, we are shown a posteriori that, amid the differences due to race, to circumstances, and to degrees of development, there are fundamental similarities of the kinds above inferred a priori. Modern Dahomey and Russia, as well as ancient Peru, Egypt, and Sparta, exemplify that owning of the individual by the state in life, liberty, and goods which is proper to a social system adapted for war. And that, with changes further fitting a society for warlike activities, there spread throughout it an officialism, a dictation, and a superintendence akin to those under which soldiers live we are shown by imperial Rome, by imperial Germany, and by England since its late aggressive activities.

Lastly comes the evidence furnished by the adapted characters of the men who compose militant societies. Making success in war the highest glory, they are led to identify goodness with bravery and strength. Revenge becomes a sacred duty with them, and, acting at home on the law of retaliation which they act on abroad, they similarly, at home as abroad, are ready to sacrifice others to self; their sympathies, continually deadened during war, cannot be active during peace. They must have a patriotism which regards the triumph of their society as the supreme end of action; they must possess the loyalty whence flows obedience to authority; and, that they may be obedient, they must have abundant faith. With faith in authority and consequent readiness to be directed, naturally goes relatively little power of initiation. The habit of seeing everything officially controlled fosters the belief that official control is everywhere needful, while a course of life which makes personal causation familiar and negatives experience of impersonal causation produces an inability to conceive of any social processes as carried on under self-regulating arrangements. And these traits of individual nature, needful concomitants, as we see, of the militant type, are those which we observe in the members of actual militant societies.

THE INDUSTRIAL TYPE OF SOCIETY

Having nearly always to defend themselves against external enemies while they have to carry on internally the processes of sustentation, societies, as remarked above, habitually present us with mixtures of the structures adapted to these diverse ends. Disentanglement is not easy. According as either structure predominates, it ramifies through the other: instance the fact that, where the militant type is much developed, the worker, ordinarily a slave, is no more free than the soldier, while, where the industrial type is much developed, the soldier, volunteering on specified terms, acquires insofar the position of a free worker. In the one case the system of status, proper to the fighting part, pervades the working part, affects the fighting part. Especially does the organization adapted for war obscure that adapted for industry. While, as we have seen, the militant type as theoretically constructed is so far displayed in many societies as to leave no doubt about its essential nature, the industrial type has its traits so hidden by those of the still dominant militant type that its nature is nowhere more than very partially exemplified. Saying thus much to exclude expectations which cannot be fulfilled, it will be well also to exclude certain probable misconceptions.

In the first place, industrialism must not be confounded with industriousness. Though the members of an industrially organized society are habitually industrious and are, indeed, when the society is a developed one, obliged to be so, yet it must not be assumed that the industrially organized society is one in which, of necessity, much work is done. Where the society is small and its habitat so favorable that life may be comfortably maintained with but little exertion, the social relations which characterize the industrial type may coexist with but very moderate productive activities. It is not the diligence of its members which constitutes the society an industrial one in the sense here intended, but the form of cooperation under which their labors, small or great in amount, are carried on. This distinction will be best understood on observing that, conversely, there may be, and often is, great industry in societies framed on the militant type. In ancient Egypt there was an immense laboring population and a large supply of commodities, numerous in their kinds, produced by it. Still more did ancient Peru exhibit a vast community purely militant in its structure, the members of which worked unceasingly. We are here concerned, then, not with the quantity of labor, but with the mode of organization of the laborers. A regiment of soldiers can be set to construct earthworks, another to cut down wood, another to bring in water, but they are not thereby reduced for the time being to an industrial society. The united individuals do these several things under command and, having no private claims to the products, are, though industrially occupied, not industrially organized. And the same holds throughout the militant society as a whole in proportion as the regimentation of it approaches completeness.

The industrial type of society, properly so called, must also be distinguished from a type very likely to be confounded with it—the type, namely, in which the component individuals, while exclusively occupied in production and distribution, are under a regulation such as that advocated by Socialists and Communists. For this, too, involves in another form the principle of compulsory cooperation. Directly or indirectly, individuals are to be prevented from generally and independently occupying themselves as they please, are to be prevented from competing with one another in supplying goods for money, are to be prevented from hiring themselves out on such terms as they think fit. There can be no artificial system for regulating labor which does not interfere with the natural system. To such extent as men are debarred from making whatever engagements they like, they are to that extent working under dictation. No matter in what way the controlling agency is constituted, it stands toward those controlled in the same relation as does the controlling agency of a militant society. And how truly the regime which those who declaim against competition would establish is thus characterized we see both in the fact that communistic forms of organization existed in early societies which were predominantly warlike and in the fact that at the present time communistic projects chiefly originate among and are most favored by the more warlike societies.

A further preliminary explanation may be needful. The structures proper to the industrial type of society must not be looked for in distinct forms when they first appear. Contrariwise, we must expect them to begin in vague, unsettled forms. Arising, as they do, by modification of pre-existing structures, they are necessarily long in losing all trace of these. For example, transition from the state in which the laborer, owned like a beast, is maintained that he may work exclusively for his master's benefit, to the condition in which he is

completely detached from master, soil, and locality and free to work anywhere and for anyone, is through gradations. Again, the change from the
arrangement proper to militancy, under which subject persons receive, in
addition to maintenance, occasional presents, to the arrangements under which,
in place of both, they receive fixed wages or salaries or fees, goes on slowly
and unobtrusively. Once more, it is observable that the process of exchange,
originally indefinite, has become definite only where industrialism is con-
siderably developed. Barter began not with a distinct intention of giving one
thing for another thing equivalent in value, but it began by making a present
and receiving a present in return, and even now in the East there continue
traces of this primitive transaction. In Cairo the purchase of articles from a
shopkeeper is preceded by his offer of coffee and cigarettes, and, during the
negotiation which ends in the engagement of a *dahabeah,* the dragoman brings
gifts and expects to receive them. Add to which that there exists under such
conditions none of that definite equivalence which characterizes exchange
among ourselves—prices are not fixed, but vary widely with every fresh transaction. [Thus] throughout our interpretations we must keep in view the truth
that the structures and functions proper to the industrial type distinguish
themselves but gradually from those proper to the militant type.

Having thus prepared the way, let us now consider what are, a priori, the
traits of that social organization which, entirely unfitted for carrying on defense against external enemies, is exclusively fitted for maintaining the life
of the society by subserving the lives of its units. As before, in treating of the
militant type, so here, in treating of the industrial type, we will consider first
its ideal form.

While corporate action is the primary requirement in a society which has to
preserve itself in presence of hostile societies, conversely, in the absence of
hostile societies, corporate action is no longer the primary requirement.

The continued existence of a society implies, first, that it shall not be
destroyed bodily by foreign foes and implies, second, that it shall not be destroyed in detail by failure of its members to support and propagate themselves. If danger of destruction from the first cause ceases, there remains only
danger of destruction from the second cause. Sustentation of the society will
now be achieved by the self-sustentation and multiplication of its units. If his
own welfare and the welfare of his offspring is fully achieved by each, the
welfare of the society is by implication achieved. Comparatively little corporate
activity is now required. Each man may maintain himself by labor, may exchange his products for the products of others, may give aid and receive payment, may enter into this or that combination for carrying on an undertaking,
small or great, without the direction of the society as a whole. The remaining
end to be achieved by public action is to keep private actions within due
bounds, and the amount of public action needed for this becomes small in
proportion as private actions become duly self-bounded.

[Thus], whereas in the militant type the demand for corporate action is intrinsic, such demand for corporate action as continues in the industrial type is mainly extrinsic, is called for by those aggressive traits of human nature which chronic warfare has fostered, and may gradually diminish as, under enduring peaceful life, these decrease.

In a society organized for militant action, the individuality of each member has to be so subordinated in life, liberty, and property that he is largely or completely *owned* by the state, but in a society industrially organized no such subordination of the individual is called for. There remain no occasions on which he is required to risk his life while destroying the lives of others; he is not forced to leave his occupation and submit to a commanding officer; and it ceases to be needful that he should surrender for public purposes whatever property is demanded of him.

Under the industrial regime the citizen's individuality, instead of being sacrificed by the society, has to be defended by the society. Defense of his individuality becomes the society's essential duty. That, after external protection is no longer called for, internal protection must become the cardinal function of the state and that effectual discharge of this function must be a predominant trait of the industrial type may be readily shown.

For it is clear that, other things equal, a society in which life, liberty, and property are secure and all interests justly regarded must prosper more than one in which they are not, and, consequently, among competing industrial societies, there must be a gradual replacing of those in which personal rights are imperfectly maintained by those in which they are perfectly maintained. [Thus] by survival of the fittest must be produced a social type in which individual claims, considered as sacred, are trenched on by the state no further than is requisite to pay the cost of maintaining them or, rather, of arbitrating among them. For the aggressiveness of nature fostered by militancy having died out, the corporate function becomes that of deciding between those conflicting claims the equitable adjustment of which is not obvious to the persons concerned.

With the absence of need for that corporate action by which the efforts of the whole society may be utilized for war, there goes the absence of need for a despotic controlling agency.

Not only is such an agency unnecessary, but it cannot exist. For since, as we see, it is an essential requirement of the industrial type that the individuality of each man shall have the fullest play compatible with the like play of other men's individualities, despotic control, showing itself, as it must, by otherwise restricting men's individualities, is necessarily excluded. Indeed, by his mere presence an autocratic ruler is an aggressor on citizens. Actually or potentially exercising power not given by them, he insofar restrains their wills more than they would be restrained by mutual limitation merely.

Such control as is required under the industrial type can be exercised only by an appointed agency for ascertaining and executing the average will, and a representative agency is the one best fitted for doing this.

Unless the activities of all are homogeneous in kind, which they cannot be in a developed society with its elaborate division of labor, there arises a need for conciliation of divergent interests, and, to the end of ensuring an equitable adjustment, each interest must be enabled duly to express itself. It is, indeed, supposable that the appointed agency should be a single individual. But no such single individual could arbitrate justly among numerous classes variously occupied, without hearing evidence; each would have to send representatives setting forth its claims. Hence the choice would lie between two systems under one of which the representatives privately and separately stated their cases to an arbitrator on whose single judgment decisions depended and under the other of which these representatives stated their cases in one another's presence while judgments were openly determined by the general consensus. Without insisting on the fact that a fair balancing of class interests is more likely to be effected by this last form of representation than by the first, it is sufficient to remark that it is more congruous with the nature of the industrial type since men's individualities are in the smallest degree trenched upon. Citizens who, appointing a single ruler for a prescribed time, may have a majority of their wills traversed by his during this time surrender their individualities in a greater degree than do those who, from their local groups, depute a number of rulers, since these, speaking and acting under public inspection and mutually restrained, habitually conform their decisions to the wills of the majority.

The corporate life of the society being no longer in danger and the remaining business of government being that of maintaining the conditions requisite for the highest individual life, there comes the question: What are these conditions?

Already they have been implied as comprehended under the administration of justice, but so vaguely is the meaning of this phrase commonly conceived that a more specific statement must be made. Justice then, as here to be understood, means preservation of the normal connections between acts and results —the obtainment by each of as much benefit as his efforts are equivalent to— no more and no less. Living and working within the restraints imposed by one another's presence, justice requires that individuals shall severally take the consequences of their conduct, neither increased nor decreased. The superior shall have the good of his superiority, and the inferior, the evil of his inferiority. A veto is therefore put on all public action which abstracts from some men part of the advantages they have earned and awards to other men advantages they have not earned.

That from the developed industrial type of society there are excluded all forms of communistic distribution, the inevitable trait of which is that they tend to equalize the lives of good and bad, idle and diligent, is readily proved. For when, the struggle for existence between societies by war having ceased, there remains only the industrial struggle for existence, the final survival and spread must be on the part of those societies which produce the largest number of the best individuals—individuals best adapted for life in the industrial state. Suppose two societies, otherwise equal, in one of which the superior are allowed to retain for their own benefit and the benefit of their offspring the entire proceeds of their labor, but in the other of which the superior have taken from them part of these proceeds for the benefit of the inferior and their off-spring. Evidently the superior will thrive and multiply more in the first than in the second. A greater number of the best children will be reared in the first, and eventually it will outgrow the second. It must not be inferred that private and voluntary aid to the inferior is negatived, but only public and enforced aid. Whatever effects the sympathies of the better for the worse spontaneously produce cannot, of course, be interfered with and will, on the whole, be beneficial. For while, on the average, the better will not carry such efforts so far as to impede their own multiplication, they will carry them far enough to mitigate the ill fortunes of the worse without helping them to multiply.

Otherwise regarded, this system, under which the efforts of each bring neither more nor less than their natural returns, is the system of contract.

We have seen that the regime of status is in all ways proper to the militant type. It is the concomitant of that graduated subordination by which the combined action of a fighting body is achieved and which must pervade the fighting society at large to ensure its corporate action. Under this regime the relation between labor and produce is traversed by authority. As in the army the food, clothing, and so on received by each soldier are not direct returns for work done, but are arbitrarily apportioned while duties are arbitrarily enforced, so throughout the rest of the militant society the superior dictates the labor and assigns such share of the returns as he pleases. But as, with declining militancy and growing industrialism, the power and range of authority decrease while uncontrolled action increases, the relation of contract becomes general, and in the fully developed industrial type it becomes universal.

Under this universal relation of contract when equitably administered, there arises that adjustment of benefit to effort which the arrangements of the industrial society have to achieve. If each, as producer, distributor, manager, adviser, teacher, or aider of other kind, obtains from his fellows such payment for his service as its value, determined by the demand, warrants, then there results that correct apportioning of reward to merit which ensures the prosperity of the superior.

Again changing the point of view, we see that, whereas public control in the militant type is both positively regulative and negatively regulative, in the industrial type it is negatively regulative only. To the slave, to the soldier, or to other members of a community organized for war, authority says, "Thou shalt do this; thou shalt not do that." But to the member of the industrial community, authority gives only one of these orders, "Thou shalt not do that."

For people who, carrying on their private transactions by voluntary cooperation, also voluntarily cooperate to form and support a governmental agency
are, by implication, people who authorize it to impose on their respective
activities only those restraints which they are all interested in maintaining—
the restraints which check aggressions. Omitting criminals (who under the
assumed conditions must be very few, if not a vanishing quantity), each citizen will wish to preserve uninvaded his sphere of action, while not invading
others' spheres, and to retain whatever benefits are achieved within it. The
very motives which prompt all to unite in upholding a public protector of
their individualities will also prompt them to unite in preventing any interference with their individualities beyond that required for this end.

Hence it follows that, while in the militant type regimentation in the army
is paralleled by centralized administration throughout the society at large, in
the industrial type administration, becoming decentralized, is at the same time
narrowed in its range. Nearly all public organizations save that for administering justice necessarily disappear since they have the common character that
they either aggress on the citizen by dictating his actions or by taking from
him more property than is needful for protecting him or by both. Those who
are forced to send their children to this or that school; those who have,
directly or indirectly, to help in supporting a state priesthood; those from
whom rates are demanded that parish officers may administer public charity;
those who are taxed to provide gratis reading for people who will not save
money for library subscriptions; those whose businesses are carried on under
regulation by inspectors; those who have to pay the costs of state science- and
art-teaching, state emigration, and so on—all have their individualities
trenched upon either by compelling them to do what they would not spontaneously do or by taking away money which else would have furthered their
private ends. Coercive arrangements of such kinds, consistent with the militant
type, are inconsistent with the industrial type.

With the relatively narrow range of public organizations, there goes in the
industrial type a relatively wide range of private organizations. The spheres
left vacant by the one are filled by the other.

Several influences conspire to produce this trait. Those motives which, in
the absence of that subordination necessitated by war, make citizens unite in
asserting their individualities subject only to mutual limitations are motives
which make them unite in resisting any interference with their freedom to
form such private combinations as do not involve aggression. Moreover, beginning with exchanges of goods and services under agreements between
individuals, the principle of voluntary cooperation is simply carried out in a
larger way by individuals who, incorporating themselves, contract with one
another for jointly pursuing this or that business or function. And yet again,
there is entire congruity between the representative constitution of the public
combination which we see is proper to the industrial type. The same law of

organization pervades the society in general and in detail. [Thus] an inevitable trait of the industrial type is the multiplicity and heterogeneity of associations—political, religious, commercial, professional, philanthropic, and social—of all sizes.

Two indirectly resulting traits of the industrial type must be added. The first is its relative plasticity.

So long as corporate action is necessitated for national self-preservation; so long as, to effect combined defense or offense, there is maintained that graduated subordination which ties all inferiors to superiors as the soldier is tied to his officer; so long as there is maintained the relation of status, which tends to fix men in the positions they are severally born to—there is ensured a comparative rigidity of social organization. But with the cessation of those needs that initiate and preserve the militant type of structure and with the establishment of contract as the universal relation under which efforts are combined for mutual advantage, social organization loses its rigidity. No longer determined by the principle of inheritance, places and occupations are now determined by the principle of efficiency, and changes of structure follow when men, not bound to prescribed functions, acquire the functions for which they have proved themselves most fit. Easily modified in its arrangements, the industrial type of society is therefore one which adapts itself with facility to new requirements.

The other incidental result to be named is a tendency toward loss of economic autonomy.

While hostile relations with adjacent societies continue, each society has to be productively self-sufficing, but with the establishment of peaceful relations this need for self-sufficingness ceases. As the local divisions composing one of our great nations had, while they were at feud, to produce each for itself almost everything it required but now, permanently at peace with one another, have become so far mutually dependent that no one of them can satisfy its wants without aid from the rest, so the great nations themselves, at present forced in large measure to maintain their economic autonomies, will become less forced to do this as war decreases and will gradually become necessary to one another. While, on the one hand, the facilities possessed by each for certain kinds of production will render exchange mutually advantageous, on the other hand, the citizens of each will, under the industrial regime, tolerate no such restraints on their individualities as are implied by interdicts on exchange or impediments to exchange.

With the spread of industrialism, therefore, the tendency is toward the breaking down of the divisions between nationalities and the running through them of a common organization, if not under a single government, then under a federation of governments.

As with the militant type, then, so with the industrial type three lines of evidence converge to show us its essential nature. Let us set down briefly the several results that we may observe the correspondences among them.

On considering what must be the traits of a society organized exclusively for carrying on internal activities so as most efficiently to subserve the lives of citizens, we find them to be these. A corporate action subordinating individual actions by uniting them in joint effort is no longer requisite. Contrariwise, such corporate action as remains has for its end to guard individual actions against all interferences not necessarily entailed by mutual limitation, the type of society in which this function is best discharged being that which must survive since it is that of which the members will most prosper. Excluding, as the requirements of the industrial type do, a despotic controlling agency, they imply, as the only congruous agency for achieving such corporate action as is needed, one formed of representatives who serve to express the aggregate will. The function of this controlling agency, generally defined as that of administering justice, is more specially defined as that of seeing that each citizen gains neither more nor less of benefit than his activities normally bring, and there is thus excluded all public action involving any artificial distribution of benefits. The regime of status proper to militancy having disappeared, the regime of contract which replaces it has to be universally enforced, and this negatives interferences between efforts and results by arbitrary apportionment. Otherwise regarded, the industrial type is distinguished from the militant type as being not both positively regulative and negatively regulative, but as being negatively regulative only. With this restricted sphere for corporate action comes an increased sphere for individual action, and, from that voluntary cooperation which is the fundamental principle of the type, arise multitudinous private combinations akin in their structures to the public combination of the society which includes them. Indirectly it results that a society of the industrial type is distinguished by plasticity and also that it tends to lose its economic autonomy and to coalesce with adjacent societies.

The question next considered was whether these traits of the industrial type as arrived at by deduction are inductively verified, and we found that in actual societies they are visible more-or-less clearly in proportion as industrialism is more-or-less developed. Glancing at those small groups of uncultured people who, wholly unwarlike, display the industrial type in its rudimentary form, we went on to compare the structures of European nations at large in early days of chronic militancy with their structures in modern days characterized by progressing industrialism, and we saw the differences to be of the kind implied. We next compared two of these societies, France and England, which were once in kindred states, but of which the one has had its industrial life much more repressed by its militant life than the other, and it became manifest that the contrasts which, age after age, arose between their institutions were such as answer to the hypothesis. Lastly, limiting ourselves to England itself and first noting how recession from such traits of the industrial type as had shown themselves occurred during a long war period, we observed how, during the subsequent long period of peace beginning in 1815, there were numerous and decided approaches to that social structure which we concluded must accompany developed industrialism.

We then inquired what type of individual nature accompanies the industrial type of society with the view of seeing whether, from the character of the unit as well as from the character of the aggregate, confirmation is to be derived. Certain uncultured peoples whose lives are passed in peaceful occupations proved to be distinguished by independence, resistance to coercion, honesty, truthfulness, forgivingness, kindness. On contrasting the characters of our ancestors during more warlike periods with our own characters, we see that, with an increasing ratio of industrialism to militancy, have come a growing independence, a less marked loyalty, a smaller faith in governments, and a more qualified patriotism; and while, by enterprising action, by diminished faith in authority, by resistance to irresponsible power, there has been shown a strengthening assertion of individuality, there has accompanied it a growing respect for the individualities of others, as is implied by the diminution of aggressions upon them and the multiplication of efforts for their welfare.

To prevent misapprehension it seems needful, before closing, to explain that these traits are to be regarded less as the immediate results of industrialism than as the remote results of nonmilitancy. It is not so much that a social life passed in peaceful occupations is positively moralizing as that a social life passed in war is positively demoralizing. Sacrifice of others to self is in the one incidental only, while in the other it is necessary. Such aggressive egoism as accompanies the industrial life is intrinsic. Though generally unsympathetic, the exchange of services under agreement is now to a considerable extent, and may be wholly, carried on with a due regard to the claims of others, may be constantly accompanied by a sense of benefit given as well as benefit received; but the slaying of antagonists, the burning of their houses, the appropriation of their territory, cannot but be accompanied by vivid consciousness of injury done them and a consequent brutalizing effect on the feelings, an effect wrought not on soldiers only, but on those who employ them and contemplate their deeds with pleasure. The last form of social life, therefore, inevitably deadens the sympathies and generates a state of mind which prompts crimes of trespass, while the first form, allowing the sympathies free play if it does not directly exercise them, favors the growth of altruistic sentiments and the resulting virtues.

▶▶▶ ◀◀◀

HAROLD D. LASSWELL

*The Garrison State**

. . . The purpose of this article is to consider the possibility that we are moving toward a world of "garrison states"—a world in which the specialists on
violence are the most powerful group in society. From this point of view the
trend of our time is away from the dominance of the specialist on bargaining,
who is the businessman, and toward the supremacy of the soldier. We may distinguish transitional forms, such as the party propaganda state, where the
dominant figure is the propagandist, and the party bureaucratic state, in which
the organization men of the party make the vital decisions. There are mixed
forms in which predominance is shared by the monopolists of party and market
power.[1]

All men are deeply affected by their expectations as well as by their desires.
We time our specific wants and efforts with some regard to what we reasonably
hope to get. Hence, when we act rationally, we consider alternative versions of
the future, making explicit those expectations about the future that are so often
buried in the realm of hunch.

In the practice of social science, as of any skill in society, we are bound to
be affected in some degree by our conceptions of future development. There are
problems of timing in the prosecution of scientific work, timing in regard to

* Reprinted from Harold D. Lasswell, "The Garrison State," pp. 455–468, *The American
Journal of Sociology*, XLVI (1941), by permission of The University of Chicago Press.
    [1] For a preliminary discussion of the garrison state see my "Sino-Japanese Crisis: The
Garrison State versus the Civilian State," *China Quarterly*, XI (1937), 643–649.

availability of data and considerations of policy. In a world where primitive societies are melting away, it is rational to act promptly to gather data about primitive forms of social organization. In a world in which the scientist may also be a democratic citizen, sharing democratic respect for human personality, it is rational for the scientist to give priority to problems connected with the survival of democratic society. There is no question here of a scientist deriving his values from science; values are *acquired* chiefly from personal experience of a given culture, *derived* from that branch of culture that is philosophy and theology, *implemented* by science and practice.

The picture of the garrison state that is offered here is no dogmatic forecast. Rather, it is a picture of the probable. It is not inevitable. It may not even have the same probability as some other descriptions of the future course of development. What, then, is the function of this picture for scientists? It is to stimulate the individual specialist to clarify for himself his expectations about the future as a guide to the timing of scientific work. Side by side with this construct of a garrison state there may be other constructs; the rational person will assign exponents of probability to every alternative picture.[2]

Expectations about the future may rest upon the extrapolation of past trends into the future. We may choose a number of specific items—like population and production curves—and draw them into the future according to some stated rule. This is an "itemistic" procedure. In contrast, we may set up a construct that is frankly imaginative though disciplined by careful consideration of the past. Since trend curves summarize many features of the past, they must be carefully considered in the preparation of every construct. Correlation analysis of trend curves, coupled with the results of experiment, may provide us with partial confirmation of many propositions about social change; these results, too, must be reviewed. In addition to these disciplined battalions of data, there is the total exposure of the individual to the immediate and the recorded past, and this total exposure may stimulate productive insight into the structure of the whole manifold of events which includes the future as well as the past. In the interest of correct orientation in the world of events, one does not wisely discard all save codified experience. (The pictures of the future that are set up on more than "item" basis may be termed "total.")

To speak of a garrison state is not to predict something wholly new under the sun. Certainly there is nothing novel to the student of political institutions about the idea that specialists on violence may run the state. On the contrary, some of the most influential discussions of political institutions have named the military state as one of the chief forms of organized society. [Auguste]

---

[2] We use the term "subjective probability" for the exponent assigned to a future event; "objective probability" refers to propositions about past events. The intellectual act of setting up a tentative picture of significant past-future relations is developmental thinking (see my *Word Politics and Personal Insecurity* [New York and London: Whittlesey House, 1935], chap. i; Karl Mannheim, *Man and Society in an Age of Reconstruction: Studies of Modern Social Structure* [New York: Harcourt, Brace, 1940]), Part IV.

Comte saw history as a succession (and a progression) that moved, as far as it concerned the state, through military, feudal, and industrial phases. [Herbert] Spencer divided all human societies into the military type, based on force, and the industrial type, based on contract and free consent.

What is important for our purposes is to envisage the possible emergence of the military state under present technical conditions. There are no examples of the military state combined with modern technology. During emergencies the great powers have given enormous scope to military authority, but temporary acquisitions of authority lack the elements of comparative permanence and acceptance that complete the garrison state. Military dictators in states marginal to the creative centers of Western civilization are not integrated with modern technology; they merely use some of its specific elements.

The military men who dominate a modern technical society will be very different from the officers of history and tradition. It is probable that the specialists on violence will include in their training a large degree of expertness in many of the skills that we have traditionally accepted as part of modern civilian management.

The distinctive frame of reference in a fighting society is fighting effectiveness. All social change is translated into battle potential. Now there can be no realistic calculation of fighting effectiveness without knowledge of the technical and psychological characteristics of modern production processes. The function of management in such a society is already known to us; it includes the exercise of skill in supervising technical operations, in administrative organization, in personnel management, in public relations. These skills are needed to translate the complicated operations of modern life into every relevant frame of reference—the frame of fighting effectiveness as well as of pecuniary profit.

This leads to the seeming paradox that, as modern states are militarized, specialists on violence are more preoccupied with the skills and attitudes judged characteristic of nonviolence. We anticipate the merging of skills, starting from the traditional accouterments of the professional soldier, moving toward the manager and promoter of large-scale civilian enterprise.

In the garrison state, at least in its introductory phases, problems of morale are destined to weigh heavily on the mind of management. It is easy to throw sand in the gears of the modern assembly line; hence, there must be a deep and general sense of participation in the total enterprise of the state if collective effort is to be sustained. When we call attention to the importance of the human factor in modern production, we sometimes fail to notice that it springs from the multiplicity of special environments that have been created by modern technology. Thousands of technical operations have sprung into existence where a few hundred were found before. To complicate the material environment in this way is to multiply the focuses of attention of those who live in our society. Diversified focuses of attention breed differences in outlook, preference, and loyalty. The labyrinth of specialized "material" environments generates profound ideological divergencies that cannot be abolished, though they can be mitigated, by the methods now available to leaders in our society. As long as modern technology prevails, society is honeycombed with cells of separate experience, of individuality, of partial freedom. Concerted action under such conditions depends upon skillfully guiding the minds of men; hence the enormous importance of symbolic manipulation in modern society.

The importance of the morale factor is emphasized by the universal fear which it is possible to maintain in large populations through modern instruments of warfare. The growth of aerial warfare in particular has tended to abolish the distinction between civilian and military functions. It is no longer possible to affirm that those who enter the military service take the physical risk while those who remain at home stay safe and contribute to the equipment and the comfort of the courageous heroes at the front. Indeed, in some periods of modern warfare, casualties among civilians may outnumber the casualties of the armed forces. With the socialization of danger as a permanent characteristic of modern violence, the nation becomes one unified technical enterprise. Those who direct the violence operations are compelled to consider the entire gamut of problems that arise in living together under modern conditions.

There will be an energetic struggle to incorporate young and old into the destiny and mission of the state. It is probable that one form of this symbolic adjustment will be the abolition of the "unemployed." This stigmatizing symbol will be obsolete in the garrison state. It insults the dignity of millions, for it implies uselessness. This is so whether the unemployed are given a dole or put on relief projects. Always there is the damaging stigma of superfluity. No doubt the garrison state will be distinguished by the psychological abolition of unemployment—"psychological" because this is chiefly a matter of redefining symbols.

In the garrison state there must be work—and the duty to work—for all. Since all work becomes public work, all who do not accept employment flout military discipline. For those who do not fit within the structure of the state, there is but one alternative—to obey or die. Compulsion, therefore, is to be expected as a potent instrument for internal control of the garrison state.

The use of coercion can have an important effect upon many more people than it reaches directly; this is the propaganda component of any "propaganda of the deed." The spectacle of compulsory labor gangs in prisons or concentration camps is a negative means of conserving morale—negative since it arouses fear and guilt. Compulsory labor groups are suitable popular scapegoats in a military state. The duty to obey, to serve the state, to work—these are cardinal virtues in the garrison state. Unceasing emphasis upon duty is certain to arouse opposing tendencies within the personality structure of all who live under a garrison regime. Everyone must struggle to hold in check any tendencies, conscious or unconscious, to defy authority, to violate the code of work, to flout the incessant demand for sacrifice in the collective interest. From the earliest years youth will be trained to subdue—to disavow, to struggle against—any specific opposition to the ruling code of collective exactions.

The conscience imposes feelings of guilt and anxiety upon the individual whenever his impulses are aroused, ever so slightly, to break the code. When the coercive threat that sanctions the code of the military state is internalized in the consciences of youth, the spectacle of labor gangs is profoundly disturbing. A characteristic response is self-righteousness—quick justification of coercive punishment, tacit acceptance of the inference that all who are subject to coercion are guilty of antisocial conduct. To maintain suspended judgment, to absolve others in particular instances, is to give at least partial toleration to countermores tendencies within the self. Hence, the quick substitute responses —the self-righteous attitude, the deflection of attention. Indeed, a characteristic psychic pattern of the military state is the "startle pattern," which is carried over to the internal as well as to the external threat of danger. This startle pattern is overcome and stylized as alert, prompt, commanding adjustment to reality. This is expressed in the authoritative manner that dominates military style—in gesture, intonation, and idiom.

The chief targets of compulsory labor service will be unskilled manual workers together with counterelite elements who have come under suspicion. The position of the unskilled in our society has been deteriorating, since the machine society has less and less use for unskilled manual labor. The coming of the machine was a skill revolution, a broadening of the role of the skilled and semiskilled components of society.[3] As the value of labor declines in production, it also declines in warfare; hence, it will be treated with less consideration. (When unskilled workers are relied upon as fighters, they must, of course, share the ideological exultation of the community as a whole and receive a steady flow of respect from the social environment.) Still another factor darkens the forecast for the bottom layers of the population in the future garrison state. If recent advances in pharmacology continue, as we may anticipate, physical means of controlling response can replace symbolic methods. This refers to the use of drugs not only for temporary orgies of energy on the part of front-line fighters, but in order to deaden the critical function of all who are not held in esteem by the ruling elite.

For the immediate future, however, ruling elites must continue to put their chief reliance upon propaganda as an instrument of morale. But the manipulation of symbols, even in conjunction with coercive instruments of violence, is not sufficient to accomplish all the purposes of a ruling group. We have already

[3] See T. M. Sogge, "Industrial Classes in the United States," *Journal of the American Statistical Association*, June, 1933; and Colin Clark, "National Income and Outlay," in A. C. Pigou, *Socialism versus Capitalism* (London: Macmillan & Co., Ltd., 1937), pp. 12–22. Sogge's paper is a continuation of an earlier investigation by Alvin H. Hansen.

spoken of the socialization of danger, and this will bring about some equalitarian adjustments in the distribution of income for the purpose of conserving the will to fight and to produce.

In addition to the adjustment of symbols, goods, and violence, the political elite of the garrison state will find it necessary to make certain adaptations in the fundamental practices of the state. Decisions will be more dictatorial than democratic, and institutional practices long connected with modern democracy will disappear. Instead of elections to office or referendums on issues, there will be government by plebiscite. Elections foster the formation and expression of public opinion, while plebiscites encourage only unanimous demonstrations of collective sentiment. Rival political parties will be suppressed, either by the monopolization of legality in one political party (more properly called a political "order") or by the abolition of all political parties. The ruling group will exercise a monopoly of opinion in public, thus abolishing the free communication of fact and interpretation. Legislatures will be done away with, and, if a numerous consultative body is permitted at all, it will operate as an assembly—that is, it will meet for a very short time each year and will be expected to ratify the decisions of the central leadership after speeches that are chiefly ceremonial in nature. Plebiscites and assemblies thus become part of the ceremonializing process in the military state.

As legislatures and elections go out of use, the practice of petition will play a more prominent role. Lawmaking will be in the hands of the supreme authority and his council; and, as long as the state survives, this agency will exert effective control. ("Authority" is the term for formal expectations, "control" is the actual distribution of effective power.)

This means that instrumental democracy will be in abeyance, although the symbols of mystic "democracy" will doubtless continue. Instrumental democracy is found wherever authority and control are widely dispersed among the members of a state. Mystic "democracy" is not, strictly speaking, democracy at all, because it may be found where authority and control are highly concentrated yet where part of the established practice is to speak in the name of the people as a whole. Thus, any dictatorship may celebrate its "democracy" and speak with contempt of such "mechanical" devices as majority rule at elections or in legislatures.

What part of the social structure would be drawn upon in recruiting the political rulers of the garrison state? As we have seen, the process will not be by general election, but by self-perpetuation through co-option. The foremost positions will be open to the officers corps, and the problem is to predict from what part of the social structure the officers will be recruited. Morale considerations justify a broad base of recruitment for ability rather than social standing. Although fighting effectiveness is a relatively impersonal test that favors ability over inherited status, the turnover in ruling families from generation to generation will probably be low. Any recurring crisis, however, will strengthen the tendency to favor ability. It seems clear that recruitment will be much more for bias and obedience than for objectivity and originality. Yet, as we shall presently see, modern machine society has introduced new factors in the military state—factors tending to strengthen objectivity and originality.

In the garrison state all organized social activity will be governmentalized; hence, the role of independent associations will disappear, with the exception of secret soceities. (Specifically, there will be no organized economic, religious, or cultural life outside of the duly constituted agencies of government.) Government will be highly centralized, though devolution may be practiced in order to mitigate "bureaucratism." There is so much outspoken resistance to bureaucratism in modern civilization that we may expect this attitude to carry over to the garrison state. Not only will the administrative structure be centralized, but at every level it will tend to integrate authority in a few hands. The leadership principle will be relied upon; responsibility as a rule will be focused upon individual "heads."

We have sketched some of the methods at the disposal of the ruling elites of the garrison state—the management of propaganda, violence, goods, practices. Let us consider the picture from a slightly different standpoint. How will various kinds of influence be distributed in the state? [4] Power will be highly concentrated, as in any dictatorial regime. We have already suggested that there will be a strong tendency toward equalizing the distribution of safety throughout the community (that is, negative safety, the socialization of threat in modern war). In the interest of morale there will be some moderation of huge differences in individual income, flattening the pyramid at the top, bulging it out in the upper-middle and middle zones. In the garrison state the respect pyramid will probably resemble the income pyramid. (Those who are the targets of compulsory labor restrictions will be the principal recipients of negative respect and hence will occupy the bottom levels.) So great is the multiplicity of functions in modern processes of production that a simple scheme of military rank is flagrantly out of harmony with the facts. Even though a small number of ranks are retained in the military state, it will be recognized that the

---

[4] Influence is measured by control over values (desired events). For purposes of analysis we have classified values as income, safety, and deference. To be deferred to is to be taken into consideration by the environment. Deference, in turn, is divided into power and respect. Power is measured by degree of participation in important decisions. A decision is a choice backed by the most severe deprivations at the disposal of the community (usually death). The making of these decisions in a community is the *function* of government. The *institution* of government is what is called government by those who live in a given community during a specified period of time; it is the most important secular decision-making institution. It is clear that the function of government may be exercised by other than governmental institutions, that is, by "government" and by monopolistic "big business." (A state is one of the most influential communities in world politics.) Respect is measured by reciprocal intimacy. Society can be divided into different classes on the basis of each value—or of value combinations. In the most inclusive sense politics studies conditions affecting the distribution of most values; in a narrower sense it studies power.

diversity of functions exercised by each rank is so great that the meaning of a specific classification will be obscure. Summarizing, the distribution of safety will be most uniform throughout the community; distribution of power will show the largest inequalities. The patterns of income and respect will fall between these two, showing a pronounced bulge in the upper-middle and middle strata. The lower strata of the community will be composed of those subject to compulsory labor, tending to constitute a permanent pariah caste.

What about the capacity of the garrison state to produce a large volume of material values? The elites of the garrison state, like the elites of recent business states, will confront the problem of holding in check the stupendous productive potentialities of modern science and engineering. We know that the ruling elites of the modern business state have not known how to control productive capacity; they have been unwilling to adopt necessary measures for the purpose of regularizing the tempo of economic development. Hence, modern society has been characterized by periods of orgiastic expansion, succeeded by periods of flagrant underutilization of the instruments of production.[5]

The rulers of the garrison state will be able to regularize the rate of production, since they will be free from many of the conventions that have stood in the way of adopting measures suitable to this purpose in the business state. The business elite has been unwilling to revise institutional practices to the extent necessary to maintain a continually rising flow of investment. The institutional structure of the business state has called for flexible adjustment between governmental and private channels of activity and for strict measures to maintain price flexibility. Wherever the business elite has not supported such necessary arrangements, the business state itself has begun to disintegrate.

Although the rulers of the garrison state will be free to regularize the rate of production, they will most assuredly prevent full utilization of modern productive capacity for nonmilitary consumption purposes. The elite of the garrison state will have a professional interest in multiplying gadgets specialized to acts of violence. The rulers of the garrison state will depend upon war scares as a means of maintaining popular willingness to forego immediate consumption. War scares that fail to culminate in violence eventually lose their value; this is the point at which ruling classes will feel that bloodletting is needed in order to preserve those virtues of sturdy acquiescence in the regime which they so much admire and from which they so greatly benefit. We may be sure that if ever there is a rise in the production of nonmilitary consumption goods, despite the amount of energy directed toward the production of military equipment,

---

[5] For the magnitude of these production losses see, for example, Chart I, "Loss in Potential Real National Income due to Depression, Unemployment of Men and Machines, 1930–1937," in National Resources Committee, *The Structure of the American Economy* (Washington, D.C.: U.S. Government Printing office, 1939), p. 2. The estimated loss of potential income was $200,000,000.

the ruling class will feel itself endangered by the growing "frivolousness" of the community.[6]

We need to consider the degree to which the volume of values produced in a garrison state will be affected by the tendency toward rigidity. Many factors in the garrison state justify the expectation that tendencies toward repetitiousness and ceremonialization will be prominent. To some extent this is a function of bureaucracy and dictatorship. But to some extent it springs also from the preoccupation of the military state with danger. Even where military operations are greatly respected, the fighter must steel himself against deep-lying tendencies to retreat from death and mutilation. One of the most rudimentary and potent means of relieving fear is some repetitive operation—some reiteration of the old and well established. Hence the reliance on drill as a means of disciplining men to endure personal danger without giving in to fear of death. The tendency to repeat, as a means of diminishing timidity, is powerfully reinforced by successful repetition, since the individual is greatly attached to whatever has proved effective in maintaining self-control in previous trials. Even those who deny the fear of death to themselves may reveal the depth of their unconscious fear by their interest in ritual and ceremony. This is one of the subtlest ways by which the individual can keep distracted from the discovery of his own timidity. It does not occur to the ceremonialist that in the spider web of ceremony he has found a moral equivalent of war—an unacknowledged substitute for personal danger.

The tendency to ceremonialize rather than to fight will be particularly prominent among the most influential elements in a garrison state. Those standing at the top of the military pyramid will doubtless occupy high positions in the income pyramid. During times of actual warfare it may be necessary to make concessions in the direction of moderating gross-income differences in the interest of preserving general morale. The prospect of such concessions may be expected to operate as a deterrent factor against war. A countervailing tendency, of course, is the threat to sluggish and well-established members of the upper crust from ambitious members of the lower officers' corps. This threat arises, too, when there are murmurs of disaffection with the established order of things on the part of broader components of the society.

It seems probable that the garrison state of the future will be far less rigid than the military states of antiquity. As long as modern technical society

6 The perpetuation of the garrison state will be favored by some of the psychological consequences of self-indulgence. When people who have been disciplined against self-indulgence increase their enjoyments, they often suffer from twinges of conscience. Such self-imposed anxieties signify that the conscience is ever vigilant to enforce the orthodox code of human conduct. Hence, drifts away from the established order of disciplined acquiescence in the proclaimed values of the garrison state will be self-correcting. The guilt generated by self-indulgence can be relieved through the orgiastic reinstatement of the established mores of disciplined sacrifice.

endures, there will be an enormous body of specialists whose focus of attention is entirely given over to the discovery of novel ways of utilizing nature. Above all, these are physical scientists and engineers. They are able to demonstrate by rather impersonal procedures the efficiency of many of their suggestions for the improvement of fighting effectiveness. We therefore anticipate further exploration of the technical potentialities of modern civilization within the general framework of the garrison state.

What are some of the implications of this picture for the research program of scientists who, in their capacity as citizens, desire to defend the dignity of human personality?

It is clear that the friend of democracy views the emergence of the garrison state with repugnance and apprehension. He will do whatever is within his power to defer it. Should the garrison state become unavoidable, however, the friend of democracy will seek to conserve as many values as possible within the general framework of the new society. What democratic values can be preserved, and how?

Our analysis has indicated that several elements in the pattern of the garrison state are compatible with democratic respect for human dignity. Thus, there will be some socialization of respect for all who participate in the garrison society (with the ever present exception of the lowest strata).

Will the human costs of a garrison state be reduced if we civilianize the ruling elite? Just how is it possible to promote the fusion of military and civilian skills? What are some of the devices capable of overcoming bureaucratism? To what extent is it possible to aid or to retard the ceremonializing tendencies of the garrison state?

It is plain that we need more adequate data from the past on each of these problems and that it is possible to plan to collect relevant data in the future. We need, for instance, to be better informed about the trends in the skill pattern of dominant elite groups in different parts of the world. In addition to trend data we need experimental and case data about successful and unsuccessful civilianizing of specialists on violence.[7]

Many interesting questions arise in connection with the present sketch about transition to the garrison state. What is the probable order of appearance— Japan, Germany, Russia, United States of America? What are the probable combinations of bargaining, propaganda, organization, and violence skills in elites? Is it probable that the garrison state will appear with or without violent revolution? Will the garrison state appear first in a small number of huge continental states (Russia, Germany, Japan [in China], United States) or in a single world-state dominated by one of these powers? With what symbol pat-

---

[7] For analysis of trends toward militarization in modern society consult Hans Speier, whose articles usually appear in *Social Research*, reprinted in *Social Order and the Risks of War* (New York: G. W. Stewart, 1952).

terns will the transition to the garrison state be associated? At the present time there are four important ideological patterns.

FOUR WORLD-SYMBOL PATTERNS

In the Name of	Certain Demands and Expectations Are Affirmed
1. National democracy (Britain, United States)	Universalize a federation of democratic free nations
2. National antiplutocracy (also antiproletarians) (Germany, Russia, Japan, Italy)	Universalize the axis of National Socialistic powers
3. World proletariat (Russia)	Universalize Soviet Union, Communist International
4. True world proletariat (no state at present)	New elite seizes revolutionary crisis to liquidate "Russian betrayers," all "National Socialisms," and "plutocratic democracies"

The function of any developmental construct, such as the present one about the garrison state, is to clarify to the specialist the possible relevance of his research to impending events that concern the values of which he approves as a citizen. Although they are neither scientific laws nor dogmatic forecasts, developmental constructs aid in the timing of scientific work, stimulating both planned observation of the future and renewed interest in whatever past events are of greatest probable pertinence to the emerging future. Within the general structure of the science of society, there is place for many special sciences devoted to the study of all factors that condition the survival of selected values. This is the sense in which there can be a science of democracy or a science of political psychiatry within the framework of social science. If the garrison state is probable, the timing of special research is urgent.[8]

[8] Robert S. Lynd is concerned with the timing of knowledge in *Knowledge for What?* (Princeton: Princeton University Press, 1939). The book is full of valuable suggestions; it does not, however, specify the forms of thought most helpful to the end he has in view.

◄◄◄ ►►►

ALEXIS DE TOCQUEVILLE

*On War, Society, and the Military**

WHY DEMOCRATIC NATIONS ARE NATURALLY DESIROUS OF PEACE AND DEMOCRATIC ARMIES, OF WAR

The same interests, the same fears, the same passions which deter democratic nations from revolutions deter them also from war; the spirit of military glory and the spirit of revolution are weakened at the same time and by the same causes. The ever increasing numbers of men of property—lovers of peace, the growth of personal wealth which war so rapidly consumes, the mildness of manners, the gentleness of heart, those tendencies to pity which are engendered by the equality of conditions, that coolness of understanding which renders men comparatively insensible to the violent and poetical excitement of arms— all these causes concur to quench the military spirit. I think it may be admitted as a general and constant rule that among civilized nations the warlike passions will become more rare and less intense in proportion as social conditions shall be more equal. War is nevertheless an occurrence to which all nations are subject, democratic nations as well as others. Whatever taste they may have for peace, they must hold themselves in readiness to repel aggression, or in other words they must have an army.

Fortune, which has conferred so many peculiar benefits upon the inhabitants of the United States, has placed them in the midst of a wilderness where they

* Reprinted from Alexis de Tocqueville, *Democracy in America,* trans. Henry Reeve, (Cambridge: Sever & Francis, 1863), II.

have, so to speak, no neighbors; a few thousand soldiers are sufficient for their wants—but this is peculiar to America, not to democracy. The equality of conditions and the manners as well as the institutions resulting from it do not exempt a democratic people from the necessity of standing armies, and their armies always exercise a powerful influence over their fate. It is therefore of singular importance to inquire what are the natural propensities of the men of whom these armies are composed.

Among aristocratic nations, especially amongst those in which birth is the only source of rank, the same inequality exists in the army as in the nation. The officer is noble, the soldier is a serf; the one is naturally called upon to command, the other to obey. In aristocratic armies, the private soldier's ambition is therefore circumscribed within very narrow limits. Nor has the ambition of the officer an unlimited range. An aristocratic body not only forms a part of the scale of ranks in the nation, but it contains a scale of ranks within itself: the members of whom it is composed are placed one above another in a particular and unvarying manner. Thus one man is born to the command of a regiment, another to that of a company; when once they have reached the utmost object of their hopes, they stop of their own accord and remain contented with their lot. There is, besides, a strong cause which, in aristocracies, weakens the officer's desire of promotion. Among aristocratic nations, an officer, independently of his rank in the army, also occupies an elevated rank in society; the former is almost always in his eyes only an appendage to the latter. A nobleman who embraces the profession of arms follows it less from motives of ambition than from a sense of the duties imposed on him by his birth. He enters the army in order to find an honorable employment for the idle years of his youth and to be able to bring back to his home and his peers some honorable recollections of military life, but his principal object is not to obtain by that profession either property, distinction, or power, for he possesses these advantages in his own right and enjoys them without leaving his home.

In democratic armies all the soldiers may become officers, which makes the desire of promotion general and immeasurably extends the bounds of military ambition. The officer, on his part, sees nothing which naturally and necessarily stops him at one grade more than at another, and each grade has immense importance in his eyes, because his rank in society almost always depends on his rank in the army. Among democratic nations it often happens that an officer has no property but his pay and no distinction but that of military honors: consequently, as often as his duties change, his fortune changes, and he becomes, as it were, a new man. What was only an appendage to his position in aristocratic armies has thus become the main point, the basis of his whole condition. Under the old French monarchy, officers were always called by their titles of nobility; they are now always called by the title of their military rank. This little change in the forms of language suffices to show that a great revolution has taken place in the constitution of society and in that of the army. In democratic armies the desire of advancement is almost universal —it is ardent, tenacious, perpetual; it is strengthened by all other desires and only extinguished with life itself. But it is easy to see that, of all armies in the world, those in which advancement must be slowest in time of peace are the armies of democratic countries. As the number of commissions is naturally limited while the number of competitors is almost unlimited and as the strict law of equality is over all alike, none can make rapid progress—many can make no progress at all. Thus the desire of advancement is greater, and the opportunities of advancement fewer, there than elsewhere. All the ambitious spirits of a democratic army are consequently ardently desirous of war, because war makes vacancies and warrants the violation of that law of seniority which is the sole privilege natural to democracy.

We thus arrive at this singular consequence: that, of all armies, those most ardently desirous of war are democratic armies and, of all nations, those most fond of peace are democratic nations. And what makes these facts still more extraordinary is that these contrary effects are produced at the same time by the principle of equality.

All the members of the community, being alike, constantly harbor the wish and discover the possibility of changing their condition and improving their welfare; this makes them fond of peace, which is favorable to industry and allows every man to pursue his own little undertakings to their completion. On the other hand, this same equality makes soldiers dream of fields of battle, by increasing the value of military honors in the eyes of those who follow the profession of arms and by rendering those honors accessible to all. In either case, the inquietude of the heart is the same, the taste for enjoyment as insatiable, the ambition of success as great—the means of gratifying it are alone different.

These opposite tendencies of the nation and the army expose democratic communities to great dangers. When a military spirit forsakes a people, the profession of arms immediately ceases to be held in honor, and military men fall to the lowest rank of the public servants; they are little esteemed and no longer understood. The reverse of what takes place in aristocratic ages then occurs; the men who enter the army are no longer those of the highest, but of the lowest, rank. Military ambition is only indulged in when no other is possible. Hence arises a circle of cause and consequence from which it is difficult to escape—the best part of the nation shuns the military profession because that profession is not honored, and the profession is not honored because the best part of the nation has ceased to follow it. It is then no matter of surprise that democratic armies are often restless, ill-tempered, and dissatisfied with their lot although their physical condition is commonly far better, and their discipline less strict, than in other countries. The soldier feels that he occupies an inferior position, and his wounded pride either stimulates his taste for hostilities which would render his services necessary or gives him a turn for revolutions during which he may hope to win by force of arms the political influence and personal importance now denied him. The composition of democratic armies makes this last-mentioned danger much to be feared. In democratic communities almost every man has some property to preserve, but democratic armies are generally led by men without property, most of whom have little to lose in civil broils. The bulk of the nation is naturally much more afraid of revolutions than in the ages of aristocracy, but the leaders of the army much less so.

Moreover, as among democratic nations (to repeat what I have just remarked) the wealthiest, the best educated, and the most able men seldom adopt the military profession, the army, taken collectively, eventually forms a small nation by itself where the mind is less enlarged, and habits are more rude, than in the nation at large. Now, this small uncivilized nation has arms in its possession and alone knows how to use them, for, indeed, the pacific temper of the community increases the danger to which a democratic people is exposed from the military and turbulent spirit of the army. Nothing is so dangerous as an army amid an unwarlike nation; the excessive love of the whole community for quiet continually puts its constitution at the mercy of the soldiery.

It may therefore be asserted, generally speaking, that, if democratic nations are naturally prone to peace from their interests and their propensities, they are constantly drawn to war and revolutions by their armies. Military revolutions, which are scarcely ever to be apprehended in aristocracies, are always to be dreaded among democratic nations. These perils must be reckoned among the most formidable which beset their future fate, and the attention of statesmen should be sedulously applied to find a remedy for the evil.

When a nation perceives that it is inwardly affected by the restless ambition of its army, the first thought which occurs is to give this inconvenient ambition an object by going to war. I speak no ill of war—war almost always enlarges the mind of a people and raises its character. In some cases it is the only check to the excessive growth of certain propensities which naturally spring out of the equality of conditions, and it must be considered as a necessary corrective to certain inveterate diseases to which democratic communities are liable. War has great advantages, but we must not flatter ourselves that it can diminish the danger I have just pointed out. That peril is only suspended by it, to return more fiercely when the war is over, for armies are much more impatient of peace after having tasted military exploits. War could only be a remedy for a people which should always be athirst for military glory. I foresee that all the military rulers who may rise up in great democratic nations will find it easier to conquer with their armies than to make their armies live at peace after conquest. There are two things which a democratic people will always find very difficult—to begin a war and to end it.

Again, if war has some peculiar advantages for democratic nations, on the other hand it exposes them to certain dangers which aristocracies have no cause to dread to an equal extent. I shall only point out two of these. Although war gratifies the army, it embarrasses and often exasperates that countless multitude of men whose minor passions every day require peace in order to be satisfied. Thus there is some risk of its causing, under another form, the disturbance it is intended to prevent. No protracted war can fail to endanger the freedom of a democratic country. Not, indeed, that after every victory it is to be apprehended that the victorious generals will possess themselves by force of the supreme power, after the manner of Sulla and Caesar: the danger is of another kind. War does not always give over democratic communities to military government, but it must invariably and immeasurably increase the powers of civil government; it must almost compulsorily concentrate the direction of all men and the management of all things in the hands of the administration. If it lead not to despotism by sudden violence, it prepares men for it more gently by their habits. All those who seek to destroy the liberties of a democratic nation ought to know that war is the surest and the shortest means to accomplish it. This is the first axiom of the science.

One remedy, which appears to be obvious when the ambition of soldiers and officers becomes the subject of alarm, is to augment the number of commissions to be distributed by increasing the army. This affords temporary relief, but it plunges the country into deeper difficulties at some future period. To increase the army may produce a lasting effect in an aristocratic community because military ambition is there confined to one class of men and the ambition of each individual stops, as it were, at a certain limit, so that it may be possible to satisfy all who feel its influence. But nothing is gained by increasing the army among a democratic people because the number of aspirants always rises in exactly the same ratio as the army itself. Those whose claims have been satisfied by the creation of new commissions are instantly succeeded by a fresh multitude beyond all power of satisfaction, and even those who were but now satisfied soon begin to crave more advancement, for the same excitement prevails in the ranks of the army as in the civil classes of democratic society and what men want is not to reach a certain grade, but to have constant promotion. Though these wants may not be very vast, they are perpetually recurring. Thus a democratic nation, by augmenting its army, only allays for a time the ambition of the military profession, which soon becomes even more formidable because the number of those who feel it is increased. I am of the opinion that a restless and turbulent spirit is an evil inherent in the very constitution of democratic armies and beyond hope of cure. The legislators of democracies must not expect to devise any military organization capable by its influence of calming and restraining the military profession; their efforts would exhaust their powers, before the object is attained.

The remedy for the vices of the army is not to be found in the army itself, but in the country. Democratic nations are naturally afraid of disturbance and of despotism; the object is to turn these natural instincts into well-digested, deliberate, and lasting tastes. When men have at last learned to make a peaceful and profitable use of freedom and have felt its blessings—when they have conceived a manly love of order and have freely submitted themselves to discipline—these same men, if they follow the profession of arms, bring into it, unconsciously and almost against their will, these same habits and manners. The general spirit of the nation being infused into the spirit peculiar to the army tempers the opinions and desires engendered by military life or represses them by the mighty force of public opinion. Teach but the citizens to be educated, orderly, firm, and free, [and] the soldiers will be disciplined and obedient. Any law which, in repressing the turbulent spirit of the army, should tend to diminish the spirit of freedom in the nation and to overshadow the notion of law and right would defeat its object; it would do much more to favor than to defeat the establishment of military tyranny.

After all and in spite of all precautions, a large army amid a democratic people will always be a source of great danger; the most effectual means of diminishing that danger would be to reduce the army, but this is a remedy which all nations have it not in their power to use.

WHICH IS THE MOST WARLIKE AND MOST REVOLUTIONARY CLASS IN DEMOCRATIC ARMIES?

It is a part of the essence of a democratic army to be very numerous in proportion to the people to which it belongs, as I shall hereafter show. On the other hand, men living in democratic times seldom choose a military life. Democratic nations are therefore soon led to give up the system of voluntary recruiting for that of compulsory enlistment. The necessity of their social condition compels them to resort to the latter means, and it may easily be foreseen that they will all eventually adopt it. When military service is compulsory, the burden is indiscriminately and equally borne by the whole community. This is another necessary consequence of the social condition of these nations and of their notions. The government may do almost whatever it pleases provided it appeals to the whole community at once; it is the unequal distribution of the weight, not the weight itself, which commonly occasions resistance. But, as military service is common to all the citizens, the evident consequence is that each of them remains but for a few years on active duty. Thus it is in the nature of things that the soldier in democracies only passes through the army, while among most aristocratic nations the military profession is one which the soldier adopts, or which is imposed upon him, for life.

This has important consequences. Among the soldiers of a democratic army, some acquire a taste for military life, but the majority, being enlisted against their will and ever ready to go back to their homes, do not consider themselves as seriously engaged in the military profession and are always thinking of quitting it. Such men do not contract the wants, and only half partake in the passions, which that mode of life engenders. They adapt themselves to their military duties, but their minds are still attached to the interests and the duties which engaged them in civil life. They do not therefore imbibe the spirit of the army—or rather, they infuse the spirit of the community at large into the army and retain it there. Among democratic nations the private soldiers remain most like civilians; upon them the habits of the nation have the firmest hold, and public opinion, most influence. It is by the instrumentality of the private soldiers especially that it may be possible to infuse into a democratic army the love of freedom and the respect of rights if these principles have once been successfully inculcated on the people at large. The reverse happens among aristocratic nations, where the soldiery have eventually nothing in common with their fellow citizens and where they live among them as strangers and often as enemies. In aristocratic armies the officers are the conservative element because the officers alone have retained a strict connection with civil society and never forego their purpose of resuming their place in it sooner or later; in democratic armies the private soldiers stand in this position and from the same cause.

It often happens, on the contrary, that in these same democratic armies the officers contract tastes and wants wholly distinct from those of the nation—a fact which may be thus accounted for. Among democratic nations the man who becomes an officer severs all the ties which bound him to civil life—he leaves it forever; he has no interest to resume it. His true country is the army, since he owes all he has to the rank he has attained in it; he therefore follows the fortunes of the army, rises or sinks with it, and henceforward directs all his hopes to that quarter only. As the wants of an officer are distinct from those of the country, he may perhaps ardently desire war or labor to bring about a revolution at the very moment when the nation is most desirous of stability and peace. There are nevertheless some causes which allay this restless and warlike spirit. Though ambition is universal and continual among democratic nations, we have seen that it is seldom great. A man who, being born in the lower classes of the community, has risen from the ranks to be an officer has already taken a prodigious step. He has gained a footing in a sphere above that which he filled in civil life, and he has acquired rights which most democratic nations will ever consider as inalienable.[1] He is willing to pause after so great an effort and to enjoy what he has won. The fear of risking what he has already obtained damps the desire of acquiring what he has not got. Having conquered the first and greatest impediment which opposed his advancement,

---

[1] The position of officers is, indeed, much more secure among democratic nations than elsewhere; the lower the personal standing of the man, the greater is the comparative importance of his military grade and the more just and necessary is it that the enjoyment of that rank should be secured by the laws.

he resigns himself with less impatience to the slowness of his progress. His ambition will be more and more cooled in proportion as the increasing distinction of his rank teaches him that he has more to put in jeopardy. If I am not mistaken, the least warlike, and also the least revolutionary part, of a democratic army will always be its chief commanders.

But the remarks I have just made on officers and soldiers are not applicable to a numerous class which in all armies fills the intermediate space between them—I mean the class of noncommissioned officers. This class of noncommissioned officers, which has never acted a part in history until the present [nineteenth] century, is henceforward destined, I think, to play one of some importance. Like the officers, noncommissioned officers have broken in their minds all the ties which bound them to civil life; like the former, they devote themselves permanently to the service and perhaps make it even more exclusively the object of all their desires. But noncommissioned officers are men who have not yet reached a firm and lofty post at which they may pause and breathe more freely ere they can attain further promotion. By the very nature of his duties, which are invariable, a noncommissioned officer is doomed to lead an obscure, confined, comfortless, and precarious existence. As yet he sees nothing of military life but its dangers; he knows nothing but its privations and its discipline—more difficult to support than dangers. He suffers the more from his present miseries, from knowing that the constitution of society and of the army allow him to rise above them; he may, indeed, at any time obtain his commission and enter at once upon command, honors, independence, rights, and enjoyments. Not only does this object of his hopes appear to him of immense importance, but he is never sure of reaching it until it is actually his own. The grade he fills is by no means irrevocable; he is always entirely abandoned to the arbitrary pleasure of his commanding officer, for this is imperiously required by the necessity of discipline. A slight fault, a whim, may always deprive him in an instant of the fruits of many years of toil and endeavor; until he has reached the grade to which he aspires, he has accomplished nothing, not until he reaches that grade does his career seem to begin. A desperate ambition cannot fail to be kindled in a man thus incessantly goaded on by his youth, his wants, his passions, the spirit of his age, his hopes, and his fears. Noncommissioned officers are therefore bent on war—on war always and at any cost; but if war be denied them, then they desire revolutions to suspend the authority of established regulations and to enable them, aided by the general confusion and the political passions of the time, to get rid of their superior officers and to take their places. Nor is it impossible for them to bring about such a crisis, because their common origin and habits give them much influence over the soldiers, however different may be their passions and their desires.

It would be an error to suppose that these various characteristics of officers, noncommissioned officers, and men belong to any particular time or country;

they will always occur at all times and among all democratic nations. In every democratic army the noncommissioned officers will be the worst representatives of the pacific and orderly spirit of the country, and the private soldiers will be the best. The latter will carry with them into military life the strength or weakness of the manners of the nation; they will display a faithful reflection of the community. If that community is ignorant and weak, they will allow themselves to be drawn by their leaders into disturbances, either unconsciously or against their will; if it is enlightened and energetic, the community will itself keep them within the bounds of order.

CAUSES WHICH RENDER DEMOCRATIC ARMIES WEAKER THAN OTHER ARMIES AT THE OUTSET OF A CAMPAIGN AND MORE FORMIDABLE IN PROTRACTED WARFARE

Any army is in danger of being conquered at the outset of a campaign after a long peace; any army which has long been engaged in warfare has strong chances of victory—this truth is peculiarly applicable to democratic armies. In aristocracies the military profession, being a privileged career, is held in honor even in time of peace. Men of great talents, great attainments, and great ambition embrace it; the army is in all respects on a level with the nation and frequently above it. We have seen, on the contrary, that among a democratic people the choicer minds of the nation are gradually drawn away from the military profession to seek by other paths distinction, power, and especially wealth. After a long peace—and in democratic ages the periods of peace are long—the army is always inferior to the country itself. In this state it is called into active service, and, until war has altered it, there is danger for the country as well as for the army.

I have shown that, in democratic armies and in time of peace, the rule of seniority is the supreme and inflexible law of advancement. This is not only a consequence, as I have before observed, of the constitution of these armies, but of the constitution of the people, and it will always occur. Again, as among these nations the officer derives his position in the country solely from his position in the army and as he draws all the distinction and the competency he enjoys from the same source, he does not retire from his profession or is not superannuated until toward the extreme close of life. The consequence of these two causes is that, when a democratic people goes to war after a long interval of peace, all the leading officers of the army are old men. I speak not only of the generals, but of the noncommissioned officers, who have most of them been stationary or have only advanced step by step. It may be remarked with surprise that, in a democratic army after a long peace, all the soldiers are mere boys and all the superior officers in declining years, so that the former are wanting in experience, the latter, in vigor. This is a strong element of defeat, for the first condition of successful generalship is youth: I should not have ventured to say so if the greatest captain of modern times had not made the observation.

These two causes do not act in the same manner upon aristocratic armies. As men are promoted in them by right of birth much more than by right of seniority, there are in all ranks a certain number of young men who bring to their profession all the early vigor of body and mind. Again, as the men who seek for military honors among an aristocratic people enjoy a settled position in civil society, they seldom continue in the army until old age overtakes them. After having devoted the most vigorous years of youth to the career of arms, they voluntarily retire and spend at home the remainder of their maturer years.

A long peace not only fills democratic armies with elderly officers, but it also gives to all the officers habits both of body and mind which render them unfit for actual service. The man who has long lived amid the calm and luke-warm atmosphere of democratic manners can at first ill adapt himself to the harder toils and sterner duties of warfare, and, if he has not absolutely lost the taste for arms, at least he has assumed a mode of life which unfits him for conquest.

Among aristocratic nations, the ease of civil life exercises less influence on the manners of the army because, among those nations, the aristocracy commands the army, and an aristocracy, however plunged in luxurious pleasures, has always many other passions besides that of its own well-being and [because], to satisfy those passions more thoroughly, its well-being will be readily sacrificed.

I have shown that, in democratic armies in time of peace, promotion is extremely slow. The officers at first support this state of things with impatience—they grow excited, restless, exasperated—but in the end most of them make up their minds to it. Those who have the largest share of ambition and of resources quit the army; others, adapting their tastes and their desires to their scanty fortunes, ultimately look upon the military profession in a civil point of view. The quality they value most in it is the competency and security which attend it; their whole notion of the future rests upon the certainty of this little provision, and all they require is peaceably to enjoy it. Thus not only does a long peace fill an army with old men, but it frequently imparts the views of old men to those who are still in the prime of life.

I have also shown that among democratic nations in time of peace the military profession is held in little honor and indifferently followed. This want of public favor is a heavy discouragement to the army; it weighs down the minds of the troops, and, when war breaks out at last, they cannot immediately resume their spring and vigor. No similar cause of moral weakness occurs in aristocratic armies; there the officers are never lowered either in their own eyes or in those of their countrymen, because, independently of their military greatness, they are personally great. But even if the influence of peace operated on the two kinds of armies in the same manner, the results would still be different. When the officers of an aristocratic army have lost their warlike spirit and the desire of raising themselves by service, they still retain a certain respect for the honor of their class and an old habit of being foremost to set an example. But when the officers of a democratic army have no longer the love of war and the ambition of arms, nothing whatever remains to them.

I am therefore of opinion that, when a democratic people engages in a war after a long peace, it incurs much more risk of defeat than any other nation, but it ought not easily to be cast down by its reverses, for the chances of success for such an army are increased by the duration of the war. When a war has at length, by its long continuance, roused the whole community from its peaceful occupations and ruined its minor undertakings, the same passions which made it attach so much importance to the maintenance of peace will be turned to arms. War, after it has destroyed all modes of speculation, becomes itself the great and sole speculation to which all the ardent and ambitious desires which equality engenders are exclusively directed. Hence it is that the selfsame democratic nations which are so reluctant to engage in hostilities sometimes perform prodigious achievements when once they have taken the field. As the war attracts more and more of public attention and is seen to create high reputations and great fortunes in a short space of time, the choicest spirits of the nation enter the military profession—all the enterprising, proud, and martial minds, no longer of the aristocracy solely, but of the whole country, are drawn in this direction. As the number of competitors for military honors is immense and war drives every man to his proper level, great generals are always sure to spring up. A long war produces upon a democratic army the same effects that a revolution produces upon a people; it breaks through regulations and allows extraordinary men to rise above the common level. Those officers whose bodies and minds have grown old in peace are removed or superannuated, or they die. In their stead a host of young men are pressing on, [men] whose frames are already hardened, whose desires are extended and inflamed by active service. They are bent on advancement at all hazards—and perpetual advancement; they are followed by others with the same passions and desires, and after these are others yet unlimited by aught but the size of the army. The principle of equality opens the door of ambition to all, and death provides chances for ambition. Death is constantly thinning the ranks, making vacancies, closing and opening the career of arms.

There is, moreover, a secret connection between the military character and the character of democracies, [a connection] which war brings to light. The men of democracies are naturally passionately eager to acquire what they covet and to enjoy it on easy conditions. They for the most part worship chance and are much less afraid of death than of difficulty. This is the spirit which they bring to commerce and manufactures, and this same spirit, carried with them to the field of battle, induces them willingly to expose their lives in order to secure in a moment the rewards of victory. No kind of greatness is more pleasing to the imagination of a democratic people than military greatness—a greatness of vivid and sudden luster obtained without toil by nothing but the risk of life. Thus, while the interests and the tastes of the members of a democratic community divert them from war, their habits of mind fit them for carrying on war well; they soon make good soldiers when they are roused from their business and their enjoyments. If peace is peculiarly hurtful to democratic armies, war secures to them advantages which no other armies ever possess, and these advantages, however little felt at first, cannot fail in the end to give them the victory. An aristocratic nation which in a contest with a democratic people does not succeed in ruining the latter at the outset of the war always runs a great risk of being conquered by it.

SOME CONSIDERATIONS ON WAR IN DEMOCRATIC COMMUNITIES

When the principle of equality is in growth not only among a single nation, but among several neighboring nations at the same time, as is now the case in Europe, the inhabitants of these different countries, notwithstanding the dissimilarity of language, of customs, and of laws, nevertheless resemble each other in their equal dread of war and their common love of peace.[2] It is in vain that ambition or anger puts arms in the hands of princes; they are appeased in spite of themselves by a species of general apathy and good will which makes the sword drop from their grasp and wars become more rare. As the spread of equality, taking place in several countries at once, simultaneously impels their various inhabitants to follow manufactures and commerce, not only do their tastes grow alike, but their interests are so mixed and entangled with one another that no nation can inflict evils on other nations without those evils falling back upon itself, and all nations ultimately regard war as a calamity almost as severe to the conqueror as to the conquered. Thus, on the one hand, it is extremely difficult in democratic ages to draw nations into hostilities, but, on the other hand, it is almost impossible that any two of them should go to war without embroiling the rest. The interests of all are so interlaced, their opinions and their wants so much alike, that none can remain quiet when the others stir. Wars therefore become more rare, but, when they break out, they spread over a larger field. Neighboring democratic nations not only become alike in some respects, but they eventually grow to resemble each other in

[2] It is scarcely necessary for me to observe that the dread of war displayed by the nations of Europe is not solely attributable to the progress made by the principle of equality among them; independently of this permanent cause several other accidental causes of great weight might be pointed out, and I may mention before all the rest the extreme lassitude which the wars of the Revolution and the Empire have left behind them.

almost all.[3] This similitude of nations has consequences of great importance in relation to war.

If I inquire why it is that the Helvetic Confederacy made the greatest and most powerful nations of Europe tremble in the fifteenth century while at the present day the power of that country is exactly proportioned to its population, I perceive that the Swiss have become like all the surrounding communities, and those surrounding communities, like the Swiss, so that, as numerical strength now forms the only difference between them, victory necessarily attends the largest army. Thus one of the consequences of the democratic revolution which is going on in Europe is to make numerical strength preponderate on all fields of battle and to constrain all small nations to incorporate themselves with large states or at least to adopt the policy of the latter. As numbers are the determining cause of victory, each people ought, of course, to strive by all the means in its power to bring the greatest possible number of men into the field. When it was possible to enlist a kind of troops superior to all others, such as the Swiss infantry or the French horse of the sixteenth century, it was not thought necessary to raise very large armies; but the case is altered when one soldier is as efficient as another.

The same cause which begets this new want also supplies means of satisfying it, for, as I have already observed, when men are all alike, they are all weak, and the supreme power of the state is naturally much stronger among democratic nations than elsewhere. Hence, while these nations are desirous of enrolling the whole male population in the ranks of the army, they have the power of effecting this object; the consequence is that in democratic ages

3 This is not only because these nations have the same social condition, but it arises from the very nature of that social condition which leads men to imitate and identify themselves with each other. When the members of a community are divided into castes and classes, they not only differ from one another, but they have no taste and no desire to be alike; on the contrary, everyone endeavors, more and more, to keep his own opinions undisturbed, to retain his own peculiar habits, and to remain himself. The characteristics of individuals are very strongly marked. When the state of society among a people is democratic—that is to say, when there are no longer any castes or classes in the community and all its members are nearly equal in education and in property—the human mind follows the opposite direction. Men are much alike, and they are annoyed, as it were, by any deviation from that likeness; far from seeking to preserve their own distinguishing singularities, they endeavor to shake them off in order to identify themselves with the general mass of the people, which is the sole representative of right and of might to their eyes. The characteristics of individuals are nearly obliterated. In the ages of aristocracy even those who are naturally alike strive to create imaginary differences between themselves; in the ages of democracy even those who are not alike seek only to become so and to copy each other—so strongly is the mind of every man always carried away by the general impulse of mankind. Something of the same kind may be observed between nations: two nations having the same aristocratic social condition might remain thoroughly distinct and extremely different because the spirit of aristocracy is to retain strong individual characteristics, but, if two neighboring nations have the same democratic social condition, they cannot fail to adopt similar opinions and manners because the spirit of democracy tends to assimilate men to each other.

armies seem to grow larger in proportion as the love of war declines. In the same ages, too, the manner of carrying on war is likewise altered by the same causes. Machiavelli observes in *The Prince* "that it is much more difficult to subdue a people which has a prince and his barons for its leaders, than a nation which is commanded by a prince and his slaves." To avoid offense, let us read public functionaries for slaves, and this important truth will be strictly applicable to our own time.

A great aristocratic people cannot either conquer its neighbors or be conquered by them without great difficulty. It cannot conquer them because all its forces can never be collected and held together for a considerable period; it cannot be conquered because an enemy meets at every step small centers of resistance by which invasion is arrested. War against an aristocracy may be compared to war in a mountainous country: the defeated party has constant opportunities of rallying its forces to make a stand in a new position. Exactly the reverse occurs among democratic nations: they easily bring their whole disposable force into the field, and, when the nation is wealthy and populous, it soon becomes victorious. But if ever it is conquered and its territory invaded, it has few resources at command, and, if the enemy takes the capital, the nation is lost. This may very well be explained: as each member of the community is individually isolated and extremely powerless, no one of the whole body can either defend himself or present a rallying point to others. Nothing is strong in a democratic country except the state; as the military strength of the state is destroyed by the destruction of the army and its civil power paralyzed by the capture of the chief city, all that remains is only a multitude without strength or government, unable to resist the organized power by which it is assailed. I am aware that this danger may be lessened by the creation of provincial liberties and consequently of provincial powers, but this remedy will always be insufficient. For after such a catastrophe, not only is the population unable to carry on hostilities, but it may be apprehended that they will not be inclined to attempt it.

In accordance with the law of nations adopted in civilized countries, the object of wars is not to seize the property of private individuals, but simply to get possession of political power. The destruction of private property is only occasionally resorted to for the purpose of attaining the latter object. When an aristocratic country is invaded after the defeat of its army, the nobles, although they are at the same time the wealthiest members of the community, will continue to defend themselves individually rather than submit, for, if the conqueror remained master of the country, he would deprive them of their political power to which they cling even more closely than to their property. They therefore prefer fighting to subjection, which is to them the greatest of all misfortunes, and they readily carry the people along with them because the people have long been used to follow and obey them and, besides, have but little to risk in the war. Among a nation in which equality of conditions prevails, each citizen, on the contrary, has but a slender share of political power and often has no share at all; on the other hand, all are independent, and all have something to lose, so that they are much less afraid of being conquered, and much more afraid of war, than an aristocratic people. It will always be extremely difficult to decide a democratic population to take up arms when hostilities have reached its own territory. Hence the necessity of giving to such a people the rights and the political character which may impart to every citizen some of those interests that cause the nobles to act for the public welfare in aristocratic countries.

It should never be forgotten by the princes and other leaders of democratic nations that nothing but the passion and the habit of freedom can maintain an advantageous contest with the passion and the habit of physical well-being. I can conceive nothing better prepared for subjection in case of defeat than a democratic people without free institutions.

Formerly it was customary to take the field with a small body of troops, to fight in small engagements, and to make long, regular sieges. Modern tactics consist in fighting decisive battles and, as soon as a line of march is open before the army, in rushing upon the capital city in order to terminate the war at a single blow. Napoleon, it is said, was the inventor of this new system, but the invention of such a system did not depend on any individual man, whoever he might be. The mode in which Napoleon carried on war was suggested to him by the state of society in his time; that mode was successful because it was eminently adapted to that state of society and because he was the first to employ it. Napoleon was the first commander who marched at the head of an army from capital to capital, but the road was opened for him by the ruin of feudal society. It may fairly be believed that, if that extraordinary man had been born three hundred years ago, he would not have derived the same results from his method of warfare or, rather, that he would have had a different method.

I shall add but a few words on civil wars, for fear of exhausting the patience of the reader. Most of the remarks which I have made respecting foreign wars are applicable a fortiori to civil wars. Men living in democracies are not naturally prone to the military character; they sometimes assume it when they have been dragged by compulsion to the field, but to rise in a body and voluntarily to expose themselves to the horrors of war, especially of civil war, is a course which the men of democracies are not apt to adopt. None but the most adventurous members of the community consent to run into such risks; the bulk of the population remains motionless. But even if the population were inclined to act, considerable obstacles would stand in their way, for they can resort to no old and well-established influence which they are willing to obey— no well-known leaders to rally the discontented as well as to discipline and to lead them, no political powers [which are] subordinate to the supreme power of the nation [and] which afford an effectual support to the resistance directed against the government. In democratic countries the moral power of the majority is immense, and the physical resources which it has at its command are out of all proportion to the physical resources which may be combined against it. Therefore the party which occupies the seat of the majority, which speaks in its name and wields its power, triumphs instantaneously and irresistibly over all private resistance; it does not even give such opposition time to exist, but nips it in the bud. Those who in such nations seek to effect a revolution by force of arms have no other resource than suddenly to seize upon the whole engine of government as it stands, which can better be done by a single blow than by a war, for, as soon as there is a regular war, the party which represents the state is always certain to conquer. The only case in which a civil war could arise is if the army should divide itself into two factions, the one raising the standard of rebellion, the other remaining true to its allegiance. An army constitutes a small community, very closely united together, endowed with great powers of vitality, and able to supply its own wants for some time. Such a war might be bloody, but it could not be long, for either the rebellious army would gain over the government by the sole display of its resources or by its first victory and then the war would be over, or the struggle would take place and then that portion of the army which should not be supported by the organized powers of the state would speedily either disband itself or be destroyed. It may therefore be admitted as a general truth that in ages of equality civil wars will become much less frequent and less protracted.[4]

[4] It should be borne in mind that I speak here of sovereign and independent democratic nations, not of confederate democracies; in confederacies, as the preponderating power always resides, in spite of all political fictions, in the state governments and not in the federal government, civil wars are, in fact, nothing but foreign wars in disguise.

◄◄◄ ►►►

MORRIS JANOWITZ

Military Elites and the Study of War*

Can war and war-making be seen as a special case of a general theory of social conflict? General theories of social conflict attempt to encompass forms as diverse as family, community, ethnic, and class conflict.[1] Clearly the understanding of war would be a crucial test of any general theory of social conflict.[2] Despite aspirations for generalized explanations of social conflicts, social scientists cannot overlook the highly distinctive aspects of war as a process of social change.

First, as of the second half of the twentieth century, wars are unique forms of social conflicts because they are waged only by nation-states. War implies social conflict between nation-states with their ideologies for legitimizing the use of violence in the national interest. The nation-state is a territorially based social system which monopolizes the use of the instruments of violence for both internal and external objectives. This is not to exclude from consideration armed conflict between established imperial nation-states and revolutionary political groups seeking to establish new and independent nation-states. In the

* Reprinted from Morris Janowitz, "Military Elites and the Study of War," pp. 9–18, *Journal of Conflict Resolution*, I (1957), by permission of the publisher.
[1] Kenneth Boulding, "Organization and Conflict," *Journal of Conflict Resolution*, I (1957), 122–130; Lewis Coser, *The Functions of Social Conflict* (Glencoe, Ill.: Free Press, 1956); Georg Simmel, *Conflict*, trans. Kurt H. Wolff (Glencoe, Ill.: Free Press, 1955).
[2] See Quincy Wright, *A Study of War* (Chicago: University of Chicago Press, 1942).

past two decades important political movements of national independence have been able to arm themselves. In the process of expelling imperial powers, these revolutionary political movements only create new nation-states which become potential and actual war-makers.

Second, war is differentiated from other forms of social conflict because war-making relies on a highly professionalized and specialized occupation, the professional soldier. By contrast, for example, conflict in the family, in community affairs, and even in wide aspects of economic relations involves no or little specialization of personnel. In these arenas the personnel are the same in conflict and in nonconflict situations. Nevertheless, in most nation-states— totalitarian and democratic—the decision to threaten war or to make war involves politicians and civilian leaders with broad manipulative skills and not primarily the military professionals. Regardless of the political power of the military elite, the classical forms of absolute military dictatorship are not applicable to a modern mass-industrialized social structure.

Third, the transition from peace to war and from war to peace is determined by a calculus which cannot be found in other types of social conflict. The essential calculus of war-making does not rest on the postulate that any prolongation of peace will increase the probabilities for the further prolongation of peace. On the contrary, given the dynamics of the traditional arms race, the prolongation of peace brings with it increased uncertainty about the enemy's war-making potential and therefore may increase the probability of war in order to maintain existing advantages.[3] In other forms of social conflict, social inertia and the postponement of decisions may contribute to the nonviolent resolution of conflict and differences.

In the language of social science, simple equilibrium models are difficult to apply to the process of war-making.[4] Instead, a process or developmental analysis which highlights the voluntaristic efforts and calculations of the elites within each nation-state is more appropriate. These considerations lead to the analysis of the organization of political and military elites as a crucial mechanism in the analysis of war and war-making.

Is it possible to identify different models of political-military elite organization—models which are reflective of different social structures? Can the consequences of the vast technological developments in war-making on the organization of elites be traced out in order to infer emerging trends? Can important uniformities in the motivational and ideological components of differing political and military elites be established?

---

[3] Harold D. Lasswell, *World Politics and Personal Insecurity* (Glencoe, Ill.: Free Press, 1950).

[4] For a discussion of equilibrium models and social change, see Barrington Moore, Jr., "Sociological Theory and Contemporary Politics," *The American Journal of Sociology,* LXI (1955), 107–115.

MODELS OF POLITICAL-MILITARY ELITES

Four models of political-military elites can be identified—aristocratic, democratic, totalitarian, and garrison state. For a baseline, it seems appropriate to speak of the aristocratic model of political-military elite structure. The *aristocratic model* is a composite estimate of Western European powers before industrialism began to have its full impact.[5] In the aristocratic model, civilian and military elites are socially and functionally integrated. The narrow base of recruitment for both elites and a relatively monolithic power structure provide the civilian elite with a method of "subjective control" of the military.[6]

There is a rigorous hierarchy in the aristocratic model which delineates both the source of authority and the prestige of any member of the military elite. The low specialization of the military profession makes it possible for the political elite to supply the bulk of the necessary leadership for the military establishment. The classical pattern is the aristocratic family which supplies one son to politics and one to the military. Birth, family connections, and common ideology ensure that the military will embody the ideology of the dominant groups in society. Political control is civilian control only because there is an identity of interest between aristocratic and military groups. The military is responsible because it is a part of the government. The officer fights because he feels that he is issuing the orders.

In contrast to the aristocratic model stands the democratic one. Under the democratic model the civilian and military elites are sharply differentiated. The civilian political elites exercise control over the military through a formal set of rules. These rules specify the functions of the military and the conditions under which the military may exercise its power. The military are professionals in the employ of the state. They are a small group, and their careers are distinct from the civilian careers. In fact, being a professional soldier is incompatible with any other significant social or political role. The military leaders obey the government not because they believe in the goals of the war, but because it is their duty and their profession to fight. Professional ethics as well as democratic parliamentary institutions guarantee civilian political supremacy. The officer fights because of his career commitment.

The democratic model is not a historical reality, but rather an objective of political policy. Elements of the democratic model have been achieved only in

5 Alfred Vagts, *The History of Militarism* (New York: W. W. Norton & Co., 1937).

6 Samuel P. Huntington, "Civilian Control of the Military: A Theoretical Statement," in Heinz Eulau, Samuel Elderseveld, and Morris Janowitz, eds., *Political Behavior: A Reader in Theory and Research* (Glencoe, Ill.: Free Press, 1956).

certain Western industrialized countries, since it requires extremely viable parliamentary institutions and broad social consensus about the ends of government. The democratic model assumes that military leaders can be effectively motivated by professional ethics alone, and this is most difficult. Paradoxically enough, certain types of officers with aristocratic backgrounds have made important contributions to the development of the democratic model.

In the absence of a development toward the democratic model, the totalitarian model tends to replace the aristocratic one.[7] The totalitarian model, as it developed in Germany, in Russia, and to a lesser degree in Italy, rests on a form of subjective control, as did the older aristocratic model. But the subjective control of the totalitarian model arises not from any natural or social unity of the political and military elites. On the contrary, a revolutionary political elite of relatively low social status and based on a mass authoritarian political party fashions a new type of control of the military elite. The revolutionary elite, bedecked with paramilitary symbols and yet forced into temporary alliance with older military professionals, is dedicated to reconstituting the military elites. Subjective control of the totalitarian variety is enforced by the secret police, by infiltrating party members into the military hierarchy, by arming its own military units, and by controlling the system of officer selection. Under subjective control of the totalitarian variety, the organizational independence of the professional military is destroyed. The officer fights because he has no alternative.[8]

The garrison-state model, as offered by Prof. Harold D. Lasswell, is the weakening of civil supremacy which can arise even out of an effective democratic structure.[9] While the end result of the garrison state approximates aspects of the totalitarian model, the garrison state has a different natural history. It is, however, not the direct domination of politics by the military. Since modern industrial nations cannot be ruled merely by the political domination of a single small leadership bloc, the garrison state is not a throwback to a military dictatorship. It is the end result of the ascent to power of the military elite under conditions of prolonged international tension. Internal freedom is hampered, and the preparation for war becomes overriding. The garrison state is a new pattern of coalition in which military groups directly and indirectly wield unprecedented amounts of political and administrative power. The military retain their organizational independence provided that they make appropriate alliances with civil political factions. The officer fights for national survival and glory.

---

[7] Hans Speier, *Social Order and the Risks of War* (New York: G. W. Stewart, 1952).

[8] The totalitarian model which developed in Western Europe is not the same as the survival of feudal-like military dictatorship still found in parts of South America, in which a military junta directly dominates civilian military life. The Perón model was a strange combination of the old-style military dictatorship plus the newer devices of the totalitarian model.

[9] H. D. Lasswell, "The Garrison State," *supra*.

It cannot be assumed that all forms of militarism involve "designed militarism." "Designed militarism"—the type identified with Prussian militarism —involves the modification and destruction of civilian institutions by military leaders acting directly and premeditatedly through the state and other institutions. Equally significant and more likely to account for crucial aspects of the garrison state, as well as for contemporary American problems, is "unanticipated militarism." "Unanticipated militarism" develops from a lack of effective traditions and practices for controlling the military establishment, as well as from a failure of civilian political leaders to act relevantly and consistently. Under such circumstances a vacuum is created which not only encourages an extension of the tasks and power of military leaderships but actually forces such trends.

The threats to the democratic model cannot be meaningfully analyzed merely from the point of view of designed militarism. Designed militarism emphasizes the impact of military leadership on the civil social structure. Unanticipated militarism requires an analysis of the manner in which the military profession responds and reacts to the developments in civilian society. The technology of war, which is the advanced technology of civilian society, lies at the root and sets the preconditions in the trends toward unanticipated militarism.

CONSEQUENCES OF TECHNOLOGICAL TRENDS

The long-term technological development of war and war-making required the professionalization of the military elite. Such technological developments were compatible with the democratic model of political-military elites, since this model rests on the differentiation of the functions of politicians and soldiers. However, the current continuous advance in the technology of war begins to weaken the possibility of the democratic elite model.

The vast proliferation of the military establishments of the major industrialized nations is a direct consequence of the continuous development of the technology of warfare. The "permanent" character of these vast military establishments is linked to the "permanent" threat of war. It is well recognized that under these conditions the tasks which military leaders perform tend to widen. Their technological knowledge, their direct and indirect power, and their heightened prestige result in their entrance, of necessity, into arenas which have in the recent past been preserved for civilian and professional politicians. The result is the tremendous stress on the traditional assumptions about the effectiveness of the democratic model for regulating political-military relations. The need that political leaders have for active advice from professional soldiers about the strategic implications of technological change serves only to complicate the task of redefining spheres of competence and responsibility. Totalitarian as well as democratic nations are faced with these problems.

The impact of the technological development of warfare over the past half-century leads to a series of propositions about social change.

A larger percentage of the national income of modern states is spent for the preparation, executing, and repair of the consequences of war.

There is more nearly total popular involvement in the consequences of war and war policy, since the military establishment is responsible for the distribution of a larger share of civilian values and since the destructiveness of war has increased asymptotically.

The monopolization of legal armed violence held by the military has increased so greatly that the task of suppressing internal violence has declined, as compared with the external tasks of the national security.[10]

The rate of technological change has become accelerated, and a wider diversity of skill is required to maintain the military establishment.

The previous periodic character of the military establishment (rapid expansion, rapid dismantlement) has given way to a more permanent maintenance or expansion.

The permanent character of the military establishment has removed one important source of political-military conflict, that is, the civilian tendency to abandon the military establishment after a war. Instead, because of the high rate of technological change, internal conflicts between segments of the military elite have been multiplied.

The diversification and specialization of military technology have lengthened the time of formal training required to acquire mastery of military technology, with the result that the temporary citizen army will become less important and a completely professional army more vital.

The complexity of the machinery of warfare and the requirements for research, development, and technical maintenance tend to weaken the organization line between the military and the nonmilitary.

Because of these technological and large-scale administrative developments, civilian society as well as the military establishment is undergoing basic transformation. The contemporary tension in political-military organization within the major industrialized powers has a common basis to the degree that the technological requirements of war are highly universal. Yet the differences in the amount or character of political power exercised by military leaders and the methods for resolving conflicts between political and military leaders as between the major nation-states cannot be explained primarily or even to any great extent by differences in the technological organization of their armed forces. This is not to deny that each weapons system—land, sea, or naval—tends to develop among its military managers characteristic orientations toward politics based on the technical potentialities of their weapons. The political outlook of any military establishment will be influenced by whether it is an

[10] Katherine Chorley, *Armies and the Art of Revolution* (London: Faber & Faber, 1943).

organization dominated by army, navy, or air force. Nevertheless, technological developments merely set the limits within which the civilian and military elites will share power. National differences in the influence patterns of
military elites must be linked to national differences in social structure and
elite organization.

These technological trends in war-making have necessitated extensive common modification in the military profession in both democratic and totalitarian
systems and regardless of national and cultural differences. The changes in the
military reflect organizational requirements which force the permanent military establishment to parallel other civilian large-scale organizations. As a
result, the military takes on more and more the common characteristics of a
government or business organization. Thereby the differentiation between the
military and the civilian—an assumed prerequisite for the democratic elite
model—is seriously weakened. In all these trends the model of the professional
soldier is being changed by "civilianizing" the military elite to a greater extent
than "militarizing" of the civilian elite.

What are some of these modifications in the military profession? They include (a) democratization of the officer recruitment base, (b) a shift in the
basis of organization authority, and (c) a narrowing of the skill differential
between military and civilian elites. Propositions concerning these trends for
the United States military during the past fifty years are applicable in varying
form to the military establishment of the other major industrialized nations.[11]

Democratization of the Officer Recruitment Base

Since the turn of the century the top military elites of the major industrialized nations have been undergoing a basic social transformation. The
military elites have been shifting their recruitment from a narrow, relatively
high-status social base to a broader, lower-status, and more representative
social base.

The broadening of the recruitment base reflects the demand for large numbers of trained specialists. As skill becomes the basis of recruitment and advancement, democratization of selection and mobility increases. This is a
specific case of the general trend in modern social structure of the shift from
criteria of ascription to those of achievement. In Western Europe the democratization of the military elites displaced the aristocratic monopoly of the
officer corps; in the United States an equivalent process can be observed, although social lines are generally less stratified and more fluid. The sheer increase in size of the military establishment contributes to this democratiza-

---

[11] M. Janowitz, *The Professional Soldier and Political Power: A Theoretical Orientation
and Selected Hypotheses* (University of Michigan: Bureau of Government, Institute of
Public Administration, 1953).

tion. The United States Air Force, with its large demand for technical skill, offered the greatest opportunity for rapid advancement.

From the point of view of the democratic model, democratization of social recruitment of military leaders is not necessarily accompanied by democratization of outlook and behavior. By "democratization of outlook and behavior" is meant an increase in accountability or an increase in the willingness to be accountable. In fact, the democratization of the military profession carries with it certain opposite tendencies. The newer strata are less aware of the traditions of the democratic model. Their opportunities for mobility make them impatient and demanding of even greater mobility. Their loyalty to the military establishment begins to depend more and more on the conditions of employment rather than on the commitment to the organization and its traditions.

The increased representativeness of social background of the military profession also results in an increased heterogeneity of the top leaders within the various military services. Under these conditions it is more difficult to maintain organization effectiveness and at the same time enforce the norms of civilian political control. (In a totalitarian society, it likewise becomes more difficult to maintain organization effectiveness and enforce party loyalty.) Of course, any large-scale organization develops devices for overcoming these forms of disruption. The military profession emphasized honor as a unifying ideology, and intraservice marriage patterns have been a power device for assimilating newcomers into the military establishment. But requirements of bureaucratic efficiency corrode honor, and military marriage, like civilian marriage, is currently more limited in its ability to transmit traditions.

Even more fundamental, the new democratization changes the prestige position of the military profession. The older traditional soldier has his social prestige regulated by his family of origin and by the civilian stratum from which he came. What society thought was of little importance as long as his immediate circle recognized his calling. This was true even in the democratic model. The British officer corps, with its aristocratic and landed-gentry background and its respectable middle-class service families, is the classic case in point. In varying degrees before World War II it was true for the United States Navy, with its socialite affiliations, and even the United States Army, with its Southern military family traditions. But with democratization of the profession, the pressure develops for prestige recognitions by the public at large. A public-relations approach must supplant a set of personal relations. Public relations becomes not merely a task for those specialists assigned to developing public support for military establishment policies. Every professional soldier, like every businessman or government official, must represent his establishment and work to enhance the prestige of the professional military. In turn, a military figure becomes a device for enhancing a civilian enterprise. Under these circumstances objective control gives way to subjective identity.

Shift in the Basis of Organization Authority

It is common to point out that military organization is rigidly stratified and authoritarian in character because of the necessities of command. Moreover, since military routines are highly standardized, it is generally asserted that promotion is in good measure linked to compliance with existing procedures and existing goals of the organization. (These characteristics are found in civilian bureaucracies but supposedly not with the same high concentration and rigidity.) Once an individual has entered into the military establishment, he has embarked on a career within a single pervasive institution. Short of withdrawal, he thereby loses the freedom of action that is associated with occupational change in civilian life.

From such a point of view, the professional soldier is thought to be authoritarian in outlook. Status and the achievement of status are thought to be fundamental motivations. The organizing principle of authority is domination —the issuing of direct commands. The professional soldier is seen as limited in his ability and skill to participate in civilian political affairs which require flexibility, negotiation, and the art of persuasion.

However, it is not generally recognized that a great deal of the military establishment resembles a civilian bureaucracy as it deals with problems of research, development, supply, and logistics. Even in those areas of the military establishment which are dedicated primarily to combat or to the maintenance of combat readiness, a central concern of top commanders is not the enforcement of rigid discipline, but rather the maintenance of high levels of initiative and morale. This is a crucial respect in which the military establishment has undergone a slow and continuing change since the origin of mass armies and rigid military discipline.[12]

Initiative rather than the enforcement of discipline is a consequence of the technical character of modern warfare, which requires highly skilled and highly motivated groups of individuals. Often these formations must operate as scattered and detached units, as opposed to the solid line of older formations. It is also a consequence of the recruitment policies of modern armies, which depend on representative cross sections of the civilian population rather than on volunteers. Modern armies increasingly draw their recruits from urbanized and industrialized populations and less from illiterate agricultural groups, for whom response to discipline is a crucial and effective form of control. Tolerance for the discomforts of military life decreases. The rationality and skepticism of urban life carry over into military institutions to a greater degree than in previous generations. The rationalization of military life makes necessary the supplying of more explicit motives. Social relations, personal

---

[12] S. L. A. Marshall, *Men against Fire: The Problem of Battle Command in Future War* (Washington, D.C.: Infantry Journal, 1947).

leadership, material benefits, ideological indoctrination, and the justice and meaningfulness of war aims are now all component parts of morale.

Short of complete automation, specialized units manning the crucial technical instruments of war must display fanatically high morale in order to achieve successful military offensive action. Although military formations are still organized on the basis of discipline, military command now involves an extensive shift from domination to manipulation as a basis of authority. Manipulation implies persuasion, negotiation, and explanation of the ends of the organization. Direct orders give way to the command conference. Since manipulation involves high social interaction, differences in status are tempered by morale objectives. Shifts from domination to manipulation, from status to morale, are present in many aspects of civilian society. However, the peculiar conditions of combat have obscured the extent to which morale leadership is especially required for military formations. This is not to imply that the military establishment has found a formula for approximately balancing domination and manipulation.

Narrowing the Skill Differential between Military and Civilian Elites

The consequences of the new tasks of military management imply that the professional soldier is required more and more to acquire skills and orientations common to civilian administrators and even political leaders. He is more interested in the interpersonal techniques of organization, morale, negotiation, and symbolic interaction. He is forced to develop political orientations in order to explain the goals of military activities to his staff and subordinates. Not only must the professional soldier develop new skills necessary for internal management; he must develop a public-relations aptitude in order to relate his formation to other military formations and to civilian organizations. This is not to imply that these skills are found among all the top military professionals, but the concentration is indeed great and seems to be growing. The transferability of skills from the military establishment to civilian organizations is thereby increased. Within the military establishment, conflicts occur and deepen with greater acceleration between the old, traditionally oriented officers and the new, who are more sensitized to the emerging problems of morale and initiative.

TRENDS IN INDOCTRINATION

In the past, institutional indoctrination of the military professional in the United States avoided discussion of human factors in the military establishment and the political consequences of military operations. (It is, of course, difficult, if not impossible, to intellectualize at any length about the enforcement of discipline.) Before World War II, the United States professional military had a schooling which supplied little realistic orientation except to emphasize a simple mechanical version of ultimate civilian supremacy. However, even before the outbreak of World War II, slowly and painfully, important sectors of the military elite had to reorient themselves on these matters. Reorientation came about as a result of the realities of the war. Of course, much of the crucial work merely devolved upon lower-rank staff officers and technical specialists, with the top military cadre not fully in sympathy.

In the absence of institutional indoctrination for these tasks, impressive indeed is the extent to which self-indoctrination succeeded in producing the number of officers capable of functioning in these areas. Nevertheless, the military establishment continues to be characterized by deep inner tensions because of its new responsibilities and because of the absence of a sufficiently large cadre of top officers sensitized to deal effectively with its broad administrative and political tasks.

Before World War II, whatever training and indoctrination existed for handling the complexities of civil-military relations and political tasks was primarily a self-generated mission. Some deviant career officers were not only sensitive to the emerging problems within the military establishment, but many of these officers sought to indoctrinate themselves about emerging problems of civil-military relations and of the political aspects of military operations. They often accepted specialized assignments of a quasi-political nature or those involving communications skills which supplied relevant opportunities for indoctrination and training. (These assignments included military attaché, foreign-language officer, intelligence officer, and public relations.) Voluntary acceptance or pursuit of these assignments represented genuine efforts at self-indoctrination and thereby selected out for training those who felt inclined and had potentials for growth. In the United States especially, before 1939, these assignments had relatively low prestige. In fact, they were seen as interfering with one's career, and therefore they were avoided by all except those who had sufficient foresight to see their high relevance. For many, these assignments did involve risk and short-term disadvantages. However, the results of such assignments in crucial cases were just the contrary. They assisted officers in entering the very top of the military elite, since they did, in fact, represent realistic indoctrination for emerging tasks.

Since the end of World War II, at all levels of the military establishment institutional indoctrination encompasses much wider perspectives—social and political. Although much of the new indoctrination appears to be oriented to the broader problems of the military establishment—internal and external—it is very much an open question as to what the consequences are likely to be for civil-military relations in a democratic society.

Ideological indoctrination is now designed to eliminate the civilian contempt for the military mind. The military mind has been charged with a lack of inventiveness and traditionalism. The new indoctrination stresses initiative and continuous innovation. This is appropriate for the career motives of the new recruits and is important in creating conditions for overcoming bureaucratic inertia. The military mind has been charged with an inclination toward ultra-nationalism and ethnocentrism. Professional soldiers are being taught to de-emphasize ethnocentric thinking, since ethnocentrism is detrimental to national and military policy. The military mind has been charged as being disciplinarian. The new indoctrination seeks to deal with human factors in combat and in large-scale organization in a manner similar to contemporary thought on human relations in industry. In short, the new indoctrination is designed to supply the professional soldier with an opinion on all political, social, and economic subjects which he feels obliged to have as a result of his new role.

The new intellectualism is a critical capacity and a critical orientation. The military officer must be realistic, and he must review the shortcomings of the past and contemporary record of political-military relations. Will the growth of critical capacities be destructive, or will it be productive of new solutions? The consequence could be a growth in hostility toward past arrangements, in particular toward past political leadership of the military establishment and toward the dogmas of civilian supremacy. The military profession runs the risk of confusing its technical competency with intellectual background. As a result, it could become critical and negative toward the military bureaucracy and toward civilian political leadership in the same way that Joseph Schumpeter speaks of the university-trained specialist becoming critical of the economic system. In the United States at least, such hostility is hardly likely to lead to open disaffectation, but more to passive resentment and bitterness.

In the long run, under either the democratic or the totalitarian model, the military establishment cannot be controlled and still remain effective by civilianizing it. Despite the growth of the logistical dimensions of warfare, the professional soldier is, in the last analysis, a military commander and not a business or organizational administrator. The democratic elite model of civilian supremacy must proceed on the assumption that the functions of the professional military are to command soldiers into battle. There is no reason to believe that the characteristics of the ideal professional soldier as a military commander are compatible with the ideal professional soldier as an object of civilian control, although the differences seem to be growing less and less as the automation of war continues. The quality of political control of the professional soldier is not to be judged by examining those aspects of the military establishment which are most civilian, but rather those which are least civilian. Here the willingness to submit to civilian control, rather than the actuality of civilian control, is most crucial.

There is no reason to believe, in a democratic society, that the military can be controlled by offering them the conditions of employment found in civilian society. In the long run, civilian establishment would draw off all the best talent, especially in a business-dominated society. To achieve the objectives of the democratic elite model, it is necessary to maintain and build on the differentiation between civilian and military roles. A democratic society must accord the professional soldier a position based on his skill and on his special code of honor. He must be integrated because his fundamental differentiation is recognized. Under these circumstances standards of behavior can be established and political directives enforced. The current drift toward the destruction of the differentiation of the military from the civilian cannot produce genuine similarity, but runs the risk of creating new forms of hostility and unanticipated militarism.

◄◄◄ ►►►

RAYMOND ARON

*War and Industrial Society**

We are too much obsessed by the twentieth century to spend time in speculat-
ing about the twenty-first. Long-range historical predictions have gone out of
fashion. George Orwell's portrait of 1984 depicted too faithfully the last years
of Stalinism to have any great value as an anticipation. Atomic weapons seem
to confront us with a simple choice between permanent peace and universal
suicide, and they are as discouraging to pacifist dreams as to militaristic
nightmares. The Third Reich, instituted for a thousand years, collapsed in
ruins at the end of twelve years; the Soviet regime, founded by revolutionaries in the name of Western humanism and the classless society, ended in the
totalitarianism which Mr. [Nikita] Khrushchev described in the style of Alfred
Jarry's *Ubu Roi* at the Twentieth Congress of the Bolshevik Party. Mankind's
intimate and tragic experience of these two millennial realms is such that
political aspirations are unlikely, in the immediate future, to take again the
form of a secular religion.

The thinkers of last century had a stronger feeling of living in a period of
transition, and they did not hesitate to make prophecies whose boldness and
dogmatism astound us. I am reminded of the remark of an historian of religion on the subject of Roman Catholicism: "The wind of the coming century

* Reprinted from Raymond Aron, *War and Industrial Society* ("Auguste Comte Lecture
No. 3" [London: Oxford University Press, 1958]), by permission of the London School of
Economics and Political Science (Copyright 1958, London School of Economics and
Political Science).

will scatter its ashes." Equally imprudent today appears the assurance with which Auguste Comte wrote in 1842: "At last the time has come when serious and lasting war must disappear completely among the human elite." [1] In that lecture Comte heralded the approach of peace and asserted the absolute incompatibility between the military spirit and industrial society. It seemed to me that there could be no worthier tribute to the memory of a great man than a consideration of one of his mistakes. In the history of thought errors are often more instructive than truths; the latter become platitudes and are integrated into the general body of knowledge, while the former, when they are not forgotten, remain isolated and open to investigation. They call for an explanation and bear witness to the limitation of even the greatest intellects.

I

In the first half of last century sociologists and philosophers who reflected upon the course of history were all struck by the development of industrial society, that is, by the concurrent processes of construction of factories, extension of the use of machinery, concentration of the working class in towns, increase in world population, and the drift to the towns of men who had become useless in the countryside. These phenomena, which we a hundred years later can see in truer perspective than contemporaries were able to do, provoked diverse attitudes and were judged in contradictory ways.

The optimists marveled at the progress of science and technology and the ever-increasing productive capacity, and they visualized an era of prosperity and peace resulting from the extension of an exchange economy. The pessimists drew attention to the misery of the working class and to the unequal distribution of wealth produced in common. Some of them doubted whether the workers' standard of living could ever rise appreciably; a rise in wages would encourage an increase in population which would soon reduce them again.

During this period there emerged the great doctrines whose impact dominated ideological controversies and, to some extent, scientific thought itself up to the war of 1939. Does the system of free enterprise and competition allow an indefinite expansion of production, or is it doomed to periodic crises and, indeed, condemned sooner or later to a total paralysis which will render inevitable the emergence of a new system? Will the incontestable growth in the means of production lead to an era of abundance, or will the increase in wealth merely lead to a growth of population so that the achievements of human ingenuity benefit only a minority?

Among the doctrines formulated and diffused in this period (which we might call the first phase of industrialization), the most famous is that of

[1] *Cours de philosophie positive*, VI, lect. 57, 239.

Marx, which combines optimism and pessimism in a striking manner. Optimism, perhaps excessive, about the contribution of capitalism to powers of production is allied with pessimism, certainly excessive, about the condition of the masses in an economy based upon private property and competition. Unbounded optimism about the fate of humanity after the liberating revolution accompanies a pessimistic view, not yet justified, of the ability of capitalism to overcome its own contradictions. Elsewhere I have characterized Marxism as "catastrophic optimism" in order to indicate one of the unique features which has contributed so much to its propaganda value. With regard to industrial civilization itself, Marx shares the confidence of the optimistic school and perhaps even carries it further; with regard to the future of capitalism and the fate of the masses under this system, he shares the fears of the pessimistic school. The industrial reserve army will prevent wages from rising, crises will become more and more violent, the class struggle will become more intense. History must pass through the purgatory of civil war before attaining the paradise of plenty and a humanity reconciled with itself thanks to its victory over nature.

These doctrinal controversies have not entirely disappeared in the mid-twentieth century. One still finds, in the West, fanatical supporters of planning or of the market mechanism, economists and sociologists who place all their hopes in one system and all their fears in the other. But on the whole, the ideological response has been gradually replaced by scientific analysis. It has been possible to distinguish the phenomena common to the initial stages of industrialization, whatever the regime, to note the variations of these phenomena according to the methods used, and to attempt a comparison of the relative cost of industrialization in different places. Instead of predicting the stability, rise, or fall of wage levels with the development of productive forces, we measure the rate of economic growth necessary to balance or surpass the growth of population. Global prophecies are replaced by correlations and by probability calculations for a particular country or a particular situation.

The nineteenth-century predictions concerning peace and war also oscillated between optimism and pessimism. But the two schools disagreed less about the evolution of industrial society itself than about the place of industrial society in world history and the significance of industrialism in modern civilization. The optimistic school, to which Auguste Comte and (with some qualifications) Herbert Spencer belonged, saw history as a unilinear movement from one type of society to another; military society and industrial society represented two fundamentally different types of social organization. The predominance of the second type would diminish warfare, which is essentially connected with the predominance of the first. On the other hand, the pessimistic school, represented by Nietzsche, [Jacob] Burckhardt, and [Oswald] Spengler (who wrote in the twentieth century but before the outbreak of 1914), saw in so-called industrial societies only another version of the urban societies, the popular mass civilizations, whose rise in antiquity was marked by the civil wars at the end of the Roman Republic. When Nietzsche predicted that the twentieth century would be one of great wars, it seems to me that his prescience was based on two observations: that urban mass civilizations are bellicose and not pacific and that the spread of Western civilization over the globe would offer the contending great powers an immense prize— world domination.

If this analysis is correct, the contrast between the two schools, that which foresees peace and that which predicts great wars, derives from a more profound disagreement—that between a progressive and a cyclical conception of history. Industrial society, in Auguste Comte's opinion, gave promise of peace because it was the culmination of a unique development. Industrial society was going to be the scene of one of the greatest wars in history, according to Spengler, because the concentration of the masses in towns, the rule of money, the disintegration of communities based on kinship, and the domination of demagogues and plutocrats made inevitable clashes between the different wills to power, concealed by changing ideologies.

If this is so, the problem of the bellicose or pacific nature of industrial societies has certainly not been resolved by the tragic experiences of the first half of the twentieth century. In economic matters the past half-century, it seems to me, has strengthened the case of those who take a middle position. Science and industry have upset the organization of human groups and have not entirely justified either optimism (capitalist or Socialist) or pessimism, still less catastrophic optimism. But we now know approximately the circumstances in which societies can take advantage of knowledge and technique to provide better material conditions for a growing proportion of people. We do not know if and when the whole of humanity will succeed in creating these conditions.

With regard to peace and war, the middle position seems excluded by the existence of atomic weapons. If the efficiency of these weapons is as great as scientists say, would not a single war, carried out with all the available weapons, destroy at one blow civilization as we know it? And if the optimists are not absolutely right, will not the pessimists be vindicated by events or even appear to have been insufficiently pessimistic?

Since the question as to whether industrial civilizations are inherently pacific remains unanswered, it is worth while to examine more closely the proofs of their pacific character which were offered a century ago by Auguste Comte and to test these proofs by the historical events of the period between Comte and ourselves.

The fundamental idea in Auguste Comte's theory—the radical opposition between the military spirit and the industrial spirit—was a commonplace in the first half of last century. It was first formulated by Saint-Simon and was suggested by the obvious changes in Western societies. Work was becoming the principal activity of the immense majority of men, and the activity which pre-eminently conferred wealth, power, and prestige. From that time the real elite in society was composed of bankers, industrialists, engineers, and scientists, not of aristocrats. But the hierarchy of values which is established by the ruling class must surely make an impression upon society as a whole and upon the course of social development. In the view of bankers, industrialists, and engineers, wars are an anachronism, a survival of former times. They squander wealth, whereas the function of work is to create it, and the major concern of those who direct the collective labor of society is to prevent waste and encourage creative activity.

This fundamental antithesis of military civilization and the civilization of labor, of the spirit of conquest and the spirit of industry, was projected by Comte into history, the former into antiquity and the latter into modern times. In antiquity, work was the duty of slaves, and free men were available for war. The primitive aversion from a life of labor made the use of force unavoidable in the first phase of man's education. The unification of the ancient world by a conquering empire was the inevitable outcome of the warlike ardor of free men.

> The primitive institution of permanent slave labour had, by its very nature, a twofold aim; on the one hand, to allow military activity a sufficient growth to accomplish properly its first great mission in the process of social evolution, and on the other hand, to establish the only general means of education which, by an invincible pressure, could overcome the radical antipathy felt by most men at first for the habit of regular work.[2]

"The first great mission" was the expansion of human societies.

> There was no other means, in the early stages, to bring about the indispensable expansion of human society, and to restrain within society, a sterile warlike ardour incompatible with an adequate growth of productive work, except the gradual incorporation of civilised populations into one conquering nation.[3]

In the ancient world, therefore, work was subordinate to war, first, because the slave was constrained by force and thus by the warrior; second, because the latter performed the essential function of extending human groups by conquest; and finally, as a result of the Roman Empire. But Comte argues—and here he is in agreement with Hegel's *Phenomenology of Mind*—that a complete reversal occurred between antiquity and modern times. Then labor was subordinate to war; the epochs of modern times are stages in the subordination of war to labor. In the first phase, industrial society developed purely

[2] *Cours de philosophie positive*, VI, lect. 56, 23.
[3] *Ibid.*, lect. 57, 287.

spontaneously, "helped only by fortunate natural alliances with various ancient powers."[4] In the succeeding phase, industry was favored as an indispensable means to military supremacy. In the third phase, industrial development was "finally established as a permanent goal of European politics which nevertheless has regularly made use of war."[5] First industry in the service of war, then war in the service of industry, and the final synthesis in the ultimate form of society will be peace through industry.

Like Spencer and the other optimists, Auguste Comte saw clearly that industry could be used as an instrument of the will to power and as a tool of political ambition. We have still to inquire why he regarded these two phases, industry subordinate to the military spirit and militarism utilized to further industrial prosperity, as transitory. After all, the Marxist theory of imperialism means regarding this second phase as inescapable, at least while capitalism itself endures. As to the first phase, that of industry in the service of war, the Spengler school of pessimists believes this to be coextensive with industrial civilization, a characteristic of the Faustian West. What are the arguments, general and historical, explicit and implicit, with which Comte supports his view?

The argument, at once implicit and fundamental, derives from the way in which industry and the industrial spirit are defined. Comte did not use the word industry in its narrow sense to distinguish it from agriculture and commerce; industry includes agriculture, factory production, commerce, and finance. It is defined, first and foremost, by regular, free labor. Industrial solidarity is "essentially founded on universal emancipation."[6] It puts an end to the regime of classes and hereditary occupations and encourages everyone to choose his work according to his ability or inclination. In other words, industrialization as interpreted by Comte is primarily defined not by the development of productive forces or the use of machinery, but by the substitution of labor (or action on nature) for war as the predominant activity and by the substitution of liberty for slavery or serfdom. This essential incompatibility does not, however, justify any historical prediction (unless associated with the extremely optimistic view that what is useless will disappear and that what has no function will not be produced). Why, then, did Comte believe that the wars of earlier stages will not be repeated?

In the third phase there was

> . . . a final series of wars, the commercial wars, in which the military spirit tended, at first spontaneously and soon systematically, to subordinate itself to the formerly inferior industrial spirit, in order to retain a permanent active role, and thereafter attempted to integrate itself into the

---

[4] *Ibid.*, p. 80.
[5] *Loc. cit.*
[6] *Ibid.*, p. 71.

new social economy by demonstrating its special ability either to conquer useful trading centres for all nations or to destroy their principal sources of dangerous foreign competition.[7]

In short, why should we suppose that the period of imperialist wars (in Lenin's sense) has come to an end?

Wars of this type—colonial wars and wars in the service of the national economy—took place in the eighteenth century. But according to Comte, the colonial regime was now in complete decline, "the separation of the American colonies was bringing about its destruction in such a way as to prevent any serious renewal of the major wars to which it had previously given rise." [8] Comte acknowledged that England was exceptional in enjoying, with its empire, a unique prosperity. But he urged the other nations of the European republic not to take offense at the anomaly "which corresponded to needs and abilities which could not exist elsewhere to the same degree."

The wars of the Revolution and the Empire must have aroused anxiety in the mind of the founder of Positivism. But he saw in them the confirmation of the opposition between modern social relations and the military spirit, because it was "for the temporary re-establishment of a regime radically antipathetic to the corresponding social milieu" that Napoleon plunged into "vast military activities." Far from renewing the work of the Roman Republic or of Charlemagne, the Emperor misunderstood the necessities of history, and he stimulated "nations to join the king in repulsing foreign invasion, and thus destroyed the sympathy and admiration that our revolutionary initiative and popular defence had everywhere aroused among our western fellow citizens." [9]

This "tremendous warlike aberration" is henceforth impossible

. . . since ideological wars, which alone remain conceivable, have been radically checked by the growth of revolutionary activity in the West. This has become for Europe today an assurance of temporary peace by continuously occupying all the attention of governments and all the activity of their numerous armies to prevent internal disturbance.[10]

Beyond this peace which fear of the people and the growth of revolutionary activity must impose on governments, "the true intellectual reorganization" will intervene to establish genuine peace.

Only one kind of war remains conceivable, that which aims "to establish directly, in the ultimate interest of universal civilization, the material preponderance of more advanced over less advanced populations.[11] Such a tendency, which Comte resolutely condemned, might "cause the mutual oppression

[7] *Ibid.*, p. 73.
[8] *Ibid.*, p. 236.
[9] *Ibid.*, p. 215.
[10] *Ibid.*, p. 237.
[11] *Loc. cit.*

of nations" and finally "precipitate various cities upon one another according to their unequal social progress." [12] With undaunted optimism, Comte tries to dispel "all irrational anxiety," puts his confidence in "the instinct characteristic of modern social relations," and refuses to envisage that this will to conquest, which justifies itself by the superiority of the white race, could become "a new source of general war entirely incompatible with the most steadfast inclinations of all civilized populations.[13]

The above quotations show that, if Comte believed that the time of peace had come for the elite of humanity, it was not because he failed to observe the possible causes of war in his time: colonial wars in which overseas territories conquered by European nations would be the stake and which had occupied the eighteenth century and ideological wars whose justification would be the superiority of European nations and which would culminate in the extension of colonial slavery in the guise of spreading civilization. Comte recognized the possibility and even the danger of all the kinds of war which have occupied the years since the Positivist doctrine foretold the coming of peace. But he dispelled "the irrational anxiety" and refused to envisage the return of the "aberrations" because his whole interpretation of history was bound up with two ideas: first, the radical opposition between military society and industrial society and, second, the inevitable disappearance of phenomena not in accord with the spirit of the time. Comte could not envisage the case of a society which would destroy itself by its own folly, and he could not admit the hypothesis of a phenomenon attaining its extreme form at the point where it had lost all its usefulness. Moreover, he was led to discover a proof of the pacifism of European societies in facts which apparently suggested a contrary interpretation.

Was conscription becoming not a revolutionary improvisation but a permanent institution? Comte was sure that it provided proof of the antimilitarist feelings of modern populations. There are still volunteer officers but not volunteer soldiers. The military profession is losing its specialization and prestige, and civilians in uniform wait for their freedom and rebel increasingly against "the temporary burden." [14] The maintenance of great armies in peacetime? They are only "great political police forces," the "last function of order allotted to the military body at a time when true warfare is about to disappear forever." [15] In the same way, the Revolutionary and Imperial crisis has shown that "the popular will" is sufficient to ensure the success of a defensive action and that the most skillful tactics, if not supported by such a purpose, will ultimately fail. Henceforth there is no need to rely on the warlike virtues or to be obsessed by military successes.

[12] *Ibid.*, p. 238.
[13] *Loc. cit.*
[14] *Ibid.*, p. 239.
[15] *Ibid.*, p. 241.

Paradoxically enough, Comte finds the best proof of this fundamental pacifism of industrial society in the inferiority of the weapons used in comparison
with those that are possible.

It is clear that the means of warfare are infinitely inferior to the powerful
and rapid increase in the stock of destructive machinery that our knowledge and resources would permit if modern nations could ever experience,
in exceptional circumstances, even a temporary stimulus similar to that
which moved the whole of the ancient world.[16]

In fact, Comte was not mistaken on this last point. The "exceptional circumstances" of 1914–1918 subjected Europeans to a "temporary stimulus."
Armored vehicles and aircraft emerged transformed from these "exceptional
circumstances." World War II, which began with the weapons of 1918, ended
with the first two atomic bombs. The apparatus of destruction had, as Comte
would have said, undergone a "powerful increase."

II

Western society, which was to have guided humanity by way of peace to its
final destination, was the birthplace and nursery, but also the victim, of the
great wars of the twentieth century which pessimistic observers had seen loom-
ing on the horizon. The only question worthy of examination concerns the
nature of these modern wars: Are they colonial wars, ideological wars, or
imperialist wars?

In my view, World War I belongs to none of these categories; it is characterized less by its immediate causes or its explicit purposes than by its extent
and the stakes involved. It affected all the political units inside one system of
relations between sovereign states. Let us call it, for want of a better term, a
war of hegemony,[17] hegemony being, if not the conscious motive, at any rate
the inevitable consequence of the victory of at least one of the states or groups.
The victory of the Central Powers would have established the hegemony of
Germany over Europe. The victory of Athens in the fifth century B.C. would
have given domination of the whole Greek world to the city of Pericles. The
victory of the Western nations resulted in the restoration, at least temporarily,
of the "liberties" of the European states, as that of Sparta restored the liberties
of the Greek cities.

Comte declared that clashes between European nations had become impossible,[18] yet such conflicts have filled the first half of the twentieth century. He

---

[16] *Ibid.*, p. 57.

[17] Such wars could also be called wars of equilibrium if they were defined with reference
to the side which is on the defensive.

[18] Because of "universal internal agitation."

imagined the nations of Europe (England, Germany, Italy, Spain, and France) uniting into one Western republic and by their example guiding the rest of humanity without any wish to conquer it by force of arms. How different the reality has been from these prophecies, and how obvious it now seems that the prophecies were wiser and more in accord with the interests of everybody than were the actual events. A Franco-German war was necessary in order that the German nation should be united. In the last quarter of the nineteenth century the nations of Europe chose the way which the founder of Positivism had advised against: they assumed "the white man's burden"; they spread civilization by conquest and invoked their superiority to justify their dominance. Overseas possessions were probably not the cause, but inevitably they seemed one of the stakes in the conflicts between the metropolitan states. All the European nations were swept along by the development of industrial civilization, but, while the conflict could not be reduced to the antithesis of the *ancien régime* and the Revolution, neither were the European nations unified under the banner of a single philosophy. The ideologies of the European nations remained diverse enough not to cause national clashes, but to aggravate them. No one in England or France would have thought of beginning a war in order to overthrow the absolutist regimes (which were, in fact, limited) of imperial Germany or Austria-Hungary. But once war was declared, democracy could be extolled against absolutism.

If the "national clashes" which Comte declared impossible nevertheless took place, then those factors which tended to extend wars, which the pacifism of industrial society should have prevented, would come into operation. If conscript armies ceased to be police forces, they would provide the war lords with an almost inexhaustible human material (if one may use this abominable term). If the entrepreneurs, engineers, and scientists began to devote their talents to the apparatus of destruction instead of the instruments of production, what diabolical marvels they could pour out from the factories and machines.

Why did the European nations embark in 1914 upon a war of hegemony? The question has been hotly discussed because, perhaps for the first time in history, the belligerents had a vague sentiment that war itself was absurd and ruinous to their common civilization and that those who began it were therefore criminals. The search for these war criminals was unrewarding because in fact nobody had wanted a war of this kind—cataclysmic, all-devouring, and increasingly devoid of purpose as it developed. Was the chief fault committed by those who wanted to teach a lesson to little Serbia or by those who had brought into operation the system of alliances and thus generalized the conflict? Or should the blame be distributed according to the war aims of the two sides? In that case, whatever treaty terms a victorious Germany would have dictated, she was the most guilty (like Athens in the Peloponnesian War) because in the event of victory she would have become the dominant power.

The European nations had not been pacified by industrialism. In August, 1914, they were rich and prosperous, and no revolutionary agitation seriously threatened them. Amid popular enthusiasm they entered upon a war which they probably imagined would be like so many others in the past. Nationalist conflicts in Southeastern Europe and Austro-Russian rivalry in the Balkans were the immediate causes of the outbreak. But this would have been impossible if, after a half-century of peace in Europe, the nations had not retained intact their warlike fervor and had not regarded their independence, as against the dictatorship of a single power, as a benefit worthy of the greatest sacrifices. Societies whose armies are made up of civilians in uniform are not necessarily peace-loving.

World War I, which originated in a minor diplomatic conflict, was generalized by the system of alliances and assumed gigantic proportions as a result of conscription and the resources of industry. It was also the cause of World War II, because the victors were unwilling to impose their own hegemony and were unable to establish a real equilibrium. The United States, which had given the *coup de grâce* to the Central Powers, retired from the game. Great Britain, having failed to recover its prosperity and being uncertain of the morality of the Versailles Treaty, left France to maintain equilibrium. And equilibrium could only be maintained, against the interests of the two great continental powers, Russia and Germany, by the permanent disarmament of Germany.

The second war of this century, even more vast than the first, was not essentially a war of hegemony. It was an ideological war, since the two sides invoked conflicting ideologies, and it was also an imperialist war, since Hitler's Germany aimed not perhaps at extending its conquests beyond Europe, but at subjecting the other European nations to the kind of rule which these same nations had imposed overseas upon the so-called inferior or less-advanced populations.

The inevitable result of what Comte would probably have called a "temporary and tragic aberration" was the general ruin of those nations which should have constituted the Western republic and which live today, reconciled but not united, under the protection of the American republic.

This interpretation of the last half-century may perhaps be summarized as follows: European politics have developed in the twentieth century in accordance with precedent and tradition, as though industrial civilization had brought nothing new. The European nations were unable either to unite in a single state or to live peacefully together as sovereign states united in the same civilization. Germany, the last to achieve national unity, was tempted in her turn by dreams of empire. Like Spain and France before her and in spite of industrialism, she plunged or was drawn into the struggle for hegemony.

Whatever the uniqueness of the present state of affairs, the first half of the twentieth century favors the thesis of the pessimists who expected from the future nothing that they had not known in the past. Antiquity gave us the spectacle of a war to the death between sovereign states of the same civilization, fought all the more bitterly because the states were so close to each other.

A number of thinkers—among them [Thorstein] Veblen, [Joseph] Schumpeter, and the Marxists—have tried to explain this "tragic aberration" in such a way as to maintain the pacific character of industrial societies.

It has hardly been noticed, in fact, but it seems to me incontestable, that Veblen's and Schumpeter's interpretations of imperialism are inspired by Positivism. Modern societies would be more prone to conquest and war the more numerous the institutional and moral survivals of the feudal or aristocratic spirit. Germany and Japan have been the disturbing elements of this century because industrial society developed there in a framework inherited from the *ancien régime* and under the direction of a managerial class loyal to military values. Veblen, as is well known, predicted the flowering of Japanese imperialism as we in fact experienced it in the Asian coprosperity sphere.

Undoubtedly the comparison is striking. Germany and Japan were the only two great industrial powers of our time governed by an aristocracy whose ethic and social attitudes dated from the preindustrial period. The reformers of the Meiji Era understood (as Chinese civil servants and scholars refused to understand) that it was necessary to adopt the industrial system of the West in order to preserve the independence and greatness of the Empire. These reformers came from the class of nobles which had been subject to the authority of the Shogun during the two centuries of the Tokugawa Period but which had not been destroyed. From this class were recruited the civil servants, teachers, business leaders, and officers who learned from the West and accomplished the most remarkable work of modernization of a non-Western country that we have seen up to the present time. The reformers did not stop at adopting weapons and factories or even the organization of armies and factories; they also introduced universal compulsory education, changed the legal system to adapt it to the needs of a modern economy, created universities of a Western type, and, in short, tried to give to the various classes of the nation the intellectual training required by economic development.

This process of Westernization was excluded from only two spheres, that which concerned the position of the family, children's education, and the traditional organization of personal relations and that which concerned the emperor as the source of power and descendant of the gods. The traditionalistic restoration of Shintoism seemed to the modernists to provide a counterweight to technical Westernization. Japan retained intact its ancestral spirit and culture in the age of submarines, skyscrapers, and internal combustion engines.

This combination of an industrial society and an *ancien régime,* to use the language of Comte, culminated in the catastrophe of 1945, after half a century of brilliant and uninterrupted success.

The reformers had created industry to preserve Japan's independence. The power which resulted inspired them with the desire to conquer. The easy victories over China and Korea followed by the resounding success over Russia gave them an exaggerated idea of their country's resources. Meanwhile, the increase of population fostered by governments anxious to acquire the force of numbers had reached such a point that their agriculture, in spite of exceptionally rapid progress, could no longer feed all the Japanese. The export of manufactured goods really became a matter of life and death. Tens of millions of people lived by industrial work, and this required the import of raw materials which could only be financed by the export of manufactured products. Impediments to export appeared as so many threats to the very existence of the Empire of the Rising Sun.

The conquest of territory in the islands or on the continent was not the only way of solving the problem of the Japanese economy. The protection of the flag is not indispensable for commercial expansion, and trade is possible without the acquisition of sovereignty. A coprosperity area would have been conceivable without domination by the stronger power and probably even without a common currency. Conquest appeared to some members of the ruling class as a means of balancing the budget and of feeding a growing population, but the increase of population had been encouraged. The conquest of Formosa and of Korea had preceded the alleged need for raw materials and trade outlets.

In seventy years from 1870 to 1940, Japan lived through the equivalent of four centuries of European history as seen by Comte: it began by setting up industry to strengthen its army, like the states of Europe in the fifteenth and sixteenth centuries; afterward it put its army at the service of the Asian coprosperity sphere, thus reviving the colonial enterprises of eighteenth-century Europe. Since the defeat, it has been cured of these two compounds of the military spirit and the industrial spirit, which were the source of war for four centuries in Europe and for seventy years in Asia.

Japanese imperialism can be explained fairly simply in the framework and within the concepts of Comte's theory. In relation to Japan's past it seems a mystery. Japanese militarism had been chiefly feudal in spirit, "defensive militarism," to use Comte's term. Unification under the authority of the Shoguns had condemned the class of nobles to internal and external peace. The policy of isolation, population stability, and the maintenance of the social hierarchy all tended, during the Tokugawa Period, toward the permanence of order in a closed society. From the time of the Meiji Era all was movement: increase of population, economic growth, increase of territory and of national strength. Having entered into competition with the West, Japan wanted to be first. The traditional militarism, armed by modern industry in an expanding universe, was transformed into the ambition to conquer. The European nations were great in proportion to their colonies. Japan wanted to compete and to surpass them. Thus the foolish decision of 1941, without appearing inevitable, becomes intelligible. Japan, unable to conquer the vast area and the masses of China, attacked the world's greatest industrial power.

The spirit of the *ancien régime* was certainly not the only force in the formation of modern Germany. She has passed through all the characteristic stages of European history, has played an important part in all Western intellectual movements, and has experienced all the social classes and all the industrial activities characteristic of Western civilization. Nevertheless, imperial Germany differed profoundly from the Western democracies. After the defeat of 1848 the liberal bourgeoisie was eliminated from the political scene and left the principal role to the civil servants and Prussian officers. German unity was achieved by Prussia's military victories, not by deliberative assemblies and popular enthusiasm. Up to 1914 the Prussian electors voted by estates, not by universal suffrage; the monarchy was constitutional, not parliamentary. The system of values and the way of thinking characteristic of the governing class were not so much those of an industrial or commercial bourgeoisie as those of aristocratic functionaries, civil servants, and officers.

The facts which Veblen and Schumpeter can quote in support of their theory are not open to doubt. The survivals of the *ancien régime* were stronger in Germany and Japan than in Great Britain or France. In both countries there was this combination of a property-owning class and a military caste which can be regarded as the chief cause of imperialism.

The article published by Veblen in 1915, "The Opportunity of Japan," in retrospect seems prophetic:

It is in this unique combination of a high wrought spirit of feudalistic fealty and chivalric honour with the material efficiency given by the modern technology that the strength of the Japanese nation lies. In this respect—in being able anachronistically to combine the use of modern technical ways and means with the mediaeval spirit of servile solidarity —the position of the Japanese government is not unique except in the eminent degree of its successful operation. The several governments of Europe are also, and with a varying measure of success, endeavoring similarly to exploit the modern state of the industrial arts by recourse to the servile patriotism of the common man, and for the purposes of a dynastic politics that is substantially of a mediaeval character; but in respect of the measure of success which this anachronistic enterprise meets with, these European powers, while differing greatly among themselves, each and several fall short of the Japanese pattern by a long interval.[19]

[19] *Essays in Our Changing Order* (New York: Viking Press, 1934), p. 251.

But Veblen did not think such a combination would last. In the long run the industrial system must ruin the mental and institutional structure of old Japan. The existing rulers would have their chance of conquest—and would probably seize it—during the intervening period.

> The opportunity of Imperial Japan as a fearsome power in the world's concert of dynastic politics may by consequence confidently be expected to lie within the historical interval that so intervenes between Japan's acquirement of the western state of the industrial arts and its consequent, slower but inevitable, falling into line with those materialistic, commercial, and spendthrift conceptions of right and honest living that make the outcome among the (Christian) peoples that have gone before along the road of industrial dominion and individual self-help.[20]

Veblen did not attribute to imperial Germany the responsibility for World War I in the same sense as the Allies' propaganda had done.[21] In Veblen's opinion there was, after all, only a difference of degree between the foreign policy of Germany and that of the other European powers.

> Had there been no Imperial Germany included in the concert of nations, the outcome might not have been substantially different in the long run, so far as regards Europe's eventual fortunes in respect of peace and war; but with Germany included there has been no room to doubt that, whenever this prospective war should break out, Germany would be the seat of the disturbance, whether on the offensive or defensive.[22]

Veblen and Schumpeter, putting aside the interminable quarrel about responsibility, justly remarked that the militaristic spirit surviving from the past dominated the "dynastic state" of imperial Germany more than the state in England, where absolutism had been defeated centuries before, or the French republic born of popular revolution. But they did not claim that this imperialist survival was the only cause of the outbreak or that the rivalry between sovereign states, even nonimperialist ones, would be essentially peaceful. Of all the European states, Germany was the only one capable of conceiving an ambition to dominate, the only one that could, if victorious, impose its rule over the whole of the old continent. She behaved as the other dominant nations of the continent had done before her.

[20] *Ibid.*, p. 255.
[21] "There can be no harm in recognizing the entire disingenuousness of all parties to the controversy. That the German volume of prevarication is the larger is something of a fortuitous circumstance, due to their more urgent diplomatic need. With the same opportunities and provocation it is doubtful if British diplomacy would not have done just as well, and it is not doubtful that the Russians would have done better" (*Imperial Germany and the Industrial Revolution* [New York: Macmillan Co., 1915], note, p. 258).
[22] *Ibid.*, p. 259.

Would she have escaped this imperial temptation if she had been more purely capitalistic and less feudal, if the bourgeoisie of the Rhineland, Bavaria, or Westphalia, instead of the junkers of Mecklenburg or East Prussia, had held first place? Let us put the question in terms of the future instead of the past. Would the dominant state in an international system refrain from abusing its power, and would it succeed in not arousing envy if it were entirely civil and if industrialism had obliterated all trace of the *ancien régime*? Is the will to conquest or to power, which Comte thought already anachronistic in his time, like to be recognized for what it is by the governing classes and by the people once the old prejudices have disappeared? The desire for collective glory, the pride of participation in national greatness, even as one of the lowest of citizens or servants, may well survive in the age of cannons, skyscrapers, and underground stations adorned with marble.

Moreover, neither German imperialism, which burst out in 1939, nor Japanese imperialism, which culminated in 1941, is, in its latest stages, the expression of a feudal class or of the spirit of the *ancien régime*. Here and there a small part of the old governing class opposed totalitarianism out of respect for liberal or Christian values and repugnance for the relapse into barbarism. The picture of a simple duality—past against future, imperialism against industrial society—does not represent the complexity of the real situation. Imperialists are no more recruited exclusively from the old classes in modern Europe than they were in ancient Rome. The charismatic leaders of popular factions are driven further by the delirium of power than are the inheritors of the feudal spirit and of "defensive militarism." The militarism of the masses is more violent and more dangerous than that of the traditional nobility.

The war of 1914 was initially the result of a diplomatic failure magnified by alliances into a war of hegemony, rather than the consequence of a German will to conquest. The peoples who had been freed by industrialism and the accidents of political history from the heritage of the *ancien régime* showed scarcely less enthusiasm for war than those who had retained a military caste and respect for aristocratic values. The cult of violence and the lust for power became most intense at a time when, as a result of wars and revolutions, a popular elite had finally suppressed the old aristocracy.

The other theory which enables us to ignore the lessons of the twentieth century and to maintain a belief in the pacific nature of industrial civilization is that of Marx or, rather, of the Marxists, according to whom wars are the inevitable outcome of the contradictions of capitalism. According to them, the concept of industrial society is misleading since it includes two fundamentally different regimes, capitalism and Socialism. The first is essentially bellicose; the second, pacific. Comte was not mistaken, and Marx basically agrees with him, in opposing two alternatives: man's struggle with nature and the struggle of men with each other. When the former has ended in victory, the latter will abate of its own accord. Once men are able to exploit the forces of nature, they will no longer wish to fight and kill or enslave each other. In fact, industrialism is essentially incompatible with militarism. But the essence of industrial society will not be revealed until classes and the class war have been overcome and the exploitation of man by man has been eliminated.

In the writings of Marx the theory is not without ambiguity. Is it the control over nature, that is, scientific and technological progress, which is decisive, or is it the elimination of classes which is to bring about social and international peace? If the coming of Socialism depended upon the development of productive forces, this question would not be important. Socialism—the triumph of the proletariat—could not precede economic and social maturity, that is, the establishment, in the heart of the old society, of the relations of production of the society of the future. But this exact correspondence, which is another form of the belief in providence (men only set themselves problems which they can solve), has not been maintained. Consequently, the question inevitably arises: Is one type of industrial society as such bellicose and the other pacific?

The necessary relation between capitalism and war has usually been demonstrated in two stages: capitalism implies imperialist expansion, and this, in turn, culminates inevitably in war between empires. An enormous literature has been devoted to this theory. To what extent, and in what sense, is a regime based on private ownership of the instruments of production and the mechanisms of the market constrained to territorial expansion? In order to show the necessity of territorial expansion, the economist must prove, in a formal analysis, that such an economy cannot function as a closed system, that it cannot procure either the raw materials or the outlets that it needs. The first hypothesis—the need for raw materials—calls for a factual verification or refutation, and in any case it does not connect expansion with the regime but with the lack of resources of a country whatever the form of government. The second hypothesis is that of a market economy which would be essentially incapable of absorbing its products and which would therefore be obliged to have resort to noncapitalist countries for dumping surplus producer goods or consumer goods which purchasing power within the capitalist zone was inadequate to absorb.

Such a demonstration, which was attempted by Rosa Luxemburg, always takes the form of positing a certain rate of surplus value and of accumulation of surplus value in the two sectors (production goods and consumption goods) and of concluding that, at a certain stage in the economic cycle, a disharmony will emerge between the structure of production and the distribution of purchasing power. If this is so, one may infer that the rate of accumulation is not the same in the two sectors or that the relative importance of the sectors should continually change. The model does not even allow us to conclude that these readjustments necessarily take place through economic crises.[23]

On the other hand, it is very easy to explain, in historical terms, the tendency to territorial expansion of a system based upon private property and a market economy. The entrepreneur, whose specific aim is profit, tries to sell at the highest price and to buy at the lowest. The underdeveloped countries have often provided an opportunity for especially high profits. European industries found in them both raw materials and outlets for manufactured products. It cannot be demonstrated that the English economy in the nineteenth century could not have functioned if it had not sold its cotton goods in India. But it is a fact that, in the primary period of industrialization, it is convenient to have dependable outlets for commodities which the low wages necessitated by a high rate of investment would have difficulty in absorbing.

If territorial expansion was, though not theoretically inevitable, historically connected with the capitalist system, how far can it be regarded as a source of conflict between different economies? So far as expansion results in conditions which approach the ideal market, the capitalist countries would theoretically have no motives for conflict. But in fact expansion has usually been preceded, accompanied, or followed by the assumption of political sovereignty. This produces more-or-less substantial advantages for the metropolis and disadvantages for the countries which are excluded. In this sense, colonial empires are a cause of conflicts since different powers use political means to retain, in the territories under their control, privileges in the supply of raw materials or in access to markets.

Colonial conquests are not the only causes of conflict brought about by economic competition between nations. Schumpeter, in his study of imperialism, not only emphasized the survivals of feudalism in imperial Germany, but pointed out the role of trusts and showed how heavy industry monopolized the internal market, sold its products there above the market price, and had to sell abroad at dumping prices to increase output to the maximum. Such practices, which violate the rules of honest competition, are as inimical as colonial conquest to harmonious and peaceful relations among capitalist countries.

Economic expansion (the search for raw materials, high rates of profit, and markets) and the attempt to obtain, by economic or political means, illegitimate advantages over competitors are phenomena which undoubtedly existed during the centuries of capitalist development. But the Marxist theory of imperialism goes far beyond these incontestable facts. It claims to relate imperialism to a definite stage of capitalism (monopoly capitalism) and to connect European wars with the struggle to share out the world. Now these relationships, whether they are expressed in terms of historical trends or cause-effect relations, are extremely dubious.

[23] The need to include noncapitalist countries in the economic process does not imply the establishment of political sovereignty over them.

Europe's colonial conquests occupy a period from the sixteenth to the twentieth century. European imperialism could not have been wholly the expression of monopoly capitalism, since it largely preceded it.[24] The domination of finance capitalism (a term borrowed from [Rudolf] Hilferding) was much less general than Lenin asserted. Neither the banks nor the international combines divided the world between them, and they were not committed to unleashing a general war if they failed to agree upon the division. Historical study does not reveal the alleged interdependence between the various series of events.

Europe was the world's banker in the nineteenth century, especially in the second half of the century. France had about forty billion gold francs invested abroad on the eve of World War I, and Great Britain two and one-quarter times as much. In the decade before 1914 the latter country invested abroad every year 5–6 per cent of its national income. Undoubtedly, these capital movements, whose extent seems to us half a century later almost incredible, were connected with a certain distribution of income within the country. The monetary stability, which lasted for a century, favored the possessors of capital and tended to increase inequality. But this diffusion of European capital was on the whole neither the cause nor the effect of colonial conquests, since for the most part French, English, and German capital was placed outside the territories under the sovereignty of these three countries. The greater part of French capital was used as an instrument of diplomacy, English capital was looking for high rates of profit, and German capital was serving the interests of foreign trade as well as of the lenders. Colonial conquest was not necessary to clear the way for investments at high interest rates, and it was rarely the consequence of such investments or a measure taken to protect them.

It is true that at the end of the nineteenth century the countries of Europe plunged into the scramble for Africa and that this continent was divided between the capitalist powers, Asia being no longer available and America being closed to European enterprise by the decision of the United States. One cannot dogmatically deny all connection between the development of capitalism in Europe and the expansion of colonial empires in Africa. But there is even greater difficulty in discerning a necessary relation. France had neither surplus population nor an industry in need of markets; she had surplus capital but hardly invested it at all in her empire. Germany, in spite of her high birthrate and economic growth, was the last to become interested in colonies. The civil servants of the Wilhelmstrasse were much more excited than were the bankers or industrialists about Morocco. In each particular case of colonial conquest, one could discover sectional interests of a firm or a bank or a large company, and one may visualize the representatives of these interests laying siege to min-

[24] This concept, moreover, seems to me itself unacceptable. Capitalism at the end of the nineteenth century and the beginning of the twentieth was neither defined nor dominated by the "monopolies."

isters and extracting their support. But, considered as a whole, the conquest of Africa by the European nations seems as much the counterpart of continental peace as the effect of a desire for economic exploitation. In the case of France, officers, explorers, adventurers, and missionaries cleared the way and found a career open to their ambition; the ministers and diplomats followed. When one country had secured the sovereignty of a certain African territory, the unwritten law of European rivalry implied that the other countries should obtain compensation. Thus the division of Africa was the by-product of diplomatic practices and of the European balance of power. France had a large share not because she needed it economically, but because Germany, saturated on the Continent, was delighted that the attention of the French should be turned away from the blue line of the Vosges.

Colonial imperialism is still less the cause of European war. Lenin dogmatically asserts that wars are waged on the continent, but the stakes are overseas possessions. He offers no argument to support this assertion. Now, it can be established that:

1. The capitalist countries were not driven to the war by internal contradictions or by the need for expansion.

2. All the diplomatic crises which had colonial conflicts as their cause or their background were resolved peacefully.

3. The war broke out when a conflict in the Balkans aroused national passions and upset the European balance of power. The nations of the Old Continent, which dominated the world, had every interest in avoiding a struggle to the death. When Comte spoke of the Western republic and when [Ernest] Renan evoked the amity of Germany, England, and France, they were not predicting the actual course of history, but they expressed historical reason. If useless or catastrophic events never occurred, the war of 1914 would not have taken place.

Could it at least be argued that a Socialist industrial civilization, without either private ownership of the instruments of production or international competition, would escape such emotional entanglements and would eliminate the economic-political conflicts of imperialism? Since all the relations between economies—foreign trade and capital movements—would be public, the conflicts produced by competition between capitalist concerns or by measures taken against a foreign private company would by definition disappear. But the public character of international economic relations would not eliminate every motive of conflict.

It has been convincingly shown that market prices are not always equitable and that the power which results from the economic importance of each party influences the conditions of exchange. A developed country is in a position to exploit the underdeveloped country when buying food or raw materials not below the market price, but at a freely established price favorable to the industrialized country, which is purchasing primary products whose price is subject to great variations owing to the nonelasticity of demand. The market, it is true, does not guarantee equity, which is, moreover, difficult to define. But the suppression of a market and the determination of price by agreement between governments gives no greater guarantee. Yugoslavia and Poland have protested against the prices at which the Russians buy their raw materials. After October, 1956, the price of Polish coal was raised retrospectively. Yet there remains in this case one relatively objective method of determining the value of commodities: prices in the capitalist market. If this objective measure were eliminated, how arbitrarily prices might be determined by negotiations between Socialist countries of unequal power.

It may be objected that conflicts limited to the determination of prices would not arouse popular passions or provoke a serious crisis. If the conditions of exchange between Socialist countries alone were in question there would be no ground for resorting to violence. But capitalist countries, in spite of the legends, have not made great wars in order to save their investments or to buy at the lowest price and to sell at the highest. Great Britain has remained the ally of the United States, which has robbed her of the first place in the world economy. The spread of Socialism would only guarantee peace on condition that the domination of weak by strong states was also abolished and that the rivalry between independent sovereign states was effaced by a new feeling of brotherhood between peoples and nations.

Whatever the social system, industrial society gives rise to many causes of conflict, but never to causes for a struggle to the death, since the common interest in peace is always greater than the limited or marginal interests which oppose it. But no economic system by itself excludes the risk of war, because none ends the state of nature which reigns among rival sovereign states. None guarantees that states will cease to attribute to each other sinister designs or that they will prefer cooperation to domination and compromise to combat. At the beginning of the century it was not capitalism, but international life itself, with its commercialized nationalisms, ideological imperialisms, and the rival wills to power which bore war within itself as the sea bears the tempest.

III

Auguste Comte treated Europe as the center of the world and the nations of Western Europe as the vanguard of history. The Western republic, which was to reconcile and unite France, England, Germany, and Spain, would serve as a model and guide to the rest of humanity. A century later, this republic is not so far from existing (apart from the exclusion of Spain, whose regime, which is neither liberal nor democratic, is inspired by the *ancien régime*), but it does not occupy the first rank in the competition between states. The U.S.A. is both richer and more powerful, the U.S.S.R. is more powerful.

In spite of this historical decline with regard to the relations between powers, Western Europe illustrates one of the possible methods of pacification as a consequence of industrialism. This pacification does not differ fundamentally from the peace of the positive era as it was conceived by Comte. The nation, conscious of itself, has become a state; frontiers are no longer matters of passionate contention; the different classes of society collaborate; social mobility permits the rise of the most gifted; the inheritance of occupations has disappeared; the transmission of privileges from one generation to the next has been, not eliminated (for this is probably neither possible nor desirable in any society), but diminished or compensated by the chances of promotion offered to many people.

Neither in the Scandinavian democracy nor in the British is there a military caste. Something of the spirit of the *ancien régime* survives in the castles of the British countryside, in the House of Lords, and in the coronation ceremony, but the aristocratic past no longer dominates everyday politics. As for transcendent religion, it has been so impregnated and transformed by modern ideas that it renders some of the services which Comte expected of the Positivist religion. It does not turn men away from the just organization of communal life on earth, and it inculcates a spirit of reform without bestowing upon any party or theory the seal of the absolute. Bringing down the mighty and raising the humble, careful to recall but not to excuse the imperfections in any human order, religion performs a social function without abandoning its dogmas (which Comte thought anachronistic).

The British or Swedish welfare state and the *soziale Marktwirtschaft* of the German Federal Republic differ in many respects from the positive society of which Comte dreamed. He had little sympathy with parliaments, and even that of Westminster would not perhaps have obtained his unqualified approval. Neither public opinion nor intellectuals nor churches provide the equivalent of the spiritual power which was to regulate feelings and bring men together. Without doubt, the founder of Positivism would have considered that in Western democracies the desire for gain overcomes devotion to the community. The acquisitive society has not yet been controlled and regulated by an altruistic morality.

In spite of these reservations, the example of Germany [25] is the most striking example of historical change from militarism to industrialism. The old military class having been eliminated, the vanquished seem to have become more peace-loving than their conquerors. Protests against rearmament increase in Germany (and in Japan), as if the nations which had suffered most from the evil had been most completely cured of it. The country which was the cradle of

[25] And also of Japan. The parallel between Germany and Japan has continued since World War II.

imperialism in Europe has plunged into peaceful industrialism with an ardor equal to that which formerly inspired its soldiers.

The pacification of Western Europe is still of too short duration to permit any general conclusions to be based upon it. Above all, it is too easily explained by circumstances for us to dare to see in it the beginning of a new era. After the collapse of the dreams of empire, men turned to other work, desires, and ambitions. The pacification of the Western republic might be the result of defeat and the expression of historical resignation. The peace which reigns within and among the nations of Western Europe may well be, in the post-World War II situation, an exception to the spirit of the time, rather than its symbol.

Since 1945 there has probably been no year without war and, even apart from war in the legal meaning of the term (conflict between internationally recognized states), violence has been rampant, revolutions have multiplied, and men have been massacred in hundreds of thousands, sometimes in millions.[26]

In Asia, Indonesia and Indochina have attained their independence by a war against the colonial power. The countries which achieved independence without war (Burma, India, Pakistan) have experienced civil war (Burma is still in its throes) or a half war between the successor states (the question of Kashmir is still not settled). After the civil war had ended in China, Korea became the scene of a conflict between the two pseudostates of the North and South, encouraged and extended by the rivalry between the Soviet Union and China on the one hand and the U.S.A. on the other. The troubles have now reached the Near East and Africa (Kenya and Algeria). The revolt of the Mau-Mau has not initiated a war according to the meaning of the word in international law any more than has the Algerian rebellion. On the day when the Algerian rebels form a "free government" in Cairo or Tunisia and when this government is recognized by some foreign states, the Algerian guerrilla army will assume a different legal form without changing its nature.

If the pacification of Western Europe does not justify optimism about the future, neither does the violence raging in the underdeveloped countries justify pessimism, if one refers to the categories of Comte. Those regions of the world which are not at peace are backward in relation to modern civilization. As yet, neither the formation of nation-states nor industrialism has overcome the conflicts of the past. Religion divides rather than unites groups, sects are arrayed against each other, and rival minorities claim to represent nations which would require decades or centuries to create and which the impatience of the masses and the weariness of the European powers call forth from one day to the next.

After all, Comte did not state the precise route which non-Western man

26 Millions were massacred after the declaration of independence of India and Pakistan.

would follow in order to join its avant-garde, any more than Karl Marx specu-
lated on the different ways in which the nations would achieve Socialism. Violence in Asia, the Near East, and Africa is born of the contradictions between
the traditional regimes and Western influences. It is comparable with that
which raged in Europe in previous centuries. The Japanese attempt at conquest was in part an imitation of the example given by the Europeans who
profited from their industrial progress to colonize other nations. The existence
of violence which results from the development of industrialism and whose
end is the constitution of nations does not refute the Positivist theory of the
peaceful vocation of modern civilization.

Where should we seek the confirmation or refutation of Comte's theses? It
would seem that only the behavior of those nations which are most advanced
on the road of industrialism and which have not been reduced to passivity by
recent defeats can provide an answer.

It is, however, an ambiguous answer, since the antagonism of the two giants
suggests that industrial civilization offers no fewer occasions for ideological
warfare than past civilizations and also that the apparently fundamental hostility does not inevitably degenerate, in our era, into war to the death. The
pessimist will emphasize the irreducible hostility, and the optimist the strange
alliance against war which seems to unite the U.S.A. and the Soviet Union in
spite of their many obvious disagreements. Is it industrialism which halts the
two great powers on the road to war? Is it industrialism which creates between
them an insuperable antagonism?

In the geometry of diplomatic relations, the present situation so far as
Europe and America are concerned does not present any very original features.
Two states peripheral to Western Europe, the cradle of industrial civilization,
have, because of their size and because of the European wars, come to dominate the scene. Any bipolar structure is by itself unstable. A shared hegemony
is a contested hegemony. The same diplomatic geometry which accounts for the
cold war also explains the temporary absence of violence. Neither of the two
great powers is in mortal peril. Neither sees its vital interests threatened. Only
the passion to rule could draw them into a death struggle. Two-thirds of humanity remain outside the European-American system, and the nation which
gained control of this system would not at once become master of the masses
of Asia or Africa.

If one thinks in military terms, the winner of a third world war would apparently have attained universal domination. He would not encounter any rival
worthy of him. But appearances are deceptive here. It is idle to recall that modern methods of administration and domination are so superior to those of the
Roman or Chinese empires that a universal empire in the conditions of the
twentieth century would not be larger than that of the Antonines or the Mings.
There is a major difference resulting from industrialism. The societies of the
past were economically stagnant. Of course they experienced at certain times

periods of economic progress, but the increase of the means of production and the raising of living standards were not a constant aim nor an essential characteristic of their civilization. The emperor who, thanks to his absolute power and an authoritarian bureaucracy, maintained order and permitted the peasant masses to live had done his duty. He unscrupulously exploited his own subjects and those of other races which he had enslaved. There is nothing like this in our own time.

Industry provides the means for destroying masses of people, as Hitler's example has shown. If the fancy took him, the conqueror could exterminate whole nations, millions, tens of millions, of human beings. But the principal ambition of conquerors is not to exterminate but to enslave. And enslavement in our time no longer pays.[27] For work to pay dividends it must be skilled, and, for it to be skilled, the worker must have had a minimum of education. But slaves cannot be taught without acquiring a desire to escape from their slavery. Hitler carried to an extreme the conqueror's anachronistic madness in the century of industrial civilization—to exterminate evil races, to treat what were held to be inferior peoples as subhuman and to confine them to the servile occupations. Imperialism had to degenerate into racialism and to fall below the level of ancient or Asiatic imperialisms in order to have any meaning in a century in which industrialism invites all the nations to work together and offers them the distant prospect of equality.

The Soviet Union has continued, in Eastern Europe, the imperialism of Hitler and has imposed a system which is perhaps in some ways as detestable as that of the Third Reich. But there is a difference; the Soviet Union keeps abreast of the times. Her ideology, if not her institutions, is that characteristic of industrial civilization. For this very reason she cannot escape the contradictions inherent in imperialism in the age of democracy and machine production.

After the victory of 1945 the Soviet armies did not reject the traditional benefits of conquest; they subjected the vanquished to the pleasure of the soldiery, they pillaged, dismantled machinery, and appropriated the products of the factories. Industrialism does not exclude these traditional processes of enrichment. But what are these levies compared with the volume of goods which each year results from collective work? If one wants to prolong the pillage, one must appropriate without payment, or at very low prices, the raw materials, producer goods, and manufactured goods of the conquered people. The Soviet rulers, imprisoned in an ideology in which they believe after a fashion, aimed, in instituting regimes modeled on that of imperial Russia, to promote what they call Socialism and, in any case, to establish a heavy industry and to develop natural and human resources. In the long run, the combination of these two undertakings—exploitation by the parent state and a high rate of investment—results in an intolerable reduction of the standard of

[27] At least in the majority of cases.

living in the satellite states. Since 1956 the Soviet Union has been obliged to aid those countries which she has colonized. That domination is costly instead of being profitable is a new fact and derives from the conditions of industrial society. It cannot but influence international relations.

Analogous phenomena, only even more pronounced, have appeared in the Western world. The hegemony exercised by the United States was at once reflected in unprecedented budgets for foreign aid. Since the end of World War II, the European nations have expended in their colonies, empires, or overseas possessions, however one chooses to call them, as much or more than they have received from their American protector. France, apart from the war in Indochina and Algeria, has spent every year in the French Union two to three hundred billion francs at 1955 prices or seven to nine hundred million dollars. When political domination involves the obligation to promote social development and thus to raise the standard of living of the population, it ceases to enrich the metropolitan power. In this century the glory of governing has to be its own reward.

The two giants proclaim the right of peoples to self-determination and the duty of rich nations to help poor ones. Ideological considerations do not prevent the Soviet Union from refusing to Hungary the right of secession any more than they have prevented her from exploiting the people's democracies. States have never been absolutely faithful to the ideas by which they claim to be directed, but nor are they ever entirely uninfluenced by them. Legally and formally the states of Eastern Europe are independent, and legal forms are not without real consequences in the long run. The Soviet rulers are driven to reduce their levies on the satellite economies so as not to weaken the so-called Socialist regimes they have established, because these regimes need an ideology and the practice of exploitation ends by discrediting the ideology. Similarly, the U.S.A. can here and there buy raw materials at a price lower than the underdeveloped countries or an impartial observer would deem equitable. But a universal empire would none the less impose on the U.S.A., even if they were not threatened by the Soviet Union and were the sole rulers of the planet, more obligations than economic advantages.

In still another way industrialism tends to divert the great powers from a fight to the death. Comte saw the proof that pacifism was peculiar to industrial society in the mediocrity of the "destructive machines" available to states. He was right about the French armies of his time, which, since the Restoration, had made no progress beyond the armies of the Empire and indeed tended to regress as a result of the traditionalism of the general staffs. Since that time, war has stimulated the engineers and military leaders. The nations have fully exploited scientific and technical resources in the development of "destructive machines." The present situation is thus the opposite of that which Comte observed. The technical stagnation of the armies seemed to him proof of the pacifism of industrial societies. Atomic and hydrogen bombs, stratospheric bombers and rockets, demonstrate the excessive interest which the nations take in the engines of war. But once these weapons are available, they may perhaps reduce the risk of an outbreak by the fear which they inspire. Even if the fruits of victory were world hegemony—and what kind of hegemony would there be over ruined towns, vast provinces contaminated by radioactive dust, and men scattered in search of an impossible protection—the dangers and the cost would be sufficient to dissuade any leader who retained his common sense or thought in economic terms from such an adventure. Nobody is insane enough to let loose voluntarily a thermonuclear war.[28]

Is industrial society responsible for the antagonism itself, which it contains within certain limits? The two ideologies, Soviet and Western, both originated in industrial society. They have many points in common: the secularization of aspirations, the cult of technology, the organization of the masses, indefinitely increasing production, and the transformation of the future. The conflict of the two ideologies reproduces the nineteenth-century conflict between liberal optimism and the catastrophic optimism of the Marxists. But in spite of appearances, the two schools have drawn closer together because the so-called revolutionary ideology, embodied in imperfect regimes, has lost the prestige of the unknown, the transcendent, that which has never been seen.

As the object of faith becomes increasingly immanent and beliefs are more and more concerned with the organization of the collectivity, political ideologies clash in the industrial period as did religions in the theological epoch. Comte only imagined an ideological war between the survivors of the *ancien régime* and the supporters of the progressive spirit. But the latter is no more unified than was the theological or metaphysical spirit. Societies dispute about the definition of the good society as much as about the notion of the true God.

Thus the bellicose peace between the two great powers, while not lacking precedents, none the less presents some original features. The U.S.A. and the Soviet Union are both masters of half the economically developed world; they are rivals who cannot agree officially on the division of the European-American region, but who prefer not to engage in a struggle to the death. The course of a war is unpredictable, but, whatever the outcome, the ruins would be piled monstrously under an empty sky. Neither of these states needs a universal empire, nor is the existence of either of them threatened. Industrialism contributes both to the impossibility of agreement and to the refusal to make the supreme test. The new powers of destruction make the bravest hearts tremble, the responsibility for economic growth reduces the attraction of conquest, and the ideology of each great power for the time being prohibits reconciliation.

At the end of the first half of the century those pessimists who predicted a conflagration into which rich and powerful European societies would insanely

---

[28] Unless he could be certain of destroying the enemy's means of retaliation, that is, of striking the other dead and of being spared himself.

plunge their youth and their wealth seemed to be justified by events; neither industry nor the bourgeoisie had prevented European nations from following in the path of the Greek cities and ruining each other in warfare. Twelve years after the end of World War II, twelve years after the destruction of Hiroshima and Nagasaki, hope revives, or at least a doubt emerges. After all, may there not be some truth in Comte's optimism?

It is not that we are living in a time of peace. As we have seen, the under-developed countries are ravaged by armed strife and the machine gun has more influence there than the ballot paper. But the underdeveloped countries live on the threshold of industrial civilization. The nations of Europe, in spite of their diminished power and the loss of their empires, enjoy a standard of living higher than at any time in their glorious past. They have discovered the vanity of conquest, and within nations all social classes share in the hardships and the profits of labor. What is the use of violence when the future may satisfy the dreams of the unprivileged without involving the ruin of those who are considered today as privileged?

As for the two giants, a conflict of principles arrays one against the other, but the community of industrial civilization restrains them from crossing the line which separates a bellicose peace from a fight to the death, limited war from total war. The winner of a third world war would hold sway over ruins, and probably the only victor would be the country, if there were such a one, which had remained on the fringe of the battlefield. Or, in other words, there would be no victor, only survivors. With Europe and America devastated by thermonuclear bombs, China would continue the adventure of mankind.

In the first half of the century wars were typical of industrial civilization, but of an initial phase of this civilization. The excess of production in rela-tion to the basic needs of the population made available for warfare immense resources of men and materials. All the belligerents proceeded to total mobiliza-tion, and workers in field and factory made a contribution no less indispensable than soldiers at the front. Throwing in the whole of their forces, the conflicting sides sought total victory not in the sense of destroying the enemy state, but in the more limited meaning of enforcing its capitulation. The armistice of 1918 left the German empire at the mercy of the allies. The unconditional capitula-tion of 1945 temporarily suspended the existence of the German state and, to some extent, of Japanese sovereignty.

In spite of this total mobilization and victory, the industrial wars of the twentieth century resembled those of the past. In certain respects they were even less destructive, for destruction is measured not absolutely, but relatively, and the capacity for recuperation, human and material, had increased more than the power of destructive machines. After the Thirty Years' War the Ger-man population had diminished by half. The war of 1914 cost the equivalent of the additional population which would have resulted from ten years of peace. The French and the German populations were larger in 1950 than in

1939. Ten years after the end of the war, the German towns are rebuilt, and production and living standards are higher than before the catastrophe.

The consequences of wars cannot be measured only in figures. It is true, as is often said, that Europe has lost its world leadership on the battlefields of the Marne and Flanders and in the plains of Poland and Russia and that it has received injuries there of which the disintegration of overseas empires is the inevitable consequence. In a more subtle and profound way, the Fascist and Communist despotic regimes, which before 1914 would have seemed contrary to historical evolution, have reflected the monstrous growth in the power of the state with the mobilization of materials, men, and knowledge that total war required.

The total war of the recent past, more destructive spiritually than materially, reflected the technology of coal, steel, and the railway and later of the internal combustion engine and aviation. The energy came from the soil (oil, petrol), and explosives were of a chemical kind. The destructive machines were relatively simple. Wars were already economically irrational so far as the mass of the population was concerned, but the latter's views might be mistaken. The identification of territorial conquests with trade outlets and of extension of sovereignty with increase of wealth, though not rationally justified, was not absurd. The hesitations of judgment between the cost of a war and the benefits of domination which would have made the Germans the master race were psychologically intelligible. After all, ordinary citizens seem to find joy and pride in the victories of their sportsmen; why should they be indifferent to military victories?

From 1945 we enter upon a different technological era. A war conducted at the level of modern technology would use explosives fired by atomic energy— also electronic and ballistic weapons. This means a reversal of the relationship between destructive power and capacity to recover. The damage caused by a thermonuclear war fought to the finish could not be repaired in a few years. In World War I the industrial organization of the factories was practically undamaged and continued to supply the colossal war machine to the very end. During World War II, in spite of bombing, war production in Germany increased up to 1945. The destruction of residential areas did not prevent the continuation of work in the factories. It needed the proximity of the air bases and daytime precision bombing to paralyze Germany's industrial machine in the spring of 1945 by the destruction of transport and certain carefully selected factories.

All that we know of the power of the atomic and hydrogen bombs indicates that the fabric of industrial civilization would not stand up to attacks with thermonuclear weapons. It would no longer be a question of progressive mobilization or of maintaining fighting strength by the work of millions of men. If the unimaginable horror of such a total war (that is, waged with all available weapons) were to come about in spite of everything, no one can predict what would happen after the initial stage (a few days or hours). Everyone knows that industrial civilization would be threatened with annihilation by its inordinate destructive power.

The present situation is almost the exact opposite of that envisaged by Comte. He saw the proof of the fundamental pacifism of modern societies in the mediocrity of their "destructive machines," so inferior to what science could invent and manufacture. Today a conflict of principle and power arrays the two giants against each other. The populations of Africa and Asia feel an obviously strong resentment against the white minority which was dominant yesterday and is today still privileged. We are not deceived by the hope of a rapid pacification. The peace required by the logic of industrial civilization, peace within a universal system of belief or based upon mutual respect for each other's beliefs and upon the exploitation in common of natural resources for the benefit of all, is at present ruled out by passions and by ideologies. Between the absurdity of total war and the impossibility of real peace, the hopes of humanity are confined to the possibility of limiting warfare.

The industrial civilization of coal and steel allowed the mobilization of soldiers, tanks, and airplanes. Industrial civilization in the electronic and atomic era can only escape suicide by the limitation of warfare—limiting the number of belligerents, the area of operations, resources used, and objectives pursued—but there is one limitation which conditions all the others. If neither side is to push the use of force to an extreme, it is necessary that neither should feel in danger of extinction, that neither should want to extort unconditional surrender from the other, and that neither should attempt to attain objectives incompatible with the vital interests of the other. In short, limited war implies the resolve of the great powers to tolerate each other.

Industrial civilization whose cities, weapons, and rockets are all characterized by lack of restraint can only escape the apocalypse by moderation.

Thus we have arrived at the anxieties of the present day. Can we legitimately forget them and, like the philosophers of last century, speculate about what the future may bring? I am aware of the audacity of this attempt, which is contrary to the Positivist approach, not as Comte conceived it, but as it is understood by contemporary sociologists. To diminish my responsibility, I shall disclaim in advance any pretension to foresee the future. I do not know whether the industrial civilization of the atom and of electronics will accomplish that limitation of war which the industrial civilization of coal and steel could not achieve. I shall merely make a mental experiment: in what conditions is it possible to conceive the transition from nontotal war, founded on mutual fear, to a peace based upon the desire for nonviolence?

The principal conditions appear to me to be three in number: a diminution of the gulf between the privileged minority and the mass of humanity which remains sunk in poverty; the constitution of nations ready to accept each other within an international community; and the end of the conflict between the two great powers and the two dominant ideologies, which implies that the various countries concerned would be ready to recognize the kinship between the different types of industrial civilization.

The first condition—diminution of the gap between the standard of living of the Western minority on the one hand and the African and Asiatic masses on the other—does not in theory seem unrealizable. In this connection it would be a mistake to return to the classical controversy of last century between optimists and pessimists. That controversy concerned historical predictions, not theoretical problems.

We can now specify exactly the circumstances in which industrialism actually improves the lot of the greatest number and, on the other hand, the circumstances in which it creates little islands of modernity while increasing the misery of those who do not escape from the traditional institutions. In abstract terms, one may say that it is necessary and sufficient that the rate of economic development should surpass that of demographic growth. No system, whether of private or public ownership, whether it has a market or a planned economy, can escape this fundamental requirement. The product per head of population never ceased to grow in Japan between the beginning of the Meiji Era and 1930 in spite of the rapid increase in population. The product per head in India has probably been increasing for the past few years although there is no assurance that the subcontinent has definitely emerged from the vicious circle of poverty.

International organizations have calculated the number of millions of dollars of investments necessary, given a certain rate of demographic growth, for the product per head (or the standard of living) to rise by a certain percentage. I do not attach any great significance to this kind of statistics. No one knows exactly what is the average rate of return on capital for the whole of the so-called underdeveloped countries. A solution would not be miraculously achieved by converting present military expenditure to economic aid. In order to break the vicious circle of poverty, it is not sufficient to put millions of dollars at the disposal of millions of men. The latter must also be in a position to spend the millions on sound investments, and this requires that machines be available in developed countries and the programs, workshops, and technicians ready in the underdeveloped countries. Economic aid can certainly reduce the sufferings of primary industrialization and make good for a few years the deficit in the balance of trade in a country such as India. But to build an industrial civilization nations must change their ways of life and thought and adopt legal and political institutions often incompatible with their centuries old customs. A colonial power may impose this revolution from without, as the Soviet Union has done in central Asia or as France had briefly the inclination to do in Africa. But once colonialism has been eliminated, the essential task can only be carried out by the governments of nations which have achieved their independence.

In the short run the prospects are far from favorable. Decolonization in certain regions of the world involves a return of capital and technicians to Europe and a lowering of the quality of the administration. Nations emerge which have not reached the level of industrial civilization and which are the more jealous of their independence the less they have of material means to assure it and more suspicious of their ex-rulers the more they need them.

At the same time the increase of population continues, sometimes at an accelerated rate, so greatly does medical progress outpace economic development and so much greater are the returns on investments in hygiene than on those in industry. Probably the number of men who are trapped in the vicious circle of poverty is greater than the number who have entered on the cumulative process of growth.

But the peoples living in poverty are no longer condemned to passivity. One might have thought that in the industrial age, when wealth and power are based on technology, the nations enjoying prosperity would easily escape the attacks of nations drawn to adventure and dreams of greatness by hunger and austerity. But this is by no means the case. The Soviet Union has strikingly shown that the greater part of the increase in production, after the satisfaction of basic needs, can be used for the construction of heavy industry and the maintenance of military forces rather than for improving the condition of the masses in proportion to the increase of total resources. The same method can be used by China and other Asian countries. Unable to compete with those in the van, the bulk of humanity can embark upon the pursuit of power which industrial civilization offers as an alternative to the pursuit of abundance.

Even if the wealthy nations are protected from invasion by the weapons of mass destruction, they are not protected from guerrilla warfare. In our time, the war of partisans has changed the map of the world more than the classical or atomic destructive machines. A resolute minority can make life unbearable for a ruling class as soon as the masses are more-or-less sympathetic to it. The cost of fighting against terrorism and partisans soon becomes prohibitive for democratic industrial countries. Constantly menaced by inflation, the latter would need to impose unpopular measures in order to finance repression. The doubts of those groups in which economic calculation is habitual are added to the ideological preferences of the anticolonialists. Partisan warfare has given the *coup de grâce* to European overseas empires. Will it cease once anticolonialism has triumphed? Will the governments of liberated nations end a reign of terror which they began in order to get rid of the conquerors? It is to be feared that the return or the achievement of the rule of law is not yet at hand for a part of the human race.

Besides these difficulties we should not forget the significance of the first condition we have formulated. The cumulative process of growth cannot continue indefinitely for any nation (at least in the present state of technology) owing to lack of land. As long as food is not manufactured industrially from raw materials in unlimited supply and men have to rely upon wheat, rice, meat, or fish that nature produces and reproduces slowly, we cannot imagine societies becoming wealthier or being able to assure permanently to all their members the standard of living of the present-day American middle class, unless we assume a stationary population. In the short run, the increase of population in the privileged Western minority is not incompatible with either a higher standard of living or the pacification of international relations (it may even be favorable to these two desirable results). It is in the underdeveloped countries that the maintenance of the traditional birthrate, with modern or semimodern conditions of hygiene, prevents the increase in productive capacity from leading to an improvement in the conditions of the masses. Confident in their Western experience, many observers believe that economic progress will have the same consequences in Asia, Africa, and South America as it had in Europe and that it will result in such a decline in the birthrate that the standard of all will rise as everyone's labor becomes more productive.

Even if we accept this optimistic view (and in any case it cannot be verified for decades), a halt in the demographic growth of the whole of humanity must be made some day or other if we are to prevent the disproportion between needs and resources from inciting individuals and communities to seek their own salvation at the expense of others.

However far off it may be, this first condition does not seem *essentially* unrealizable. In the U.S.A. one can see approximately what the stationary situation would be; in other words, the volume of goods that could be assured and the hours of work that would be necessary in order to provide for the fundamental needs (food, housing, clothing, education) and the division of labor between the various occupations which results from the unequal productivity of industrial, agricultural, and (in the broad sense) administrative work. A stationary population is not unlikely in a society which has attained such a stationary economic state.

On the other hand, the second condition we formulated, the constitution of a world community of nations which mutually accept each other, is ambiguous. It suggests an idea rather than a complex of institutions. The pacification of Western Europe provides a possible model: with their roots in history, the nations wish to retain their identity without regarding each other as enemies. But one may ask whether the renunciation of power politics on the part of the European nations is not an expression of their weakness and of their subordination to the really dominant states. In other words, can one imagine the world completely pacified by the extension and reinforcement of national communities satisfied with their lot and not envious of others?

Probably such a peace, which would be neither imposed from above nor a result of the balance of power nor due to fear, would require a lowering of barriers between nations, demilitarization, and the transfer of some state powers to a supranational organization. If we suppose the first condition realized, purely economic conflicts would disappear, the supply of raw materials to each community would no longer be endangered, and natural resources would be exploited in common. The "commercialized nationalism" of which Thorstein Veblen spoke would disappear, as did the nationalism of dynastic states and of the feudal tradition before it. From that stage different types of organization are conceivable, and they all point in the same direction; nations no longer dream of making war, and, the economy being less and less confined within national boundaries, national sovereignties tend to fade away or to become administrative units which the citizens are more willing to accept the nearer they are to them. Community of culture and historic unity dedicated to power politics are no longer identical. Sovereign states no longer use industry as their tool and no longer declare that the prosperity of the national industry is their objective. World prosperity being no longer incompatible with the prosperity of individual nations or, rather, the prosperity of all being regarded as necessary to the prosperity of each, communities admit the essentially international (or, if you prefer, nonnational) character of the economic order.

This recognition involves in its turn the fulfillment of the third condition—the disappearance of the conflict of ideologies and of power between today's two giants (or any other giants of the future). The U.S.A. and the Soviet Union, the West and China, no longer judge each other's ideals as deceptive and their institutions as criminal. They no longer suspect each other of desiring the death of his rival; they understand the kinship of their dreams and the interdependence of their destiny.

How, it may be objected, will such a reconciliation be possible? Would it not be even more contrary to the facts than the abuse exchanged by the protagonists in this drama? It is not a matter of underestimating the violence or the stakes of contemporary conflict. It would be naïve to expect an early peace. But we should delude ourselves just as much if we thought that the conflict between Communism and Western democracy (or between Socialism and capitalism) could not be resolved. These two types of industrial society have more characteristics in common than the doctrinaires in the two camps wish to admit and—passions apart—more reasons for coming to an agreement than for destroying each other.

Let us not forget that the Soviets and the West, representing the two types of industrial society, claim to be guided by the same values; both aim to exploit natural resources, to raise the standard of living, and to achieve an economy of abundance. Politically they declare themselves democratic, partisans of the liberation of nations and the rule of the common man. Between Marxists and the West the argument is about the merits of the institutions—property systems, economic methods, political systems—which provide the framework of industrialism. Since the two industrial societies accept the same criteria, it is not impossible to determine their relative value. Economically, a high rate of investment is perhaps desirable for the sake of future generations, but the watchword "Save, save; this is the law and the prophets" is, according to Marx himself, that of capitalism, not of Socialism. That this formula remains indispensable to the East is proof that the Soviet system is temporarily backward in industrialism, not necessarily permanently inferior to that of the West, which is already capable of distributing to the masses many benefits of technological progress. The Soviets could claim that the higher rate of investment, involving a higher rate of growth and a slower rise in consumption, will in time give the man advantage over the West, which sacrifices the future to the present. This claim is rather unconvincing because of the low productivity of the collective farms, an increase in food supply being the essential condition for an improvement in the condition of the masses.

Politically, the Soviets are obliged to claim that the single party and the unconditional authority of the general staff of the party is equivalent to the dictatorship of the proletariat (which is absurd). Moreover, this dictatorship itself can only be justified historically; it is only a transitory phase, not the final regime. Is not the citizens' inability to choose their representatives even farther from the democratic ideal than the partial manipulation of free elections? A community which needs the monopoly of a single party thereby shows that it cannot tolerate open controversy and free discussion between individuals or groups. Leaving aside the dictatorship of the party, which is called dictatorship of the proletariat, what will democratization comprise if not the relaxation of ideological orthodoxy or the rise of a multiparty system?

It does not much matter whether or not one agrees with these opinions on the relative value of the two types of industrial society. The essential thing is to admit the kinship between them. If we admit that the ends are the same, the controversy about the advantages of collective or private property, of a planned or a market economy, concerns the means and is really technical and not metaphysical, even though passion and ideology transform it into a metaphysical, almost a religious, quarrel.

The large American corporations differ more from traditional private property, the ownership of a patch of land or a small shop, than from the Soviet trusts. A capitalist regime in which the state is responsible for full employment and the volume of investment distributes to the masses the surplus production resulting from increasing productivity and allows trade unions the political role of discussing with employers' federations is more like what was called Socialism in the nineteenth century than the image of capitalism which the old-fashioned propagandists of the day of judgment persist in retaining. The economic aspect of the conflict between the Soviet Union and the West calls for compromise and a gradual reconciliation of the two sides of the Iron Curtain rather than war to the death.

The political aspect has quite a different significance. If the West believes that its very existence is threatened, this is not, whatever the doctrinaires of the Soviet system may say, through attachment to free enterprise or to free competition as such. From a technical viewpoint, a certain amount of private property and competition seems to us preferable to the concentration of power, property, and planning which is theoretically for the benefit of the state, but [is] in fact for the benefit of the few men who govern the state. But the essential point is that the Soviet regime has brought with it up to now a state ideology and a single-party system; it destroys freedom of thought, individual security, rivalry between parties, and the guarantees of a constitutional authority. Obviously peace does not require that the Soviets should confess their sins and hail the parliamentary democracies as the culmination of human history. But it does at least require that they should no longer claim the single-party system and ideological orthodoxy as the supreme expression of democracy and as a necessary stage on the royal road of humanity.

At the present time the truth or falsity of the Western and Soviet interpretations of the situation has less influence on events than the fact that these interpretations exist, are passionately accepted by millions of people, and are radically opposed. The elements which Comte included in the concept of industrial society are henceforth dissociated. A Soviet regime favors science, industry, and machines, not free inquiry and rational research, which are the essence of industrial society and of the Western spirit. The doctrine which, according to the Soviets, ought to direct the reorganization of society is not Positivism, which preached class cooperation, but Marxism, which declares inevitable the struggle between proletarians and capitalists and sees no hope of peace except in the total victory of the former. Such a doctrine divides humanity, exalts those regimes which accept it, and mercilessly condemns the others; in short, it fosters what Comte called ideological warfare.

The re-establishment of human unity presupposes the universal diffusion or the progressive relaxation of this doctrine. Would the conversion to the Soviet system of the whole of humanity result in peace? If the gap between productive forces and standards of living remained, would the U.S.A. and the Soviet Union, governed by parties paying lip service to Marxism-Leninism, accept their inequality of wealth in an idyllic peace? Until doctrinaire passion, which is today expressed in Marxism-Leninism or Stalinism, has given place to a spirit of scientific inquiry, the interpretation of the ideology officially adopted by the whole of humanity would create almost as many occasions for quarreling as does the conflict of ideologies in our era. Only the second alternative offers real hope; the Soviet societies, as they progress, should relax the orthodoxy of which they are at present prisoners and should admit that there are different roads to Socialism and that the different stages are characterized less by the nationalization of large enterprises than by the accumulation of capital and the rise in the productivity of labor.

While the differences between standards of living in the West, the Soviet countries, and the underdeveloped countries remain so great, it will be useless to expect the two worlds to accept each other. Anti-Western passions are both expressed and concealed by the doctrine that Socialism comes after capitalism in the course of history, whereas the slight development of productive forces and the merciless processes of tyranny in the so-called Socialist countries suggest an inverse relation. In other words, the third condition implies the first. While the differences in resources are immense, the resentment of the underprivileged and the attempt to catch up are inevitable. Ideologies like that of the Soviet Union facilitate effort, camouflage resentment, and substitute ideological progress for economic backwardness. The more the Soviet regimes can give to their citizens the benefits enjoyed by the citizens of capitalist democracies, the less inclined they will be to deny the claims and the real achievements of the latter.

Let it be clearly understood that I do not assert that the equalization of productive capacity or standards of living will suffice to re-establish peace between states and between ideologies. The wars of the twentieth century have been waged between states belonging to the same civilization and having comparable living standards. There is nothing to indicate that the Soviet rulers would renounce their doctrine after the disappearance of the poverty which provides the rational motive we discern in their madness.

If, in our mental experiment, it has seemed possible to realize the three conditions, there are plenty of objections even to such an abstract and hypothetical optimism.

It is true that industrial civilization is favorable to cooperation between classes and nations, that it makes war irrational and peace the interest of all. But it fails to abolish the causes of conflict.

Domination, we have said, no longer pays. The master cannot keep the slave poor indefinitely, and he can only raise the living standards of poor nations by costly investments. But there are exceptions to this rule. Great Britain's protectorate in Bahrein and Kuwait is certainly profitable. France's sovereignty in the Sahara would be a source of profit if millions of tons of petroleum lay hidden beneath the burning sands. The ideal colony in the twentieth century is a desert containing black gold. The various emirates of the Arabian peninsula come close to this ideal.

Even if we ignore these marginal cases, any politicization of the economy engenders friction and harms certain interests. If trade between states is planned, will not the strongest impose prices which the weakest will regard as inequitable? If there is free trade, will not the country whose industry loses a market because the goods of a competitor are cheaper be tempted to defend itself by methods which will set up a chain reaction of resentment and suspicion? While states suspect each other of hostile intentions, they are alert to assure, even by force, their supplies of energy and metals. It is even conceivable that wars will (in the long run) be justifiable once more when reserves of raw materials are inadequate to satisfy all needs.[29]

The latter is a very long-term contingency. The other possibilities do not weaken the fundamental proposition that a major war is irrational in the age of industrial civilization once the whole of humanity has embarked upon the cumulative process of enrichment.

From a political viewpoint, the formation of nations comes up against the obstacle of heterogeneous communities. In Algeria there are a million French people whose average income is at about the same level as that of the French in metropolitan France and eight million Algerians, three-quarters of whom have an income seven or eight times lower. The dominant French minority would not think of submitting to the laws of an Algerian republic, and the Mohammedan majority, inspired by nationalism, thinks only of forming an independent state similar to that of Tunisia or Morocco. In the African continent there are many cases of overlapping communities. Even if the populations of European or Asian extraction agreed to return to their countries of origin (which is inconceivable), any large state would have a heterogeneous population, since Africa as a whole has not gone through the process of transition from tribe to nation.

The uncertainty of the results of our mental experiment turns on the third condition. The ideological conflict between the Soviet system and capitalism is not insoluble, because both are aiming at the same objectives and lay claim to the same values. The nature of the conflict is not the same as between the *ancien régime* and the revolution or between the feudal and the industrial spirit. The Soviet system and capitalism are two versions of industrial civilization and, according to the logic of industry, ought to recognize their kinship. But is this logic socially and humanly compelling?

Thus we reach the final uncertainty. Industrial society, as defined by Comte, comprised a way of thinking, a social organization, and a system of government, and the whole system was incompatible with the spirit of war. Schumpeter and Veblen also consider that the spirit of industrial society was foreign to the prejudices or superstitions which are essential to the survival of feudal hierarchy, the dynastic state, or aggressive imperialism. Veblen put the blame for war on what he called "commercialized nationalism," while the Marxists blamed "monopoly capitalism." In the present phase, the survivors of the *ancien régime* use the power of industry to embark upon conquest, with the collusion or at the instigation of commercial or financial interests. Beyond this stage—which is a new formulation of Comte's intermediate stage—the Socialists envisaged an economic organization which would prevent rivalry of interests and the methods of power politics. Veblen, after World War I, sug-

[29] Or, again, if the cost of exploiting mineral resources available to both parties is so different that it is worth establishing sovereignty over the rich areas with a low cost of production.

gested a league of peaceful nations which would liquidate both feudal survivals and capitalist speculation.

No one had clearly perceived the major difficulty. The exchanges between politicoeconomic units are partly distorted by import duties, export subsidies, cartels for maintaining internal prices, dumping, and the search for high rates of profit, which Marxist critics untiringly denounced at the beginning of this century. But if private enterprise and market mechanisms were abandoned, the exchange of goods between economic units with separate sovereignties would become political acts. There is a danger that conditions of exchange fixed by governments will reflect power relations and fail to satisfy all parties. Veblen and the Marxists, struck by the disadvantages of a commercial system to some extent distorted by the capitalists, did not realize that the only alternative to the commercial system was political planning. The industrial system of production does not contain within itself any regulating or distributing mechanism. Such a mechanism is inevitably commercial or political or, rather, both, but in unequal proportions.

Veblen and the Socialists, when they conceived a situation in which feudalism and capitalism had been abolished, assumed the existence of governments which would express faithfully and with absolute impartiality the aspirations and interests of the masses. It was assumed that these aspirations were peaceful, that the interests of all nations were in accord, and that free exchange, organized by a supranational power, would correspond both to men's aspirations and to their interests. This optimistic view failed to recognize what historians, reasoning by analogy, had observed: that industrial society does not exclude authoritarian or despotic regimes.

These despotisms are not and will not be mere temporary survivals of the dynastic state; they reveal one of the permanent possibilities of technical or mass civilization. These despotisms, which profess allegiance to conflicting ideologies, will be arrayed one against the other, each proclaiming peace and democracy as their watchwords. But the peace of one is war in the eyes of the other, and the democracy of one is tyranny to the other. Worse still, the adherence of the masses to these despotisms will perhaps be gained by employing a combination of terror and propaganda. If atomic weapons did not make a major war an act of madness, it is even possible that the masses would follow their despots along the path of conquest. By participating in collective power, men find satisfactions which sweep aside economic calculations and make sacrifices meaningful. The desire for power and pride in surpassing other men are no less profound impulses than the desire for worldly goods. This will to power can be satisfied in and through the community. If power is an end in itself and not just a means, will industry suffice to make peace reign between men who care less about living than ruling?

Let us reiterate briefly the stages of our analysis.

The events of the first half of the century have largely confirmed the prophecies of philosophers who judged the possibilities of the future in terms of what had happened in the past. In retrospect, the past two wars seem to us to be civil wars of the Western republic, but, in the time of the Macedonian hegemony or the Roman Empire, the Peloponnesian War must also have looked like a Greek civil war. All wars which preceded the imperial unification of an area of civilization became in retrospect civil wars in the eyes of citizens of the established empire. Probably these are the real wars and the most ruthless. Strangers have no reason to fight; at the very most they kill each other when land or food is lacking. Only crusades or religious wars have the bitterness of civil wars.

Moreover, perhaps the Greeks regretted having broken up the city system by fighting the Peloponnesian War to a finish. No Englishman regrets having paid for resisting Hitler by the breakup of the Empire. One does not like to ask whether a compromise peace concluded in 1916, even if it gave the domination of the continent to imperial Germany, would not have been preferable to the most costly and sterile of victories.

Neither the survivals of the *ancien régime* in Germany and Japan nor the imperialist conflicts between the European home countries were the principal causes of the two wars. The spirit of the *ancien régime* has only degenerated into barbarism when revived by the passions of a popular movement. The will to conquer and pride in domination are not a monopoly of the nobility; millions of men may dream of enjoying them by participating in a national community: "The kneeling slave dreams of ruling the world." [30]

Waged by nations which wanted to be peaceful and believed themselves to be so and by soldiers who were only civilians in uniform, the European wars, more than those of any other century, were "wars to end war," accompanied by a tumult of competing propaganda slogans. Conscript armies, when they ceased to be police forces, became mass armies which could undergo and inflict immense losses, supported by the efforts of entire nations. The characteristic of the second stage of modern civilization, which was, according to Comte, the subordination of industry to war and the use of the resources provided by industry for military strength, became the major characteristic of all societies which were, to a greater degree than ever before, military and industrial at the same time. The worker and the soldier: two symbolic figures, complementary and no longer antithetic.

The fact that the European countries were also the possessors of vast empires in Asia and Africa was neither the remote nor the immediate cause of the outbreak. But the European wars assumed a universal dimension and significance because of Europe's place in the world. Indians, Senegalese, Vietnamese, and Algerians came to fight and to die in Flanders and Lorraine, while Frenchmen, Germans, and Englishmen clashed in equatorial forests or

[30] Marquis de Custine.

in the deserts of the Near East. Europeans did not fight to the death to share out the world, but, because they had fought to the death, together they lost the domination of the world.

The pattern of the European war of 1914–1945 may be compared with that of the Peloponnesian War, which was divided into two periods by the armistice of Nicias, and it has historical precedents; but the weapons used, the size of the theater of operations, and the stakes involved in the conflict give this unique complex of events its specific features. The bipolar structure of the diplomatic situation in the European–American complex is also not without precedent. The impossibility of peace and the rejection of war is not a radically new phenomenon. Empires—Rome and the Parthians, Byzantium and the Arabs— have coexisted for centuries, not without peripheral conflicts, but without war to the death. Failing a joint domination, the two great powers must in reason prefer the limited hazards of an armed peace to the measureless risk of total war.

The present situation has none the less certain new characteristics connected with industrial society. Henceforth the fruits of victory for the great powers are derisory in relation to the inevitable cost of the war. The common interest of states possessing atomic weapons in not fighting far outweighs the separate interests which oppose them in this or that area of the world.

The Soviet-American rivalry, created by circumstances rather than by men's ambitions or passions, is concerned not with the territory of either of the two states, but with the destiny of other nations, old nations of Europe or countries of Africa or Asia previously colonized or dominated. While Europe seems to be the object of the Soviet-American antagonism, the latter resembles the conflicts which have frequently occurred between two claimants to an empire. But once the U.S.A. and the Soviet Union oppose each other not because the two states want to destroy or enslave each other, but because their ideologies are incompatible and the other states too weak to defend themselves alone, the situation becomes unique. Never before has diplomacy been world-wide, as it has been since the second European war, and never before have the two dominant states of an international system competed simultaneously for hegemony over the other parts of the world. The rejection of war is not connected only with the destructive power of nuclear weapons, but also with the purposes of the conflict. Total war between the U.S.A. and the Soviet Union would not settle once and for all the fate of the rest of the world.

The consequences of industrialism are contradictory, some aspects being favorable to war, some to peace. Nuclear weapons make any major war insane, and the responsibility for development makes domination costly. But ideological war, to return to Comte's expression, remains possible, since, instead of the clash between the *ancien régime* and a new spirit, we see a clash between two versions of the new spirit.

These contradictory aspects of the present situation explain the caution of the prophets. How can one prophesy peace when so many people are committed to violence and when a single atomic war might well render part of the world uninhabitable? How can one prophesy war when the great powers have so many motives for fighting and nevertheless refuse to do so? For the next few years one hopes for a limitation of warfare. Further than that, it is impossible to see.

Nevertheless, even beyond this transitional phase, uncertainty remains. What would be required then to confirm the pacific nature of industrial society? The raising of the living standards of the least-favored nations, the slowing down of demographic growth and the acceleration of economic progress, the formation and strengthening of political unities, the appeasement of ideological passions and the acceptance of the partial legitimacy of the various economic and political regimes—these are the conditions, easy to imagine but difficult to realize, in which the spread of industrial society would in theory cease to foster new conflicts as fast as it settles old ones.

Is this theory itself correct? Would men cease to hold exclusive ideologies when there were no longer differences in living standards to conceal? Would men of all races recognize each other's humanity and equality when they effectively shared in the same material civilization?

If one supposes that all the difficulties of the transitional period were surmounted, would industrial society be a permanent source of war or an opportunity for peace? Is industry "the weapon of a beast of prey," as Spengler said, or an apprenticeship to reason?

It seems to me that the answer is contained in the question. Industrial society *may* teach people to be reasonable if it ceases to be regarded as the instrument of a beast of prey. Comte was wrong to confuse the military spirit with that of a military caste; the disappearance of professional soldiers does not imply the triumph of pacifism. He misjudged the danger of national collisions; the avant-garde of humanity, against the advice of the founder of Positivism, set out to conquer the backward peoples. Whatever the number of Comte's errors or omissions, the same inescapable question remains: Has war still a function when there is no longer a military caste, when work is the only source of wealth, when the whole of humanity is united in exploiting natural resources, and when destructive weapons threaten the very basis of civilization? At the present time, small wars may still have a function in the stage when nations are being formed and when there are great disparities in the industrial development of the different countries. The ideological rivalry of the two great powers, which is also contemporaneous with the period of transition in which industrial civilization has to coexist with incompatible traditions, may easily transform a local conflict into a total war. At a later stage, when the whole of humanity and not merely a part of it has entered on an era of continuous expansion, why should not the peace which has been achieved by the Western republic be extended to the rest of humanity?

There is no guarantee that there will be anything beyond what we may, with Comte, call the transitional stage. But if the peoples of Asia within the next hundred years overcame the vicious circle of poverty, if the Soviet states, without giving up a planned economy, and [if] the Western states, without abandoning the principle of a pluralist regime, recognized that they constitute species of the same civilization—in other words, if the ideologies were no longer at war and if all nations were reaping the benefits of productive work— what would be the sense of great wars?

Man has not changed, the psychologist would reply; he remains capable of aggression, he has been and will remain a beast of prey. To be sure; but while individual aggression is perhaps a permanent condition, it is not a sufficient cause of wars and violence between groups. The individual can satisfy his fighting instincts elsewhere than on the battlefield where armies meet. Societies have not changed, the anthropologist would reply; they establish themselves by conflict, and each society consolidates its unity by an image of the world or a system of values which inevitably brings it into conflict with other societies. Millennial religions preach the brotherhood of all men precisely because temporal communities divide humanity. The churches themselves follow a path which leads inevitably to discord although their doctrine knows no frontiers. It may be, indeed, that the antagonism between the earthly city and the city of God, between the gospel and the church, will continue for ever. Perhaps human communities are destined to singularity and, in consequence, to ethnic conflicts and religious wars. But pacification does not presuppose nonviolence and love between nations. Unless the object of the conqueror is the extermination of the vanquished, reasonable statesmen, knowing the cost of an industrial war and the necessity for the master to maintain the standard of living of the slave, will prefer peace to military adventures.

Let me repeat—there may be nothing beyond the transitional stage during which the diffusion of industrial society comes up against the resistance of age-old traditions, upsets the stable order of the past, spreads misery among countless multitudes, and increases the cause of conflict. But if there is something beyond, it seems to me that there is no proof that Homo sapiens must finish his earthly career in an insane catastrophe. The Faustian spirit, we are told, inspires the search for scientific truth, the eagerness to produce, and the will to power. I agree. It was a mistake to believe, as in the nineteenth century, that the domination over nature would rid men of the desire to dominate each other. But is it right to believe that men will be as anxious to dominate when mastery brings nothing but the glory of ruling? It is true that industrial societies are inspired by a passion to know, to possess, and to enjoy. If peace on earth can be based only on detachment and asceticism, modern societies are certainly farther from it than any in the past. But the attempts to bring about peace by changing men's hearts have all failed. The endeavor to which humanity is condemned today is without precedent. The transformation of all men into workers, all workers into citizens, and all citizens into members of a universal community of labor—this is the meaning of the industrial society which Comte imagined.

Comte certainly did not foresee, nor would he have approved, the unbridled and unqualified technological progress which forces men to choose between collective suicide and peace. In his view, the essence of industrial society was not the power to produce or to destroy, but the extinction of the military caste and the pre-eminence of work. He dreamed of restoring social stability by the permanence of a true doctrine, of offering men the prospect of constantly increasing wealth, but also of a perpetual readaptation to an unpredictable technology.

If Comte's theory is treated as a prophecy, then it is reasonable to dismiss ironically the teaching of a man who declared inevitable a future which has not come to pass. But neither Comte, nor, for that matter, Marx, is one of those philosophers who were condemned by Sir Isaiah Berlin in a previous Auguste Comte Memorial Lecture and who seek in an allegedly inevitable future an excuse for their own resignation.

Neither Comte nor Marx claimed to justify the unjustifiable by declaring it to be inevitable. The chief fault of both is optimism. They assumed, implicitly or explicitly, that phenomena which no longer have any meaning or function necessarily disappear. They did not conceive that the absurd might survive (although Marx's well-known formula, "Socialism or barbarism," suggests such an eventuality). Marx predicted Socialism in order to encourage the proletariat in the revolutionary action which he believed to be necessary for the good of humanity. Comte predicted the coming of a Positivist society in order to make men conscious of what was required for the stability of industrial civilization. The enunciation of an inevitable future emerges in one case as an appeal to action, in the other as an appeal to moral responsibility.

Comte's appeal to moral responsibility takes on an added significance in present circumstances. Technological progress ends not by accident, but by a logical development, in giving men the power to destroy themselves. Man has always had the means to kill his fellow man. With hydrogen bombs and rockets, societies have the means to make the world uninhabitable.

Comte was wrong to believe that wars would no longer occur because they would have no function. But should we be justified in going to the other extreme and seeing no difference between what is sensible and what is insane, between the reasonable and the absurd? Should we be right to maintain that universal catastrophe is as probable as salvation? Those who confine their hopes to this world cannot but choose the universal community of work which those whom we call optimists dreamed of in the past century. Today we are more aware of the sacrifices it involves, of its improbability in the short run, and yet, in spite of everything, of the remote possibility of achieving it.

We have lost our taste for prophecies; let us not forget the duty of hope.

Selected Bibliography

GENERAL STUDIES

ARON, RAYMOND. *The Century of Total War*. Boston: Beacon, 1955.

CLARKSON, J. D., and COCHRAN, T. C. *War as a Social Institution*. New York: Columbia University Press, 1941.

NEF, JOHN U. *War and Human Progress*. Cambridge: Harvard University Press, 1950.

ROPP, THEODORE. *War in the Modern World*. Durham, N. C.: Duke University Press, 1959.

VAGTS, ALFRED. *A History of Militarism*. New York: Meridian, 1959.

WALTZ, KENNETH. *Man, War and the State*. New York: Columbia University Press, 1959.

WRIGHT, QUINCY. *A Study of War*. 2 vols. Chicago: University of Chicago Press, 1942.

INSTINCT THEORIES AND COMPARATIVE PSYCHOLOGY

BEACH, F. A. "The Snark Was a Boojum," *American Psychologist*, V (1950), 115–124.

FREUD, SIGMUND. *Civilization and Its Discontents*. London: Hogarth Press, 1957.

HEBB, D. O. *The Organization of Behavior*. New York: John Wiley & Sons, 1949.

LORENZ, KONRAD Z. *King Solomon's Ring*. New York: Thomas Y. Crowell Co., 1952.

SCOTT, JOHN PAUL. *Aggression*. Chicago: University of Chicago Press, 1958.

THORPE, W. H. *Learning and Instinct in Animals*. Cambridge: Harvard University Press, 1956.

PSYCHIATRIC PERSPECTIVES

ALEXANDER, FRANZ. "Psychiatric Aspects of War and Peace," *The American Journal of Sociology*, XLVI (1941), 504–520.

ERIKSON, ERIK H. *Young Man Luther*. New York: W. W. Norton & Co., 1958.

FAIRBAIRN, W. RONALD D. "The War Neuroses—Their Nature and Significance," in *idem. An Object Relations Theory of Personality*. New York: Basic Books, Inc., 1962.

GLOVER, EDWARD. *War, Sadism and Pacifism*. London: George Allen & Unwin, Ltd., 1935.

MURPHY, GARDNER. *Human Nature and Enduring Peace*. New York: Houghton Mifflin, 1945.

SAGER, CLIFFORD J. "The Concept of Aggression in Modern Psychiatry," *Mental Hygiene*, XXXVI (1952), 210–219.

STRACHEY, ALIX. *The Unconscious Motives of War*. London: George Allen & Unwin, Ltd., 1957.

ZILBOORG, GREGORY. *History of Medical Psychology*. New York: W. W. Norton & Co., 1941.

SOCIAL LEARNING AND INTERGROUP RELATIONS

ADORNO, T. W., FRENKEL-BRUNSWIK, ELSE, *et al. The Authoritarian Personality*. New York: Harper, 1950.

ALLPORT, GORDON W. *The Nature of Prejudice*. Cambridge: Addison-Wesley Publishing Co., 1954.

BROWN, J. F. "The Theory of Aggressive Urges and Wartime Behavior," *Journal of Social Psychology*, XV (1942), 355–380.

CANTRIL, HADLEY. *Tensions That Cause Wars*. Urbana: University of Illinois Press, 1950.

DOLLARD, J., DOOB, C. W., *et al. Frustration and Aggression*. New Haven: Yale University Press, 1939.

DOLLARD, J., and MILLER, N. E. *Personality and Psychotherapy*. New York: McGraw-Hill, 1950.

GUTHRIE, E. R. *The Psychology of Human Conflict*. New York: Harper, 1938.

JANIS, IRVING L., and KATZ, DANIEL. "The Reduction of Intergroup Hostility," *Journal of Conflict Resolution*, III (1959), 85–100.

KELMAN, HERBERT C., ed. "The Relevance of Social Research for War Prevention," *Journal of Human Relations*, II (1954), 7–22.

KLINEBERG, OTTO. *Tensions Affecting International Understanding*. New York: Social Science Research Council, 1950.

LEWIN, KURT. *Field Theory and Social Science*. New York: Harper, 1951.

MCNEIL, ELTON. "Personal Hostility and International Aggression," *Journal of Conflict Resolution*, V (1961), 279–290.

MILLER, JAMES G. "Psychological Approaches to the Prevention of War," in Wayne Dennis *et al. Current Trends in Social Psychology*. Pittsburgh: University of Pittsburgh Press, 1948.

PEAR, T. H. "Peace, War and Culture Patterns," in T. H. Pear, ed. *Psychological Factors of Peace and War*. London: Hutchinson & Co., Ltd., 1950.

WHITING, JOHN W. M. *Becoming a Kwoma*. New Haven: Yale University Press, 1941.

SELECTED STUDIES IN SOCIOLOGY AND ANTHROPOLOGY

ABEL, THEODORE. "The Element of Decision in the Pattern of War," *American Sociological Review*, VI (1941), 853–859.

ANDRZEJEWSKI, STANISLAUS. *Military Organization and Society*. 4 vols. London: Routledge & Kegan Paul, 1954.

BERNARD, LUTHER LEE. *War and Its Causes*. New York: H. Holt & Co., 1944.

COOLEY, CHARLES HORTON. "Social Control in International Relations," *Publications of the American Sociological Society*, XII (1917).

COSER, LEWIS. *The Functions of Social Conflict*. Glencoe, Ill.: Free Press, 1956

DAVIE, MAURICE. *The Evolution of War*. New Haven: Yale University Press, 1929.

FRIED, MORTON H. "Warfare, Military Organization, and the Evolution of Society," *Anthropologica*, III (1961).

GINSBURG, MORRIS. "The Causes of War," *Sociological Review*, XIII (1939).

SCHNEIDER, JOSEPH. "On the Beginnings of Warfare," *Social Forces*, XXXI (1952), 68–74.

SOROKIN, P. A. *Social and Cultural Dynamics*. 4 vols. New York: American Book Co., 1937, III.

SPEIER, HANS. *Social Order and the Risks of War*. New York: G. W. Stewart, 1952.

Selected Bibliography

TURNEY-HIGH, H. H. *Primitive War: Its Practice and Concepts.* Columbia, S. C.: University of South Carolina Press, 1949.

SELECTED STUDIES ON WAR, LIBERAL DEMOCRACY, AND INDUSTRIAL SOCIETY

ARON, RAYMOND. *On War.* New York: Anchor Books, 1963.
COMTE, AUGUSTE. *The Positive Philosophy of Auguste Comte.* Translated by Harriet Martineau. New York: William Gowans, 1869. Book VI.
EMERSON, RUPERT. *From Empire to Nation.* Cambridge: Harvard University Press, 1960.
HAYES, CARLETON J. *Nationalism: A Religion.* New York: Macmillan, 1960.
JANOWITZ, MORRIS. *The Professional Soldier,* Glencoe, Ill.: Free Press, 1960.
LASSWELL, HAROLD D. "The Garrison-State Hypothesis Today," in Samuel P. Huntington, ed. *Changing Patterns of Military Politics.* New York: Free Press of Glencoe, 1962.
————. *World Politics and Personal Insecurity.* Glencoe, Ill.: Free Press, 1950.
MANNHEIM, KARL. *Man and Society in an Age of Reconstruction.* New York: Harcourt, Brace, 1950.
MILLS, C. WRIGHT. *The Power Elite.* New York: Oxford University Press, 1956.
ORTEGA Y GASSET, JOSÉ. *The Revolt of the Masses.* New York: W. W. Norton & Co., 1932.
SPENGLER, OSWALD. *The Decline of the West.* New York: A. A. Knopf, 1947.
TOYNBEE, ARNOLD. *War and Civilization.* New York: Oxford University Press, 1950.
WALLER, WILLARD, ed. *War in the 20th Century.* New York: Dryden Press, 1940.
WRIGHT, QUINCY, EVAN, WILLIAM M., and DEUTSCH, MORTON. *Preventing World War III: Some Proposals.* New York: Simon & Schuster, 1962.

SELECTED LITERARY STUDIES OF WAR

BABEL, ISAAC. "Red Cavalry," in *Collected Stories.* New York: Meridian Fiction, 1960.
CHURCHILL, WINSTON. *My Early Life: A Roving Commission.* New York: Scribner's, 1951.
CRANE, STEPHEN. *The Red Badge of Courage.* New York: Appleton-Century-Crofts, 1952.
EBERHART, RICHARD, and RODMAN, SELDEN. *War and the Poet.* New York: The Devin-Adair Co., 1945.
FINLEY, JOHN H., JR. *Thucydides.* Cambridge, Mass.: Harvard University Press, 1942.
FORD, FORD MADOX. *Parade's End.* New York: A. A. Knopf, 1950.
GIRAUDOUX, JEAN. *Tiger at the Gates.* New York: Oxford University Press, 1955.
GRAVES, ROBERT. *Goodbye to All That.* Garden City: Doubleday, 1957.
GRAY, J. GLENN. *The Warriors.* New York: Harcourt, Brace, 1959.
HEMINGWAY, ERNEST. *For Whom the Bell Tolls.* New York: Scribner's, 1940.
HERSEY, JOHN. *Hiroshima.* New York: A. A. Knopf, 1946.
HOMER. *The Iliad.* Translated by Richmond Lattimore. Chicago: University of Chicago Press, 1961.
MAILER, NORMAN. *The Naked and the Dead.* New York: Rinehart, 1948.
ORWELL, GEORGE. *Homage to Catalonia.* New York: Harcourt, Brace, 1952.
PLIEVIER, THEODORE. *Stalingrad.* New York: Appleton-Century-Crofts, 1948.
REMARQUE, ERICH MARIA. *All Quiet on the Western Front.* Boston: Little, Brown, 1958.
THUCYDIDES. *The Peloponnesian War.* New York: Modern Library, 1934.
TOLSTOI, LEO. *War and Peace.* London: Oxford University Press, 1951.
————. *Sebastopol.* Ann Arbor, Mich.: University of Michigan Press, 1961.
WILSON, EDMUND. *Patriotic Gore.* New York: Oxford University Press, 1962.

Index